Personal Bankruptcy For Dummies®

What Bankruptcy Usually Can Do For You

- Bring to a halt almost any lawsuit.
- Prevent creditors from grabbing a chunk of your paycheck.
- Stop evictions and foreclosures.
- Prevent the loss of your driver's license because of an unpaid fine.
- Keep the IRS at bay, for a while.

What Bankruptcy Usually Can't Do For You

- Stop a criminal prosecution.
- Protect someone who cosigned your loan.
- Eliminate your child support or alimony obligations.

What You Shouldn't Do Before Talking to a Lawyer

- Borrow any more money.
- Get married.
- Get divorced.
- Transfer assets to relatives or friends.

What Bills You Should Pay First When You Can't Pay Everyone

- Rent (unless you plan to move)
- Utilities
- Car (if you want to keep it)
- Mortgage (if you want to keep your home)
- Fines
- Child support and spousal support
- Income taxes

For Dummies: Bestselling Book Series for Beginners

Personal Bankruptcy For Dummies®

Cheat Sheet

What You Can Do to Buy Some Time

- Sell off assets to feed the debt monster.
- Negotiate with creditors.
- Refinance your home at a lower interest rate.
- Get a home equity loan.

What Debt Collectors Can't Do

- Call you early in the morning, late at night, or at any other unreasonable time or place.
- Harass you.
- Contact you at work if your employer prohibits personal calls.
- Threaten you.
- Tell anyone (other than your spouse, lawyer, or co-signer) that you're in debt.
- Bug you once you've told them to bug off.

What to Do When Debt Collectors Break the Rules

First, tell them you know what the Fair Debt Collection Practices Act is and how to use it. Then, use it by filing a complaint to the:

Federal Trade Commission
Correspondence Branch
600 Pennsylvania NW
Washington, D.C. 20580

For Dummies: Bestselling Book Series for Beginners

Personal Bankruptcy

FOR

DUMMIES®

Kort M.

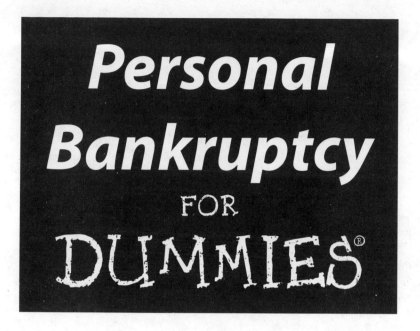

Personal Bankruptcy FOR DUMMIES®

by James P. Caher and John M. Caher

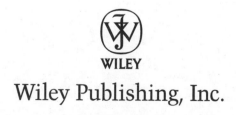

Wiley Publishing, Inc.

Personal Bankruptcy For Dummies®

Published by
Wiley Publishing, Inc.
111 River Street
Hoboken, NJ 07030
www.wiley.com

Copyright © 2003 by Wiley Publishing, Inc., Indianapolis, Indiana

Published by Wiley Publishing, Inc., Indianapolis, Indiana

Published simultaneously in Canada

For general information on our other products and services or to obtain technical support, please contact our Customer Care Department within the U.S. at 800-762-2974, outside the U.S. at 317-572-3993, or fax 317-572-4002.

Wiley also publishes its books in a variety of electronic formats. Some content that appears in print may not be available in electronic books.

Library of Congress Control Number: 2002114838

ISBN: 0-7645-5498-0

Manufactured in the United States of America

10 9 8 7 6 5 4 3 2

1B/RU/QS/QT/IN

WILEY is a trademark of Wiley Publishing, Inc.

About the Authors

James P. Caher, a practicing attorney with more than 25 years of experience, is a nationally recognized expert on consumer bankruptcies.

Jim coauthored, with his brother John, *Debt Free! Your Guide to Personal Bankruptcy Without Shame* (Henry Holt, 1996) and two highly regarded books for lawyers: *Discharging Marital Obligations in Bankruptcy* (LRP, 1997) and *Discharging Credit Card Debts in Bankruptcy* (LRP, 1998).

In addition, Jim has published scores of articles for bankruptcy professionals and was labeled the "online guru" by a national legal weekly because of his regular appearances on the Internet as an expert analyst on bankruptcy law. Jim also serves on the editorial board of the American Bankruptcy Institute.

Jim graduated from Niagara University and then earned his law degree from Memphis State University Law School, where he was a member of the Law Review and recipient of the American Jurisprudence Award for Excellence in the field of debtor-creditor relations. He filed his first consumer bankruptcy case shortly after graduating in 1975. Jim lives and practices in Eugene, Oregon.

John M. Caher is a legal journalist who has written about law and the courts for most of his 20-year career.

Currently the Albany bureau chief for the *New York Law Journal*, John previously was state editor and legal affairs reporter for the *Times Union* of Albany, New York. His legal reportage has won more than two dozen awards, including prestigious honors from the American Bar Association, the New York State Bar Association, the Associated Press, and the Hearst Corporation.

John coauthored, with his brother Jim, *Debt Free! Your Guide to Personal Bankruptcy Without Shame* (Henry Holt, 1996). He is the author of *King of the Mountain: The Rise, Fall and Redemption of Chief Judge Sol Wachtler* (Prometheus Books, 1998). In addition, John was the principal writer assisting former U.S. Treasury Secretary William E. Simon in preparation of his memoirs. Mr. Simon's autobiography will be published posthumously in 2003 by Regnery.

John is a 1980 graduate of Utica College of Syracuse University, where he received his bachelor's degree in journalism, and a 1993 graduate of Rensselaer Polytechnic Institute, where he earned a master's degree in technical communications/graphics. John lives in Clifton Park, New York.

Dedication

This book is dedicated to the memory of our parents — Big Jim and Fitz — who died before their time but left us with their own life examples of personal responsibility, fairness, justice, affinity for the underdog, basic decency, and common sense. It is also dedicated to the five grandchildren they should have known and would have adored and enjoyed beyond measure: Sean and Brendan Caputi, and Erin, Kerry, and Norah Caher.

Authors' Acknowledgments

Working with editors and publishers usually is a love-hate ordeal for a writer, with more hate than love. But our experience with Pam Mourouzis and her wonderful staff of editors at Wiley Publishing, Inc. was truly a delight. They know what they want, articulate it, and do what they say they'll do. They're efficient. They're smart. They're pros. Every one of their suggestions made this book better, and working with them was genuinely a collaborative effort. For a writer, it just doesn't get any better than that. Thanks to our project editor Marcia L. Johnson, our initial project editor Allyson Grove, and our copy editor Neil Johnson. And a special thanks to our agent, Sheree Bykofsky of Sheree Bykofsky Associates in Manhattan, for steering us to the perfect publisher and doing what needed to be done to make this happen.

We owe an enormous debt of gratitude to Michael J. O'Connor, a partner at O'Connor O'Connor Mayberger & First PC in Albany, New York. Mike, an outstanding bankruptcy attorney, and a real good guy, provided the much appreciated technical review.

And finally, and most importantly, we acknowledge the love and support of our respective mates — Kate Donnelly and Kathleen Caher — who were there for us every step of the way.

Publisher's Acknowledgments

We're proud of this book; please send us your comments through our Dummies online registration form located at www.dummies.com/register/.

Some of the people who helped bring this book to market include the following:

Acquisitions, Editorial, and Media Development

Project Editor: Marcia L. Johnson

Acquisitions Editor: Pamela Mourouzis

Copy Editor: E. Neil Johnson

Technical Editor: Michael O'Connor

Editorial Manager: Jennifer Ehrlich

Editorial Assistant: Elizabeth Rea

Cartoons: Rich Tennant, www.the5thwave.com

Production

Project Coordinator: Kristie Rees

Layout and Graphics: Amanda Carter, Carrie Foster, LeAndra Johnson, Stephanie D. Jumper, Erin Zeltner

Proofreaders: John Tyler Connoley, Andy Hollandbeck, Carl William Pierce, TECHBOOKS Production Services

Indexer: TECHBOOKS Production Services

Special Help
Allyson Grove, Greg Pearson, Chad Sievers

Publishing and Editorial for Consumer Dummies

Diane Graves Steele, Vice President and Publisher, Consumer Dummies

Joyce Pepple, Acquisitions Director, Consumer Dummies

Kristin A. Cocks, Product Development Director, Consumer Dummies

Michael Spring, Vice President and Publisher, Travel

Brice Gosnell, Publishing Director, Travel

Suzanne Jannetta, Editorial Director, Travel

Publishing for Technology Dummies

Andy Cummings, Vice President and Publisher, Dummies Technology/General User

Composition Services

Gerry Fahey, Vice President of Production Services

Debbie Stailey, Director of Composition Services

Contents at a Glance

Introduction 1

Part 1: Bankruptcy: The Big Picture 5
Chapter 1: Considering Bankruptcy 7
Chapter 2: Stopping the Bleeding 25
Chapter 3: Meeting the Players 45
Chapter 4: Deciding Which Type of Bankruptcy Is Best for You 55
Chapter 5: Getting from Here to There: The Bankruptcy Process 69

Part 11: Avoiding Bankruptcy 87
Chapter 6: Considering Alternatives to Bankruptcy 89
Chapter 7: Handling Bill Collectors 107
Chapter 8: Negotiating with the IRS 117

Part 111: Keeping Your Stuff 125
Chapter 9: Understanding Which Assets Are Off-limits to Creditors 127
Chapter 10: Dealing with Secured Debts 145
Chapter 11: Saving Your Home 157

Part 1V: Getting Rid of (Most of) Your Debt 173
Chapter 12: Lingering Obligations 175
Chapter 13: A House of Cards: Wiping Out Credit-Card Debts 187
Chapter 14: Give unto Caesar: Using Bankruptcy to Deal with Tax Debts 197
Chapter 15: The Devil Made Me Do It: Fines, Fraud, and Other Foibles ..207
Chapter 16: Till Debt Due Us Part: Bankruptcy and Divorce 215
Chapter 17: Student Loans and Other Mind Games 229

Part V: Strategies for a Successful Bankruptcy 243
Chapter 18: Avoiding Troubles with Your Trustee 245
Chapter 19: Living on the Edge in Chapter 13 Bankruptcy 255

Part VI: Enjoying Your Fresh Start 275
Chapter 20: Repairing Your Credit 277
Chapter 21: Staying Out of Financial Trouble 289

Part VII: The Part of Tens 297

Chapter 22: Ten Common Bankruptcy Mistakes 299

Chapter 23: Ten Things You Can Do Right Now to Ease Your Financial Woes 303

Chapter 24: Ten Common Questions about Bankruptcy 307

Appendix A: Glossary 311

Appendix B: Exemption Laws 327

Index 347

Table of Contents

Introduction 1
   The Jim/John Solution 1
   How This Book Is Organized 2
      Part I: Bankruptcy: The Big Picture 2
      Part II: Avoiding Bankruptcy 2
      Part III: Keeping Your Stuff 2
      Part IV: Getting Rid of (Most of) Your Debt 3
      Part V: Strategies for a Successful Bankruptcy 3
      Part VI: Enjoying Your Fresh Start 3
      Part VII: The Part of Tens 3
      The Appendixes 3
   Icons (Signposts) Used in This Book 4

Part 1: Bankruptcy: The Big Picture 5

Chapter 1: Considering Bankruptcy 7
   Viewing Bankruptcy in Historical Context 8
   Debunking Bankruptcy Myths 10
      Bankruptcies are at epidemic levels 10
      People who go bankrupt are sleazy deadbeats 10
      Bankruptcy is the easy way out for folks
         who can pay their bills 12
      Bankruptcy threatens the ethical foundations of our society 12
      Honest folks pay a "tax" to support those who are bankrupt 13
   Understanding What You Can Gain Through Bankruptcy 14
      Stopping creditors in their tracks 15
      Wiping out most of your debts 16
      Catching up on back mortgage and car payments 16
      Filing bankruptcy to pay some debts over time 16
      Using bankruptcy to pay all your debts 17
   Knowing What You Can Lose in Bankruptcy 18
   Considering Alternatives to Bankruptcy 19
   Introducing the Different Types of Personal Bankruptcy 20
      Liquidations (Chapter 7) 20
      Consumer reorganizations (Chapter 13) 21

Weighing the Consequences of Not Filing Bankruptcy 21
    Claims secured by your car 22
    Claims secured by your home 22
    Student loans 22
    Support obligations 22
    Fines and restitution 23
    Taxes 23
    Lawsuits 23
Using the Statute of Limitations 23

Chapter 2: Stopping the Bleeding **25**
Preventing Further Damage Now 26
Comparing Your Income with Your Spending 27
    Focusing on how much income you have 28
    Coming to grips with where your money goes 29
Assessing Your Spending Habits 34
    The devil's in the details: Scrutinizing your expenses 34
    Are you a spendaholic? 35
Getting a Handle on What You Own 36
Figuring Out How Much You Owe 39
Coming Out of the Financial Closet 41
    Telling parents 42
    Talking to mates 42
    Explaining the situation to offspring 44

Chapter 3: Meeting the Players **45**
Finding Professional Help 45
    Answering why a lawyer is a must 46
    Finding a good lawyer 47
    Understanding what to expect from your lawyer 48
    Paying the piper 48
Getting to Know the Players 50
    Bankruptcy judge 50
    Case trustee 51
    U.S. Trustee 52
    Creditors 53

Chapter 4: Deciding Which Type of Bankruptcy Is Best for You **55**
Deciding Whether to Go Solo or As a Married Couple 55
Looking at Your Probable Bankruptcy Choices 56
    Chapter 7: Straight bankruptcy 57
    Chapter 13: Debt repayment plans 59
Deciding Between Chapter 7 and Chapter 13 62
    Recognizing when Chapter 7 is best 62
    Considering Chapter 13 as your number-one option 63

Considering Other Types of Bankruptcy 66
    Chapter 11: Large reorganizations 66
    Chapter 12: Reorganizations for family farmers 66
    Chapter 20: Adding Chapters 7 and 13 67
Changing Your Mind 67

Chapter 5: Getting from Here to There: The Bankruptcy Process ... 69

Getting Organized before Talking to a Lawyer 69
    Doing your financial homework 70
    Tracking down your creditors 72
Meeting Your Lawyer for the First Time 73
Completing the Paperwork 74
Filing Your Bankruptcy Case 74
    Using the automatic stay 75
    Exceptions to the automatic stay 76
    Receiving notice of the creditors' meeting 78
Working Your Way through Chapter 7 79
    The 341 meeting 79
    Dealing with secured creditors 80
    Amending paperwork 81
    Adding creditors 81
    Sweating out key deadlines 81
    Attending a discharge hearing 82
    Closing no-asset cases 82
    Administering asset cases 82
    Anticipating complications 83
Working Your Way through Chapter 13 83
    Filing your plan and beginning your payments 83
    The 341 meeting 84
    Confirming your repayment plan 84
    Going through valuation hearings 85
    Looking at the claims process 85
Comparing the Chapter 7 and Chapter 13 Processes 85

Part II: Avoiding Bankruptcy 87

Chapter 6: Considering Alternatives to Bankruptcy 89

Appreciating the Negative Consequences of Bankruptcy 90
    The drawbacks of bankruptcy 90
    Reasons not to file bankruptcy 90
    Reasons to delay filing bankruptcy 91

Looking at Remedies Other Than Bankruptcy 92
    Budgeting 92
    Allowing your family to bail you out 92
    Selling your assets 93
    Transferring credit-card balances 94
    Restructuring home mortgages 94
    Tapping your retirement plan 98
Choosing Which Bills to Pay First (If at All) 98
    Deciding whether to pay your mortgage 100
    Considering whether to make car payments 100
    Dealing with alimony and child support payments 101
    Deciding whether you should pay your taxes 101
Negotiating with Your Creditors 101
    Work-out agreements 102
    Threatening bankruptcy 102
Considering Credit Counseling Services 103
Simply Ignoring Creditors 104

Chapter 7: Handling Bill Collectors 107

Taming the Toothless Tiger: The Bill Collector 108
Invoking Federal Law 109
    When debt collectors can contact you 111
    Where debt collectors can't contact you 112
    When debt collectors may contact others about your debt 112
    Dirty tricks are outlawed 113
    Your remedies under the FDCPA 113
Tapping State Laws 113
    State statutes 114
    Common law remedies 114
Keeping Your Dukes Up 114

Chapter 8: Negotiating with the IRS 117

Looking at the Tax Collection Process 117
    Service centers 118
    Automated Collection System (ACS) 118
    Local revenue officers 118
Making Nice with the Touchy-Feely IRS 119
    Your due process 120
    Negotiating an installment agreement 120
    Knowing when to get professional help 121
    Gaining "uncollectible" status 122
    Planning bankruptcy while pursuing
        an installment agreement 122
Submitting an Offer in Compromise 123
Getting Help from a Taxpayer Advocate 124

Part III: Keeping Your Stuff *125*

**Chapter 9: Understanding Which Assets
Are Off-limits to Creditors** **127**

Grasping the Legal Concepts 127
    Digging through the property of the estate 128
    Understanding how exemptions work 131
Determining the Value of Your Stuff 132
Understanding How the Courts View Certain Assets 132
    Homesteads 133
    Automobiles 134
    Household goods 134
    Inheritances and life insurance benefits 135
    Divorce settlements 135
    Spendthrift trusts 135
    Rent receipts 136
    Security deposits 137
    Wages 137
    Bank accounts 137
    Severance and vacation pay 138
    Sales commissions 138
    Real estate commissions 139
    Insurance commissions 139
    Suits to recover money 140
    Income tax refunds 140
    Earned income credits 141
    Retirement accounts 141
Creating Exemptions 143

Chapter 10: Dealing with Secured Debts **145**

Getting the Lowdown on Liens 146
    Perfecting liens 146
    Seeing liens as double-edged swords 146
Identifying Different Kinds of Liens 147
    Consensual liens 147
    Nonconsensual liens 149
Dealing With Liens in Bankruptcy 149
    Freeing your household goods and tools from liens 149
    Redeeming (getting back) your property 150
    Reaffirming your debts 150
    Dealing with rent-to-own contracts 151
Figuring Out What Will Happen to Your Car 151
Applying Lien Laws to Household Goods 154
Banging the Gavel on Judgment Liens 155

Chapter 11: Saving Your Home 157

Your Home, Your Castle — and Sometimes Your Hassle 157
    Figuring out how much your home is worth 158
    Deducting mortgages and other liens
        that affect your share of the pie 158
    Understanding the homestead exemption 159
Dealing with Jointly Owned Property 160
    Example 1: When the homestead exemption
        is larger than your equity 161
    Example 2: When your equity is larger than
        your homestead exemption 161
Understanding How Foreclosures Work 162
Heading off the Homewreckers 163
    Keeping your home in Chapter 7 163
    Keeping your home in Chapter 13 163
    Comparing Chapter 7 and Chapter 13 167
Using Truth-in-Lending Laws 169
Coping When Your Dream Home Becomes a Nightmare 170

Part IV: Getting Rid of (Most of) Your Debt *173*

Chapter 12: Lingering Obligations 175

Recognizing (Possibly) Indelible Debts 175
    Confronting obligations enforceable by court orders 176
    Debts arising after bankruptcy 177
    Unlisted debts 178
    Debts preserved under sections of the Bankruptcy Code . . . 179
Sweating Out the 60-day Bar Date 181
Avoiding the Urge to Borrow to Pay Nondischargeable Debts 182
Understanding Reaffirmation Agreements 183
    Reasons to reaffirm 183
    Changing your mind 184
Having Your Discharge Denied or Revoked 184
    Grounds for denial of a Chapter 7 discharge 185
    Protecting your discharge 185
    Revoking your discharge 186

Chapter 13: A House of Cards: Wiping Out Credit-Card Debts 187

Playing the Credit-Card Game 187
Seeing What Judges See 189
Examining Your Mind-set When You Incurred the Debt 190
Forcing the Credit-Card Company to Prove Its Case 191
Explaining Presumptively Fraudulent Charges 192
Defending Against False Financial Statement Allegations 192
Using Credit-Card Advances for Gambling 193

Bullying the Credit-Card Bullies 193
Transferring Credit-Card Balances 194
Having a Bankruptcy Dismissed for Credit-Card Abuse 195

**Chapter 14: Give unto Caesar: Using Bankruptcy
to Deal with Tax Debts** **197**

Dealing with the Federal Tax Man 197
    Watching out for recently assessed taxes 201
    Coping with interest and penalties 201
    Confronting federal tax liens 202
    Making the trustee pay your taxes 202
    Paying taxes over time in Chapter 13 203
    Keeping on top of postpetition taxes 203
    Paying taxes before bankruptcy 204
    Using the statute of limitations to escape taxes 204
    Facing the consequences if you've been a tax protestor 204
Dealing with the State Tax Man 204
Addressing Taxes Other Than Income Taxes 205
    Paying trust fund employment taxes 205
    Deciding whether to pay real and personal property taxes 205
Obtaining Loans to Pay Your Taxes 206

**Chapter 15: The Devil Made Me Do It: Fines, Fraud,
and Other Foibles** **207**

Dealing with Debts Resulting from Fraud 208
    Charges on the eve of bankruptcy 208
    False financial statements 208
    Bad checks 209
    Receiving undeserved welfare and unemployment benefits 209
    Willful and malicious behavior 210
    Theft 212
Covering Fines, Penalties, and Restitution Orders 212
    Criminal fines 212
    Restitution 213
    Noncriminal fines and penalties 213
    Motor-vehicle fines 214
Accepting Responsibility for Drunken-driving Injuries 214

Chapter 16: Till Debt Due Us Part: Bankruptcy and Divorce **215**

Introducing Key Points 215
Planning Your Strategy 216
    Exploring your financial obligations 217
    Doing what's best for both spouses 218
    Completing property transfers 219
    Timing it right 219

Understanding How Support Obligations
Are Treated in Bankruptcy 220
Support obligations in Chapter 7 220
Support obligations in Chapter 13 221
Figuring out which obligations are in "the nature of" support 221
Focusing on financial conditions at the time of your divorce 222
Looking at factors that some courts consider 223
Understanding How Property Divisions Are Treated in Bankruptcy 224
Determining your "ability to pay" 225
Ability to pay — over what period of time? 226
Tipping the relative suffering scales 226
Remembering the 60-day bar date 227
Other grounds for bankruptcy-proof marital debts 227

Chapter 17: Student Loans and Other Mind Games **229**
Tracing Your Loans 230
What They Can Do If You Don't Pay 231
Managing Student Loans with Bankruptcy 231
Proving your insufferable need for a break 232
Wiping out part of your student loans 235
Paying student loans under a Chapter 13 plan 235
Using a "Chapter 20" strategy 236
Addressing medical school loans 237
Getting stuck even when you're only a cosigner 238
Clicking your clock into The Hardship Zone 238
Managing Student Loans without Bankruptcy 239
Consolidating your loans 239
Requesting a reasonable and affordable payment plan 240
Getting a deferment 241
Accepting a forbearance 242
Going for an administrative discharge 242

Part V: Strategies for a Successful Bankruptcy **243**

Chapter 18: Avoiding Troubles with Your Trustee **245**
Playing by the Rules and Telling the Truth 245
Accurately Listing Your Assets 247
Appreciating the Trustee's Ability to Recover Assets 247
Fraudulent transfers 247
Preferential transfers 249
Unperfected liens 251
Special problems with manufactured homes 252
Protecting Your Discharge 254

Chapter 19: Living on the Edge in Chapter 13 Bankruptcy 255
    Creating a Realistic Plan 256
        Why Chapter 13 plans fail 256
        Paying the bare minimum 256
    Keeping Your Lawyer in the Loop 257
    Blowing It . . . Again? Not! 258
        Suspending your payments 259
        Modifying your plan 260
        Requesting a "hardship discharge" 261
        Converting to a Chapter 7 262
        Dismissing your Chapter 13 and filing a new Chapter 7 262
        Dismissing your Chapter 13 and filing a new Chapter 13 264
        Understanding when the 180-day rule applies 264
    Tackling Car and Mortgage Payments Outside the Plan 265
        Doing nothing 265
        Proposing a new plan that includes missed payments 266
        Working out drop-dead agreements 267
        Asking for time to sell your property 267
    Addressing Debts Incurred After You File 268
        Nonemergencies 268
        Emergencies 269
        Automobiles 269
        Support obligations 269
        Income taxes 270
    Sinking Your Ship before It Arrives 270
    Tying Things Together 271

Part VI: Enjoying Your Fresh Start 275

Chapter 20: Repairing Your Credit 277
    Realizing that You've Already Taken the First Step
      by Filing Bankruptcy 278
    Using the Fair Credit Reporting Act to Your Advantage 278
    Getting Your Credit Reports after Bankruptcy 279
        Getting credit reports for free 280
        Correcting mistakes on your credit reports 280
        Making sure your credit reports properly reflect
          your bankruptcy 282
    Obtaining New Credit 283
        Applying for an unsecured credit card 283
        Settling for secured credit 284
        Informing credit bureaus of your good work
          when the creditor doesn't 285
        Taking it easy when building new credit 285

Watching Out for Credit-repair Scams 286
Establishing Good Credit When You're Married 286

Chapter 21: Staying Out of Financial Trouble 289

Addressing Compulsive Spending 289
    Admitting that you have a problem 290
    Enrolling in Debtors Anonymous 290
Building a Consensus with Loved Ones 290
    Establishing common ground with your mate
        on money matters 291
    Creating realistic expectations from your offspring 291
Using a Budget 291
    Developing a system for tracking what you spend 291
    Sticking to the plan 292
Avoiding Temptation 292
    Reducing credit-card solicitations 292
    Removing your name from direct-marketing lists 293
    Reigning in telemarketers 293
Making a Few Lifestyle Changes 293
    Figuring out your priorities 294
    Thinking about ways to save money 294
    Discovering how to live without credit 294
    Discovering cheap ways to have fun 295
Recognizing Danger Signs 295
    Watching for telltale signals 295
    Living without savings 295
    Using debt-to-income and equity ratios 296

Part VII: The Part of Tens 297

Chapter 22: Ten Common Bankruptcy Mistakes 299

Borrowing Money from Relatives 299
Repaying Money Owed to Relatives 300
Chipping Away at Debts with a Home-equity Loan 300
Draining Retirement Accounts to Pay Debts 300
Neglecting to Accurately List All Creditors 301
Concealing Your Assets 301
Transferring Assets to Keep Them Away from Creditors 301
Making Payments that You Can't Afford to Make 301
Thinking that Bankruptcy Is Your Last Resort 302
Filing Bankruptcy Too Soon 302

**Chapter 23: Ten Things You Can Do Right Now
to Ease Your Financial Woes** **303**
    Stop Feeling Guilty 303
    Cut Up Your Credit Cards 304
    Order Your Credit Reports 304
    Keep Track of Everything You Buy 305
    Get Your Name off Any Joint Accounts 305
    Stop Making Partial Payments on Credit-card Bills 305
    Call a Lawyer Now If You're Being Sued or Foreclosure
      Is Underway 305
    Find Out How Much Your Home and Car Are Worth 306
    Empty Accounts in Banks Where You Owe Money 306
    Sharpen Your Pencil and Start Filling Out the Worksheets
      in Chapter 2 306

Chapter 24: Ten Common Questions about Bankruptcy **307**
    Will Bankruptcy Damage My Credit Rating? 307
    Will Bankruptcy Affect My Job? 308
    Will I Lose My Home? 308
    Will I Lose My Personal Belongings? 308
    Will I Ever Be Able to Buy a House? 308
    Does My Spouse Have to File Bankruptcy Too? 309
    Can I Keep Some Debts Off My Bankruptcy and
      Deal with Them Separately? 309
    Can I Cancel My Bankruptcy If I Change My Mind? 310
    Is Filing Bankruptcy a Long, Protracted Process? 310
    Does It Cost a Bundle to File? 310

Appendix A: Glossary *311*

Appendix B: Exemption Laws *327*
    Choosing between Federal and State Exemptions 327
    Identifying Bankruptcy Code Exemptions 328
    Surveying State Exemptions 330

Index *347*

Introduction

Welcome to *Personal Bankruptcy for Dummies* — your nuts-and-bolts tool-box of practical utensils for wrenching your way out of financial hell.

Only a dummy would think bankruptcy is simple, easy, or painless. But with a little know-how, you can get through this process with a minimum of headache, heartache, and indigestion. We'll show you how, and we aim to serve as your partner every step of the way — regardless of whether you ultimately conclude that bankruptcy's your best bet.

We know you're not a dummy, and the fact that you're taking responsibility for your troubles and considering your legal options proves the point. This book helps you sort out all the possibilities, with a clear understanding of what's to gain and what's to lose. We're not going to preach, and we're not going to teach. What we are going to do is give you the information and ammunition to intelligently and confidently choose your own best path.

The Jim/John Solution

If you ever go to Ireland, an Irish phrase that you just have to know is: "It's clearly signposted all the way." It usually comes up in a tavern, or anywhere else you may stop to ask for directions. Invariably, you'll be sent on your merry way with these promising words.

Now, the ignorant may assume that means the way to your destination is obvious and prominent signs are everywhere that you can make a wrong turn. But, what a foolish assumption! What it really means is that no such signs are anywhere to be found, and you're going to get hopelessly lost, prob-ably for the remainder of your natural life.

What's that have to do with bankruptcy? Nothing, except that most of the bankruptcy books we've encountered are "clearly signposted all the way" and about half as understandable as an Irish roundabout. Do you go around the traffic circle to the left or right when you drive on the left, and how come there's a cow in the passing lane? You just can't get there from here without wading through a mountain of manure.

So we, The Brothers Caher, decided to make the world of bankruptcy a little more intelligible and a little more navigable. Yeah, we thought about fixing Ireland first, but getting lost adds to the fun and charm of our ancestral homeland. Nothing's fun or charming about getting lost in the dragon-plagued dungeons of bankruptcy law.

How This Book Is Organized

So you're thinking that perhaps, just perhaps, bankruptcy is the way to go. Maybe it is. Maybe it isn't. We'll guide you through all the thickets of bankruptcy law, so you can figure that one out for yourself. This book covers everything you need to know, and we've tried real hard to organize a ton of material so you can immediately put it to practical use. Here's a brief rundown of what you'll find in each section of the book.

Part I: Bankruptcy: The Big Picture

Torn over the question of whether bankruptcy is for you? Worried about your reputation? Losing sleep over the endless hemorrhaging from your billfold or purse? The aim of this first part is simply to put your mind at ease and get you to evaluate the bankruptcy option on a simple, objective, intelligent standard: Do the benefits outweigh the drawbacks? We explain the process and the pitfalls and, as an added bonus, we describe some quick and effective ways to immediately stop the financial bloodletting.

Part II: Avoiding Bankruptcy

Most folks will do almost anything to avoid bankruptcy, and all too many only make matters worse by putting off that day of reckoning. We understand your reluctance to file bankruptcy and respect your good-faith effort to do whatever you can to avoid that indignity (without conceding for a nanosecond that filing bankruptcy betrays a lack of integrity). Although in our experience, people who qualify are usually better off filing bankruptcy sooner rather than later, in this section, we explain a variety of debt-busting techniques to keep the bill collectors off your back until you get on your feet again.

Part III: Keeping Your Stuff

The credit industry would have you believe that when you file bankruptcy an army of predators and scavengers descends on the tranquility of your homestead and yanks the bowl of porridge right out from under your kids' spoons. Well, the fact of the matter is that although you may — *may* — lose some of your possessions in bankruptcy, the really important stuff is strictly off-limits to your creditors. This section spells out what's yours, what's potentially at stake, and what you can do to make sure your most important possessions remain in your own good hands.

Part IV: Getting Rid of (Most of) Your Debt

Bankruptcy eliminates most of your debts, but some problems (like taxes, child support and school loans) may stick around even if you file. In this section, we explore those lingering obligations and explain what you can do to get the biggest bang for your bankruptcy buck.

Part V: Strategies for a Successful Bankruptcy

With apologies to Yogi Berra, "It ain't over 'til it's over" — and in some cases it ain't even over when it's over. You have to put in a little effort to get the most relief from your bankruptcy filing. This section offers oodles of suggestions about how you can make the process run smoothly and effectively, and how you can avoid some troublesome traps.

Part VI: Enjoying Your Fresh Start

Phew! You made it. You survived bankruptcy, and you're determined to never return to the bad old days of debts, delinquencies, and diabolical collection agents. Thanks to the American tradition of justice, fair play, and sympathy for the underdog, you have a new lease on your financial life. Here, we work on restoring your credit and, once and for all, putting all your bad financial experiences behind you.

Part VII: The Part of Tens

Hey, this wouldn't be a *For Dummies* book without the tens — and we've included such nuggets as the ten most common questions that we get about bankruptcy and the ten things you can do right now to ease your mind. In fact, you may want to scan the common questions right now.

The Appendixes

Here's some good stuff — including a thorough glossary (which, given the lawyerly talent for making anything complicated, was a must) and a rundown on how the rules on exempt property vary from state to state. The exemption thing is a biggy, because some property that may be completely protected in some states is completely at jeopardy in others. You'll want to know the score for your state.

Icons (Signposts) Used in This Book

Your road to financial salvation has many twists and turns, and you have to know when to zig and when to zag. So we've included a bunch of eye-catching, head-bopping iconic reminders to draw attention to particular points or hazards and to warn you in advance of the boring technical stuff.

These little bull's-eyes point out helpful tidbits and strategic moves you or your lawyer may want to consider.

This icon points out the legal and logistical bombs that may blow up in your face if you're not minding your p's and q's.

These icons are reminders of points made previously. An awful lot of information is included in this book, and we don't expect you to keep it all in your head. This is a gentle reminder.

Yikes, some complicated, convoluted information is coming your way! We've made it as easy to understand as possible, but some stuff is just plain mind boggling. Dive in at your own peril. We won't be offended, however, if you skip ahead. Well, Jim (the lawyer) may be offended. Forget about him.

The rules for what's called a Chapter 7 bankruptcy — one where you wipe out all your debts and surrender certain assets — are different from the other most common consumer bankruptcy, a Chapter 13. When you see this icon, you'll know we're talking only about Chapter 7.

The rules for what's called a Chapter 13 bankruptcy — one where you pay off a portion of your debts over time — are different from the other most common consumer bankruptcy, a Chapter 7. When you see this icon, you'll know we're talking only about Chapter 13.

Legal principles are much easier to understand when you can see how they apply in the real world. We've included plenty of examples and identified them with this icon.

Part I

Bankruptcy: The Big Picture

The 5th Wave   By Rich Tennant

"I'm not sure HOW I became bankrupt. I know life's a crap shoot, and you've got to play the hand you're dealt, so I spun the wheel and hoped for aces. But my horse came in last place and suddenly I'm behind the 8-ball. Now, according to my attorney, all bets are off."

In this part . . .

Is bankruptcy for you? What happens when you file? What happens if you don't? Do you need a lawyer? How can you stop the hemorrhaging? Where do you even start? If you don't already know the answers to these questions — and maybe even if you think you do — start your journey here. Many people begin with the assumption that even considering bankruptcy is an admission of failure. Don't make that assumption! Read this part to recognize that bankruptcy is a viable and legitimate financial relief tool and to understand the implications of choosing that particular escape hatch.

Chapter 1

Considering Bankruptcy

In This Chapter

▶ Understanding the history and tradition of bankruptcy

▶ Dispelling myths about bankruptcy

▶ Discovering what you can gain in bankruptcy

▶ Recognizing what you may lose in bankruptcy

▶ Knowing the consequences of not filing bankruptcy when you qualify

Maybe you were socked with an unexpected and uninsured medical expense, and you didn't have the savings to cover the bills. Perhaps you lost your job, and you can no longer juggle your car and mortgage payments. Maybe you dipped into personal assets in a desperate (and futile) bid to salvage your business. Perchance your husband split and left you holding a big bag of joint debts. You likely bought into the easy-credit, instant-gratification, shop-till-you-drop mentality encouraged by lenders and retailers, and found yourself mired in financial quicksand.

In any case, things got out of hand and now you're up to your ears in debt.

Finance companies are warning that if you don't pay up, and soon, they're going to take your home and car. Credit-card firms are threatening to haul your butt into court. Debt collectors are pursuing you relentlessly. Your finances are a disaster. Your personal and professional relationships are strained. You're losing sleep, and you're becoming a perfect candidate for ulcers. Welcome to the club. Millions of Americans are in the same leaky boat.

Thankfully, you have a way — a perfectly legitimate way — to stop foreclosures and repossessions, put an end to lawsuits, protect your paycheck from garnishments, get those menacing debt collectors off your back, and regain control of your life: Bankruptcy.

But bankruptcy is shrouded in myth and prejudice. You may have even felt a few twinges of embarrassment when buying this book.

If you're like many folks, the first step on the road to financial recovery is overcoming your feelings of inadequacy, shame, guilt, and fear of the unknown.

In this chapter, we encourage you to put myth and prejudice aside and look calmly at the advantages and disadvantages of bankruptcy. Then, and only then, can you make a rational decision about whether bankruptcy is the best choice for you and your loved ones. You have things to gain, and things to lose, in bankruptcy. This chapter gives you a glimpse of what's at stake with bankruptcy in kind of a broad way and serves as a gateway to the rest of the book.

Viewing Bankruptcy in Historical Context

In the United States, the concept of bankruptcy is unique. Here, bankruptcy is viewed — legally and perceptually — as a means to an end, and not as "the end" of a debtor's financial life. America's Founding Fathers provided for bankruptcy right in the Constitution. A series of laws passed (and sometimes repealed) by Congress during the 1800s shaped the America view of bankruptcy as not only a remedy for creditors, but also as a way to give honest but unfortunate debtors financial rebirth. The Bankruptcy Act of 1898 established that debtors had a basic right to financial relief without creditor consent or court permission. American bankruptcy laws have come to be recognized as far more compassionate and much less punitive to debtors than the laws of other countries.

Like much of American law, the country's bankruptcy statutes reflect the constant tension between the competing interests of debtors and creditors. Think of it as a perpetual tug of war, with each side striving mightily but never pulling their opponent all the way over the line. To this day, the balance of influence between creditors and debtors is in an ever-present state of flux. Sometimes debtors have the upper hand. Other times, creditors get the edge. The constant, however, is that Americans have always been (and remain) entitled to a fresh start. The obstacles that you must clear to obtain this fresh start are not constant; they're always changing.

Modern day bankruptcy is rooted in the Bankruptcy Code of 1978, a federal law that was produced after more than ten years of careful study by judges and scholars. Since then, influential credit industry interest groups have pressured Congress to pass various procreditor amendments. The credit industry groups aim to completely rewrite bankruptcy law in their favor. Despite massive lobbying, and some incredibly generous campaign donations, the creditors have not yet succeeded, and bankruptcy remains a viable tool at your disposal. The practical application of this tool is governed by almost 300 volumes of opinions written by judges who interpret the Bankruptcy Code and attempt to apply its provisions to circumstances foreseen and unforeseen by the Code's drafters.

Bankruptcy's roots

The word *bankruptcy* evolved from an Italian phrase, *banca ratta,* that means "broken bench or table." In medieval times, when a merchant failed to pay his debts, creditors would ceremoniously break the bench or table from which he conducted his business. The forgiveness of debts, on the other hand, has biblical roots.

Consider the Old Testament: "At the end of every seven years, you are to cancel the debts of those who owe you money. This is how it is done. Everyone who has lent money to his neighbor is to cancel the debt: he must not try to collect the money: the Lord himself has declared the debt canceled." (Deuteronomy 15: 1–2).

Debt forgiveness also is a prominent New Testament theme. In Matthew 18:21–27, Jesus relates the story of a servant who was indebted to his master. The master ordered the servant and his entire family into slavery but, upon reconsideration, he forgave the debt. Jesus used the parable to explain the virtue of debt forgiveness. (On the other hand, the apostle Paul admonishes debt in Romans 13:8, "Render therefore to all their dues . . . owe no man any thing." So maybe we can't afford to get too pious here.)

In any case, throughout history creditors have not exactly displayed an attitude of Judeo-Christian charity toward debtors. Neither have governments.

The early Romans hacked up and divided the bodies of people who didn't pay their debts. In early England, people who were in over their heads financially were tossed in dungeons. The initial bankruptcy law, passed in 1542 during the reign of Henry VIII (the guy who kept beheading his wives), viewed debtors as quasi criminals but, for the first time, provided remedies other than imprisonment or mutilation.

Apparently, creditors finally realized that killing, maiming, or imprisoning debtors only ensured that they'd never get their money and that even if the debtor survived, he'd never be able to support himself and his family or become a productive member of society.

During the more enlightened reign of Queen Elizabeth I, a comprehensive bankruptcy law was passed (one that remained in effect for more than a century). The aim of the 1570 bankruptcy law was most certainly *not* to grant relief to debtors. Rather, it was designed to help creditors. It applied only to merchants (ordinary debtors still were imprisoned) and essentially laid out procedures by which a bankruptcy commissioner could seize the debtor's assets, sell them, and divide the proceeds among creditors. Debtors who did not cooperate had one of their ears lopped off.

The very idea of a bankruptcy law aiding debtors or forgiving debts remained a somewhat unimaginable concept until 1705, when Parliament enacted the first law that enabled a person to wipe out unpaid financial obligations. However, the terms were rather harsh: Consent of the creditor was required, and anyone who fraudulently sought bankruptcy relief faced the death penalty.

Before the United States won its independence, the various colonies handled bankruptcy their own respective ways, and little uniformity existed from colony to colony — except for the fact that settlers generally maintained the British tradition of jailing debtors (which extended to one of the British Empire's greatest literary stars: Charles Dickens. Bah humbug!). In fact, Robert Morris, known as the "financier of the American revolution" and a signer of the Declaration of Independence, spent three years in debtors' prison (and six years in the United States Senate). Supreme Court Justice James Wilson fled Pennsylvania to avoid a similar fate.

Debunking Bankruptcy Myths

In its relentless attack on American-style bankruptcy, the credit industry makes the same tiresome and disproved claims of the past as it lobbies for special privileges and attempts to shame people out of filing bankruptcy. You need to be aware of their claims and understand why they're full of baloney (with a capital "B"). Bankruptcy is an economic decision, not a morality play, and you needn't be deceived into viewing it as anything else. The following sections look at some of the usual red herrings that are cast about by the creditors' lobby.

Bankruptcies are at epidemic levels

People file for bankruptcy because they're in debt. The more debt there is, the more bankruptcies there are. Well, duh! It really is that simple.

When compared to the level of borrowing, the rate of bankruptcy has remained fairly steady. In 1977, 74 bankruptcies were filed for every $100 million of consumer debt. In 1997, 73 bankruptcies were filed for every $100 million of consumer debt.

Bankruptcy isn't the cause of debt but rather is the result. And it isn't the disease but rather is the cure. Restricting access to bankruptcy court won't solve the problem of debt any more than closing the hospitals will cure a plague.

People who go bankrupt are sleazy deadbeats

The credit industry stereotypes folks who file bankruptcy as worthless deadbeats taking advantage of a loophole-ridden legal system to dump their moral obligations on the backs of the rest of us. This stereotype is false, discriminatory, and manifestly unfair. Sure, bankruptcies have increased dramatically along with consumer debt, but it isn't because of some evil substrata of our culture.

From the 1970s to the 1980s, filings virtually doubled. The pace continued to increase in the 1990s, with bankruptcy filings setting new records year after year, even with a seemingly robust economy and near full employment. In fact, by the mid-1990s, bankruptcy filings, on a per capita basis, were running some eight times ahead of those of the Great Depression.

And who are these people filing for bankruptcy? Chances are they're your neighbors regardless of what neighborhood you live in. Bankruptcy is an equal opportunity phenomenon that strikes every socioeconomic bracket.

American bankruptcy

Our forefathers had radical ideas when it came to bankruptcy.

The founders of this country foresaw the possibility that honest people might suffer severe economic misfortune or make poor choices (Thomas Jefferson, certainly one of the most productive and accomplished individuals in the history of the world, was perpetually on the brink of bankruptcy during his latter years) and had the wisdom to provide for bankruptcy in the U.S. Constitution.

After the Constitutional Convention of 1787, the framers of the Constitution added a bankruptcy clause empowering Congress to pass uniform bankruptcy laws to prevent some states from establishing debtors' havens. In 1800 — 11 years after the ratification of the Constitution — Congress passed (by a single vote) a national bankruptcy law that enabled debtors to wipe out unpaid debts. But the provision was repealed three years later because of creditor complaints. Consequently, states began passing their own bankruptcy laws, a practice that was struck down by the U.S. Supreme Court.

By 1833, the federal government abolished debtors' prisons. Honest debtors would no longer be incarcerated. But bankruptcy was still viewed as a remedy for creditors, not debtors.

The tide began to shift when Congress, spurred by the powerful oratory of Daniel Webster, passed the Bankruptcy Act of 1841, a seminal event that established clearly that bankruptcy law was for debtors and for creditors. For the first time in history, the advocates for debtors had prevailed over the interests of creditors.

The victory, however, was short lived. Only three years later, creditors succeeded in having the law withdrawn. A similar choreography occurred just after the Civil War: Congress passed the Bankruptcy Act of 1867, which again enabled debtors to wipe out their debts. Eleven years later, creditors got it repealed. The threshold problem was this: Debt elimination was viewed as a privilege, dependent on creditor consent or court permission, not a fundamental right.

In the late 1890s, a revolutionary and uniquely American idea emerged — namely, that bankruptcy relief needed to be available to an honest person without consent or permission from others. This concept, which has come to be known as the *unconditional discharge,* was carved into the Bankruptcy Act of 1898.

Regardless of the long history and legal tradition underlying the unconditional discharge, creditors never cease trying to turn the clock back to the days when your bankruptcy relief required their permission.

Whenever the political climate appears favorable, creditors predictably scamper to Congress, whine about their losses, and claim that the "crisis" of "out-of-control" bankruptcies threatens to undermine the whole of Western civilization.

Yawn!

(See Charles Jordan Tabb, *The History of the Bankruptcy Laws in the United States,* American Bankruptcy Institute Law Review, Vol. 3:5, 1995.)

In any case, the image of the sleazy, deadbeat bankruptcy filer is a phantom and a scapegoat for irresponsible lending. The bankruptcy filer can be more accurately described as an ordinary, honest, hardworking, middle-class consumer who fell for aggressive and sophisticated credit marketing techniques, lost control, and unwittingly surrendered his financial soul to the devil that is debt.

Bankruptcy is the easy way out for folks who can pay their bills

Creditors have been making this claim since the 1800s, and it's as demonstrably wrong today as it was back then.

In recent years, the credit industry funded several *studies* — a handy euphemism for propaganda, the more accurate description — that supposedly supports their argument. Every one of these self-serving reports has been debunked by independent sources. Every single one. Several of these studies were even discredited by two financial arms of Congress, the General Accounting Office and the Congressional Budget Office.

Bankruptcy threatens the ethical foundations of our society

Gee, you'd think that bankruptcy was the greatest threat to apple pie and motherhood since Elvis Presley and bell-bottom jeans!

Credit-card companies furiously push plastic on virtually anyone willing to take it. At present, more than one billion credit cards are in circulation — that's about a dozen for every household in America. Lenders mail out billions of credit-card solicitations every year. Low- and moderate-income households, high school students, and the mentally disabled are popular targets of lenders.

According to the Administrative Office of the United States Courts, consumers between the ages of 18 and 25 are one of the largest growing segments of new bankruptcy filers. This statistic is disturbing. The main culprit for this trend is the readily accessible credit that is dispensed with abandon to students and other young people who lack the maturity and resources to handle debt.

Anyone with a brain can figure out that extending credit to irresponsible, immature, or even mentally incompetent people is kind of dumb (not to mention morally questionable). But creditors are more than willing to ignore the dangers of tomorrow so that they can reap exorbitant interest rates today. They're counting on — literally banking on — your ignorance of the situation. They encourage robbing Peter to pay Paul by using credit-card advances to pay off credit-card bills. They convince many middle-class consumers to bleed all the equity out of their homes through aggressively marketed home-equity loans — with much of it going to finance consumable products (mall junk) rather than the homestead of the American Dream. That hundreds of solid, middle-class folks find themselves in bankruptcy court isn't surprising.

Judges and legislators on bankruptcy

American law has long recognized the plight of debtors and strived to help folks get back on their feet. The attitudes of lawmakers and judges are etched in American history, and their comments attest to the legitimacy of bankruptcy as a means of achieving freedom from debt:

✔ **1897:** "This vast number [of debtors] constitutes an army of men crippled financially — most of them active, aggressive, honest men who have met with misfortune in the struggle of life, and who, if relieved from the burden of debt, would reenter the struggle with fresh hope and vigor and become active and useful members of society. . . . (The fresh start of bankruptcy) will lift these terrible and hopeless burdens and restore to the business and commercial circles of the country the active and aggressive elements that have met with misfortune and are now practically disabled for the battle of life. . . ." 55th U.S. Congress.

✔ **1904:** "Systems of bankruptcy are designed to relieve the honest debtor from the weight of indebtedness which has become oppressive and permit him to have a fresh start in . . . life, freed from the obligation and responsibilities which may have resulted from . . . misfortune." U.S. Supreme Court in *Wetmore v. Markoe.*

✔ **1934:** "The power of the individual to earn a living for himself and those dependent upon him is in the nature of a personal liberty quite as much if not more than it is a property right. . . . From the viewpoint of the wage-earner, there is little difference between not earning at all and earning wholly for a creditor. Pauperism may be the necessary result of either." U.S. Supreme Court in *Local Loan Co. v. Hunt.*

✔ **1991:** "A central purpose of the Code is to provide a procedure by which certain insolvent debtors can reorder their affairs, make peace with their creditors, and enjoy a new opportunity in life with a clear field for future effort, unhampered by the pressure and discouragement of preexisting debt." U.S. Supreme Court in *Grogan v. Garner.*

Although the rules of bankruptcy can and do shift with the political and societal winds, the basic premise — that honest folks deserve a second chance — has remained unchanged throughout American history.

But why, in the face of increasing credit-card losses, does the credit industry continue dispensing credit with utterly reckless abandon? The answer is simple: Because it's profitable . . . extremely profitable.

Honest folks pay a "tax" to support those who are bankrupt

That honest taxpayers are supporting people who are bankrupt is nothing short of an outright, bald-faced lie. The theory, espoused in press releases and by lobbyists, is that hundreds of thousands of Americans routinely ignore their obligations, intentionally or recklessly drive up their debts, and then declare themselves insolvent, stiffing creditors, and ultimately, every God-fearing, bill-paying, hard-working, patriotic American. The credit industry alleges that of the 1.37 million people who filed for bankruptcy in 1997, somewhere between 15 percent and 25 percent could have paid their debts.

Creditors note that they write off about $40 billion in debts annually, which works out to about $400 to $500 for every American household. Thus, the reasoning goes, if access to bankruptcy were restricted, the credit industry wouldn't suffer losses that it must pass along to consumers.

The fact of the matter is the credit industry would sustain the same $40 billion in losses even if the entire Bankruptcy Code were repealed. The reason? Most of the debt is owed by people who — the credit industry knows — are dead broke and wouldn't be able to pay under any circumstances. You just can't take blood from a stone, even if, by golly, you hold a press conference!

Understanding What You Can Gain Through Bankruptcy

If you have no way of paying your bills, bankruptcy certainly needs to be a consideration. If you have an income but cannot repay your debts in full within three years while maintaining a reasonable standard of living, bankruptcy may be a wise option (the tables in Chapter 2 help you calculate your potential to pay your debts based on current income and expenses).

Bankruptcy isn't the solution when your motive is anything other than reasonable relief from your debts. The U.S. Bankruptcy Code was established to assist *honest debtors* (those who adhere to the reasonable-relief maxim), not to provide a haven for chiselers and charlatans. If your aim is to jerk some creditor around, weasel out of debts you can easily pay, evade child support, or generally just stiff someone, bankruptcy is the wrong route. Bankruptcy should not be used for vengeance or as a stopgap measure. It should not be used as a ploy or a bargaining chip. You should not file bankruptcy unless you are serious about following through.

Bankruptcy can:

- ✔ Halt almost every kind of lawsuit
- ✔ Prevent garnishment of any wages you earn after filing
- ✔ Stop evictions — at least temporarily
- ✔ Avert repossessions

- Stop foreclosures
- Prevent your driver's license from being yanked for unpaid fines or judgments
- Bring IRS seizures to a skidding stop

Bankruptcy generally *won't* prevent:

- Criminal prosecutions
- Proceedings against someone who cosigned your loan, unless you file a "Chapter 13" repayment plan and propose paying the loan in full (See Chapter 4)
- Contempt of court hearings
- Actions to collect back child support or alimony, unless you file Chapter 13 and propose to pay that obligation off during the life of your plan (See Chapter 16)
- Governmental regulatory proceedings

In recent years, some self-proclaimed "mortgage consultants" and "foreclosure service" outfits have made a business out of essentially tricking their clients into filing bankruptcy. These con artists exploit the bankruptcy laws to delay foreclosure, collect rents from the property during the delay, and then head for the hills. In the end, unsuspecting clients usually lose their homes and wind up with a bankruptcy on their records without realizing they'd even filed for bankruptcy. Bottom line: Discuss your options with an experienced bankruptcy attorney, not some fly-by-night flimflam operation. See Chapter 3 for tips on finding a good lawyer.

Stopping creditors in their tracks

The moment that you file a bankruptcy petition, a legal shield called the *automatic stay* kicks in, prohibiting creditors from contacting you, suing you, repossessing your property, or garnishing your wages.

After you file, a creditor can ask for permission to proceed with a repossession, foreclosure, or eviction. But the creditor must obtain permission in advance, and the bankruptcy court judge may very well turn them down, if you propose a reasonable plan for paying that particular debt. (The following sections cover filing bankruptcy to eliminate some bills and pay others.)

Whenever a creditor is foolish enough to ignore the automatic stay, he'll have a federal judge on his back and may well get zapped with a fine and an order to pay your attorney fees.

Wiping out most of your debts

Bankruptcy wipes out or *discharges* most debts. Credit cards, medical bills, phone charges, loans, and judgments all are usually *dischargeable*. However, some obligations generally are not eliminated in bankruptcy and these *nondischargeable* debts include:

- Student loans (see Chapter 17)
- Alimony and child support (see Chapter 16)
- Damages for a personal injury you caused while driving illegally under the influence of drugs or alcohol (see Chapter 15)
- Debts from fraud (see Chapters 13 and 15)
- Financial obligations imposed as part of a criminal conviction (see Chapter 15)
- Taxes arising during the past three years (see Chapter 14)

Catching up on back mortgage and car payments

Sometimes, even dischargeable debts may continue to haunt you when they are tied to one of your essential possessions. For example, you can wipe out loans secured by your home or car, but the creditor can still foreclose on your house or repossess your vehicle if you don't pay.

In a Chapter 13 bankruptcy (one where you pay what you can toward your debts and the remainder is forgiven), you can propose a partial repayment plan to avoid foreclosure and make up back mortgage payments over a five-year span. You can prevent repossession of your car by gradually paying what it's worth — rather than the whole loan balance. (See Chapters 10 and 11.)

Filing bankruptcy to pay some debts over time

Although some debts are not dischargeable, filing a Chapter 13 reorganization enables you to pay debts such as support obligations or back taxes over a five-year period and protects you from being hassled while you're paying down the balances. You can also gradually catch up on missed mortgage payments. In the meantime, most of your other debts are just eliminated while you just pay for current expenses and keep current on future house and car payments.

Noncitizens of the U.S. of A.

You don't even have to be an American citizen to qualify for a fresh start. Neither citizenship nor even formal resident-alien status is required. Bankruptcy is available whenever you live in the United States or have a business or property in the U.S.

But there's a catch.

Your right to keep *exempt assets* (those that cannot be taken by creditors) is determined by the law of the state that is your permanent home. If you're in the United States on a temporary basis, the courts may say that no place in the United States qualifies as your permanent home. Therefore, although a tourist may be eligible to file bankruptcy, he may not be entitled to the benefit of any exemptions. Of course, that's no problem when he has no assets anyway. A person doesn't even have to live in

the U.S. to be eligible for bankruptcy if he does business or has property here.

But courts disagree on just what "property in the United States" constitutes, and some have rejected attempts by foreigners to create eligibility by simply obtaining a U. S. mailbox or establishing a nominal bank account. Others take a more liberal view.

For example, Ernestine didn't live in the U.S., didn't work in the U.S., and didn't do any business in the U.S., but she had a few hundred bucks in a bank account. The court said Ernestine was eligible to file bankruptcy in the United States — and expressed bewilderment as to why American credit-card companies would offer massive amounts of credit to a foreigner whose only asset in this country was $522.

Using bankruptcy to pay all your debts

Sometimes filing bankruptcy actually provides a way of paying all your debts rather than escaping them.

If the value of your property is sufficient to pay all your debts if only you had enough time to sell your assets, bankruptcy can be used to hold aggressive lenders at bay until your property is sold for the benefit of all your creditors — and possibly producing a surplus for you.

Here's how it works. Say, for example, that you own investment property worth $150,000, on which you have a mortgage of $100,000, and that you have other debts totaling $25,000.

If you can sell the property, you can pay off the mortgage and other debts, and still have something left over for yourself. But if the mortgageholder forecloses, neither you nor your creditors are likely to receive a cent. Although the property *is* put up for public auction in a foreclosure, bidders rarely show up, and the only bidder typically is the mortgageholder, which merely bids the amount that's owed on the mortgage. In other words, the mortgage company ends up owning the property without paying any cash. Filing bankruptcy interrupts the foreclosure so that the property can be sold for everyone's benefit. See Chapter 11 for more on how foreclosures work and how you can actually use the bankruptcy process to save your home.

Knowing What You Can Lose in Bankruptcy

Although bankruptcy may be that miracle cure you sought for your financial woes, you may encounter some unpleasant side effects. The disadvantages of filing bankruptcy are:

- **You can lose assets.** Depending on how much your home is worth and where you live, it is possible, but unlikely, that you'll lose it by filing bankruptcy. (If you're really worried about what will happen to your stuff, check out Part III, especially Chapter 9.) In most bankruptcies, debtors don't have to give up any of their belongings, but . . . .

- **Bankruptcy is a matter of public record.** As more and more records are stored on computers and accessible on the Internet, searching that data will become easier and easier for anyone who's interested. In other words, if your nosey neighbor wants to know whether you filed bankruptcy, how much you owe, and who you owe it to, the information is all in a public file and available for the asking.

- **Bankruptcy affects your credit rating.** Bankruptcy may have a negative effect on your credit rating, but that fact may well fall into the "So what?" category for you. Even with a bankruptcy on your record, your odds of obtaining credit are very good. When you talk to people who've actually filed bankruptcy, you'll discover that with a little work and perseverance, you can reestablish credit almost immediately. Some credit-card companies actually target folks right after bankruptcy, because they know that these people are free of all their existing debts and won't be likely to file another bankruptcy any time soon. So, don't pay too much attention to the horror stories bill collectors tell you about the disastrous effect bankruptcy has your credit. (In Chapter 20, we'll walk you through rebuilding your credit after bankruptcy.)

- **Friends and relatives can be forced to give back money or property.** If you repaid loans to friends or relatives or gave them anything within the past year, they can be forced to repay a trustee the money they received, if you don't know what to watch out for. (We tell you what to watch out for in Chapter 18.) You can usually avoid these kinds of problems by carefully timing your bankruptcy filing.

- Bankruptcy can strain relations with loved ones, especially parents who were raised in a different era. (In Chapter 2, we give you some pointers on easing the strain.)

- A stigma may still be attached to filing bankruptcy. This drawback is especially true in small communities but is much less likely to be a problem in cities where newspapers don't even bother printing the names of nonbusiness bankruptcies.

- Bankruptcy may cause more problems than it solves when you've transferred assets to keep them away from creditors. (More about this problem can be found in Chapter 18.)

- You can suffer some discrimination. Although governmental agencies and employers aren't supposed to discriminate against you for filing bankruptcy, they may still do so in a roundabout way. Prospective employers may also refuse to hire you (see Chapter 24 for more on employment discrimination).

Considering Alternatives to Bankruptcy

Bankruptcy isn't for everyone, and sometimes better solutions are available. We explain them in Chapter 6. If it appears that the negatives outweigh the positives, another route may be your best choice. Depending on your situation, the best alternative may be:

- Selling assets to pay debts in full

- Negotiating with creditors to reduce your debts to a manageable level.

- Restructuring your home mortgage

- Taking out a home-equity loan

- Doing nothing at all if you have nothing, expect to acquire nothing, and don't care about your present or future credit rating

In any event, you need to weigh your decision on a simple, rational scale. Ask yourself whether the benefits outweigh the drawbacks. Many people, ravaged by guilt and shame, think they need to fully exhaust every alternative before considering bankruptcy, including:

- Making payments that never reduce the principal balance owed

- Taking out second mortgages to pay credit-card debts

- Borrowing against pensions

- Obtaining loans from friends and relatives

- Taking second jobs

You must think seriously about the strain your financial distress places on your health, marriage, and family. Granted, bankruptcy is a very serious step that you shouldn't take lightly, but that doesn't mean you have to wait until you've lost everything. Think of it in these terms: If you have some blocked arteries, it just may be smarter to have bypass surgery *before* you have a heart attack. The same is true of bankruptcy.

Introducing the Different Types of Personal Bankruptcy

Consumer bankruptcies are covered mainly under two parts of the U.S. Bankruptcy Code:

- ✔ *Chapter 7 liquidation,* which enables you to eliminate most of your debts but may require you to forfeit some of your assets for distribution to creditors.

- ✔ *Chapter 13 reorganization,* which enables you to pay off all or a portion of your debts during a three-to-five-year time span but doesn't require you to forfeit any of your belongings or assets to pay *unsecured debts* (those that are not secured by property, such as your car or another valuable asset). See Chapter 10 for more on the difference between secured and unsecured debts.

Likewise, special kinds of bankruptcy exist. Chapter 12 bankruptcy, which is similar to Chapter 13 bankruptcy, addresses the unique problems faced by family farmers. And finally, Chapter 11 bankruptcy is available to individuals but primarily is used for business reorganizations. As a practical matter, almost all consumer cases are covered under Chapter 7 or Chapter 13 of the code.

Liquidations (Chapter 7)

Chapter 7, commonly referred to as *straight bankruptcy,* is often what people mean or think of when they use or hear the term generically.

In its simplest form, Chapter 7 wipes out most of your debts and, in return, you may have to surrender some of your property. Chapter 7 doesn't include a repayment plan. Your debts are simply eliminated forever. If you buy a lottery ticket the day after filing and hit the jackpot, yippee! for you and tough beans for your creditors. You obviously can voluntarily pay back your creditors if you suddenly strike it rich, but legally you don't owe a dime after your debt is discharged.

Theoretically a debtor's assets can be seized and sold for the benefit of creditors. All nonexempt assets owned on the petition date are fair game. They can be sold, with the proceeds distributed to your creditors. But in practice, 96 percent of consumer bankruptcies are *no-asset cases,* meaning that no property is taken away from the debtor because it's all exempt or worth so little that it's not worth the trouble.

Consumer reorganizations (Chapter 13)

Chapter 13 involves a repayment plan in which you pay all or part of your debts during a three- to five-year period. In a Chapter 13, you propose a debt repayment plan that requires court approval and thereafter keeps creditors at bay as long as you keep making payments. This can be a great deal, when you're able to establish and live within the confines of a budget.

A budget plan that demands frugality to the point of misery is doomed to fail ("Frugality is misery in disguise," observed Pubilius Syrus some 2,000 years ago). One that is reasonable has a good chance of succeeding. The operative word, however, is reasonable. See Chapters 2 and 21 for more on creating and living within a budget.

Every Chapter 13 plan must pass two tests:

- ✔ The *best-interest test,* which mandates that unsecured creditors be paid at least as much as they would receive if you filed a Chapter 7 instead of a Chapter 13.

- ✔ The *best-efforts test,* which requires that you pay all your disposable income (the amount left over after paying reasonable living expenses) to the trustee for at least the first 36 months of your plan.

When you're done, you're done. Most creditors have gotten all they're going to get. Life goes on.

Weighing the Consequences of Not Filing Bankruptcy

In the same way that filing bankruptcy can have negative consequences, not filing can also have negative consequences. If you're eligible for bankruptcy, but opt against filing, creditors have a number of options they can pursue, depending on whether a particular debt is secured by your property.

Claims secured by your car

If your car secures a debt, the creditor can repossess the vehicle and sell it to cover the loan. The proceeds of a repossession sale usually are not enough to pay the debt, so you'll lose the car and still have to pay the balance that you owe on it — the worst of both worlds. See the section on autos in Chapter 9.

Although the law requires a creditor to sell a car in a "commercially reasonable" manner, that doesn't necessarily mean that the creditor will receive nearly as much as you can by selling it yourself. Before allowing repossession, you may want to try selling the vehicle. Your chances of getting more for the car are greater than the finance company's. See Chapter 10 for more on how bankruptcy can affect your car.

Claims secured by your home

Mortgage companies can't simply boot you out of your home and onto your derrière if you miss a few payments. They must first go through a foreclosure procedure to extinguish your ownership rights. Although not all foreclosures involve court proceedings, all do take time — at least three months in most cases and frequently much longer. You can continue to live on the property until the foreclosure is completed. Chapter 11 has more on the workings of foreclosures.

Student loans

Government agencies can *garnish* (siphon off) up to 10 percent of your disposable income without going to court. A garnishment is almost like a withholding tax — the money is gone from your paycheck before you ever see it. You also need to be aware that Congress canceled state statutes of limitations on student loans. In other words, you can't just wait it out. You must deal with student loans. They won't evaporate on their own. See Chapter 17 for more on student loans.

Support obligations

Although debtors' prisons are officially a thing of the past, a divorce court can still send you to jail for neglecting your support obligations, and some states have programs to revoke professional licenses — such as licenses for practical nurses or accountants or cosmetologists — of professionals who haven't kept up with their support. Support obligations are covered in Chapter 16.

Fines and restitution

If you've been ordered to pay a fine or make restitution in connection with a criminal proceeding, and don't pay, accommodations at the local jail may await you. Don't tempt the judge, because some of them don't need much tempting to have you hauled off to jail. See Chapter 15 for more on fines.

Taxes

The IRS has truly scary powers to seize your bank account, pension, real property, or even the shirt off your back. State taxing authorities also have similar special powers. In addition, your town or city, student loan creditors, or your ex-spouse or kids may be able to grab your tax refund whenever you owe alimony or support. Chapters 8 and 14 cover taxes.

Lawsuits

Creditors with other types of claims can't do much without first suing you and obtaining a judgment. To do this, they must serve you with legal documents and give you a chance to dispute the debt in court. If you don't respond, a default judgment can be entered against you. That means the ruling goes against you even though you never presented your case. See Chapter 15 for the lowdown on judgments.

Using the Statute of Limitations

Most debts — student loans being the most notable exception — eventually disappear simply through the passage of time. In most cases, the *statute of limitations* (the time period within which an action must be commenced) is less than six years. But whenever a judgment has been entered against you, it can be as long as 20 years.

The trick is figuring out when the statute of limitations clock begins ticking. Sometimes, just making partial payments or acknowledging a debt can start the time running all over again. And you sure don't want that to happen.

Chapter 2

Stopping the Bleeding

- -

In This Chapter

▶ Avoiding making matters worse

▶ Weighing your income against what you spend

▶ Determining whether you're a compulsive spender

▶ Covering your assets

▶ Figuring out what you own and what you owe

▶ Talking about money problems with loved ones

- -

Demoralizing debt can seem like a perpetual storm cloud hovering over your days and putting a damper on all life's pleasures. As bleak as your outlook may seem, the forecast really isn't that dismal. A ray of sunshine is striving to break through those clouds, and we're going to help you find it. Remember, however, that maintaining a positive, can-do attitude is essential. Although considering personal bankruptcy is no time for self-pity, understanding that you're not a loser, you're not alone, and that your predicament is symptomatic of a new culture that emerged during the last half century is definitely important.

If you're like most debtors, you probably feel as if you've been hemorrhaging green stuff for so long that your financial blood vessels are bone dry. And you're probably down on yourself in a big way. Although you must accept responsibility for your own mistakes — and bear the cross even when your predicament is just the result of rotten luck — you're also probably riding a crazy but predictable wave that has engulfed several million other Americans.

Lenders perpetually make pitches for more spending and more borrowing, which on the credibility scale is somewhere up there with the Boston strangler promoting the Heimlich maneuver. Even political institutions have signed on to the consumerism fad. National leaders tell us in times of economic downturn that spending more and more is our patriotic duty, further extending our debt load. What's good for the credit-card companies, apparently, is good for America — at least in the eyes of consumer lenders.

Odds are you've consciously (or subconsciously) swallowed this bait hook, line, and sinker. And odds are you've already paid the piper in the currency of stress and anxiety. It doesn't take a mind reader to predict that you (and others in your situation) are probably:

- ✔ Fighting with your spouse over money.

- ✔ Watching in helpless horror as more and more and more of your monthly income falls down the debt drain.

- ✔ Sweating even the minimum payments on your credit cards.

- ✔ Neglecting routine and preventive medical and dental care because you can't pay the doctor's bill, and even the co-pay seems daunting.

- ✔ Taking advances on one credit card to cover payments on another — the very definition of robbing Peter to pay Paul.

- ✔ Dodging calls from creditors and pretending to be someone else when they call.

- ✔ Using your credit card for small purchases, and then buying more things you don't need because you're embarrassed to go into a drugstore and charge only a bottle of aspirin.

- ✔ Saving those unsolicited cash advance checks from lenders, just in case.

- ✔ Waking up in the middle of the night worrying about money.

Welcome to the club — a really big club. Now that you're a member, you have only one thing to do: Clear your head and put a tourniquet on your wound this instant. True, the problem may not be entirely your making. It is, however, entirely your responsibility to get out of trouble, so go for it! You need to make a rational determination about what you ought to do and how you ought to do it.

Preventing Further Damage Now

Imagining things being much bleaker than they seem right now is probably difficult, but if you're on the brink of bankruptcy, you need to be extremely careful; otherwise, you'll only muck up your situation.

Until you've met with a bankruptcy lawyer and know just where you stand, do not

- ✔ **Borrow any more money.** Period. No balance transfers. No bill consolidation loans. No pension loans. No home-equity loans. And certainly no loans from friends or relatives.

- ✔ **Make any payments on debts to friends, business partners, or relatives.**

- ✔ **Call or write to any creditor who does not already know how to contact you.**

- ✔ Get married — or divorced.

- ✔ Sell any valuable assets.

- ✔ Make any gifts (other than charitable contributions that you normally make) or transfer property in an attempt to keep these assets away from creditors.

- ✔ Ignore lawsuits.

- ✔ Give any creditor a postdated check.

- ✔ Reveal to a creditor who holds the title to your car that you are considering bankruptcy.

- ✔ Agree to pay joint debts if you are in the middle of a divorce matter.

- ✔ File any past-due income tax returns. (However, have them prepared and ready to file.)

- ✔ Make any unusual or large contributions to a pension fund.

- ✔ Make any withdrawals from your pension.

- ✔ Move out of your homestead or enter into a contract to sell it.

- ✔ Allow a foreclosure sale to occur or give a creditor a deed in lieu of foreclosure.

- ✔ Leave any money on deposit in an institution where you owe money.

- ✔ Allow health insurance to lapse.

- ✔ Voluntarily leave your job.

Throughout this book, we show you how these seemingly innocent things can make your bankruptcy more complicated and cause unpleasant surprises. If you've already done some of the *don'ts*, don't despair. Just make sure to tell your lawyer, who may be able to fix things.

Now that we've covered what *not* to do, let's focus on what you *can* do to improve your situation. And the first thing to do is make an honest, objective, unemotional assessment of what you have, what you owe, and what you can do to balance the scales.

Comparing Your Income with Your Spending

Figuring out where you stand or where you're going without knowing just how much you make and spend is tough. Taking the time to complete the two worksheets outlined in Tables 2-1 and 2-2 helps you

✔ Provide insight into whether you can solve your problems without bankruptcy.

✔ Assemble the information your lawyer needs to file bankruptcy.

✔ Establish a budget for the future so you don't get into financial trouble again.

Focusing on how much income you have

Table 2-1 helps you calculate the first half of the financial equation — your monthly income.

Focusing on monthly income and expenses would be wise, so you may have to prorate some figures. *Prorating* means, for example, that when you're paid every two weeks, you double the amount of your paycheck. Whenever you receive an annual bonus, divide it by 12.

Several of the sources to which you can look for this information are

✔ Your paycheck

✔ Last year's income tax return

✔ Records of any alimony you receive (not the amount you're supposed to get, the actual amount you received)

Table 2-1	Your Net Income		
	You	*Your Mate*	*Combined Amount*
Current gross wages, salary, and commissions	$	$	
Estimated overtime pay	$	$	
Subtotal gross income			$
PAYROLL DEDUCTIONS			
Payroll taxes and social security	$	$	
Insurance	$	$	
Union dues	$	$	
Contributions to pension	$	$	
Repayments on pension loan	$	$	
Support payments deducted from pay	$	$	

	You	Your Mate	Combined Amount
Other payroll deductions	$	$	
Subtotal of payroll deductions			$
TAKE-HOME PAY	$	$	$
Gross income from business, profession, or farm (expenses of running the operation are accounted for on the expenses worksheet)	$	$	
Gross income from rental properties (expenses are accounted for on the expenses worksheet)	$	$	
Social Security and other government assistance	$	$	
Retirement income	$	$	
Other income	$	$	
TOTAL INCOME	$	$	$

Coming to grips with where your money goes

Chances are you don't really know where all your money goes. It probably seems like you just never have enough, despite living a rather modest lifestyle.

We suggest that you carry around little notebook so you can record *every* expenditure that you make for a month. You say you dropped $10 in the collection basket at church? Write it down. Maybe you picked up a box of cookies at the convenience store . . . make a note. Even if it's only a cup of coffee or a soda, record it. Sure it sounds like a hassle — and it is, but that's the point. The pain of having to write down every expenditure makes you less likely to spend the money. It just becomes more trouble than it's worth.

Keeping track of all your expenditures enables you to do the following:

- ✔ Prepare a realistic budget
- ✔ Lay the groundwork for bringing your spending under control, regardless of whether you end up filing bankruptcy
- ✔ Make a more informed decision about whether bankruptcy is the best solution
- ✔ Intelligently weigh pros and cons of a Chapter 7 liquidation versus a Chapter 13 reorganization

✔ Provide a ready record of some of the information necessary to complete bankruptcy papers, if you decide to go that route

Be sure to record expenses that are not monthly and tend to fall into the out-of-sight-out-of-mind category. Insurance, real property taxes, income taxes not withheld from wages, vacation expenses, tuition, and Christmas spending are a few examples. When you pay car insurance every six months, divide the amount of this payment by six. When you pay some bills weekly, multiply by 52 and then divide by 12 to arrive at the monthly payment amount.

Include payments on *past* credit-card charges, but as for future charges, record the items purchased.

Table 2-2 should help.

Table 2-2	Where Does My Money Go?	
Type of Expense	*Monthly Average*	*Total*
HOUSING		
Rent	$	
Mortgage payments	$	
Real property taxes (if not included in mortgage payments)	$	
Furniture/appliance purchases	$	
Home maintenance/repairs	$	
Total Housing Expense		$
UTILITIES		
Gas/electric/oil	$	
Water	$	
Regular phone	$	
Cable TV	$	
Total Utilities Expense		$
FOOD		
Groceries	$	
Eating out	$	
Total Food Expense		$

Type of Expense	Monthly Average	Total
CLOTHING EXPENSES		
New clothes	$	
Laundry	$	
Total Clothing Expense	$	
MEDICAL EXPENSES		
Doctors/Dentists/Other medical professionals	$	
Drugs	$	
Eyeglasses	$	
Other medical expenses	$	
Total Medical Expense		$
TRANSPORTATION EXPENSES		
Gasoline	$	
Maintenance/repairs	$	
License and other fees	$	
Parking	$	
Public transportation	$	
Other transportation expenses	$	
Total Transportation Expense		$
DEBT PAYMENTS		
Credit cards	$	
Auto loans	$	
Student loans	$	
Other payments		
Total Debt Payment		$
TAXES NOT DEDUCTED FROM PAY		
Estimated tax payments	$	
Taxes paid when annual return filed (remember to divide by 12)	$	

(continued)

Table 2-2 (continued)

Type of Expense	Monthly Average	Total
Payments on back taxes	$	
Other tax payments	$	
Total Tax Payment		$
RECREATION EXPENSES		
Cell phone	$	
Internet	$	
Movies, sporting events, concerts	$	
Books	$	
Vacation and travel	$	
Gifts	$	
Pet expenses	$	
Other recreational expenditures	$	
Total Recreation Expense	$	
INSURANCE		
Homeowners (unless included in mortgage payment)	$	
Auto insurance	$	
Health insurance (unless deducted from pay)	$	
Life insurance (unless deducted from pay)		
Other insurance	$	
Total Insurance Expense	$	
VICES		
Tobacco	$	
Alcohol	$	
Gambling	$	
Other	$	
Total Vice Expense		$

Type of Expense	Monthly Average	Total
PERSONAL ITEMS		
Haircuts, beauty products (including makeup)	$	
Health club memberships	$	
Other	$	
Total Personal Items Expense		$
SUPPORT AND ALIMONY PAYMENTS		
Back alimony and child support (not deducted from pay)	$	
Current alimony and child support payments	$	
Total Support Payments		$
OFFSPRING		
Allowance	$	
Tuition	$	
Day care	$	
Toys and presents	$	
Money given to adult children	$	
Other	$	
Total Offspring Expense		$
PERSONAL EDUCATIONAL EXPENSES		
Tuition	$	
Books	$	
Supplies	$	
Other	$	
Total Educational Expense		$
BUSINESS EXPENSES		
Total monthly expenses of business, profession, or farm	$	
Total monthly expenses of owning and operating rental property	$	
Other business expenses	$	
Total Business Expense		$

(continued)

Table 2-2 *(continued)*		
Type of Expense	*Monthly Average*	*Total*
OTHER EXPENSES		
Charitable contributions	$	
Miscellaneous expenses	$	
Total Other Expense		$
TOTAL MONTHLY EXPENSES		$

Assessing Your Spending Habits

Congratulations! You've just taken the most important step on the road to financial recovery. To varying degrees, we all live in a self-imposed fog when it comes to spending money. Spending becomes a comfortable habit — just the way you go about your daily business — and habits are always hard to break. But now you're on your way.

Now that you've committed yourself to recovery, we can take a close look at where your money is going, consider the possibility that overspending has become a habit and, if so, suggest ways to deal with it.

The devil's in the details: Scrutinizing your expenses

Okay, documenting your expenses has proven the obvious: You've wasted money, and probably made some lousy financial decisions. Who hasn't? But now that you have a handle on the problem, you're in position to take control. In Chapter 21, we offer some suggestions for a simpler lifestyle through financial "downshifting."

With the right attitude, eliminating unnecessary expenditures can be a little like a treasure hunt. There's extra money somewhere; you just have to find it.

While we wouldn't presume to tell you how much to spend on any particular item — that's your call — here are a few things to zero in on:

- **Credit-card payments.** If a big chunk of your monthly income is going to pay credit-card bills (and for minimum payments at that) bankruptcy may be far and away the best solution. Right now you're just spinning your wheels — paying interest without significantly reducing the principal amount of the debts.

✔ **Daily dribbles.** We all live our lives against a background of daily patterns that eventually become habits. Many times these habits include unnecessary spending that provides no real benefit or enjoyment. What seems like small stuff eventually adds up. Consider the $2 latte you get on the way to work, a $1 you put in the soda pop machine and $2.50 you spend for an afternoon snack — all without thinking about it. Over the course of a year, you've blown $1,430. To put it in perspective: If you invested this money for 20 years at 10 percent interest, you'd end up with more than $80,000!

✔ **Extravagances.** Admittedly, one person's luxury is another's necessity, but you really need to think long and hard before plopping down $100 for a restaurant meal or $60 to watch a pay-for-view prize fight on television. It's sometimes helpful — albeit painful — to figure out how much work you had to do to pay for a particular treat. For instance, if a night on the town costs you a day and a half of work, you may think twice about the return on your investment.

✔ **Impulse purchases.** A little later in this chapter we'll ask you to list all your belongings, but for now just make a trip to your attic, basement, and garage. If you're like most people — and us — you'll see tons of stuff you've bought but rarely if ever use. Simplify.

✔ **Gifts.** Studies show that many folks spend lavishly on gifts they would never buy for themselves. Christmas, of course, is the granddaddy of budget busters.

✔ **Overwhelming mortgage payments.** If you obtained your mortgage recently, most of your monthly payment goes toward the interest. So, you may not have much equity and the home may not be worth keeping — especially if it's a second mortgage. More on this in Chapter 11.

✔ **Killer car payments.** New cars are awfully pricey these days, partly because they are more dependable and longer lasting. If you're struggling to maintain payments on a new car, you may want to consider selling your expensive car and buying something more affordable. There are plenty of reliable, moderately priced, used cars on the market today.

Are you a spendaholic?

Similar to an addiction, compulsive spending can be a disease. If you are so afflicted, you may need professional assistance. Debtor's Anonymous, a group dedicated to helping folks curb excessive spending habits, has compiled a checklist of the common signs of compulsive behavior. Ask yourself the following questions:

✔ Are your debts making your home life unhappy?

✔ Does the pressure of your debts distract you from your daily work?

✔ Are your debts affecting your reputation?

- Do your debts cause you to think less of yourself?

- Have you ever given false information to obtain credit?

- Have you ever made unrealistic promises to your creditors?

- Does the pressure of your debts make you careless of the welfare of your family?

- Do you ever fear that your employer, family, or friends will find out the extent of your total indebtedness?

- When faced with a difficult financial situation, does the prospect of borrowing give you an inordinate feeling of relief?

- Does the pressure of your debts cause you to have difficulty sleeping?

- Has the pressure of your debts ever caused you to consider getting drunk?

- Have you ever borrowed money without giving adequate consideration to the rate of interest you are required to pay?

- Do you usually expect a negative response when you are subject to a credit investigation?

- Have you ever developed a strict regimen for paying off your debts, only to break it under pressure?

- Do you justify your debts by telling yourself that you are superior to the "other" people, and when you get your "break" you'll be out of debt overnight?

If you answer yes to eight or more of the previous questions, you may be a compulsive spender. An organization called Debtors Anonymous can help. You can check out their Web site at www.DebtorsAnonymous.org, call them at (781) 453-2743, or write to them at: Debtors Anonymous, General Service Office, PO Box 920888, Needham, MA 02492-0009.

You also may want to take a look at Chapter 21 to help reorder your spending priorities.

Getting a Handle on What You Own

Although you're in a mode figuring out what your spending habits and your earnings are, now also is a good time to get an equally firm grasp on what you *own*. Documenting your assets does the following:

- Creates a basis for figuring out what property you may lose by filing bankruptcy

- Lets you know if avoiding bankruptcy by selling things is a viable option

✔ Demonstrates how little you have to show for thousands of dollars of credit-card debt

Use Table 2-3 to document what you own. If you need some help figuring out how much you stuff is worth, take a look at Chapter 9.

Documenting your assets when you're close to bankruptcy is depressing.

Table 2-3	What You Own
Asset	*Value*
REAL PROPERTY	
Your home	
Other real property	
Timeshares	
MOTOR VEHICLES	
BANK ACCOUNT BALANCES	
HOUSEHOLD GOODS	
Furniture	
Appliances	
Audio and video equipment	
Computers and accessories	
Other household items	
ART OBJECTS AND COLLECTIBLES	
JEWELRY	

(continued)

Table 2-3 (continued)

Asset	Value
FIREARMS	
HOBBY EQUIPMENT	
STOCKS, BONDS, AND OTHER INVESTMENTS	
CASH VALUE OF LIFE INSURANCE	
INTERESTS IN ANY TRUSTS	
BUSINESS INTERESTS	
MONEY THAT YOU ARE OWED	
Alimony and support	
Bonuses at work	
Accounts receivable	
Claims where you can sue someone	
Commissions	
Tax refunds	

Asset	Value
MONEY YOU ARE ENTITLED TO BECAUSE SOMEONE DIED	
Life insurance	
Distributions from an estate	
PATENTS AND COPYRIGHTS	
TOOLS AND MACHINERY USED FOR WORK	
CASH VALUE OR PENSIONS	
OFFICE EQUIPMENT NOT INCLUDED IN HOUSEHOLD GOODS	
BUSINESS INVENTORY	
OTHER ASSETS	

Figuring Out How Much You Owe

Purveyors of consumer credit want you to think in terms of monthly payments instead of considering the total amount you'll owe. It's a lot easier to sell that new car when the customer focuses on a $400 monthly payment rather than on a $25,000 albatross. But when it comes to assessing your financial condition, knowing the total amount of your debts is critical.

Home and car loans should be considered separately from other debts for two reasons:

✔ These loans can be reduced or eliminated if you sell the house or car.

✔ Bankruptcy affects home and car loans differently than other debts.

You can find out how much you owe on these loans by phoning the creditor. If you are behind in payments, also find out how much it will take to bring the loan current (as opposed to the amount required to pay loan in full).

Filling the blanks in Table 2-4 helps you get a grip on what you owe.

Table 2-4	How Much Do You Owe on Mortgage and Car Loans			
	Total Balance Owed	*Monthly Payment*	*Value of Home/Car*	*Arrearage (Amount You're Behind)*
Residence				
Other real estate				
Cars				

Calculating how much you owe on other debts is a little tougher.

Ordering credit reports is one place to start. See Chapter 5 for tips on getting credit reports.

The amounts owed on judgments, child support, alimony, fines, and restitution obligations can frequently be determined from documents on file in the courthouse.

You can get a rough idea of how much you owe on income taxes by looking at copies of your income tax returns, but this won't give you the amount of penalties and interest that has accrued. See Chapter 8 and Chapter 14 for more info on dealing with tax obligations.

Hopefully, you have a rough idea of how much you owe on student loans. If not, you'll probably have to find out more than you want to about how the student loan industry works just to find out whom to ask. Check out Chapter 17.

After you know what you owe, use Table 2-5 to help you keep track of it.

If creditors don't how where you live, or have given up on you, don't ring their bell by calling them up.

Table 2-5	How Much Do You Owe on Other Debts
Type of Debt	*Total Amount Owed*
Judgments	
Income taxes	
Child support and alimony	
Student loans	
Fines and restitution obligations	
Medical bills	
Credit-card balances	
Loans to friends and relatives	

At this point, you may want to jump to Chapter 4 to discover which types of bankruptcy are available and to Chapter 6 to check out alternatives to bankruptcy.

Coming Out of the Financial Closet

Achieving permanent personal financial salvation is much easier when your family is on your side. Informing parents, mates, and offspring of your financial predicament all present unique challenges.

Telling parents

People who came of age when the Great Depression still was a vivid and painful memory tend to have little sympathy and even less understanding for someone living beyond his or her means. But many Baby Boomers and their progeny grew up with a much different financial ethos and, for better or worse, contributed more to the cultural fabric than rock'n'roll music.

You'll have an easier time with your parents when you can show them that, for better or worse, society has changed. But remember, allowing them to bail you out is almost always a lousy idea because:

- ✔ They probably can't afford it.
- ✔ It most likely will only postpone the day of reckoning and won't solve the problem.
- ✔ It may sour the relationship with your parents.
- ✔ It may backfire if you ultimately end up in bankruptcy.

Tom's parents thought they could ease his financial woes by paying off his $12,000 car loan. But even after Ma and Pa paid off the car, Tom still had to file bankruptcy because he owed $25,000 on credit cards. Because Tom then owned the car free and clear, the trustee sold it for the benefit of creditors. A far better plan would have been for Tom to file bankruptcy *first* so that Tom's parents could pay off his car loan after bankruptcy without fear of losing their investment to creditors.

Talking to mates

It's no secret that money squabbles top the list of domestic disputes. Reaching common ground with your mate may not only help to solve your debt problems, but it also may even save your relationship. And yet, starting a meaningful dialogue about money with your mate can be a pretty dicey proposition.

Typically couples:

- ✔ Discuss money only when there's a problem.
- ✔ Tend to assess blame, and then argue about who was *right* and who was *wrong* about past financial decisions, which can get in the way of any real communication.
- ✔ May have radically different views about earning, spending, and saving — not to mention bankruptcy.

Self-indulgent Yanks

Professor Juliet B. Schor explores the shifting American attitude toward consumption and debt in her book, *The Overspent American* (Basic Books, 1998). Her research indicates that:

- Keeping up with the Smiths and Joneses has become keeping up with the apparent lifestyles of favorite television characters. People no longer are content with being as successful as the people next door. They want the idealized lifestyle of the rich and famous.

- Barometers of what constitutes the good life have shifted. In 1975, people were more likely to be content with a happy marriage, healthy children, and a job where they could make a difference. By 1991, the focus was on material goods and luxuries — vacation homes, swimming pools, a second color TV, and a big-bucks job.

- Many Americans confess to *defensive spending*, or fearing that if they don't keep up their children will suffer a disadvantage. So, they join a country club they can't afford so their kids associate with the "right" people and enjoy the "right" experiences.

- As upscale consumption intensifies, family finances deteriorate and households take on record amounts of debt. The largest increases have not been among low-income households, but rather are carried by people in the $50,000 to $100,000-per-year bracket.

- Nearly one-third of American households survive from paycheck to paycheck, saving only about half what they were socking away 15 years ago. In 1995, only 55 percent of all American households were saving anything at all. The French, Germans, Japanese, and Italians save roughly three times what Americans do, and the British and Dutch save more than twice as much. Even Indian and Chinese families, many of whom are dirt poor, manage to save about a quarter of their yearly incomes.

- A growing number of *downshifters* — people working at or below their abilities and below their earning capacities — are dropping out of the rat race. About 85 percent are happy about the change they made. Downshifters are no more likely to be women than men, and they're not wealthy; almost half made $35,000 or less before making the change.

- Children, weaned on MTV and spending their Saturdays in shopping malls, are "agents of materialism," infecting family values with ever-increasing consumerism.

- People are more able to justify spending for gifts for others than necessities for themselves. According to one survey 75 percent of *pets* receive Christmas gifts.

When you just can't see eye to eye, a joint session with a reputable bankruptcy lawyer can help provide an accurate assessment of your options and at least stop you from spinning your wheels. You may find that one spouse is better off filing bankruptcy, and the other can make out better with some other plan.

The process of working out a mutually agreeable solution to a current problem also can lay the foundation for teamwork down the road in mapping a financial plan so that you'll both be on the same page regarding the lifestyle and financial priorities that the future holds.

Explaining the situation to offspring

Kids say and do the darndest things, even when they're 40 years old.

Older parents often try to support or partially support adult offspring and, as a result, find themselves at the brink of financial disaster. More often, well-meaning young parents spend themselves into trouble in an effort to provide their kids with every advantage and every joy. In either case, it may be time to make a decision about finances, about the private skating lessons, the class trip abroad, the piano tutor, the ballet tutu, the soccer camp, and so on.

Including children (even adult children) in productive family discussions about finances gives them a better understanding of lifestyle changes that are required of them and you.

Chapter 3

Meeting the Players

In This Chapter

▶ Appreciating why you need a lawyer

▶ Finding a lawyer you can trust, and figuring out how to pay her

▶ Identifying friends and foes

*I*n your pursuit of a fresh financial start, you'll encounter a rather large cast of characters, at least indirectly. One player, and only one, is unequivocally on your side: your lawyer. Others, such as the trustee, look out for the interests of your creditors. And the judge is supposed to function as a neutral arbiter. This chapter identifies the cast members, their roles on the bankruptcy stage, and how those factors relate to you and your goals. It also includes — in the sidebar at the end — a brief vocabulary list for you to look at so you can understand what everyone is talking about. For greater fluency in bankruptcy legalese, however, be sure to check out the Glossary in the back of the book.

Finding Professional Help

One of the challenges of putting your financial house in order is getting an accurate, trustworthy, and unbiased assessment of your particular options. Obtaining objective advice is absolutely essential, because you're going to be bombarded with conflicting information and opinions about bankruptcy.

Despite their best intentions, friends or relatives may mislead you. And so can the following groups of people:

> ✔ Credit counselors, who ostensibly help with budgeting and dealing with creditors, may inappropriately discourage you from filing for bankruptcy, and, instead, push for a secret agenda. Although they may appear to be independent, many of them are on creditors' payrolls, so their interests may be completely at odds with yours.

✔ Debt consolidators, offering to replace your many monthly bills with a single "low-interest, easy payment loan," sometimes use sophisticated marketing ploys to dazzle you into believing that you can get out of debt by borrowing more money.

✔ Bill collectors are willing to tell you just about anything to squeeze some money out of you.

The hugely influential credit industry constantly disseminates antibankruptcy propaganda directly and indirectly through press releases and subtle public relations ploys. Expect creditors to do everything in their power to turn filing for bankruptcy into an emotional issue and prevent you from evaluating your personal financial situation by rationally weighing the risks and rewards of bankruptcy.

You need to act with your head, and not your heart, when making a cold, calculated, harsh judgment of what truly is in your best interests. This section explains why you need a lawyer, how to find one, and how to deal with legal and other costs associated with filing bankruptcy.

Answering why a lawyer is a must

An old adage says that a lawyer who represents himself has a fool for a client. Nowhere is that statement more true than in the area of bankruptcy law, and never was it truer than today. Bankruptcy law is incredibly complex, and many attorneys with successful general practices have difficulty keeping up to date.

Although the federal statute known as the Bankruptcy Code comprises only a single book (and a dry-as-dirt one at that), since 1978, the courts have produced 300 volumes of decisions interpreting the law. That pace continues at the rate of about 18 editions a year. Document preparers, paralegals, and even many lawyers simply lack the time to keep ahead of the avalanche of interpretations, so you absolutely must find a legal representative who's up to snuff.

During the last few years, a number of paralegals and document preparation services have offered do-it-yourself bankruptcy services. They usually charge less than attorneys, so you may — and we emphasize *may* — save some money. You may be able to get by just fine without a lawyer, but we won't bet on your succeeding. Put it this way: You can try to walk across a truck route with your eyes closed, and you just may make it to the other side without becoming roadkill. But do you really want to take that chance? Do-it-yourself bankruptcy is in the same category. And all too often, using do-it-yourself services results only in the blind leading the blind.

Cheapskate Charlie learns an expensive lesson

Cheapskate Charlie figured he'd get a good deal going through the Fly-By-Night Bankruptcy Service. But after his cut-rate bankruptcy, Charlie wasn't a happy camper. He was rather surprised to discover that the trustee was suing his grandmother to recover loan repayments that he'd made to her, that the IRS still was lurking about, that his beloved Harley Davidson motorcycle was in Hog hell, and that his credit was shot to smithereens.

These things didn't need to happen.

A lawyer who knows the ropes would've advised Charlie to delay his bankruptcy for a month, so Grandma wouldn't get sued. The lawyer also would've had the sense to file under Chapter 13, so that Charlie could've paid off his taxes without interest or penalties and on a timetable he could meet.

True, it would've cost Charlie another $200 to hire a lawyer, but in the long run he would've saved that sum many times over. And he may have even been able to keep his Hog.

Finding a good lawyer

Certainly no shortage of "free" advice exists out there, but most of it is worth about what it costs — nothing — if that. When you're serious about considering bankruptcy, you need a lawyer — simple as that. So how do you go about finding one?

You can check with friends and relatives who have filed bankruptcy and, if you already know a reputable attorney whose firm does *not* handle bankruptcy cases, he or she is likely to know a good source of advice. Chances are that such a law firm refers clients with financial problems to a particular practitioner or firm, because they won't knowingly send their clients to hacks. (For tips about meeting with your lawyer, see Chapter 5.)

The mere fact that a lawyer does or does not advertise isn't, by itself, an indication of how dedicated he or she is. But the tone of any advertising may provide you with hints about whether a lawyer runs a committed professional practice or an assembly line operation. Remember, however, that not all high-volume practitioners are bad — not by a long shot. In fact, some conduct excellent, scrupulous, and efficient practices.

Others . . .

Well, the bottom line is that you need expert support from someone with no ulterior motives, and the only place to get that is from a reputable bankruptcy attorney.

Understanding what to expect from your lawyer

Some lawyers offer a "free" initial consultation, which means the only way that they make any money is if you end up filing bankruptcy. That approach can skew their judgment.

You're probably better off paying an attorney for an hour of his or her time, expecting to pay roughly $100 to $200 per hour. When you're paying a fee, you have every right to insist on a consultation with the attorney who actually would be handling your case, not some paralegal or assistant. Whenever a law firm won't make this commitment or tries to shift you to someone else, take your business and your money elsewhere.

Paying the piper

Filing a Chapter 7, the type of bankruptcy that does not involve any kind of repayment plan, will cost you a $200 court fee. A Chapter 13 filing, where you repay a portion of your debts over time, costs $185. Legal fees vary widely, depending on where you live and how complicated your case is. Ballpark legal fees for a Chapter 7 cost $500 to $1,000. They'll run about twice as much for a Chapter 13, simply because it's more work and takes more of the lawyer's time.

In a Chapter 7 bankruptcy, all attorney fees must be paid before filing. Fees can be paid over an extended time period in a Chapter 13 filing.

"I'll gladly pay you Tuesday for a bankruptcy today"

Until recently, many lawyers filed Chapter 7 cases and collected their fees later when their clients' financial conditions improved. The problem with that, however, is that bankruptcy wipes out unpaid attorney fees along with other debts. And lawyers, like other creditors, can face big trouble for trying to collect debts that have been wiped out in a bankruptcy.

This issue came to head when courts got wind of a bankruptcy mill that charged clients double for allowing them to make payments after

bankruptcy. The thing is, the lawyers never warned their clients that debts for legal services had actually been wiped out. In fact, they told clients that making payments improved their credit ratings.

After fining the lawyers, a bankruptcy court described their operation as an "ugly and evil enterprise." (*In re Hessinger & Associates*, 171 B.R. 366. — Volume 171, page 366 of the Bankruptcy Reporter — an official compilation of bankruptcy court decisions)

Surfing for consumer info on the Internet

Information that you glean from the Internet can be a godsend. It also can also be god-awful.

Some Web sites are sponsored by debt consolidation companies, which earn fees from debtors and creditors when they convince the former to undertake debt repayment plans; even folks with no hope of success and client's who'd be far better off in bankruptcy. For that matter, even well-intentioned sites sometimes provide erroneous information. Oops.

Still other sites that appear consumer oriented actually sell advertising to mortgage lenders and credit-card issuers. So-called experts on these sites frequently try to convince people to borrow even more, often by advising visitors to take out second and third mortgages against their homes when they actually need to file bankruptcy and start out fresh.

That said, we've found that the following Web sites are consistently reliable and informative:

- **ABI World** (www.abiworld.org): Maintained by the American Bankruptcy Institute (ABI), ABI World is the premier Internet location for bankruptcy professionals and consumers. Although ABI is careful not to provide individualized legal counseling, it nevertheless offers a wealth of useful information.

- **National Consumer Law Center** (www.ConsumerLaw.org): The National Consumer Law Center (NCLC) sponsors this Web site. It provides a ton of useful consumer information.

- **Debtors Anonymous** (www.DebtorsAnonymous.org): Debtors Anonymous provides a wealth of information about compulsive spending and offers the opportunity to chat with others about money problems without anyone trying to lend you money, sell you something, or sign you up for their debt repayment plans.

Considering your current financial situation, you're probably wondering where you're going to find money to pay for your bankruptcy filing? Here are a few suggestions:

- After you decide to file bankruptcy, you don't need to make any more payments on debts that ultimately will be eliminated (such as most credit-card debts). That alone is likely to free up a fair amount of cash to apply toward your legal and court costs.

- You can sell assets to raise the money. This is a smart move whenever you'd otherwise be forced to forfeit these assets when you file bankruptcy.

- A friend or relative can give you the money to file, if you ask nicely. An employer may even pony up bankruptcy fees to focus the employee's attention on the job rather than on his or her financial problems and avoid the hassle of dealing with creditors trying to attach or garnish the employee's wages.

Borrowing money to pay attorney fees is a dicey proposition; the idea, after all, is getting out of debt, not accumulating more. In any case, one definite is: Don't borrow money from anyone without first revealing your plan to file bankruptcy. If you do, that creditor may claim that you're guilty of fraud and try to keep the debt from being wiped out. See Chapters 13 and 15.

Getting to Know the Players

Bankruptcy, like the American judicial system in general, is an adversarial process in which individuals with competing interests struggle against one another to — it is hoped — achieve a balanced and fair result. Bankruptcy court is the playing field, and the judge is the referee. The people you can encounter in the bankruptcy system all have different roles to play.

Although the players act politely and respectfully toward each other most of the time, keep in mind that the only person responsible for looking out for your best interests is your lawyer.

Bankruptcy judge

The justice system is blessed with scores of dedicated, thoughtful bankruptcy judges who conscientiously strive to fairly balance the competing interests. Some judges, of course, are better than others, but in the scheme of things, that also means that others are downright bad. Some judges are biased, and some have agendas. And even good judges sometimes make mistakes. For those reasons, an appeals process is in place. Rulings are regularly reviewed by other federal judges — and sometimes even the United States Supreme Court.

Unlike some other federal jurists, bankruptcy judges don't enjoy lifetime appointments. The federal court must reappoint them when their 14-year terms expire. Recently, several well-respected judges were denied reappointment, because creditors' groups complained (lobbied) to powers with political muscle, claiming the judges were too sympathetic to debtors. This development can't help but influence judges who hope to be reappointed. Academics and bankruptcy practitioners — and the bankruptcy judges themselves — have long argued, but to no avail, for life tenure to avoid this problem.

Regardless, in our experience, few judges (consciously) allow outside influences to color their decision making. And the decisions of those who do tend to be reversed on appeal. In other words, be aware that the judge *may* not be as objective as you'd hope, but don't lose any sleep over it.

In all likelihood, you'll never even see the bankruptcy judge who handles your case. Other players usually can resolve issues through negotiation and settlement, and the judge is called in only when a problem is encountered.

Still, you can feel reassured in knowing that if all else fails, you can always take it to the judge and make a federal case out of it.

Case trustee

The most visible player in a bankruptcy filing is the *case trustee*. Your relationship with this trustee differs depending on whether you file a Chapter 7 liquidation or a Chapter 13 reorganization.

Chapter 7: The panel trustee

The trustee in a Chapter 7 bankruptcy is appointed at random from a panel of (usually) lawyers. You'll encounter your case trustee when you meet with creditors to answer questions at a *341 meeting* (see Chapter 5).

A Chapter 7 trustee's main mission is selling property and doling the proceeds out to creditors. Any *nonexempt property* — stuff that can be taken to satisfy your debts — is up for grabs, and so is money received within six months of filing bankruptcy from life insurance, inheritances, or divorce property divisions. The trustee also can recover some transfers and payments that you made before filing bankruptcy (see Chapter 18 for more details). For his troubles, the case trustee gets a commission based on how much money is collected.

After reviewing your bankruptcy documents, the case trustee asks you some questions to determine whether any assets can be sold to cover your debts. Although the Chapter 7 trustee isn't necessarily your friend, he needn't be your enemy either. Most case trustees are reasonable people just trying to fulfill their roles within the confines of the law. So, try not to take it personally.

Granted, the thought of someone scrounging through your belongings and putting them up for sale is kind of offensive. But you don't need to worry that the trustee will turn your living room into a Salvation Army store. In 96 percent of Chapter 7 cases, no assets actually are liquidated, because they're all exempt or because they're not worth enough to bother with.

Beware, however, that a trustee is likely to pounce on anything that looks like easy pickings — like income tax refunds for past years and the current year. But remember that he can't take future tax refunds.

If the trustee doesn't pursue an asset, it's yours after your bankruptcy case is closed — provided that you accurately described it on your bankruptcy papers. For that reason, making sure your paperwork is complete, accurate, and honest is extremely important. Besides, doing so may keep you out of jail.

Chapter 13: The standing trustee

A Chapter 13 trustees has a different role, and you'll meet him or her at your 341 meeting with your creditors. The trustee questions you about your assets and scrutinizes your income and expenses and generally tries to make sure that your repayment plan meets technical requirements and that it has a reasonable chance of succeeding.

Unlike a Chapter 7 trustee, a Chapter 13 trustee doesn't typically liquidate any property. Instead, the trustee collects monthly payments that you make under a Chapter 13 repayment plan and receives a commission based on these payments. The longer that you make required payments, the more the trustee earns. So the Chapter 13 trustee has an incentive in helping you succeed with your repayment plan.

Some Chapter 13 trustees sponsor personal financial management courses, hoping that your attending them will increase your chances for successfully completing the repayment plan. So far, the jury is out on whether debtor education leads to higher Chapter 13 success rates. But if the option is there, take it. You've nothing to lose.

U.S. Trustee

The U.S. Trustee is an employee of the U.S. Department of Justice and is an entirely different creature than the case trustee. A U.S. Trustee heads one of 21 regional offices. The head of the entire United States Trustee program, the Executive Director, is a political appointee of the U.S. Attorney General and, by extension, of the current president.

The U.S. Trustee:

- ✔ Oversees private trustees and makes sure that they properly account for all funds they receive.
- ✔ Watches out for fraud in bankruptcy cases and refers questionable matters to the U.S. Attorney for criminal prosecution.
- ✔ Conducts, in theory, 341 meetings, where debtors answer questions from creditors. In practice, this chore usually is delegated to the trustee assigned to your particular case.
- ✔ Can help whenever special accommodations must be made for the 341 meeting. For example, if you're disabled or need an interpreter, the U.S. Trustee tries to provide appropriate assistance.

On October 30, 2001, the head of the U.S. Trustee program announced a major new initiative to increase scrutiny of Chapter 7 cases. Now, whenever it appears that the debtor has the ability to pay a significant portion of his or her debts, the U.S. Trustee will ask the court to reject your bankruptcy for substantial abuse (see Chapter 4) of the system. So, as long as you play by the rules, chances are that you'll never encounter the U.S. Trustee, unless your bankruptcy filing papers indicate that your income is high and debts relatively modest. Those two factors cause warning bells to go off. For more information, you can check out the USTP Web site at www.usdoj.gov/ust.

Bumping heads with Uncle Sam

Chrissie was, like, totally not into completing the financial questionnaire her lawyer gave her. So-oh, she pretty much made up the answers while watching MTV. Chrissie didn't really mean to deceive anyone, but digging up all that stuff is a drag, and she really had more fun things to do. So, she winged it. Who'd ever care?

Chrissie's papers were so riddled with errors that the judge had a fit, refused to wipe out her debts, fined her — and referred the matter to federal prosecutors for possible criminal action. Chrissie totally couldn't deal with that!

But the U.S. Trustee could. And did.

Bum-mer!

Creditors

Although creditors certainly are players in the process, you shouldn't have much to do with them after your case if filed. They may attend the 341 meeting and ask a few questions, but most won't bother.

Any contact that you have with creditors will probably be only in the context of surrendering collateral or making arrangements to keep it after you file (see Chapter 10).

Talking the legal lingo

Legal eagles and legal beagles talk their own language, and oftentimes the legalistic meaning of a word or concept is different than the generic definition. So having a basic familiarity with legalese is a good idea so that you can communicate effectively with the lawyerly sorts you'll likely encounter whenever you decide to take this journey. (A more extensive glossary can be found at the end of this book).

Automatic stay: The instant your bankruptcy petition is filed, an automatic court order keeps the creditors at bay. They can't garnish your wages, repossess your car, start or continue foreclosure proceedings, sue you, or even contact you about your debts. And, if they do, they'll

have a federal judge — and probably an angry one at that — to answer to.

Collateral: An asset that backs up a specific debt.

Confirmation: A court order making a Chapter 13 plan binding on the debtor and all creditors.

Discharge: When your case is over, a court order wipes out or "discharges" your debts.

Exempt property: Some property is yours to keep, regardless of the bankruptcy. Those possessions are said to be *exempt* — or off limits to creditors.

(continued)

(continued)

Foreclosure: The way a creditor turns collateral into cash. When the collateral is *real property* (essentially land and buildings), an actual lawsuit sometimes (but not always) is required. Many states provide a method of nonjudicial foreclosure in which real property is sold at public auction a specified time — typically about four months — after notice of the sale has been published. When the collateral is *personal property*, a nonjudicial sale can be held with as little as ten days' notice. Foreclosure should be distinguished from repossession, which, by itself, doesn't terminate your interest in the collateral.

Joint bankruptcy: Your spouse doesn't have to file bankruptcy just because you're filing, but if both of you go that route, the petition is called a *joint bankruptcy.*

Lien: Some debts are backed up by specific assets (collateral), which the creditor can seize if you don't pay. For example, when you buy a house, the bank holds a mortgage that places a *lien* on your home as collateral for the mortgage. Similarly, your car oftentimes is used as collateral for a loan. Again, that is a *lien.*

No-asset case: A Chapter 7 case in which the value of a debtor's assets isn't high enough to bother liquidating any of them.

Personal property: Anything you own that's not attached to land — and that includes your car, household goods, bank accounts, pensions, and so on — is considered *personal property,* as opposed to *real property,* and is subject to special rules in bankruptcy. In some states, even mobile homes are considered personal property, as long as they're not permanently tied to the ground.

Petition date: The date that your bankruptcy petition is filed.

Property of the estate: Everything that you own as of the petition date is deemed *property of the estate,* and therefore is potentially at risk in bankruptcy.

Reaffirmation: Even if bankruptcy would wipe out a debt, you can promise to repay what you owe. And why would you want to do that? Good question! See Chapter 12 for situations where *reaffirmation* may make sense.

Redemption: Say you bought a refrigerator and stove for $1,500, and those appliances now are worth only $500, but you still owe $1,000. *Redemption* enables you to keep the refrigerator and stove by making a lump sum payment of $500. The remainder of the debt is wiped out.

Repossession: Where a creditor obtains possession of collateral if you don't pay.

341 meeting: About 40 days after filing your bankruptcy petition, a meeting is scheduled at which a trustee (the person who represents the interests of creditors in bankruptcy matters) and creditors can quiz you about your assets and debts. It's named a *341 meeting* after a particular section of the U.S. Bankruptcy Code.

Chapter 4

Deciding Which Type of Bankruptcy Is Best for You

In This Chapter

▶ Considering the impact of bankruptcy on your spouse

▶ Understanding your options

▶ Weighing Chapter 7 versus Chapter 13

▶ Looking at other forms of bankruptcy

▶ Changing your mind

*P*ersonal bankruptcy comes in a variety of flavors. You can find advantages and disadvantages to using any bankruptcy option, and we explore those pluses and minuses in this chapter.

The vast majority of consumers opt for *Chapter 7,* where you immediately eliminate most of your debts, surrender any *nonexempt assets* — those that can be sold off for the benefit of creditors — and go merrily on your way. Another common choice is *Chapter 13,* where you keep your stuff but have to make payments to a trustee for several years. After that, any remaining balances on most debts are wiped out.

In addition, if you can qualify as a family farmer, another option, *Chapter 12,* is probably the way to go. And finally, there's *Chapter 11,* a form of bankruptcy commonly used for business reorganizations. But it just may provide a remedy for you.

Deciding Whether to Go Solo or As a Married Couple

Many married people assume that they're automatically responsible for each other's debts. Wrong.

You are, of course, liable for your own debts and any monetary obligations that you accept by cosigning for a loan or a credit card obtained by your spouse or significant other. When you cosign, you tell the creditor that if your mate doesn't pay up, you will.

An ancient "doctrine of necessaries," stemming from the era when only husbands were the breadwinners, states that if a husband wasn't bringing home the bacon, his wife could go out and buy essential items by charging them to his credit.

In modern times, however, the doctrine of necessaries usually arises in cases like providing medical services. Hospitals frequently claim that both spouses are liable for services provided to one spouse or to one of their dependents. Although that argument is a mile wide and an inch deep (and often unsuccessful), when medical expenses overwhelm you, filing a joint bankruptcy usually is easier than battling with hospitals.

When you live in one of nine community-property states (Arizona, California, Idaho, Louisiana, Nevada, New Mexico, Texas, Washington, and Wisconsin), the rules are different. Husbands or wives frequently find themselves on the hook for their spouses' debts, because so-called community property of both is subject to debts incurred by either. *Community property* includes the earnings of either spouse and all property acquired by either the husband or the wife during the marriage, except for gifts and inheritances.

Even in situations in which you and your spouse must file bankruptcy, you don't have to file jointly. In fact, you may find advantages to filing separately (see Chapters 9 and 11).

And, just in case you're wondering, you must actually be married to file a joint bankruptcy. You and your significant other — even if you're in a long-term, committed relationship that closely resembles marriage — must file separate bankruptcies even if most of debts are joint.

Looking at Your Probable Bankruptcy Choices

Your basic choice is between a bankruptcy that doesn't involve any type of repayment plan (Chapter 7 bankruptcy), and one that does (Chapters 11, 12, and 13). You need to base your decision on what's best for you and your family, not on what you think will make your creditors happy.

Chapter 7: Straight bankruptcy

Chapter 7, which occasionally is referred to as *straight bankruptcy,* is essentially the belly-up version that most people envision when they hear the word *bankruptcy.* If you file under Chapter 7, most of your debts are eliminated, and some of your property may go to your creditors. You don't have any repayment plan; your debts simply disappear.

Assets that are *nonexempt* (or ripe for picking by creditors) may be seized and sold by the trustee, with the proceeds distributed to your creditors. In the real world, however, most consumer bankruptcies fall in the category of *no-asset* cases. In other words, you have nothing for creditors to take, except the shirt on your back and various other items that are off limits. That's a pretty nifty deal and, if things work out, you've little to lose except your debt.

The law won't let you bounce from one spending spree to another using bankruptcy as your escape valve. So, for the most part, whenever you go bankrupt, you can't discharge your debts in Chapter 7 for another six years.

You can still file under Chapter 7, even if you received a bankruptcy discharge within the past six years, but doing so makes no sense. If you had your debts wiped out in bankruptcy less than six years ago, your latest financial obligations wouldn't be discharged by a new Chapter 7 case. So, filing would be pointless.

The six-year restriction does not apply when:

- ✔ Your earlier bankruptcy was dismissed prior to its completion.
- ✔ Your previous bankruptcy was a Chapter 13 reorganization and creditors received at least 70 percent of their claims.
- ✔ You file your second case under Chapter 13.

Chapter 7 has no maximum debt restrictions, so virtually everyone is eligible for bankruptcy relief. However, courts can and do dismiss cases when your financial obligations are primarily consumer debts if they find that discharging all debts would result in substantial abuse of the bankruptcy process.

Substantial abuse

Courts agree that the most important consideration in determining whether you're trying to weasel out of your debts is finding out whether you have the *ability to pay* if you feel like it. However, they don't agree on just what ability to pay means.

One court ruled that a debtor had the ability to pay when she was capable of covering a quarter of her debts over three years. Another ruled that unless a debtor can pay 70 percent of his bills over three years, he didn't meet the ability-to-pay standard. So, without a clear legal standard, you are, to some extent, at the whim of your local bankruptcy judge.

Bankruptcy papers that you file with the court include a *Schedule I,* which lists your income, and a *Schedule J,* which lists your expenses. Of course, you need to review all your paperwork carefully before filing with the court, but you must be particularly careful when these schedules show that your income is significantly higher than your expenses. Miscalculating how much you earn or missing some expenses is very possible. If you don't try to correct these figures until a substantial abuse issue arises, you may have serious credibility problems and, therefore, have to deal with the lawyer's standard question: "Were you lying then, or are you lying now?"

In determining what percentage you can pay, the court must decide which of your expenses are legitimate and which are not — a subjective determination at best. Among the questions often asked are whether you need to:

- ✔ Help support elderly parents or adult children
- ✔ Make charitable contributions
- ✔ Save for retirement
- ✔ Repay debts to relatives
- ✔ Live in your own apartment when you could live with your parents for free
- ✔ Get a second job
- ✔ Get married

As you may expect, different judges have different views on what is or is not a legitimate expense. Many are reluctant to second-guess your basic choices, and yet others — thankfully a minority — seem to relish the opportunity to impose their views on others. Obtaining guidance from a bankruptcy specialist familiar with local judges' ideas is critically important.

Good faith

In addition to looking at your ability to pay, some judges also consider whether you're acting in *good faith.* They may ask whether:

- ✔ Your bankruptcy was necessitated by sudden illness, calamity, or unemployment.
- ✔ You made unnecessary eve-of-bankruptcy purchases far exceeding your ability to pay.
- ✔ Your bankruptcy paperwork is complete and accurate.

A committed mate saves the day

Moira and Scott lived together for 12 years. Instead of working, Moira ran the household, helped raise Scott's boys, and attended to Scott's infirm mother.

During their relationship, Scott took care of all household expenses and agreed to do so during the life of Moira's Chapter 13 bankruptcy case. The judge was so impressed by Moira's and Scott's commitment to each other that he held that Scott's voluntary contributions to Moira qualified as income for Chapter 13 purposes and approved her Chapter 13 plan.

Although you eventually must check with a bankruptcy specialist who's familiar with local judges to get a reading on what to expect, you can do one thing immediately to avert a possible good-faith problem: Make darned sure that your bankruptcy papers are accurate and that you list each and every income and each and every expense. Guesstimating just doesn't cut it. When you don't know the answer, look it up . . . don't make it up.

Chapter 13: Debt repayment plans

In filing a Chapter 13 bankruptcy, you propose a debt repayment schedule and, for the next 36 to 60 months, you pay what you can afford. The two types of payments that you may have to make are

- To a trustee, who doles out money to creditors.

- So-called *payments outside the plan,* which are payments that are coming due after you file and are paid directly to the creditor.

Creditors usually end up receiving only a small percentage of what they're owed and typically must settle for pennies on the dollar. After that, you're home free.

A big advantage to a Chapter 13 bankruptcy — other than getting out of your debts by paying a pittance of what you really owe — is known as the *super discharge.* That's a benefit that can enable you to eliminate debts for fraud, other intentional wrongdoing, marital property divisions, loans to pay federal income taxes, and then some taxes themselves — none of which are wiped out in other forms of bankruptcy.

Only individuals with regular income (no corporations, no partnerships) can file under Chapter 13. The source of your income isn't important (assuming, of course, that it isn't from some criminal activity), provided that it is regular and stable. Your income can be wages, self-employment profits, unemployment benefits, or even assistance of friends and family.

To qualify for Chapter 13, your debts must fall within specific limits. Your *unsecured debts* — those where nothing, like a car, can be repossessed if you don't pay — can't be more than $290,525. *Secured debts* can't exceed $871,550. *Note:* These debt limits are adjusted every three years on the first business day on or after April 1. The next adjustment will be April 2, 2004. You can find out more about secured and unsecured debts in Chapter 10.

Certain debts, known as *priority claims,* must be paid in full over the life of any Chapter 13 plan. The most common priority claims are support obligations and recent taxes. Really big child-support obligations that you can't possibly pay off over 60 months or tax arrearages, as a practical matter, make you ineligible for Chapter 13, because those debts must be paid in full over a maximum of 60 months. If you can't repay those bills within five years, you're better off not filing under Chapter 13.

The length of your repayment plan depends on how much you earn and whether you have any *nonexempt assets* — stuff that could be taken to satisfy the claims of creditors. Every plan must satisfy two tests: the best-interest test and the best-efforts test.

- ✔ **Best-interest test:** Unsecured creditors must receive at least as much as they'd get when you file a Chapter 7 bankruptcy rather than a Chapter 13. If all your property is exempt and unsecured creditors would receive nothing in a Chapter 7, the best-interest test isn't a factor. On the other hand, when you have nonexempt property, your plan must propose to pay at least that much.

    Look at it this way: If you own investment property worth $10,000 and file a Chapter 7 bankruptcy, the trustee probably will sell the property and distribute the proceeds among creditors. On the other hand, if you file under Chapter 13, you keep the property, but you still have to pay at least as much as creditors would otherwise receive had you gone the Chapter 7 route — their share of the $10,000.

- ✔ **Best-efforts test:** Chances are you can't possibly pay unsecured creditors in full, and the court and your creditors know that. So, although the law doesn't expect you to make good on everything, it nevertheless requires you to do the best you can. And that means that all your *disposable income* — basically the difference between your expected income and your projected expenses — goes to the trustee during at least the first 36 months of the repayment plan. Don't panic, though, you'll be left with enough for reasonable expenses. (See the "Making your best effort" sidebar for more about disposable income and reasonable expenses.)

    In Chapter 13 bankruptcy, you won't have any extra cash burning a hole in your pocket, but you will have what you need to get by. You'll even have an allowance for entertainment.

Making your best effort

Your Chapter 13 repayment plan must be proposed in good faith, and you must make your best attempt to repay as much of your debt as you reasonably can. That means all your disposable income goes into the plan for at least three years. But just what is disposable income?

On the income side of the *disposable income equation,* courts include all the money that comes into your household. So, your spouse's income is included in the calculation even if you file by yourself. Any payments that you regularly receive are counted, regardless of whether they come from a pension, Social Security, welfare, or any other source.

Courts differ on just what expenses are reasonable. Here's some general perspective on how courts view various items:

- **Charitable contributions:** A specific provision of the Bankruptcy Code allows charitable contributions of up to 15 percent of your annual gross income. But a few courts have refused to allow deductions where it appeared that debtors were planning to make charitable contributions for the sole purpose of stiffing their creditors.

- **Pension contributions:** In most cases, courts won't let you sock money into a retirement account that otherwise can apply toward repaying your debts. However, whenever you're required to make pension payments as a condition of employment, the court probably will approve those contributions. And a *few* courts allow modest pension contributions of up to 6 percent of gross income.

- **Repayment of pension loans:** Most courts won't allow you to pay back a pension loan for the same reasons that regular pension contributions aren't allowed. You shouldn't be able to build up savings at your creditors'

expense but, on the other hand, no one benefits if you get fired. So you can repay a pension loan if it's a condition of holding your job.

- **Costs of private schooling:** If the cost of private schooling is significantly higher than public schools, you'll have to show why the additional cost is necessary. When your child is disabled and has special needs that can't be met in public schools, you may get the okay for private education. Similarly, if deeply held religious beliefs require your children to attend a parochial school, that expense will probably be allowed.

- **Adult educational expenses:** Most courts wouldn't find expenses for recreational education reasonable, but they may go along with education aimed at boosting your earning potential. In other words, yoga class at the YMCA probably won't be approved — unless, of course, you intend to become a professional yoga instructor.

- **Payments for expensive toys:** You probably won't be allowed to maintain payments on luxury items like an exotic automobile or a home theater system.

- **Life insurance premiums:** Modest life insurance premiums will probably be allowed if you have a family. But the court won't allow you to sock hundreds of dollars a month into a life insurance policy that builds up a cash value.

- **Contingency funds:** Depending on the views of the local trustee and court, you may be able to deposit a reasonable amount into a fund for emergencies, or save for critical large expenses such as a new roof on your house or other necessary maintenance costs.

In calculating what you may have to pay in a Chapter 13 repayment, consider Mike. After paying routine monthly living expenses, Mike had $300 left over each month. He was $4,000 behind on mortgage payments and owed $55,000 in credit-card debts.

Mike wanted to keep the home, as well as an antique piano worth $5,000. The piano, although it was a family heirloom, was not exempt from bankruptcy. To satisfy the best-interests test under a 36-month plan, Mike would have to pay $250 per month ($4,000 + 5,000 = $9000 ÷ 36 = $250). But that's not the whole story. Mike must also pass the best-efforts test, which in this case would require that he pay $300 (all his disposable income) for 36 months. So Mike would have to pay $300 per month for 36 months. After that, his credit-card bills would be history.

Deciding Between Chapter 7 and Chapter 13

Your lawyer must take the time to fully discuss the relative advantages and disadvantages of your choice between Chapter 7 and Chapter 13, but in some situations making the right choice can be devilishly difficult. This section provides some general guidelines for you.

Recognizing when Chapter 7 is best

Chapter 7 probably is your best choice when all the following statements are true:

- You don't have any assets that you must surrender to a trustee.
- You have no need for the super discharge offered in a Chapter 13 filing. (For details, see "Chapter 13: Debt repayment plans" section earlier in this chapter.)
- You are current on home and car payments or willing to give them up.
- You don't have much money left over each month after paying expenses.
- You haven't received a bankruptcy discharge in an earlier case filed within the past six years.

Considering Chapter 13 as your number-one option

Chapter 13 is probably the way to go in any of these situations:

- ✔ You want to catch up on mortgage payments.

- ✔ You need time to pay off past-due support obligations.

- ✔ You owe tax debts that you want to pay off without interest or penalties.

- ✔ You want to preserve the option of canceling your bankruptcy if things don't pan out as expected.

- ✔ You received a discharge in a bankruptcy case filed within the past six years.

- ✔ You're concerned that excessive credit-card use may give rise to a fraud claim if you file Chapter 7.

- ✔ You earn enough money to pay monthly expenses with ease and want to do your best to repay creditors at least some amount.

Discovering the advantages of Chapter 13

We discuss the upshot of Chapter 13 in detail throughout the book, but as a general proposition the benefits are:

- ✔ You can pay taxes over time without interest or penalties.

- ✔ Your overdue alimony and child support can be stretched out and paid off over three to five years.

- ✔ You can get your house and car payments up to date over the life of the plan.

- ✔ Your car payments can actually be reduced.

- ✔ You're eligible for a super discharge.

- ✔ You can keep nonexempt property.

- ✔ You're eligible for Chapter 13 even though you received a discharge in a prior bankruptcy filed within the last six years.

- ✔ You can protect a cosigner from creditor harassment by proposing to pay the cosigned debt over the life of the plan.

Another advantage of Chapter 13 is that you can back out when you change your mind, or if things don't play out as expected. Conversely, after you file Chapter 7, you can't get out without the court's permission — and that can be pretty tough to get.

Being able to back out of Chapter 13 doesn't mean that you can bounce in and out of bankruptcy as the mood strikes you. You must wait 180 days before you can file again, if your case was dismissed at your request after a creditor asked the court for relief from the *automatic stay*, which stops collection activities after a case is filed, *or* because you disobeyed an order of the court.

Exploring disadvantages of Chapter 13

One obvious disadvantage of Chapter 13 is that it usually takes at least three years to complete. During this time:

- ✔ You may feel like you're on a leash . . . because you are.

- ✔ You'll probably have to give up your income tax refunds.

- ✔ You may receive an unexpected windfall, and then lose it to the trustee.

- ✔ You won't be allowed to incur any more debts without the trustee's consent.

- ✔ You can lose your job and your ability to maintain payments, resulting in dismissal of your case.

- ✔ You may risk your homestead exemption (See Chapters 9, 11, and 19) if you move or sell your home.

Some people claim that a Chapter 13 filing is less detrimental to your credit rating than a Chapter 7. We're skeptical. When you file under Chapter 7, you may actually be a more attractive credit risk. Reason: Your slate is clean, your old debts are gone — and you can't file a Chapter 7 to escape new debts for six years.

Another drawback is that about two-thirds of Chapter 13 plans fail and, after that happens, the debtor must permit the bankruptcy to be dismissed, allowing all those nasty debt collections tactics to resume, or, more likely, cause you to convert to Chapter 7. In Chapter 5, we guide you through a Chapter 13 filing so that your chances of success are much higher than the raw statistics would indicate.

Advantages of Chapter 13 over nonbankruptcy repayment plans

Filing Chapter 13 usually is better than repayment agreements worked out by consumer counseling outfits because:

- ✔ You pay only a small percentage of your total debts. Nonbankruptcy repayment plans usually require you to pay your debts in full (except perhaps some interest).

- ✔ You can deal with secured debts such as your home and car. Nonbankruptcy plans typically do not address those debts.

✔ You don't need the permission of the creditor to cut your obligation.

✔ You can invoke the automatic stay, which immediately stops creditors from pursuing you.

✔ You'll be allowed to catch up on back alimony and support obligations. Nonbankruptcy plans don't deal with those problems.

For a quick comparison of the eligibility requirements for Chapter 7 and Chapter 13 bankruptcies, check out Table 4-1.

Table 4-1	Comparing Eligibility Requirements for Chapter 7 and Chapter 13	
Requirement	*Chapter 7*	*Chapter 13*
Previous Chapter 7 or Chapter 13 discharge in case filed within six years	Not eligible unless the discharge was a Chapter 13 discharge and creditors in that case were paid at least 70 percent.	Does not affect eligibility.
Debt requirements	No maximum debt limit. Possible minimum if substantial abuse is found.	Maximum secured debt limit of $871,550 and unsecured debt limit of $290,525. (These amounts will be adjusted April 1, 2004.) No minimum debt requirement.
Income requirements	No maximum income limitation, unless income is so high that substantial abuse factors are present. No minimum income requirement.	No maximum income limitation, but high income may require higher plan payments. Minimum income necessary to make payments required by the plan.
Good-faith limitations	Good faith seldom is an issue, unless substantial abuse factors are present.	Good faith is required.
Effect of nondischargeable taxes, alimony, or child support	Does not affect eligibility to wipe out other debts.	Potential to indirectly affect eligibility, because plan must provide that these obligations be paid in full over a period of no longer than five years.

Considering Other Types of Bankruptcy

Although your case almost certainly falls under the Chapter 7 or 13 rubric, a few other potential options bear thinking about.

Chapter 11: Large reorganizations

One other form of bankruptcy, which rarely is an option or even a good choice for most nonbusiness debtors, is Chapter 11. Whenever you don't qualify for Chapter 13 and you have substantial assets that you want to continue to control, Chapter 11 may be worth looking into. But a Chapter 11 proceeding is extremely complicated and expensive.

A Chapter 11 filing is a bankruptcy specialty in its own right. Many lawyers specializing in consumer bankruptcy don't have much experience with Chapter 11 cases. If you go this route, make sure that your lawyer is an experienced Chapter 11 practitioner.

Chapter 12: Reorganizations for family farmers

Chapter 12 is a special type of bankruptcy reserved for family farmers. Congress recognizes that family farmers play a unique role in our culture and economy that is deserving of special treatment.

If you qualify as a family farmer, Chapter 12 provides most of the benefits of a Chapter 13, and then some. Repayment plans aren't restricted to five years, and you have fewer limitations on the your ability to restructure home mortgages. The downside of a Chapter 12 is that dischargeable debts are limited to those dischargeable in a Chapter 7. So, you don't get the super discharge available with a Chapter 13 filing.

To qualify as a farmer, you must meet each of the following requirements:

- Debts may not exceed $1.5 million.
- Eighty percent of those debts (excluding your home mortgage) must be from farming operations.
- Fifty percent of income from the preceding year must have come from farming operations.

But what exactly is a farmer? One debtor, whose sole income (less than $10,000) for the year, before bankruptcy, came from the firewood he chopped on his land, was deemed a family farmer. As a result, the court approved a repayment plan that actually reduced the mortgage on his home so that it would be paid off in 10 rather than 15 years.

Chapter 20: Adding Chapters 7 and 13

Although no Chapter 20 filing is included the Bankruptcy Code, that term *is* used to describe the practice of filing Chapter 7 and Chapter 13 at the same time to reap the benefits of both.

For example, if you owe a bunch of credit-card bills and you are under an order to pay restitution under a criminal sentence, you can file Chapter 7 to get rid of the credit-card bills, and then file Chapter 13 to pay the restitution over three to five years. We take a closer look at Chapter 20 bankruptcy in Chapter 17.

Changing Your Mind

After you're in Chapter 7 bankruptcy, you can't back out without the court's permission, and that may be tough to get.

For example, the day after filing Chapter 7, José crashed his car into the back of a minivan. When Soccer Dad threatened to sue, José asked the bankruptcy court to dismiss his case so he could turn around and file a new one. That way, José figured, he could file a new Chapter 7 and include any claims from the crash.

No way José! The court said José's strategy simply wasn't in the best interests of his creditors.

On the other hand, when you file Chapter 13, you can dismiss the case if you choose to, if things don't turn out as expected, or if you just change your mind.

You can also convert one type of bankruptcy to another, if you realize that you're better off taking another route.

We take a closer look at converting from Chapter 13 to Chapter 7 in Chapter 19.

Chapter 5

Getting from Here to There: The Bankruptcy Process

In This Chapter

▶ Getting organized

▶ Meeting with your lawyer

▶ Filing your petition

▶ Navigating Chapter 7

▶ Navigating Chapter 13

▶ Comparing the Chapter 7 and Chapter 13 processes

*O*kay, you're thinking that bankruptcy just may be in the cards. What now? Although it's a bit of a journey, the process of mapping out your route and knowing where you're going need not be an excursion into a dark cave. Instead, view it as more of a self-guided tour, where you've done your homework, picked up the latest travelogue, and now you know which routes are open, which are closed, and which are littered with pot holes and construction crews. By just taking it one step at a time, you won't seem so overwhelmed.

Consider this chapter as your road map, showing you the process for the two most common forms of consumer bankruptcy — Chapter 7 liquidations and Chapter 13 reorganizations — and exposing some goblins and trolls that you may encounter along the way.

Getting Organized before Talking to a Lawyer

Just by reading this book, you'll by far be better prepared than a typical bankruptcy client. And although doing some legwork prior to meeting with your lawyer isn't required, your initial consultation will go smoother and be more productive when you do. If you're still wondering whether you need a lawyer, take a look at Chapter 3.

Doing your financial homework

To the greatest extent possible, calculate

- The amount of any income taxes that you owe and for which years
- How much you're behind on support obligations
- What your home is worth, the amount you're behind on mortgages, and the total balances owed on mortgages
- How much your cars are worth, and the amounts you owe against them
- A rough total of the balances (not monthly payments) that you owe on all your bills

You also need to gather copies of the following:

- Completed worksheets (tables) from Chapter 2.
- Your mortgage documents.
- The certificate of title for any motor vehicles you're using. If the vehicle is financed, you'll have to request a copy from the lender.
- Your most recent income tax return.
- Any court papers if a lawsuit is pending against you.
- Any divorce decrees, support orders, or marital settlement agreements.

In addition, Table 5-1 features some simple questions for which your lawyer will need answers. Check the appropriate box for each question and bring a copy of this checklist with you for your lawyer to look over.

Table 5-1	Checklist to Give to Your Lawyer	
	Yes	*No*
Is a foreclosure is pending?		
Have you been served a lawsuit in which there's still time to respond?		
Is your driver's license about to be yanked for unpaid fines or judgments?		
Are you facing eviction from your apartment?		
Is your car about to be repossessed?		
Repaid debts owed to close friends or family members within the past 12 months?		

	Yes	No
Have you repaid debts cosigned by close friends or family members within the past 12 months?		
Do you expect that in the next year someone will die (or has someone just died) leaving you an inheritance or life insurance benefits?		
Are you in the process of getting a divorce?		
Were you divorced within the past four years?		
Have you made credit-card balance transfers within the last six months?		
Have you made large debt repayments within the past 90 days?		
Do you make the mortgage payments on your home when your mate is not filing?		
Have you refinanced your house within the past 12 months?		
Have you refinanced your car or purchased a car on credit within the past 12 months?		
Do you expect to be paying higher medical expenses in the near future?		
Do you expect a large income tax refund this year?		
Have you been fined as part of a criminal proceeding?		
Are your wages being or about to be garnished?		
Have you filed all the income tax returns you were supposed to?		
Are you current with your mortgage payment?		
Are you current with your car payment?		
Have you filed bankruptcy before?		
Have you any interest in a trust?		
Have you talked to another lawyer (about any matter) in the last four years?		
Within the last four years, have you made large gifts to anyone?		
Within the last four years, have you transferred any assets or put them in other people's names?		
Within the last 60 days, have you racked up more than $1,000 to a single creditor?		

(continued)

Table 5-1 *(continued)*

	Yes	No
Have you any money on deposit at an institution where you owe money?		
Are you entitled to a bonus at work or can you cash in unused vacation pay or sick time?		
Does anyone owe you money?		
Have you made any unusual contribution to your pension or rolled over one pension into another within the past four years?		
Are you current with your child support and alimony payments?		
Have you paid someone else's debts within the past 12 months?		
In applying for a loan or credit card, have you ever overstated your income or given other false information?		
Is your home a manufactured home or a mobile home?		
Do you use your home for a nonresidential purpose?		

Tracking down your creditors

Whenever you're unsure of all your creditors, you need to obtain copies of your credit reports. For under $10, depending on where you live, you can order your credit report from:

- ✔ Equifax, P.O. Box 740241, Atlanta, GA 30374-0241; phone, 800-685-1111; Web site, www.equifax.com
- ✔ Experian, P.O. Box 2002, Allen, TX 75013; phone, 800-682-7654; Web site, www.experian.com
- ✔ Trans Union, P.O. Box 1000, Chester, PA 19022; phone, 800-851-2674; Web site, www.transunion.com

You can obtain a free credit report from any of these agencies when you request it within 60 days after being denied credit because of a bad report from that company. Sometimes, people apply for a loan knowing that they'll be turned down so they can receive a free copy of their credit report. However, they receive only a copy of the report that was used to deny their loan application, not all three reports, so the document is of limited value.

Some creditors may report to one or two of the credit bureaus, but not all three. So ordering a credit report from only one company isn't enough. For about $35, you can obtain a merged credit report, combining information from Equifax, Experian, and Trans Union with addresses for creditors, from:

- Coast to Coast Information Services, 800-877-4033, `www.fullcredit reports.com`

- True Credit, 800-493-2392, `www.truecredit.com`

Bear in mind that the only creditors who appear on a credit report are the ones that have reported you. These generally include credit-card companies, major department stores, and other large institutional creditors. Smaller creditors — such as your doctor, landlord, or local grocery store — probably don't report to the credit bureaus, at least not until the account is turned over to a collection agency.

Whenever you contact creditors or credit bureaus that don't know your whereabouts or phone number, try not to provide that information, because doing so may just tip off creditors about how to hound you for payment.

Many creditors, especially credit-card companies, list two addresses on their bills: one for correspondence and another for payments. Frequently, when anything other than money arrives at the address for payments, it goes directly into the circular file (trash), and some creditors have (unsuccessfully, so far) claimed they consequently were ignorant of any bankruptcy filing.

The National Association of Consumer Bankruptcy Attorneys (NACBA) also provides links to several sources that can help you locate your creditors' addresses (see `http://nacba.com/links.html#help`).

Meeting Your Lawyer for the First Time

Reputable bankruptcy lawyers have different styles of practice, and one isn't necessarily better than the other. Some handle a high volume of cases on an assembly line basis, thus relying heavily on paralegals. Others opt for a lower volume of cases with more personal contact between lawyer and client. Go with whichever makes you more comfortable.

By reading this book, and being prepared, you aren't the typical bankruptcy client — especially when you're willing to pay a lawyer's hourly fee just to get an unbiased assessment of your options. If you explain how you've done your homework when calling for an appointment, even a high-volume office needs to alter its procedures so that you can meet with the lawyer who is in charge of your case, rather than a nonlawyer intake person. If not, you may want to consider looking elsewhere.

Inaccuracies can be worse than embarrassing

Bill's bankruptcy documents showed that his monthly income exceeded expenses by $500. As a result, the United States Trustee charged that his Chapter 7 case needed to be dismissed because he could repay a significant amount of his debts.

Bill then discovered that he'd underestimated some of his expenses and that actually he was barely making ends meet. Uh-oh!

Although Bill amended his schedules, the court was skeptical because it looked like Bill had cooked up these additional expenses just to avoid having his case dismissed.

In your first meeting, the lawyer — after reviewing the materials you bring in and asking questions — must be able to tell you whether bankruptcy is your best choice and, if so, which type. If you answer yes to any of the questions in Table 5-1 (earlier in the chapter), expect the lawyer to inquire further. If he doesn't, you want to be sure to bring up any issues.

Completing the Paperwork

After a decision to file bankruptcy is made, you'll have to provide information so that official bankruptcy documents can be prepared. Some law offices give you a questionnaire to fill out at home; others help you fill it out on the spot, possibly with the assistance of a paralegal. Either way is fine as long as the information is accurate.

Receiving and reviewing drafts of official documents is a must. We recommend taking the drafts home and going over them very carefully at your own speed. Although documents can be amended after they're filed, your lawyer may charge you for the extra work and remember that mistakes still may come back to haunt you.

Filing Your Bankruptcy Case

When your paperwork is complete, your lawyer decides when the best time is to actually file the papers with the court. This *petition date* determines which debts and property are included in your bankruptcy and which aren't. Tactical considerations in deciding whether to file this week or next may come into play, and your lawyer can help you with making that determination.

From A to Z (well, J): Bankruptcy documents on the Web

You can take a peek at bankruptcy documents, which are similar to those a lawyer will prepare in your case by visiting www.uscourts.gov/bankform/.

The forms used in typical personal bankruptcy cases include:

- **Voluntary petition:** You provide identifying information about yourself and formally ask for bankruptcy relief.

- **Schedule A:** Lists any real property that you own, its value, and how much you owe against it.

- **Schedule B:** Covers all your personal property and its value.

- **Schedule C:** Lists any property that you claim is exempt, or out of reach of your creditors.

- **Schedule D:** Addresses secured debts — those that are backed up with collateral such as your home or car.

- **Schedule E:** Deals with priority debts. The more common ones are income taxes and support obligations.

- **Schedule F:** Covers all debts that are neither secured nor priority — in other words, the vast majority of your debts.

- **Schedule G:** For "Executory Contracts" and "Unexpired Leases" — real estate leases, car leases, and other long-term contracts.

- **Schedule H:** Identifies codebtors, where someone else also is liable for one of your debts.

- **Schedule I:** Your income.

- **Schedule J:** Your current expenses.

- **Statement of Financial Affairs:** Specific questions about your financial dealings and those of any business you have.

- **Statement of Intention:** This is the form on which you tell secured creditors how you intend to treat them when dealing with your debt (for instance, by surrendering property or making up what you owe).

In any case, the instant that your papers are filed, the pressure should be off. No more calls from debt collectors. No more collection efforts. You don't have to dread answering the phone any more. Something called an automatic stay kicks in and, when it does, you'll finally see a glimmer of light at the end of your tunnel of financial distress.

Using the automatic stay

The *automatic stay* is one of the more important benefits of bankruptcy. It is a federal court order forbidding creditors from taking any action against you without first going through the judge.

Warning aggressive creditors that you've filed

Dan phoned the finance company and left a message that he'd just filed bankruptcy. Any finance company should, and would, know that a bankruptcy filing immediately stops all collection efforts.

But somehow, Dan's message got lost, and that night the company repossessed his car. When it refused to immediately return the vehicle, Dan asked for help from the bankruptcy court. The judge not only ordered the return of the car but also fined the finance company and made it pay Dan's legal fees.

Sometimes, however, a glitch may occur, because the court doesn't notify creditors of your bankruptcy until about ten days after it's filed. So, what if a creditor doesn't know that you've filed and repossesses your car?

Your attorney can almost certainly get your car back, but doing so is likely to be an unnecessary hassle and expense. You can avoid this headache simply by informing any creditor who's likely to take immediate action that you've filed bankruptcy. That way, if they violate the automatic stay, they'll have to pay you damages and reimburse your attorney fees.

If you're in default on your car loan, we suggest not notifying the creditor until after you actually file bankruptcy. Otherwise, the lender may attempt to grab the car before the automatic stay takes effect.

After your petition is filed, do the following things:

- ✔ If a foreclosure sale is scheduled, personally attend and announce that you've filed bankruptcy and that the sale cannot legally continue. Bring a copy of your petition just in case anyone insists on verification.

- ✔ Contact anyone who's suing you and send a copy of the bankruptcy petition to any court where you're being sued.

- ✔ Although doing so may be uncomfortable, you need to inform your employer about your bankruptcy so that no more money is garnished from your pay. Antidiscrimination laws prohibit your employer from taking any action against you simply because you filed bankruptcy.

Exceptions to the automatic stay

The automatic stay is a tremendous shield, but it isn't entirely bullet proof. It won't protect you from:

- ✔ Criminal prosecution. Filing bankruptcy won't prevent you from being tried, convicted, and sent to jail if you've committed a crime.

- ✔ Proceedings to establish your paternity, or in most cases, efforts to collect child support or alimony from you.

- ✔ Government regulatory matters . . . as long as they aren't an end run to collect on a prepetition debt.

Plenty of states automatically suspend your driver's license when you fail to pay a judgment stemming from a car crash. The aim, obviously, is collecting money from you, so the automatic stay therefore applies.

On the other hand, licensing requirements that are designed to protect the public from incompetent nurses, doctors, architects, lawyers, accountants, and so on are not designed primarily to collect revenue. Consequently, the automatic stay won't stop the state from revoking your professional license when you've somehow managed to commit malpractice or violate the standards of your profession.

For spouses and relatives

The automatic stay protects pretty much only you and your property. For example, it neither stops foreclosure on your grandfather's house nor precludes repossession of your spouse's car, if he or she doesn't also file bankruptcy.

However, if you have even a partial ownership interest in an asset, the stay may very well apply.

Some sleazebags have abused the automatic stay by transferring partial ownership interests to a number of pals or siblings. That way, whenever repossession or foreclosure is on the horizon, one of them files bankruptcy just long enough for the automatic stay to take effect and then promptly gets the bankruptcy dismissed. The next time creditors get antsy, another "owner" files and does the same thing. This is a crummy tactic, and courts are becoming not only willing but also seemingly eager to impose some pretty nasty fines on people who do it. If you ever decide to play this game, well, don't say we didn't warn you.

For cosigned debts

Ordinarily the automatic stay in your case wouldn't prevent a creditor from going after someone who cosigned a loan for you.

You can, however, protect cosigners when filing under Chapter 13, if your plan proposes paying off the cosigned debt in full (although over an extended period of time). This is known as the *codebtor stay* and may be just the ticket to protect your sister, cousin, mother-in-law, rabbi, or whoever else may have cosigned for your loan.

Taking quick action to save your driver's license

When the state tried to suspend Felicity's driver's license for not paying a judgment in a lawsuit over an automobile crash, she had her lawyer immediately file a bankruptcy petition. The automatic stay stopped the license suspension proceedings so that Felicity could continue to drive.

Smart move.

Had Felicity waited until her license actually was suspended before she filed her bankruptcy petition, she wouldn't have been able to drive until after the bankruptcy discharge was entered and her license was formally reinstated.

Receiving notice of the creditors' meeting

Within about ten days of filing your bankruptcy petition, the court sends notice to all your creditors (using addresses you provide in your schedules), informing them of your case, announcing the appointment of a case trustee (who represents the interests of the creditors), and setting the date for a meeting with creditors (the so-called 341 meeting).

The court uses *your address* as the return address on notices of your filing. So, if a creditor's address is incorrect, that notice is returned to *you,* telling you that a correction must be made. But you're the only person who'll know unless you tell your lawyer.

The one and only time in most bankruptcies that you and your creditors may come face to face is at what is known as the *341 meeting.* Named for a section of the Bankruptcy Code, this session sometimes is referred to as the "First Meeting of Creditors." That's kind of a misnomer because creditors almost never show up and a second meeting rarely occurs.

The 341 meetings generally are open to the public, although few people ever attend just out of idle curiosity. However, *you* may want to consider attending a couple just to watch the process unfold. Call the bankruptcy court or the U.S. Trustee's office to find out when and where 341 meetings will take place. *Note:* Chapter 7 meetings are somewhat different than Chapter 13 meetings, so make sure that you check out what type of meeting you'll be attending in your case.

After a case is filed and the automatic stay kicks in, Chapter 7s and Chapter 13s take different paths. The next two sections take closer looks at each one separately.

Working Your Way through Chapter 7

The first thing that happens in Chapter 7 is the 341 meeting with creditors, which usually takes place 20 to 40 days after filing. The trustee conducts this meeting and, of course, you and your lawyer must attend.

Local practice may require that you bring certain things, such as bank statements, pay stubs, income tax returns, car titles, and the like to the meeting, but ideally you've already provided your lawyer with all these materials, and he or she just has to bring copies for the trustee.

In addition, you must bring a photo ID, as well as proof of your social security number.

The 341 meeting

At the 341 meeting, the trustee asks whether you were honest in listing all your assets on your bankruptcy petition and whether you have any non-exempt property that can be sold off to satisfy creditors. The trustee may also inquire about any payments you made or property that you transferred before bankruptcy. She won't browbeat you for filing or try to embarrass you. That isn't her job or her purpose. You can expect to encounter a professional person acting professionally.

Whenever creditors show up, which is unlikely, they are permitted to ask a few polite questions, but they won't be allowed to harass you or put you down. Keep in mind that the purpose of the meeting is strictly "just the facts, ma'am" informational. You don't have to explain yourself or justify your spending.

Although attending a 341 meeting is not an act of penance, you still want to keep on your toes.

Keep in mind that getting rid of debt that you rack up when knowing full well that you won't be able to pay may be difficult. Sometimes a creditor pretends to be sympathetic, trying to lead you down the garden path of admitting that you knew you couldn't pay the debt when you incurred it. Don't ever let anybody put words in your mouth! If you thought that you'd be able to pay or just didn't realize how bad things were, stick to your guns. Don't admit to things that aren't true just to be helpful. Damning admissions can inspire creditors to file papers attempting to prevent that debt from being discharged on the basis of fraud (see Chapter 15).

Moreover, the trustee asks questions to find out whether you meet local requirements for exemptions that you claimed. You'll probably be quizzed about

- ✔ The value of your home, and whether you actually live there.
- ✔ Whether you actually use tools in your trade or business.
- ✔ The value of your car.
- ✔ Your pension plan.

  Whether you'll be asked about your pension plan depends on where you live.

Your lawyer should anticipate these questions and review them with you ahead of time.

Whenever you have nonexempt assets, the trustee usually inquires if you'd be willing to pay her the value of the asset so that you can keep it. Say, for example, that you owned a personal watercraft worth $1,500. The trustee would ask you if you'd rather pay $1,500 or surrender it. If you decide to keep it, payments may be stretched out over a few months.

If you can't or don't want to buy back nonexempt assets, the trustee arranges to have them picked up for liquidation. In the case of real estate, she hires a real estate agent who then inspects the property and comes to an independent opinion as to its value. The trustee then decides whether to have the real estate agent offer the property for sale.

This applies only to *nonexempt* property, and not your home if it's fully exempt.

The trustee may also make arrangements to receive your income tax refund for the current year, or request additional information about your assets, payments, or recent transfers of property. These issues usually can be handled by your lawyer simply by sending a letter addressing any unresolved questions. Sometimes, a second meeting is necessary, but that's a rarity.

In the majority of cases, the trustee quickly concludes that you don't have enough nonexempt assets to bother with and declares your matter a no-asset case. In these cases, your involvement with the trustee usually ends at the conclusion of the 341 meeting.

Dealing with secured creditors

Aside from dealing with the trustee, you also must make arrangements with secured creditors within a month or so after the 341 meeting. You may:

- ✔ Surrender collateral
- ✔ Redeem some kinds of personal property
- ✔ Reaffirm the secured debt
- ✔ Use avoidance powers to eliminate liens

See Chapter 10 for a more in-depth look at secured debts and ways to deal with them.

Amending paperwork

If you discover that you've made inadvertent mistakes in the paperwork, the earlier you correct them, the better. Telling the trustee about errors is essential. However, when addressing a significant error, merely telling the trustee isn't enough. Significant errors mean a formal amendment needs to be filed so that the court's records show you've been forthright and truthful. Your attorney probably will charge you extra to amend your paperwork, but getting it right is crucial.

Check out Chapter 18 to get an idea of what types of errors may be considered significant enough to require formal amendment to your papers.

Adding creditors

The general rule is that debts that aren't listed aren't wiped out. But you still can add them after you've filed, if you do so promptly, and the sooner the better. Making additions to your list of debts within 30 days after the 341 meeting is preferable, and it's essential within 90 days if assets will be available to creditors in your case. (See Chapter 12 for more information about dealing with unlisted creditors.)

Sweating out key deadlines

The Bankruptcy Code mercifully establishes two deadlines, and you can breathe easier after they pass. They are:

- **30 days after the 341 meeting concludes:** The 30th day is the last day for the trustee or creditors to object to your claims of exempt property. If you've properly listed the asset, you're in the clear after that. But if you have to amend an exemption claim, the 30-day clock starts running all over again.

- **60 days after the 341 meeting:** The 60th day is the deadline for creditors to claim that certain types of debts — most notably credit-card fraud claims and nonsupport marital obligations — should not be wiped out. If the creditor fails to file in time, it's too late, and you're home free. The same deadline applies to claims that your discharge should be denied altogether because of serious misconduct. This is also the deadline for claiming that your Chapter 7 should be dismissed for substantial abuse (a term we deal with in Chapter 4) of the bankruptcy process.

Attending a discharge hearing

This hearing takes place before the judge but usually is unnecessary when an attorney represents the debtor. The purpose of a discharge hearing is to make sure a debtor who wants to *reaffirm* a debt (or allow it to continue after bankruptcy) understands the consequences.

Usually, you have to attend a discharge hearing only if you want to reaffirm a debt and your lawyer refused to sign a statement that reaffirmation is in your best interest. Understand that your lawyer is not doing this to be mean. She's actually trying to look out for your best interest despite your desires. At the discharge hearing, the judge makes sure that you really understand the consequences of reaffirming a debt.

Closing no-asset cases

Most no-asset cases close about 60 days after the 341 meeting. At that point, you're done. All assets that you listed on your schedules are yours again when the case is closed.

Administering asset cases

Asset cases remain open long enough for the trustee to liquidate your non-exempt assets, distribute the proceeds to creditors, and file a report with the court. If the trustee can't sell an asset, she abandons it, and that means that you own it again.

This whole process is referred to as the *administration of the estate,* and sometimes it takes quite a while — sometimes even years, depending on the kind of assets that are involved.

If someone owed you money on the petition date, the trustee can sue that person to collect it. If you already were in the process of suing someone, the trustee takes over the case. All this takes time, and courts are pretty indulgent in giving trustees all the time they need.

Even though an asset case can drag on, your discharge (assuming there are no complications; see the next section for details) still will be entered approximately 60 days after the 341 meeting. Still, you must cooperate with the trustee in her efforts to convert assets to cash.

Fortunately, fewer than 5 percent of Chapter 7 filings are assets cases.

Laying the foundation for credit repair

Sooner or later, you're going to want to repair your credit rating — and there's no time like the present for getting started. You can do a number of things right now that make the going easier down the road.

For instance, some banks won't allow a recent bankruptcy filer to open a checking account. You can avoid this hassle by opening a new account before bankruptcy at a bank where you don't owe any money. Just deposit the minimum amount, and don't use the account until after you file.

You may also want to consider getting a new credit card or a charge account. Although it may seem that there's nothing you need less than more credit, getting a new account is a step toward rebuilding your credit, and doing it now rather than later is easier and cleaner.

Be sure to accurately list all your debts and assets on any application, and if you succeed in getting a credit or charge card, don't use it until after you file. If you don't owe money on an account, you won't need to list it on your bankruptcy petition. Chances are the creditor won't be notified of your filing and you'll be able to use the new account to begin restoring your credit history in the future.

Anticipating complications

Not every Chapter 7 is routine, however, and complications sometimes develop. (Chapter 18 explains how to deal with the Murphy's Laws of bankruptcy.) The good news is that an experienced bankruptcy lawyer usually can tell, even before filing, whether possible problems are lurking on the horizon. If you've been completely candid with your lawyer, and she's not worried about any potential glitches, you needn't worry either.

Working Your Way through Chapter 13

Aside from the obvious fact that you'll be making payments for the next 36 to 60 months, when filing a Chapter 13 reorganization, you have a few extra hurdles to jump. Procedural requirements are designed to ensure that your plan is feasible, that it satisfies certain technical mandates, and that you do the best you can to repay creditors.

Filing your plan and beginning your payments

Although you have 15 days after your petition is filed to submit your payment plan, having it ready when you file is a better idea. Your first plan payment is due within 30 days, and it may come due even before you meet with the trustee. One concern of the trustee is whether you're willing and able to make timely plan payments. Missing the first payment makes for a dreadful start. Your lawyer should tell you how and where to make plan payments.

The 341 meeting

Many aspects of the 341 meeting with creditors are the same in Chapter 13 as they are in Chapter 7 cases, but the emphasis is different and some additional concerns exist.

The Chapter 13 trustee scrutinizes your income (Schedule I) and expenses (Schedule J) to see whether you are

- ✔ Likely to meet your monthly payment obligations. You probably won't be able to keep up with payments if you haven't been realistic in estimating your living expenses.

- ✔ Making a good faith effort to repay your creditors as much as reasonably possible. The trustee questions you to make sure that you listed all your sources of income and carefully reviews your proposed expenses. The trustee probably won't allow deductions for pension contributions or repayments of pension loans, payments for obvious luxury items, expenses for supporting adult children, or expensive private schools. And your days of eating at gourmet restaurants are over — at least for a while. Sorry.

In locations where the local practice is to conduct confirmation hearings (see the next section) immediately after the 341 meeting, more creditors may attend and ask questions along the same line as those just listed. In other locations, most creditors do not attend 341 meeting.

Confirming your repayment plan

The court decides whether to approve or reject your repayment plan at what's called the *confirmation hearing*.

In many places, if the trustee supports your plan and your creditors have no objections, you don't have to appear at the confirmation hearing, and the court will probably approve your proposal as a matter of course.

But whenever the trustee or a creditor objects, you and your lawyer have to attend. Your lawyer determines whether to proceed with a hearing and tries to convince the judge that the objections have no merit or tries negotiating with objecting creditors. If the court upholds any objection to your plan, you'll probably have an opportunity to file a modified plan and schedule another confirmation hearing. Occasionally, the judge concludes that the objection is so serious that any attempted plan modification would be futile, and simply orders that the case be dismissed.

Going through valuation hearings

Another type of hearing known as a *valuation hearing* is where secured creditors can object to how they are being treated under your plan, because the value of their collateral is different than you claim. Your lawyer usually can resolve valuation issues through negotiation but, if that fails, the judge decides.

Looking at the claims process

Whenever any creditors are entitled to receive money from your bankruptcy — that is, if you filed a Chapter 13 or a Chapter 7 asset case — be sure that the money goes toward satisfying debts that won't be discharged or that will continue to linger because of a lien.

For example, if you file Chapter 13 to catch up on your back mortgage payments, you want the money you pay to the trustee to be used for this purpose — not toward payment of debts that will just be eliminated.

But remember that a creditor can't receive any money from a bankruptcy estate unless a document called a *proof of claim* is filed with the court. Most creditors have 90 days from the 341 meeting to file such a claim. If the creditor doesn't file one, you can lodge a proof of claim on behalf of the creditor up to 120 days from the 341 meeting.

Governmental units get special treatment and are afforded 180 days after the petition date to file a proof of claim.

Certain taxes are *priority debts*. These taxes, which ordinarily would be nondischargeable, can be wiped out in Chapter 13 whenever the taxing authority doesn't file a timely proof of claim. (Obviously, you don't want to file a proof of claim for these debts.)

Comparing the Chapter 7 and Chapter 13 Processes

Table 5-2 shows what usually happens, step by step, in Chapter 7 and Chapter 13 cases.

Table 5-2	Comparing Two Main Bankruptcy Processes
Chapter 7	*Chapter 13*
1. Petition filed	1. Petition filed
2. Aggressive creditors notified immediately	2. Aggressive creditors notified immediately
3. Court sends notice to you, your, lawyer and all your creditors	3. Court sends notice to you, your lawyer, and all your creditors
4. 341 meeting	4. Payment plan must be filed with first payment due in 30 days
5. Deal with secured creditors	5. 341 meeting
6. 30 days after 341 meeting concludes, last day for objections to exemptions	6. 30 days after 341 meeting concludes, last day for objections to exemptions
7. 60 days after 341 is deadline for claiming some debts not discharged, discharge should be denied or case dismissed for substantial abuse	7. Confirmation hearing
8. Discharge hearing	8. Valuation hearing
9. Discharge usually entered about 60 days after 341 meeting	9. 120 days after 341 meeting last filed on behalf of creditor you want paid. (180 days from petition date for governmental creditors)
10. 120 days after 341 meeting last day for proof of claim to be filed on behalf of creditor you want paid. (180 days from petition date for governmental creditors)	10. 180 days after 341 meeting last day for proof of claim to be filed on behalf of governmental creditors.
11. Closing no-asset case	11. Completion of plan payments and discharge of remaining balances
12. In asset cases, trustee liquidates property, distributes proceeds to creditors, files reports, and closes case.	

Part II
Avoiding Bankruptcy

The 5th Wave   By Rich Tennant

"I'm well aware that we ask for a lot when people file for bankruptcy, Mr. Harvey. However, sarcasm is rarely required."

In this part . . .

The solution to your problem may lie in bankruptcy —
or maybe not. When you're still not sure whether
bankruptcy is the winning strategy for you, and you still
want to consider other alternatives, you have the right
book. Read on to fully understand the downsides of
bankruptcy. In this part, we offer a crash course in successful sparring with debt-collection bullies — to keep
them at bay while you make up your mind — and some
tips on negotiating the granddaddy of all debt collectors:
Good ol' Uncle Sam.

Chapter 6

Considering Alternatives to Bankruptcy

In This Chapter

▶ Understanding the downside of filing bankruptcy now — or later

▶ Considering alternatives to bankruptcy

▶ Selecting bills to pay, or not pay

▶ Dickering with creditors

▶ Considering credit counseling

▶ Ignoring creditors

*B*ankruptcy is a fantastically powerful tool for financial rebirth, and one that never should be viewed only as a last resort. Bankruptcy is a tool at your disposal, and you need to measure its usefulness by the simplest of criteria: Do the benefits outweigh the disadvantages? Too many people comply with the advice of less-than-objective debt counselors and sincere-but-ignorant friends and relatives, parting with essential assets like their homes and pensions, only to wind up in bankruptcy (where those kinds of assets may have been protected) anyhow.

But bankruptcy isn't necessarily the best or even the only solution for you. Filing bankruptcy has definite downsides, and sometimes a different strategy is more appropriate for your situation or your personality.

In this chapter, we look at some of the pitfalls of bankruptcy and alternatives such as using your home equity or pension to pay your debts.

Appreciating the Negative Consequences of Bankruptcy

Bankruptcy isn't without consequences, and some of them can be painful. You need to fully appreciate what you have to lose if you file bankruptcy, and what you stand to lose if you file at the wrong time.

The drawbacks of bankruptcy

Although the drawbacks frequently are exaggerated, filing bankruptcy *can* (note we say "can" and not "will"):

- Hurt innocent people who extended you credit
- Damage your credit rating
- Represent the ultimate admission of financial defeat
- Result in pubic humiliation in communities where newspapers print the names of bankruptcy filers (Because of the sheer volume, however, many newspapers now limit those listings to businesses and prominent individuals.)
- Subject your personal lifestyle to scrutiny in a public meeting room (rarely, however, do any curiosity seekers show up)
- Be used against you by prospective employers, particularly if your career involves being bonded (bank teller, jewelry associate, and so on)
- Cause you to lose some of your belongings
- Preclude bankruptcy as an avenue of relief if you get in even worse trouble in the near future

Reasons not to file bankruptcy

Bankruptcy may be the wrong solution for you if:

- Your debts are small enough that you can probably pay them off in full in a few years without too much trouble.
- You don't owe the money. Just because someone says you owe him money doesn't necessarily mean that you do. If you sincerely believe the debt is an error, and can prove it, fight.

✔ You won't be able to shed your most nettlesome debts by filing. Bankruptcy won't eliminate all your debts. Criminal fines, student loans, most taxes, support obligations, and personal injuries caused by drunk driving usually can't be wiped out in bankruptcy.

✔ You have valuable nonexempt assets that can be taken to satisfy creditors, and you don't want to risk losing them.

✔ Your goal is just to delay a creditor or jerk him around.

✔ Your biggest debts are secured (by your house or car, for example), and your unsecured debts are relatively insignificant.

✔ You have transferred property to or put title in someone else's name to keep it away from creditors.

Reasons to delay filing bankruptcy

Sometimes a successful bankruptcy depends on careful timing. Your lawyer may suggest that you wait if you:

✔ Expect to receive a large income tax refund. If you file before receiving the windfall, the money goes toward paying your debts. But if you wait until after you receive your refund, you'll be able to spend it on essentials (like car or house repairs) before filing.

✔ Racked up quite a bit of debt recently. If you wait for a while to file bankruptcy, it will be less likely that creditors would claim fraud and try to prevent elimination of these debts. See Chapters 13 and 15.

✔ Repaid debts to family members during the past year. If you wait for a year to expire after paying debts to family members, you protect them from having to cough up this money to a bankruptcy trustee. See Chapter 18.

✔ Are facing large medical bills in the foreseeable future. Remember that you won't be able to wipe out these bills in a Chapter 7 for six years if you file now.

✔ Filed bankruptcy within the last six years. Your debts won't be wiped out if you file Chapter 7 within six years of a prior case.

✔ Are contemplating divorce. Deciding exactly when to file bankruptcy when a divorce is looming is devilishly tricky. See Chapter 16.

✔ Owe taxes that wouldn't be dischargeable if you filed bankruptcy right now but would become dischargeable in the near future.

Looking at Remedies Other Than Bankruptcy

You don't swat a fly with a sledgehammer or use a wrench to drive in a nail — or at least you shouldn't. By the same token, you don't need to file bankruptcy just to solve a trivial financial problem or when a more targeted remedy is available. Although you never should view bankruptcy as a last-ditch solution, you probably shouldn't make it your first consideration either. If you can get out of trouble without filing, that's wonderful! In fact, this section explains a number of things that you may want to consider before deciding that bankruptcy is the way out.

Budgeting

If you can get your financial house in order through discipline and careful budgeting, go for it. The key to realistic budgeting is establishing a reasonable time frame for immediate and long-term goals and adopting a positive attitude that focuses not on what you're giving up but rather on what you're achieving.

You may also consider looking into an Employee Assistance Program (EAP), if your employer offers one. These plans provide counseling for a variety of issues, including debt problems. The EAP may also suggest ways that your company credit union can help. However, you always need to be leery of attempting to borrow your way out of debt. It's kind of like those diet plans that claim you can eat your way thin.

Allowing your family to bail you out

Frequently, a parent or other family member offers to save your hide, and accepting that generosity often is tempting. Allowing your family to bail you out may be a wise alternative to bankruptcy, but only if your Guardian Angel:

- Is ready, willing, and able to help.
- Can pay your debts without suffering financial hardship himself.
- Can truly solve your problem, not just postpone an inevitable bankruptcy. Loaning or giving money to a loved one to relieve the immediate pressure is common, but such actions ultimately are a waste of money whenever you end up in bankruptcy anyway. The money is gone, the gesture was futile, and far too often, bad feelings linger.

Selling your assets

If you own assets that you'd lose to a bankruptcy trustee, you may want to consider selling your stuff to pay your debts. If that doesn't raise enough money to pay *all* your debts, it at least helps whittle down your debt load.

Every state has laws that make certain essential assets exempt or off-limits to creditors, regardless of whether the debtor files bankruptcy. Note that we're talking about selling *nonexempt* assets — those that a creditor can get. Don't let anyone bully you into selling exempt assets, which in most cases are off-limits whenever you file bankruptcy. Most states allow you to keep:

- Homesteads up to a specified value
- Pensions
- Basic household furnishings
- A modest vehicle

Practically speaking, here's how exemptions work. Say your home is worth $100,000 and your mortgage(s) total $80,000. The equity in your home is $20,000. If the homestead exemption for your state is $25,000, the only creditors who can take your home are the ones holding your mortgages. The law says that your home is yours — unless you agree otherwise by getting another mortgage or borrowing more on your present one. In other words, selling exempt assets to pay debts is rarely a good idea. Actually, it's often downright foolish.

When selling assets, you need to:

- Sell the asset for a fair price. If you sell to someone you know, be prepared to show how you determined the price.
- Avoid repaying debts to friends or relatives if there's any possibility of bankruptcy.
- Tell your bankruptcy lawyer when you've sold assets. (Actually, it would be better to tell him beforehand if possible), and be sure that the sale is mentioned in your bankruptcy paperwork.

Some department stores take a *security interest* in items that you purchase on their charge accounts. In practical terms, that means you aren't supposed to part with an item you've charged before you fully own it. But if you've already sold it, it's probably not a big deal if you didn't know any better.

Keep in mind that the law does *not* require you to strip yourself of key assets to satisfy creditors. (We describe such exemptions in detail in Part III.) You need somewhere to live. You may need a car. Someday you'll need a pension. Bankruptcy protects all those things.

Transferring credit-card balances

Although trading high interest rates for lower rates is worth checking out, credit-card balance transfers seldom are effective. A *balance transfer* actually is a new loan with the proceeds going to pay debts that should be pretty far down on your list of priorities. Furthermore, whenever you transfer a balance and then end up in bankruptcy, you may be facing an allegation of fraud, and your creditors may fight to prevent the debts you owe them from being wiped out.

If you do decide to shop around, a Web site at www.getsmart.com can help you find a more favorable credit-card rate. Another Web site, www.bankrate.com also provides useful information about credit-card rates and mortgage rates.

Keep in mind, however, that creditors have ulterior motives. Even when monthly payments are lower, the longer the creditors continue collecting interest, the more you'll ultimately pay.

Restructuring home mortgages

You may be able to free up some cash by restructuring your home mortgage. Basically, you can do this in two ways:

- ✔ By arranging a mortgage work-out agreement
- ✔ By refinancing

If a foreclosure sale is scheduled, keep your eye on that date and, if possible, try to get it postponed. When such a sale goes forward, you're likely to lose any equity that you have in the property. See Chapter 11 to see why bankruptcy must be filed before a foreclosure sale is conducted.

Mortgage work-outs

If your only problem is that you temporarily fell behind on your mortgage payments — perhaps because of a layoff, sickness, or family emergency — your mortgageholder may allow you to catch up on back payments over an extended period of time. The bank doesn't want your house, but it definitely wants the money you promised to pay for it (or at least as much as it can get).

The sooner you contact the lender, the better. After a foreclosure begins, the amount that you eventually have to come up with increases by at least $1,000, because you have to pay the lender's attorney fees.

When you have built up significant equity in a property, selling it before a foreclosure is completed usually is better. Foreclosures rarely produce any money over and above the amount owed to the lender, but you may be able to sell the property for more than that amount. That way, you get to keep the extra.

The widespread use of mortgage insurance also offers a glimmer of hope. With this type of insurance, a mortgage insurer agrees to pay the lender any losses that it suffers if you don't pay the mortgage, and after it pays off the lender, it steps into the lender's shoes and takes over the loan.

Government agencies, such as the Federal Housing Administration (FHA), the United States Department of Housing and Urban Development (HUD), the Farmers Home Administration (FmHA), and the Veteran's Administration (VA) insure many mortgages. These agencies have programs designed to help folks avoid losing their homes. When you approach the lender about a workout agreement, ask whether the loan is insured by one of these agencies. If so, call the agency to find out what programs are available.

An often-overlooked defense to foreclosures

The Federal Truth in Lending Act (TILA — U.S. Code, vol. 15, secs 1601–1667) (volume 15, sections 1601 through 1667 of the official compilation of federal statutes known as the United States Code) can be a godsend in stopping foreclosure.

The TILA requires lenders to provide borrowers with certain precise information about the loan, at the time that it's made. If the lenders screw up — and they often do, you can rescind, or cancel, a mortgage on your home, thus ending the foreclosure. At some point you're supposed to repay the money that you borrowed, but if you don't, they can't take your home. Although the time for rescinding supposedly expires three years after the loan is made, many courts have ruled you still can rescind even beyond three years if the lender tries to foreclose.

Truth-in-lending defenses frequently are overlooked because most lawyers aren't up to speed on the Act. Public-interest law offices and legal aide counselors tend to be the most knowledgeable about this powerful weapon.

The greatest limitation to TILA defenses is that the TILA doesn't apply to mortgages taken to buy the home — probably your first mortgage.

Refinancing

By refinancing your mortgage — in effect, trading an old mortgage in for a new one with a more favorable interest rate — you can significantly cut your monthly payment, perhaps by a couple hundred dollars a month or even more. You can shop around for a better mortgage rate at `www.interest.com/mmis.html` and `www.bankrate.com`.

Generally, refinancing makes economic sense only when rates have fallen a full 2 percentage points. Otherwise, closing costs and fees eat up any potential savings. Likewise, be wary of variable-interest mortgages, which fluctuate, usually with the prime interest rate. They have a nasty tendency to go up at the worst possible time.

Home-equity loans

A world of difference exists between refinancing to get a better rate and taking a home-equity loan — which doesn't reduce the amount of your mortgage debt. All you really do with a home-equity loan is, in essence, unbuy your house, and then buy it back again.

Many companies aggressively tout home-equity loans, urging you to use the value that you've built up in your home as collateral. They claim that borrowing against your home to pay off credit cards is the greatest thing since canned beer because:

- ✔ Interest on home mortgages is tax deductible.
- ✔ Making a single monthly payment is more convenient than numerous credit-card payments.
- ✔ The interest rate is lower.
- ✔ Your monthly payment will be lower than what you're now paying on credit cards.

Sometimes the slick ads also subtly suggest that you may even have enough cash left over after paying off credit cards for you to take a much-deserved vacation or buy an expensive toy.

All this may sound pretty good, but don't forget that your home may be the most valuable and important asset that you have, and you're putting it at risk when you play the home-equity credit game. If paying credit-card bills was a struggle, making payments on a home-equity loan probably won't be much easier. To make matters worse, after your credit-card bills are paid off, your credit-card accounts will be available for more borrowing — the very thing that got you into trouble with in the first place.

You also want to keep in mind that home-equity loans usually carry a steeper interest rate than conventional mortgages, so you probably won't save much in interest. And if your plan is to take out a loan so you can pay a number of smaller bills, you're actually just exchanging many smaller bills for a large one, and probably paying some loan fees to boot.

Furthermore, remember that a home-equity loan creates a lien on your home that survives bankruptcy. Say that after sucking all the equity out of your home to pay your credit-card bills, you still end up in bankruptcy. What you've done is needlessly put your house on the line. The credit-card debts were unsecured and would've probably been eliminated in bankruptcy. But the value of your house secures the home-equity loan. No wonder lenders (and sometimes credit counselors who work openly — or not — for lenders) push home-equity loans!

Whenever you do consider refinancing, be on the alert for hidden costs, such as broker's fees, points (additional interest), and penalties for prepaying your present mortgage. These fees can negate the benefits of using home equity to consolidate your debts.

And watch out for loans that require "balloon" payments. Sometimes, these loans are structured in such a way that you fork over relatively small monthly payments until the final installment is due — and then you get whacked.

Finally, if bankruptcy is even remotely visible on your horizon, consult with an attorney *before* taking out a second mortgage. The sight of folks losing bankruptcy as a viable solution by taking out one of these loans is all too common, so you need to be quite clear about the ramifications of a second mortgage before taking that step. No competent attorney will try to push you into bankruptcy if that isn't your best choice, or if you're just not ready. But a good bankruptcy lawyer needs to be able to give you a clear picture of the potential benefits and drawbacks of your unique situation. Expect to pay a reasonable fee for the lawyer's time (between $100 and $200), and consider it a smart investment. See Chapter 3.

Reverse mortgages

So-called *reverse mortgages* usually target senior citizens, enticing them to tap into their home equity by borrowing money that doesn't have to be repaid until they move or die.

For example, say you're 65 years old, and you own your $100,000 home free and clear. With a reverse mortgage, you'd borrow up to some specified percentage of the home's value, say $80,000, and then receive portions of that money in regular intervals without having to make any mortgage payments.

Sounds like a good deal, doesn't it? Depending on your unique circumstances, it may be. Just don't lose sight of the fact that someday that loan will have to be repaid; otherwise, your house will be turned over to the lender, and that inevitability may come as quite a shock to your heirs.

Be very careful when considering a reverse mortgage and look out for outfits that prey on older people with equity in their homes. Stick with a reputable lender and be sure that you understand all the costs and fees that you'll be charged. Finding out whether and how a reverse mortgage in your particular situation may affect your eligibility for government benefits such as Social Security or Medicaid also is a good idea.

Once again, we encourage you to talk to a bankruptcy lawyer before entering into a reverse-mortgage arrangement. Depending on the available homestead exemption, you may be much better off just filing bankruptcy.

Tapping your retirement plan

In most states, creditors can't get at your pension unless you enable them to do so by withdrawing the money or taking a loan against it. Taking either of those routes seldom is a good move. You may face serious tax consequences when you take an early pension distribution or fail to repay a pension loan.

Borrowing against your retirement plan is usually a lousy idea because:

- ✔ It gives the lender a claim against your pension. Ordinarily, creditors can't get their hands on your retirement account.
- ✔ Most debts that you'd pay with the proceeds of the pension loan, such as credit card accounts, can probably be wiped out in bankruptcy.
- ✔ If you don't repay the pension loan, you'll suffer serious tax consequences.
- ✔ If you lose your job, you may have to repay the loan almost immediately.

In a few situations, tapping into your retirement fund may be a feasible way of solving your problems. But you'd do well to find out your bankruptcy options before risking your retirement nest egg.

Choosing Which Bills to Pay First (If at All)

Chances are you don't have the money to pay all your bills, at least not right away, so you'll need to decide which ones to pay. You obviously need to continue paying current bills for living expenses like food and utilities.

Amid all your personal financial turmoil, debt collectors usually give you crummy advice because all they care about is wringing as much as possible out of you, as soon as possible, and with the least amount of effort on their part. Your decisions must be based on reason and guided by what's best for you and your family and not on what makes for a happy debt collector.

Keeping that perspective when a bill collector is bullying you isn't always easy. Remember, however, that the most obnoxious collectors act the way they do because they really don't have any other weapon to use against you.

It is hoped that you plan to talk to a bankruptcy lawyer before making these decisions, but if you're not quite ready to take that step, you may want to start by asking yourself two questions:

- What can this creditor do if I don't pay?
- Will I be able to escape this debt altogether if I eventually decide to file bankruptcy?

When you can't pay everyone, you need to invest your money where it does the most good or avoids the gravest of problems. Dribbling out money to the most aggressive collectors without an overall plan is a mistake. The payments at the top of your priority list (in order) should be your:

- Rent, or mortgage, if you intend to keep your house
- Utilities
- Essential vehicle
- Fines, if nonpayment would land you in jail
- Child support and alimony
- Income taxes
- Possibly student loans (but first see whether you're eligible for one of the repayment plans described in Chapter 17)

It's no accident that credit cards, loans from finance companies, and medical bills don't make the cut in this list. That's because these types of creditors must sue you and obtain a judgment before they can take any of your property. In other words, before they can ever cause you any real trouble, they have some hurdles to jump over. Besides, these kinds of debts can be wiped out if you end up in bankruptcy.

If bankruptcy is in your future, you should neither repay any loans to close friends or family members nor loans that are cosigned by any such people. If you file bankruptcy within one year of making these types of payments, the trustee can get the money back. See Chapter 18.

As a general rule, you need to be wary of giving creditors any additional ammunition just because you think it will get them off your back. It won't. Trust us on this one. And it may cause you additional headaches in the future.

Credit counselors or *consolidators* backed by the lending industry may try talking you into taking a home-equity loan to pay off your credit cards. If you see any possibility at all that you'll eventually go bankrupt (and it is probable that you do), a home-equity loan is a terrible idea. The reason? You'd essentially transform unsecured debts (your credit-card bills) into a debt secured by your home. Then if you don't pay, they can take your home sweet home. See why the creditors like it so much?

The National Consumer Law Center publishes a guide that helps you decide which debts to pay and generally how to cope with debt outside of bankruptcy. This publication, *Surviving Debt* by Jonathan Sheldon and Gary Klein, can be obtained through many bookstores, or you can order it directly by contacting: National Consumer Law Center, 77 Summer St., 10th Floor, Boston, MA 02110-1006; phone, 617-523-8089.

Deciding whether to pay your mortgage

Although you'll probably want to make your mortgage payments if you decide to file bankruptcy, it isn't necessarily a given.

Whenever your home is worth less than what you owe on it, you may just want to save the money for a deposit on a new place to live, knowing that eventually the mortgageholder will foreclose and kick you out anyway. However, if you intend to keep your home, be sure to maintain insurance and, if possible, pay real estate taxes. If you don't, the lender may be able to foreclose even if you're making your payments.

Considering whether to make car payments

As is true with your house, the question to ask about your car is whether it is worth less than you owe on it. You'll have to make your car payments if you want to keep it. And even if you decide to surrender the vehicle, your problem may not be cured. Most car dealers sell surrendered vehicles at wholesale prices, leaving you liable for any balance due on the loan. You may try selling the vehicle yourself to raise enough to pay the loan in full and satisfy the entire obligation.

Smart cars?

Payment Protection Systems, Inc., manufactures and markets a device (known as *On Time*) that attaches to a vehicle, warns the occupant when an installment payment on the vehicle is about to be due, and disables the starting mechanism of the car when payment is overdue. When payment is made, the debtor can restart the car by entering a code in the device. Evidently, a customer is able to use the disabled vehicle in the case of an emergency. If you're interested in finding out more about this gizmo, check out www.ontime-pps.com.

Dealing with alimony and child support payments

If at all possible, you also need to get current with your alimony and child support obligations. The consequences for neglecting those obligations are serious, possibly even criminally serious if you're jailed for contempt of court. And many judges have adopted a zero-tolerance approach toward deadbeat parents.

Deciding whether you should pay your taxes

You need to pay current income taxes, and probably those from the last three years. Taxing authorities can make your life miserable if you don't, and penalties for not paying add up at an astonishing rate (see Chapter 8 for more information).

Negotiating with Your Creditors

If you can find someone who actually has the authority to negotiate, you may be able to cut a deal that works to everyone's satisfaction. But if your creditor is a large institution, you'll have difficulty getting beyond the bean counters and paper pushers; that is, if you even get past the answering machines. You're more likely to succeed if your creditor is a small organization. Regardless, attempting a nonbankruptcy solution is worth the effort.

Work-out agreements

Traditionally, a nonbankruptcy *work-out agreement* — where a debtor reaches a negotiated solution with creditors — falls into one of three categories:

- ✔ Composition arrangements where all creditors agree to accept less than full settlement of the debts
- ✔ Extension agreements that merely extend the term for repayment in full
- ✔ Combination agreements where debts are reduced and paid over an extended time period

The problem with these plans is that all your creditors must go along, and so, the more creditors you have, the harder it is to get them to agree. In addition, you'll probably need a lawyer to negotiate settlement agreements, and the legal fees may be exorbitant, if not prohibitive.

Strange as it may seem, whenever a creditor writes off a debt outside of the bankruptcy context, the amount of the write-off is taxable income to the borrower unless he was insolvent (owed debts exceeding the value of your assets) when the debt was kissed off. If you're in this situation, consider filing Form 982 with your tax return. You can get it on the IRS Web site at www.irs.ustreas.gov/formspubs/index.html (click on "Forms and Publications by Number").

Work-out agreements are more useful when you have valuable nonexempt assets that are worth enough to pay your debts but for which you need some time to sell without having to juggle creditors. In consumer cases, rarely does a debtor have enough assets to pay his debts.

Threatening bankruptcy

If you genuinely are considering bankruptcy, unsecured creditors may agree to settle for a pittance simply because when you do actually file they'd otherwise receive nothing.

Consider the following scenario:

Assume you borrowed $50,000 to start a business, which never got off the ground. There's no way you can repay this debt, and all you own is a modest home, mortgaged to the hilt, an old car and a pension. If you file bankruptcy, the lender won't receive one red cent. If you offered the creditor the money that you will otherwise spend on filing bankruptcy, about $1,000, he should (if he's thinking rationally) agree to take the money and write off the debt. A thousand dollars is still better than nothing. And you avoid having to file bankruptcy.

The success of this kind of strategy depends on convincing your creditor that you're truly prepared to file bankruptcy. The best way to accomplish that is to hire a well-known bankruptcy specialist to handle the negotiation. That way, the creditor knows that you're serious. But, don't ever bluff or threaten bankruptcy unless you're truly prepared to turn in that direction.

Considering Credit Counseling Services

You can find a number of outfits that offer credit counseling. Consumer Credit Counseling Services is the most common. CCCS offices are local non-profit debt-counseling outfits, numbering about 1,300 and joined under the National Foundation for Consumer Credit.

CCCS acts as an intermediary between you and the creditors. It often gets late fees dropped and wage garnishments revoked. Typically, you and the CCCS counselor devise a repayment schedule, and then you make regular payments to the CCCS, which forwards the money to the creditor.

Creditors pay CCCS a commission on the funds that it collects. Because of this commission, some people claim that CCCS is nothing more than a glorified bill collector. Nevertheless, fees charged to consumers are fairly nominal and usually under $25 a month. Sometimes CCCS even renders its services for free. To find a CCCS near you, call the main office at 800-388-2227, write to the headquarters at 8611 Second Ave., Suite 100, Silver Springs, MD 20910, or check out the National Foundation for Consumer Credit Web page at www. nfcc.org.

CCCS is more helpful to you in either of the following situations:

✔ When the total amount of your debts is small enough that you know you can pay if just given enough time.

✔ When you intend eventually to file bankruptcy but need to buy some time. For example, you may be waiting until past-due income taxes become dischargeable.

Although some organizations like CCCS offer valuable assistance, they're also allied with creditors and have an institutional bias against bankruptcy, even when it's in your best interest.

Some counselors are very good and, if a person's situation is truly hopeless, they immediately refer that person to a competent bankruptcy attorney. On the other hand, some counselors think that talking people out of filing bankruptcy is their duty. They vigorously push repayment plans, which often are doomed to fail. Additionally, they often fail to have the principal amount of your debts reduced and don't help much in extending payments on secured debts.

Terrible advice from a credit counselor

When Joe and Mary's little boy, Ray, was diagnosed with leukemia, they spent all their savings, incurred $50,000 in medical bills and charged $20,000 on credit cards trying to do the best for Ray. After Ray died, a credit-counseling outfit convinced Joe and Mary to sell the family home and cash in their pensions.

That was bad advice.

Even after surrendering all their assets, Joe and Mary remained $23,000 in the red and still had creditors on their tails. They ultimately ended up in bankruptcy, but by then, their home and pensions, which would have been preserved had they filed for protection earlier, were long gone.

The credit agency was looking out for creditors and, from Joe and Mary's standpoint, made a rotten situation only that much worse.

Several other organizations offer online debt counseling. Many provide advice about how to get out of debt. As is true with CCCS, however, you need to be skeptical. Debt counseling groups, even those with nonprofit status, don't necessarily have your best interests in mind, especially when filing bankruptcy is potentially in your best interest. You may also want to think twice about submitting personal financial information to a stranger.

In any case, here are some of the better-known online services and their Web sites:

- **Consolidated Credit Counseling Services:** www.debtfree.org
- **American Consumer Credit Counseling:** www.consumercredit.com
- **Myvesta:** www.myvesta.org

If your problems primarily are medical, consider Health Allies — a company that specializes in arranging payment plans for medical and hospital bills of all kinds (www.healthallies.com).

You can also check your local phone book for debt counselors, but be very careful. Some are nothing more than marketing fronts for companies trying to lend you more money.

Simply Ignoring Creditors

Sometimes doing absolutely nothing makes perfect legal and financial sense, but using that tactic needs to be a conscious and intelligent decision that is not a result of your refusal to face the music.

Whenever you live simply, have little income or property, plan to maintain that lifestyle indefinitely, and don't give a flip about your credit rating, doing nothing may just be the wisest course. You can't go to jail for failure to pay debts (other than support obligations and criminal fines). Creditors can't strip you of basic necessities, such as clothes and food. A good part of your income, as well as Social Security benefits, welfare, and unemployment are inaccessible.

You can be sued, of course, but even bill collectors can't extract blood from a stone.

If you own virtually nothing and plan to own nothing in the foreseeable future, you need to at least consider this option. Creditors recognize the futility of going after some people, don't even bother to sue them, and eventually just give up.

Although the do-nothing strategy may make sense at the moment, this strategy has some limitations.

Your long-lost uncle may leave you a bundle or maybe you'll win the lottery. If that happens, creditors may find out and try to get a piece of the action.

Even if your ship doesn't come in, you'll always have to be very careful with bank accounts. When a judgment creditor finds out where you bank (and some do periodically check), it can snatch your money. Depositing your money in someone else's account carries its own set of problems, not to mention the danger that a creditor will seize all the money and force your friend to prove just how much belongs to him. So, you may be forced to deal solely in cash or money orders.

In short, before deciding to do nothing, you need to understand and be willing to accept the possible consequences.

Chapter 7

Handling Bill Collectors

. . . .

In This Chapter

▶ Understanding that bill collectors are all bark, and no bite

▶ Using federal law to fight back

▶ Looking to state law for help

▶ Keeping your guard up when dealing with bill collectors

. . . .

*I*t probably seems like yesterday — and it probably was — that credit-card solicitors and hucksters of every stripe were just aching to be your best pal. They just couldn't wait to offer you more and more credit (at higher and higher interest rates).

Well, now that you've missed a few payments, they're singing a different tune. They've turned on you like Brutus on Caesar and unleashed their debt collectors, who play every game in the book to make you feel like a slimeball. They call all the time, suggest that you're going to get sued, and try to squeeze you for whatever they can.

Although some debt collectors are reasonable people just trying to do their jobs, face it, you incurred the debt, you promised to pay it back, and your creditor expects to be paid. Can you really blame them for trying to collect what they sincerely believe is legally theirs and, when all else fails, sending out the dogs? On the other hand, that doesn't give them the right to abuse you.

Many debt collectors, especially the ones working for professional debt collection agencies, are nothing but bullies. They really can't do much of anything, and if you stand up to them, they'll almost certainly back down.

Bill collectors have a grand total of one weapon in their arsenal: intimidation — with all the firepower of a spitball. By comparison, you have an armada in the form of federal and state debt collection laws.

The federal government has provided you with not only a shield but also a sword in the Fair Debt Collection Practices Act, and nearly every state augments that law with its own consumer protection laws.

In this chapter, we take an up close and personal look at bill collectors and review your federal and state remedies for whenever they get nasty.

Taming the Toothless Tiger: The Bill Collector

Creditors with real leverage don't waste time on endless phone calls threatening to sue you or repossess you car; they just do it. Landlords evict. Car lenders repossess. Mortgageholders foreclose. Utility companies turn off the power. Other creditors and their agents huff and puff and try to frighten you with vague promises to take further action (whatever that means), report you to credit bureaus, seize your wages, or turn the matter over to their attorneys.

The key to handling bill collectors is knowing how little power they actually have.

Bill collectors essentially can:

- ✔ Cancel your account (big deal).
- ✔ Report you to credit bureaus (they probably already have).
- ✔ Get a lawyer to sue you and get a judgment (easier said than done, which is why some debt collectors will put you on hold and pretend to consult with the nonexistent on-site attorney).

But, bill collectors can't:

- ✔ Report you to your employer.
- ✔ Publish your name in the newspaper.
- ✔ Embarrass you to family and friends.
- ✔ Take any of your property, at least not until they obtain a judgment by successfully suing you. Even then, most assets are off-limits or exempt. A creditor with a judgment may seize your bank account (if you've made the mistake of leaving money in the bank) and roughly 25 percent of your net wages. But the process is complicated, and many creditors don't bother.

When you don't have enough money to go around, the bills to pay first are the ones where creditors can do something (like take your car or foreclose on your house) when you don't pay. Bill collectors are more commonly used to convince you to pay on unsecured debts. They know they're at the bottom of the food chain and are just hoping to get something, anything, out of you.

Giving aggressive bill collectors nothing at all usually is better than giving them a small payment. Whenever they succeed in milking even a few dollars out of you, they're only inspired to keep begging. It's kind of like feeding stray mutts; keep it up, and you'll never get rid of them.

Don't let bill collectors bully you into doing things like calling them at specific times or faxing something to them. These tactics are just an intimidation game. They figure that if they can get you to obey just one command, they've established some weird sort of dominance over you and the next time you may come up with a few dollars. In short, you don't have to play games with debt collectors, and you don't have to deal with them at all. So don't.

Invoking Federal Law

Even though bill collectors have no real power, they surely can be a kick in the keister. Congress formally recognized this fact Sept. 20, 1977, when it passed the Fair Debt Collection Practices Act. The FDCPA protects consumers from abusive collection techniques and harassment.

Understanding the FDCPA — and letting your creditors know you understand it — is one of the most effective ways of abruptly putting an end to any overt bullying.

Congress enacted the law after finding abundant evidence that many debt collectors were using abusive, deceptive, and unfair debt-collection practices. It concluded that those kinds of bill-collecting tactics actually increased the number of personal bankruptcies, disrupted marriages, caused joblessness, and invaded individual privacy.

The FDCPA specifies when, where, and how professional debt collectors can contact you concerning a consumer (nonbusiness) debt. It outlaws certain dirty tricks that bill collectors regularly used to employ, and it restricts communications with third persons (such as your boss) concerning your debt.

Under the law, debt collectors can't:

- ✔ Call or contact you in any way before 8 a.m. or after 9 p.m., nor at any other unreasonable time or place, without your permission.
- ✔ Contact you by postcard.
- ✔ Make you accept collect calls or telegrams.
- ✔ Use a false name.
- ✔ Publish your name and the nature of your debt.
- ✔ Threaten to take any action, such as having your wages garnished or initiating a lawsuit, unless they have a legal basis for doing so and truly intend to follow through.
- ✔ Threaten to have you arrested.
- ✔ Collect any amount greater than your debt, unless specifically authorized to do so by other law.
- ✔ Prematurely deposit postdated checks.

The FDCPA applies only to those who regularly collect debts owed by others. It doesn't, however, apply to the original creditor.

In other words, if you owe money to the electric company, the collection activities of the electric company aren't restricted by the FDCPA (although they may well be by state statute). And yet, if the electric company hires a collection agency, the Act is triggered. Similarly, the Act doesn't restrain IRS or other governmental employees from acting in their official capacities, but it does apply to private collection agencies hired to collect debts owed to the government.

Additionally, although the original legislation specifically exempted attorneys on the theory that they were only "incidentally involved in debt collection activities," Congress repealed that exemption in 1986. Since then, courts have held lawyers to a pretty high standard. Simply put, attorneys of all people, must be pretty careful to cross all their T's and dot all their I's when it comes to debt collection. If a collections attorney contacts you, advise him right away that you know your way around the FDCPA. That way, you'll be dealing with a very careful, or a very dumb, lawyer. Either way, you come out on top.

If you believe a debt collector has violated the FDCPA, you can report her to the Federal Trade Commission Correspondence Branch, 600 Pennsylvania Northwest, Washington, DC 20580.

Depending on how badly the debt collector behaved, you may also have grounds for a lawsuit. See the section about "Your remedies under the FDCPA" later in the chapter for more details.

When debt collectors can contact you

Debt collectors can contact you only at reasonable times. They can't contact you at any time that they have reason to believe is inconvenient and, in general, may not contact you when they know an attorney represents you. Collectors must tell you that they're calling from a collection agency, and they must identify the original creditor and the amount of the balance. They must tell you that you have 30 days to dispute the debt.

If you tell a bill collector that you're busy and she doesn't terminate the call, or if she calls back when she should realize that you're still busy, she's probably in violation of the law. Ditto if the person answering the phone tells her that you're sleeping. And for the most part, bill collectors can't contact you at all — and that means no calls, no visits, no letters, and no telegrams — if you've notified them in writing to buzz off (see the sidebar, "Sending a 'bug-off' letter" for more information).

Sending a "bug-off" letter

Under the Federal Fair Debt Collection Practices Act, you can send third-party debt collectors (not the original creditor) what is known as a *cease-and-desist letter* — which is legalese for, "Yo! Take a hike, sucker!"

After receiving this notification, the debt collection agency can't communicate with you further, except to:

✔ Advise you that the debt collection efforts are being stopped

✔ Inform you that the collector or creditor intends to do something specific, like sue you

A simple letter, such as this, should do the trick:

Pursuant to the Federal Fair Debt Collection Practices Act, 15 USC§1692c(c), I ask that you stop communicating with me about my account with _____, account number _____. I will take care of this matter when I can.

Although not required, sending your notification by certified mail, return receipt requested, is a good idea, so you have proof that the bill collector received it. Send one copy to the collection agency, one to the original creditor, and one to the Federal Trade Commission.

Sending a cease-and-desist letter does not, of course, eliminate your obligation to repay the debt.

Where debt collectors can't contact you

Debt collectors may not contact you at any place that is inconvenient for you or causes you unnecessary embarrassment. They may not contact you at work, if they've been informed that your employer forbids such communication. Furthermore, a bill collector can't contact you at work if she has reason to know that a call would be inconvenient for you, regardless of whether your employer allows such interruptions.

When debt collectors may contact others about your debt

Generally, the FDCPA prohibits debt collectors from contacting *third persons*, or others, about your debt, thus outlawing the once common tactic of trying to shame people into paying a debt. But spouses and guardians aren't considered third persons. So, any time a bill collector contacts you, he can also contact spouses or guardians.

Under the statute, your parents may be contacted only if you're a minor; otherwise they're considered third persons and are off limits. Others not specifically mentioned in the law — like siblings, uncles, aunts, grandparents, or living companions — always are considered to be third persons.

A debt collector *can* contact your attorney, a credit-reporting agency, and any codebtors. She also can contact any person for the purpose of locating you or obtaining your address, phone number, or place of employment, provided that she doesn't already have that information. But she should never reveal that you owe a debt and generally may not contact the same person more than once. When the collector knows that a lawyer represents you, she must go through the attorney and can't contact others unless the lawyer is unresponsive.

If a creditor has a judgment against you, the collector can also contact others to enforce that judgment.

Collector told to take a hike

Sandy was trying her best to pay her bills but had fallen way behind. Bill collectors were harassing her, calling at all hours, and threatening to tell her employer. Finally she discovered the Fair Debt Collection Practices Act (FDCPA) and kept a copy of it by the phone.

Whenever bill collectors called, she cited the law verbatim, telling them to take a hike.

That got their attention.

Sandy turned the tables on the bill collectors and sent them running for cover.

Dirty tricks are outlawed

The FDCPA forbids debt collectors from engaging in any conduct that tends to harass, oppress, or abuse you. They can't unnecessarily leave messages with a third person for you to return a call, contact you too frequently, imply the use of force against you, use foul language, or threaten to embarrass you.

Additionally, the FDCPA prohibits false, misleading, or unfair practices by debt collectors, including a number of specific practices that creditors have traditionally used to collect debts.

These provisions are especially interesting because they highlight tactics that creditors who aren't subject to the act still may use against you, unless your state has its own law outlawing such ploys.

Of course, the underlying threat of most bill collectors is that you'll be sued if you don't pay up. But a debt collector's threat to sue you can violate this law if the collector doesn't actually intend to do so. With varying success, collectors have tried getting around this rule by saying they "can" sue, or the collector is "authorized" to sue, or recommending that you settle the debt "out of court." One court said that threats to take "drastic action" and engage in "vigorous prosecution," were disguised threats to sue, and the collector violated the law because he never really planned to do so.

Your remedies under the FDCPA

You can sue a debt collector for violating the FDCPA and recover actual damages, punitive damages up to $1,000, and attorney fees. Long shot? Maybe, or maybe not.

Consider this: A Texas jury was so outraged by a credit company's attempt to collect on a $2,000 debt that it awarded the debtors $11 million in damages. Who knows, maybe that pesky debt collector will make you a millionaire! But don't bet on it.

A debt collector still may prevail by proving that he didn't intend to violate the act, and just made an honest mistake.

You must file your suit within one year of the violation.

Tapping State Laws

Under our legal system, laws actually come from two places: legislative bodies that enact statutes and courts that issue decisions in particular cases that apply to similar situations in the future. This body of court-made law has evolved though the centuries and is known generally as the *common law*. So, although the FDCPA usually doesn't apply to creditors collecting their own debts, state laws may.

State statutes

Almost every state has a statute dealing with abuses by creditors and/or debt collectors.

Although those laws differ greatly from state to state, most states outlaw some or all the conduct that is forbidden under the FDCPA. State statutes, unlike the federal law, generally apply to creditors collecting debts that debtors owe them. You can call your state's attorney general's office or consumer protection agency for a review of local laws.

For a comprehensive analysis, look at Robert J. Hobbs's book, *Fair Debt Collection* (National Consumer Law Center, third edition, 1996). Hobbs's book is the bible for consumer rights lawyers. You can purchase a copy by contacting the National Consumer Law Center, 77 Summer St., 10th Floor, Boston, MA 02110-1006; phone, 617-523-8089.

Common law remedies

Aside from statutory prohibitions, creditors who intentionally misbehave can get into trouble by violating time-honored principles of common decency. In extreme cases, you may be able to sue a creditor or debt collector for things like: abuse of process, malicious prosecution, defamation, intentional infliction of emotional distress, and other such wrongs. Talk to a lawyer to find out whether any of these theories applies to your situation, but remember that a creditor's conduct must be pretty outrageous to give rise to a claim under common law.

Keeping Your Dukes Up

Your government — and your society — have determined that overbearing debt collection efforts won't be tolerated. Many debt collectors skirt the law by counting on your ignorance, but when you know your rights and you're ready to exercise them, chances are that overzealous bill collectors will back off in search of easier prey.

If a debt collector can't get any money out of you, she may eventually give up and leave you alone. For that reason, making small payments sometimes is worse than making no payments at all.

You need to be on guard for the following common collections ploys:

✔ Collectors typically use caller ID, so you need to be careful if you want to keep your phone number secret when you call or return a call from a bill collector. You can prevent identification by dialing *67 (1167 for rotary phones) prior to dialing the number, but check with your local phone company because procedures sometimes vary. The *67 remedy, however, won't work when you're calling an 800 or 888 (toll-free) numbers. With toll-free numbers, the only way to evade detection is by using a public phone.

✔ Any FDCPA claim must be listed as an asset in your bankruptcy. In a Chapter 7 liquidation bankruptcy case, only the trustee can prosecute the FDCPA, and any recovery, after paying you the amount of any exemption, would be distributed to your creditors. But when the Chapter 7 trustee doesn't want to bother trying to collect on the claim, she abandons it, and then you're able to prosecute the claim by yourself and keep all proceeds. In a Chapter 13 reorganization bankruptcy, instead of prosecuting the claim herself, the trustee authorizes you to do so. But any recovery you receive is paid into your Chapter 13 plan and distributed to creditors.

✔ Avoid giving a creditor or bill collector a postdated check even (perhaps especially) when they ask you to. Sometimes intentionally writing a check without sufficient funds is a crime and gives the creditor the added leverage of threatening criminal charges or challenging discharge of the debt in bankruptcy.

✔ Be careful not to agree to a payment plan when you're disputing any part of the debt. If a collection notice contains an error, write to the source requesting that the mistake be corrected before formally agreeing to anything. The FDCPA requires debt collection agencies and lawyers to stop collection efforts until they obtain verification of the debt, provided that the consumer's written request is received within 30 days of the collector's giving the consumer notice of the right to dispute the debt. If you don't raise a dispute within this period, you may confront an argument that you've "agreed" that you owe the debt.

✔ If the dispute involves a revolving account, a credit-card account, or an electronic transfer of money, federal regulations provide you 60 days after receiving an erroneous bill within which to send a letter to the creditor indicating a billing error. Even where these laws don't apply, most creditors take a second look at the account whenever the debt is disputed.

✔ Taping a bill collector's call without consent is a dicey proposition. It is, after all, illegal in many states, and unethical for lawyers. But you can refuse to talk to a bill collector unless he agrees to allow you to tape the call. And if a bill collector is dumb enough to leave an abusive message on your answering machine, by all means save that tape.

Chapter 8

Negotiating with the IRS

In This Chapter

▶ Understanding the tax-collection process

▶ Introducing the warm-and-fuzzy Internal Revenue Service

▶ Negotiating with the IRS

▶ Plotting bankruptcy while negotiating

▶ Using the taxpayer advocate

*L*ike a lingering cold or an ex-boyfriend, sometimes it seems that you just can't get rid of an old tax bill.

In some situations, bankruptcy may just do the trick (see Chapter 14), but frequently your best shot at relief is negotiating with the Internal Revenue Service (IRS) and hoping it's in a conciliatory mood. You usually can't force Uncle Sam to negotiate, but if he comes to the table, his concessions are legally binding. And, luckily for you, there's never been a better time for dealing with the taxman.

This chapter explains how the IRS goes about getting its (your?) money, describes the logistics and implications of negotiations, discusses how you can negotiate with the IRS while quietly preparing your bankruptcy, and tells you how the government's own taxpayer advocate actually can help you. Ah, your tax dollars at work!

Looking at the Tax Collection Process

The IRS uses three different, and somewhat overlapping, offices to collect taxes:

✔ **Service Centers** are where you file your tax returns. These centers are located in Andover, MD.; Atlanta, GA; Austin, TX; Cincinnati, OH; Fresno, CA; Holtsville, NY; Kansas City, MO; Memphis, TN; Ogden, UT; and Philadelphia, PA.

✔ **Automated Collection System (ACS),** which is a closed-to-the-public command center where scores of clerks sit in front of computer monitors and deal with people only by phone or letter.

> ✔ **Local offices,** staffed by revenue officers. The people in these offices have some clout, unlike those in the Automated Collection System.

Service centers

If you don't pay the tax due with your return, you'll first be sent a polite, non-threatening letter entitled "Request for Payment" or "Notice of Federal Taxes Due." It's really just a friendly reminder.

When you don't pay within about five weeks of receiving that letter, the Service Center sends the first in a series of four increasingly nasty notices. The first is identified with the number 501, and the last, 504, is a Notice of Intent to Levy (*levy* means "seize your property"). Sending you this series of letters takes about six months. Along the way, you'll receive Publication 594 (Understanding the Collection Process). If you're heading in this direction, you may want to download the document now from the IRS's Web site at www.irs.gov.

Despite the "Intent to Levy" title of the 504 notice, the IRS probably has no real intention of imposing a levy right away. And although this notice says that it's "final," that just means if you don't pay, your file will be transferred to another office. In other words, when you receive a 504 notice, you need to take it seriously without losing a whole lot of sleep.

Automated Collection System (ACS)

ACS has the power to mail further collection notices, negotiate payment arrangements, grab your bank accounts, and intercept your wages. It is essentially faceless. Collectors may not even use their real names, and you probably won't deal with the same official twice.

The ACS is the IRS's notion of efficiency, and its minions try to keep your file within this monument to Murphy's Law whenever possible. However, if you tell them that you don't understand the notices you're receiving, and that you can't agree with what the IRS says you owe, your file should be transferred to a local office. Then, you can deal with a real, honest-to-goodness bureaucrat.

Local revenue officers

If the ACS can't collect the tax, or if you've so requested, you'll be hearing from a revenue officer. Although looking at a tax collector face to face is a little scarier than just talking with someone on the phone, it may well be preferable to dealing with the ACS, especially when the officer can suspend collection activities by concluding there's no way you can pay anything.

Keeping your eye on the statute of limitations

The Internal Revenue Service essentially has ten years to collect a tax. After that, the tax vanishes. The ten-year clock normally begins ticking shortly after you filed your return when the tax is assessed.

But there's a glitch. If you don't file a return, the statute of limitations never starts, and a *dummy return,* one that's filed in your name by the IRS, doesn't count.

Figuring out when the statute of limitations begins and expires can be pretty tricky, because the clock stops and starts like so many hiccups. For example, a bankruptcy filing *tolls,*

or suspends, the statute during the period your case is pending, plus an additional six months.

You also toll the statute of limitations when you:

- ✔ Request a Taxpayer Assistance Order
- ✔ Make an Offer in Compromise (see below)
- ✔ Sign a waiver of the statute
- ✔ Ask for a Collection Due Process hearing

Although the IRS has the power to go to court to extend the statute before it expires, it won't; unless you owe a king's ransom or you've been a pain-in-the-butt chronic tax protestor.

Making Nice with the Touchy-Feely IRS

Taxpayers and courts long have complained, and with good reason, about the overbearing presence of the Internal Revenue Service. The IRS and its cadre of bureaucrats from hell seemed to relish its guilty-until-proven-innocent-and-even-then-still-guilty attitude.

A few years ago, however, Congress conducted a bunch of hearings and got an earful from constituents who felt like the IRS was treating them like axe murderers. Those hearings resulted in legislation imposing a wide range of restrictions on the collection efforts of the IRS. So now, after years of nurturing its reputation as a bulldog, the Internal Revenue Service is trying to embrace something of a teddy-bear image. It really has become far more accommodating, if not exactly cuddly.

The kinder, gentler IRS is considerably less arrogant and appreciably more humble than it once was. And with all the new procedures, IRS collection efforts have become so burdensome that authorities are more willing to settle than ever before.

As part of its new image, the IRS maintains a very useful Web site (www.irs.gov) where you can find all the official IRS forms, instructions, and other helpful information mentioned in this chapter.

Your due process

One of the reforms, known as *collection due process,* took effect in January 1999 and requires the IRS to give you at least 30 days warning before seizing your property and to notify you of your right to appeal its determinations.

The appeal, which first is heard by the IRS Appeals Office, provides you with an opportunity to claim that you're an *innocent spouse* (where your wife or husband fudged a joint tax return without telling you) or determine the appropriateness of an asset seizure and the correctness of the amount the IRS claims is due.

More important, the taxpayer can also propose alternative payment plans such as *installment agreements* or *offers in compromise* (see below). If the appeals office turns you down, you can go to federal court and have a judge review the situation. All these new procedural safeguards must take place before any of your property is actually seized.

Negotiating an installment agreement

When you owe less than $25,000, getting the IRS to accept a payment proposal actually is pretty easy. A government that can get what it wants (your money) with a minimum of hassle makes for happy bean counters.

An installment agreement requires that you:

- Make all payments on time.
- File all future tax returns and pay the taxes due on those returns in full.
- Furnish updated financial information whenever requested.
- Agree that any state or federal refunds be applied to your unpaid taxes.

If your file still is with the Service Center, you can use Form 9465 Installment Agreement Request. This form doesn't require any supporting information about your ability to pay. All you do is plug in the amount you can afford to pay each month and mail it in. The IRS normally responds within about 30 days. You may want to take a look at *Taxes For Dummies*, an annual by Eric Tyson and David Silverman (Wiley Publishing, Inc.). It includes a section about filing this form (among other tax pointers).

Your offer is likely to be accepted if the payment you propose takes care of your total tax debt, including interest and penalties that continue to accrue, within 36 months.

If, on the other hand, your file has been transferred to ACS or your local district office, you need to tell the collector that you want to make an installment agreement, and indicate how much you can afford to pay. If your offer is rejected, stop! Get professional help.

Knowing when to get professional help

If you owe $25,000 or more, or your request for an installment agreement has been denied, we suggest that you hire a lawyer or accountant who's experienced in dealing with the IRS.

At this juncture, the IRS can and does insist on detailed information about all your assets and your family's income and living expenses.

The Service Center and ACS use Form 433-F. Other offices use Form 433-A for individuals and Form 433-B for businesses and self-employed individuals. These forms generally are referred to as Collection Information Statements (CIS).

From the IRS's perspective, the CIS are good for:

- Detailing total household income and expenses.

- Measuring your expenses against IRS guidelines, which the collector may fine-tune to fit your individual situation.

- Telling the IRS where all your assets are located, which facilitates seizure in the event negotiations fall through or you end up defaulting on your agreement.

The IRS normally requires payments equal to all your net income minus *necessary living expenses*. Some collection employees have pretty bizarre notions of how much it costs to live and demand completely unrealistic payment plans. But your lawyer or accountant may be able to have such functionaries overruled by the bosses. What's the point in agreeing to a payment structure that you can't meet, especially when you complete a CIS telling the IRS exactly where to get at each of your assets?

If the CIS show that you have any liquid assets — such as cash, stock, or bonds — equal to the amount of tax you owe, the IRS demands immediate payment and may insist that you take cash advances or use credit cards to pay taxes.

Although you can now pay taxes with major credit cards, that's probably not a good idea for anyone considering bankruptcy, because:

- ✔ Loans to pay nondischargeable federal taxes also are nondischargeable.
- ✔ Credit-card issuers commonly assess special fees when the card is used to pay taxes.

Gaining "uncollectible" status

If the IRS determines that collecting the tax creates an undue hardship, it may suspend collection efforts indefinitely. (In IRS-speak, the account is "53'd," based on the number of the form the revenue officer must complete when reporting that an account is uncollectible.)

Undue hardship means that you're unable to meet necessary living expenses if required to make installment payments or if the IRS seizes your assets. The agency distinguishes between undue hardship and *mere inconvenience* — usually finding in favor of the former when it thinks pursuing you isn't worthwhile and finding the latter when going after your assets may be worthwhile.

However, even with an undue hardship, your tax isn't abated. Taxes and penalties continue to accrue, and tax liens aren't released. And, of course, the IRS continues to grab your refunds.

The ten-year statute of limitations on collection continues to run, however, and the IRS typically reopens the account right before the statute is about to expire, most likely in an attempt to intimidate you into signing a waiver of the statute of limitations. Don't do it! See a tax specialist!

Planning bankruptcy while pursuing an installment agreement

You and your lawyer need to be keenly aware of how an installment agreement can affect a bankruptcy down the road. You must consider:

- ✔ **The statute of limitations on collection:** If the term of an installment agreement expires less than one year before the ten-year statute of limitations, the IRS can insist that you agree to extend it for up to five more years, and that's something you need to consider only with extreme care. You may be better off putting up with the IRS for a little longer and letting the statute of limitations expire. Then, you're home free.
- ✔ **The time restrictions for wiping out taxes through bankruptcy:** An installment agreement doesn't extend the various time periods that must pass before taxes are rendered dischargeable in bankruptcy.
- ✔ **Tax liens:** Taxes may be much more difficult to wipe out or manage in bankruptcy when a tax lien has been filed. Under current policy, if the

amount due under an installment agreement is less than $25,000, the IRS won't file a lien (although it may already have done so under previous procedures). In other cases, the IRS can postpone filing a lien as long as you're honoring your installment agreement.

✔ **Allocating tax payments:** When you make installment payments, you designate how your payments are applied. Requiring the IRS to apply payments to the most recent years usually is best. As time goes by, taxes for the earlier years become dischargeable if you end up filing bankruptcy.

Submitting an Offer in Compromise

Unlike a payment agreement, an offer in compromise that the IRS accepts actually results in a reduction in the amount you owe. After getting its wrists slapped by Congress, the IRS is more willing to make a deal than ever before.

Checking out Forms 656 and 656-A (and their accompanying instructions), which you can download from the IRS Web site, gives you a good idea of what's required. However, you need to seek out professional help when actually preparing and submitting an offer. Some accountants and attorneys now specialize in helping folks submit offers in compromise.

The grounds (three exist) for an offer in compromise are

✔ Doubt about whether you actually owe the tax.

✔ Doubt about whether you have sufficient assets and income to pay the tax in full.

✔ Exceptional hardship or unfair or inequitable circumstances caused by payment-in-full requirements. (This last one is brand new and its contours will have to be developed.)

When determining how much it will accept in settlement, the IRS looks at your present assets and future earning ability. It calculates how much it would receive from a quick sale of all your assets and adds a lump-sum amount based on what it figures you'd have been able to pay on taxes during the next 48 months.

If you can pay this amount in a lump sum within 90 days, the IRS is likely to accept your offer. If not, you can request up to two years to pay, but the amount increases to whatever the IRS thinks you can pay over 60 months rather than 48 months. However, taxpayers who have less than four years left on the ten-year statute of limitations need offer only the amount they can pay for the period remaining under the statute. Even if you can't pay that amount, don't give up. Given its new attitude and growing backlog, the IRS may accept substantially less, so making such an offer definitely is worth a try.

The disadvantages of making an offer in compromise are:

- It doesn't resolve state tax debts.

- It may delay the time for filing bankruptcy. One condition for discharging a tax in either a Chapter 7 or Chapter 13 bankruptcy is that it had to be assessed more than 240 days before the bankruptcy is filed. If you file bankruptcy within 240 days of submitting an offer in compromise, the clock stops. In other words, you must wait for a period of time equal to the sum of 240 days, plus the time your offer was pending, plus 30 days before your taxes can be discharged in bankruptcy.

- If you later default on future tax liabilities, the tax liabilities that were forgiven are revived. The IRS will keep the offered sum and you'll have to pay that remaining balance on the original tax along with interest and penalties.

- Making an offer extends the ten-year statute of limitations by the period that your offer is under consideration plus an additional year.

Getting Help from a Taxpayer Advocate

A taxpayer advocate operates under the IRS Problem Resolution Program. Such an advocate is supposed to act on your behalf whenever you're suffering a *significant hardship* (being treated harshly or unfairly) because of the way the IRS is administering the tax laws. An advocate has authority to issue taxpayer assistance orders, which can, at least temporarily, stop collection activities.

A taxpayer advocate is at your disposal and can be reached by:

- Contacting your local taxpayer advocate office

- Calling toll free 877-777-4778

- Sending Form 911 to the local taxpayer advocate office

You can find out the address and phone number of the local taxpayer advocate office and obtain copies of Form 911 by contacting your local IRS District Office.

Disadvantages of a taxpayer assistance order are that:

- It suspends the statute of limitations for whatever amount of time the matter is under consideration.

- Any time during which a taxpayer assistance order is in effect doesn't count toward tax periods that normally would apply toward discharging taxes.

Part III
Keeping Your Stuff

The 5th Wave   By Rich Tennant

"Ronny's such a couch potato the bankruptcy court agreed to list his big screen TV as 'tools of the trade'."

In this part . . .

*I*n the not-so-good old days, creditors could literally take the shirt off your back when you couldn't pay your bills. Those days are gone, and although you may well lose some of your property if you go bankrupt, much of your stuff is off-limits to creditors. This part explains what's yours, what may go to the creditors, and what you can do to keep your most important possessions.

Chapter 9

Understanding Which Assets Are Off-limits to Creditors

In This Chapter

▶ Comprehending "property of the estate" and "exemptions"

▶ Understanding the nuts and bolts of exemptions

▶ Figuring out the value of your assets

▶ Seeing how certain assets are treated in bankruptcy

▶ Making the most of your exemptions

Although you may lose some of your property by filing bankruptcy, the days when creditors could quite literally take the shirt off your back are long gone. Much of what you need most and treasure is *exempt*, which means creditors can't touch it. So, knowing what's all yours, what isn't, and what is of equal interest to your creditors — who obviously are eager to grab anything they can get their paws on — is real important.

In this chapter, you get the scoop on which assets you can keep, which ones you may have to surrender, and how to make the most of it.

Grasping the Legal Concepts

Gaining an understanding of how bankruptcy affects your possessions means that you need to know about two legal concepts:

✔ *Property of the estate,* which includes everything you own on the *petition date* (when you file bankruptcy), some things you acquire later, and other assets that a trustee (the guy who represents the interests of creditors; see Chapter 3) can recover under some circumstances

✔ *Exemptions,* which enable you to remove certain assets from the bankruptcy process and take them out of the reach of creditors

The principles behind property of the estate and exemptions are important in Chapter 7 liquidations and Chapter 13 reorganizations.

Even when an asset isn't subject to the bankruptcy process, a creditor with a security interest may cause you grief. We take a closer look at this problem in Chapters 10 and 11.

Under Chapter 7 bankruptcy laws, you may lose any asset that is property of the estate unless it is exempt.

In a Chapter 13 reorganization, your minimum payments are determined by the value of your nonexempt property. For example, if the value of your nonexempt property were $7,500, you'd have to pay at least that much during the life of your Chapter 13 plan or sell an individual item and pay the proceeds to the trustee.

If one of your prized possessions is property of the estate, and not covered by an exemption, you can be required to give it up or pay its value to the trustee regardless of which way you file — Chapter 7 or Chapter 13. The difference is that in Chapter 7 you must pay for it in a couple of months, but in Chapter 13, you can stretch out payments for up to five years.

By answering the following three general questions about an asset, you can figure out whether a bankruptcy trustee has dibs on it or can make you pay its value:

- ✔ Is it property of the estate? In other words, do you own it?
- ✔ What is the value of your interest in the asset? The trustee doesn't care about things worth only a few dollars.
- ✔ Does an exemption protect the asset? If so, then neither trustees nor creditors (unless a particular creditor has a lien; see Chapter 10) can get their mitts on it.

Digging through the property of the estate

The first thing you need to know about an asset is whether it's considered property of the estate. That category includes:

- ✔ Just about every asset you own when you file bankruptcy.
- ✔ Proceeds from property of the estate. For example, if your rental unit is property of the estate, any rents that you receive, even after you file, also are property of the estate.
- ✔ Inheritances and life insurance proceeds, if your benefactor dies before bankruptcy or within 180 days after your filing.

> ✔ Marital property divisions that you become entitled to receive within 180 days after the petition date.
>
> ✔ Property you transferred prior to bankruptcy that was recovered when the trustee flexed his strong-arm powers to undo the transfer. See Chapter 18 for more on how trustees have the power to nullify certain transfers of property.

Figuring out your interest in the property

If you own an asset jointly with someone else, ordinarily the trustee can deal only with your chunk — not the half owned by your brother-in-law. But your piece of the pie may well be on the line.

When an asset at issue serves as collateral for a debt, the creditor has ownership rights in the item that are superior to yours or the trustee's. If, for example, your car is worth $10,000 and is subject to an $8,000 secured loan, your interest in the car is only $2,000 ($10,000 – $8,000).

Spouses frequently own their homes jointly, which means each has an undivided one-half interest.

In most states, each spouse's property interests are separate, even though an asset may be jointly owned. If you and your spouse own your home jointly, each of you has a one-half interest. So, if you file bankruptcy, your wife's share of the house won't become property of the estate, unless, of course, she also files for bankruptcy (keeping in mind that you can, but don't have to, file a joint bankruptcy petition).

Do you really own it?

An asset owned by someone else doesn't become part of your bankruptcy just because you have it in your possession, and even an asset titled to you isn't necessarily your property. The pretzel-logic of that concept is easier understood with a few examples:

✔ The chain saw that you borrowed from your neighbor isn't included in your bankruptcy just because it's stored in your shed.

✔ If you're an authorized signer on your elderly uncle's bank account, the account doesn't become part of your bankruptcy when all the money really belongs to him.

✔ Property belonging to your children isn't included in your bankruptcy.

✔ When your name is on the title to your teenager's car, you can probably convince the trustee that the vehicle doesn't actually belong to you — provided, that is, your kid used his own money to buy it. If you bought it for him, the trustee will insist that you really do own it or, even if you don't own it, that he can go after it.

Lottery winner ends up in bankruptcy

Bennie won $3 million in the state lottery, which was payable in annual installments of $128,000. During the next six years, he spent so much money that he had to file bankruptcy. The court declared the balance of Bennie's winnings property of the estate, including the installment payments that he expected to come due after bankruptcy.

However, the score's a little different when you happen to live in one of the nine community-property states — Arizona, California, Idaho, Louisiana, Nevada, New Mexico, Texas, Washington, or Wisconsin. In those states, all property acquired by either spouse during the marriage is considered community property. Common exceptions are gifts and inheritances received by one spouse during the marriage. Property acquired prior to marriage typically doesn't become community property.

In the community-property states, all community property (as well as the individual property of the filing spouse) becomes property of the estate even when only one spouse files bankruptcy. Individual property of the nonfiling spouse doesn't, however, become property of the estate.

Knowing what happens when someone owes you money

If someone owes you money on the date that you file bankruptcy, that debt is considered an asset that is property of the estate, even when it isn't paid until later. So, for example, the income tax refund you're expecting in the current year is considered property of the estate, even if you don't receive it until after the petition date.

Accrued wages likewise are included in the estate, even though you won't receive them until after the petition date. Why? They actually were earned before you filed. It sounds confusing, but thinking it through really isn't that difficult.

Let's say you have a job where you're paid weekly. Your paycheck usually covers the previous week's work, not the current one, so the employer always is a week behind. That means that if you file bankruptcy on the day after payday, your employer owes you one week's pay as of that date. For bankruptcy purposes, the wages you have earned before the petition date become property of the estate, even though you haven't yet received them.

Don't sweat it too much. As we point out in a minute, most, if not all, of that money ultimately will be covered by an exemption for wages anyhow.

Understanding how exemptions work

Determining which assets are included in your bankruptcy is kind of tricky. That's because one law may plop your stuff smack-dab into bankruptcy, but another one yanks it right out of the proceedings. It's enough to make you dizzy. And to further spin your noodle, different states have different rules for exemptions. See Appendix B for the lowdown on each state's exemption laws.

Some federal exemptions are available even in *op-out states* — states where laws have been passed denying residents the use of federal Bankruptcy Code exemptions. See Appendix B for some of the federal exemptions that still are available.

When your permanent residence was in more than one state during the 180 days prior to bankruptcy, the laws that apply are the ones in the state where you were domiciled (your permanent home) for the greater part of that 180-day period. For example, if you moved from New York to Oregon four or five months ago, the Oregon exemption law applies.

Similarly, you're not necessarily domiciled in a state just because that's where you live. Domicile is the place that you consider as your permanent home. Say you grew up in New York and went off to school in Tennessee, intending to return when your studies were complete. You always were domiciled in New York, even though you lived in Tennessee — where you never intended to settle down.

Some people have moved to take advantage of another state's more liberal exemption policies; however, courts are increasingly adopting rules that discourage this practice. As a result, that little maneuver may just backfire. We explain more about that in the "Creating Exemptions" section later in this chapter.

Buying Florida mansion backfires on Buffalo boy

Bart thought he was one clever dude when he sold his home in Buffalo, New York, and liquidated his investment portfolio in anticipation of the brilliant idea of moving to Florida, buying a mansion, and then declaring bankruptcy to exploit the Sunshine State's unlimited homestead exemption. Nice try, but it didn't work. The bankruptcy court saw through Bart's scheme and denied his homestead exemption. His mansion was sold off pronto, much to the pleasure of Bart's creditors. And now Bart's back in Buffalo, reacquainting himself with lake-effect snowdrifts.

Determining the Value of Your Stuff

After figuring out which set of exemption laws apply, you need to calculate how much your property is worth. This calculation must be based not on the cost of replacing your stuff with new items but rather on what it would cost to obtain similar things in used condition. The intangibles, loosely things such as an ongoing business or a lawsuit from which you can recover money, are extremely difficult to value. Your lawyer should be able to help you in those cases. For the simpler stuff, the following list gives you a basic idea of what your stuff is worth:

- **Household goods:** The value of household goods is what a secondhand store would charge or the asking price for similar goods offered for sale in newspaper classified ads.

- **Automobiles:** The value of an automobile frequently is based on "Blue Book" retail value with adjustments for your specific vehicle. You can get *Kelley Blue Book* figures by logging on www.kbb.com.

- **Real property:** Valuing real property depends on where you live. But, a good starting point may be finding out the figure used by your local tax assessor — commonly known as the *assessed value*. But that can be a crapshoot because in some venues, assessed values are ridiculously inaccurate. If you only recently purchased the property, a better indication is the price that you paid.

  Appraisals are great for determining value, but watch out — be careful. Appraisals that are completed for loan purposes frequently tend to be high because many lenders encourage appraisers to inflate values to justify making a loan. The same is true of listing prices. Some real estate agents overstate the value of your property to attract your business. We take a closer look at valuing your home in Chapter 11.

- **Pensions and life insurance:** You usually can place a dollar amount on your pensions and life insurance policies by calling the company.

Understanding How the Courts View Certain Assets

Special rules govern the way certain property — such as homes, cars, household items, and so on — is treated in bankruptcy. We discuss the most common in this section.

Homesteads

Almost all states have some type of homestead exemption that protects some or all the *equity* in a debtor's home. Additionally, the Bankruptcy Code provides each debtor with a homestead exemption of $17,425. The exemption is doubled for joint owners, or $34,850. This amount (as well as the amount for all the other exemptions specified in the Bankruptcy Code) is adjusted every three years by the government to reflect changes in the Consumer Price Index (CPI). The next change will take effect April 1, 2004. We discuss homestead exemptions in much more detail in Chapter 11.

Table 9-1 helps you figure out the extent to which your home is protected by a homestead exemption.

Table 9-1	Applying Your Homestead Exemption
1. Value of your home	$
2. Total amount owed on mortgages	$
3. Amount of any judgments	$
4. Unpaid real property taxes	$
5. Amount owed on any other liens	$
6. Total liens and mortgages (Add lines 2, 3, 4, and 5)	$
7. Equity (Subtract Line 1 from Line 6)	$
8. Amount of homestead exemption	$
9. Nonexempt equity (Subtract Line 7 from Line 8)	$

TECHNICAL STUFF

Tenancy by the entirety

Some jurisdictions recognize an ancient form of husband-and-wife property ownership known as *tenancy by the entirety*, which protects joint property from creditors of only one spouse. The effect of such a rule is that under some circumstances, jointly owned property may be fully exempt when only one spouse files bankruptcy (if no joint creditors are involved) or partially exempt after claims of joint creditors are satisfied.

Jurisdictions recognizing tenancy by the entirety are: Delaware, the District of Columbia, Florida, Hawaii, Illinois, Indiana, Maryland, Massachusetts, Michigan, Mississippi, Missouri, North Carolina, Pennsylvania, Rhode Island, Vermont, Virginia, and Wyoming.

Automobiles

Most states allow debtors to exempt at least one motor vehicle, but the amount of the exemption is limited. The federal exemption scheme allows each debtor to claim $2,775 in a motor vehicle.

Whenever the equity in your car exceeds your total exemption, a Chapter 7 trustee can sell the car and pay you the value of your exemption.

For example, when your motor vehicle exemption is $1,500, and your car is worth $2,500, the trustee can sell your car but has to pay you $1,500. You're usually given the opportunity to keep your car by paying the net amount that the trustee would receive from selling the vehicle.

In a Chapter 13, the trustee can't sell the car, but you'd have to pay the amount of nonexempt equity ($1,000 in the previous Chapter 7 example) over the life of the bankruptcy plan.

You also may be able to claim an exemption for your motor vehicle as a *tool of the trade* — if that's what it is. For example, a professional driver's semi rig is likely to qualify, and a specially modified pickup truck used by a carpenter probably fits the bill. But you're really pushing your luck if you try for an exemption on the Mercedes sports car that you use to impress your sales clients.

See Chapter 10 for more on what happens to your car if you file bankruptcy.

Household goods

Most states exempt household goods up to a specified dollar amount. The federal Bankruptcy Code exemption for household goods exempts single items up to a value of $425 and all items up to a total of $8,625.

Occasionally, a question is raised about whether a particular item qualifies as a household good — for example, a firearm. Several courts have said they guns don't qualify; however, another ruling indicates that a pistol used for defense of the family was a household good but that a shotgun and rifle used for sporting purposes were not.

Courts also seem to be having trouble deciding whether a computer is a household good. Some courts say that a computer qualifies, and others say the exact opposite. A local lawyer familiar with the courts in your area can be a big help in figuring out what may or may not be exempt.

Inheritances and life insurance benefits

Any inheritance or life insurance benefits left to you by someone who dies before or within 180 days after you file for bankruptcy become property of the estate.

However, if the benefactor passes away before you file bankruptcy, you may be able to find a way of preventing your inheritance from going to the trustee. In some states you can renounce an inheritance before you actually receive it so that it goes to other heirs. This strategy, however, is very tricky and features many pitfalls. It's definitely something to bring up with your lawyer.

Divorce settlements

Many times, divorce and bankruptcy go hand in hand.

If you become entitled to a divorce property settlement within 180 days after your petition date, the property can be used to pay creditors. These rules apply to property divisions (where a divorce court splits assets and allocates debts) but not to alimony or support, which usually are exempt.

Sometimes filing bankruptcy and then waiting 180 days before filing for divorce is a better strategy. And, of course, make sure that your divorce lawyer knows about your bankruptcy plans, and your bankruptcy lawyer knows about your divorce. See Chapter 16 for more about divorce settlements.

Spendthrift trusts

A trust is a time-honored way for a wise benefactor to make a generous gift to a young or reckless beneficiary without throwing caution to the wind. Legal title to the property is transferred to a trustee (not to be confused with a bankruptcy trustee) with specific instructions so the beneficiary doesn't blow the entire inheritance.

Typically, the document establishing the trust includes a *spendthrift provision*, which says the beneficiary's creditors can't touch the assets of the trust.

A beneficiary's interest in a valid spendthrift trust doesn't become property of his bankruptcy estate because:

- Creditors of the beneficiary never had any claim against the benefactor.
- The beneficiary can't force the trust's trustee to distribute trust property to him, neither can creditors or a bankruptcy trustee.

There are two kinds of trusts:

- *Intervivos trusts* — trusts that are effective while a benefactor is still alive
- *Testamentary trusts* — trusts that don't go into effect until after the benefactor dies

If you're the beneficiary of a testamentary trust, any distributions you actually receive from the trust within 180 days after filing bankruptcy become property of the estate.

In addition, any distributions you receive from either type of trust are considered disposable income in a Chapter 13 case.

Although courts show considerable deference for legitimate trusts, they are not at all fond of scams or shams. Courts won't honor spendthrift restrictions in trusts that actually are manipulations designed to protect the donor's property from his own creditors. You can't place your own property in a trust for yourself just to keep it away from your creditors. Some self-anointed "experts" touting "living trusts" may tell you differently. Don't believe them. Too often, debtors end up losing property they'd normally keep, except they tried to con their creditors. Don't get cute.

Furthermore, you can't serve as sole trustee and sole beneficiary of the trust at the same time, even when someone else sets it up. The courts aren't going to enable you to shield money when you have sole discretion over how and when it is distributed.

The most important point about trusts is that the rules are technical and extremely tricky. Your lawyer needs to review all trust documents to determine whether you're risking your interest in the trust by filing bankruptcy.

Rent receipts

Any income earned by property of the estate is itself property of the estate. So, be careful if you're a landlord — the trustee may have a claim to any rents received from your property after the petition date.

If you rent out a part of your home, rents coming in after the petition date may be covered by your homestead exemption, but check this situation out with your attorney before spending the money.

When rent comes in from property that is not part of your home, it won't be covered by a homestead exemption. You may, however, be allowed to use rent receipts to make postpetition mortgage payments on the rental property.

You need to receive the trustee's consent or your attorney's approval before using rent receipts to pay the mortgage; otherwise, you may have to reimburse the estate for any rents that you paid out after the petition date. Just imagine the predicament you'd be in if you had already spent the money for something else!

Security deposits

Occasionally, a trustee tries to claim a debtor's rent deposit, contending that the debtor must pay the amount of the deposit into the estate. Doing so, in our opinion, is tantamount to extortion, and courts tend to shoot down the trustee's claim for one of two reasons: Your landlord is entitled to continued possession of the deposit, or; it was protected under the homestead exemption.

However, before taking any action or making any assumptions, talk it over with your attorney.

Wages

As we mention in the "Knowing what happens when someone owes you money" section earlier in this chapter, wages that you have earned, but not yet received, as of the petition date are property of the estate, even when they aren't paid until afterward. Nevertheless, a large portion of your wages is exempt. Under federal law, the estate can't claim any more than 25 percent of the net wages that are due to you on the petition date. In some states, you get to keep even more.

Sometimes a question arises about whether money that is due to a debtor qualifies as wages. Courts disagree on whether accounts receivable can be considered exemptible wages, even when the debtor is sole owner of the business.

You can minimize the amount of wages that are at risk by filing your petition soon after your payday. Of course, you'll want to spend this money (your pay) before filing because the funds on hand as of the petition date would also be property of the estate.

Bank accounts

Money in your checking and savings accounts typically is property of the estate, unless you can demonstrate that all or part of the account balance belongs to someone else.

Be careful when dealing with checks that haven't yet cleared when you file bankruptcy. That money technically still is in the bank, and the trustee can make you pay the estate the amounts of any checks that clear after you've filed. For that reason, using cashier's checks or money orders to make payments (like your house payment) right before you file bankruptcy is a good idea.

You may be able to exempt all or part of a bank account, however, when the money in the account is traceable to some exempt source such as Social Security benefits. Most states also allow modest exemptions for cash and bank accounts.

Severance and vacation pay

Other factors to watch out for include whether your job entitles you to severance pay or whether you're entitled to cash in on accumulated vacation time.

The trustee can't, of course, force you to quit your job. However, if you decide to terminate your employment while your bankruptcy case still is open, the trustee may claim these kinds of benefits by arguing that they actually are compensation for services rendered prior to bankruptcy. Nevertheless, a portion of your severance pay may be covered by your exemption for wages.

However, be forewarned that a trustee may be able to cash in your vacation. Courts differ about whether a portion of vacation pay is exempt. In one case, on the petition date, the debtor was entitled to severance pay consisting of accrued wages and vacation pay. The court ruled that the portion of severance pay attributable to accrued wages qualified for the 75 percent wages exemption, but the vacation pay did not.

Sales commissions

A couple of thorny issues arise when the debtor is a commission salesperson.

The first is finding out whether an unpaid commission actually was earned prior to bankruptcy. If so, then it's property of the estate even though the debtor doesn't receive it until after the petition date. After the issue is decided in that manner, the question turns to whether a portion of the unpaid commission qualifies for exemption as wages. If the court concludes that the commission wasn't earned until after bankruptcy, then it's yours and not property of the estate. In this situation, it doesn't matter whether it would be considered as exempt wages.

Real estate commissions

Real estate sales commissions are especially tricky, because agents put a great deal of work into their deals, but don't actually receive a commission until the sale goes through. What if a real estate agent files bankruptcy before a deal actually closes?

Some courts say that a commission paid from a sale that closes after the petition date is not property of the estate, because the commission wasn't actually earned until after bankruptcy. Other courts would determine whether a commission was earned before bankruptcy by figuring out how much work the real estate agent performed prior to filing the bankruptcy petition. For example, say a real estate salesperson, in putting together a sale, performed 90 percent of the work before bankruptcy. Some courts would say that 90 percent of the commission is property of the estate.

Insurance commissions

Similar issues come up when an insurance agent files bankruptcy. Typically, insurance agents automatically receive a commission every time one of their policyholders renews.

Trustees frequently try to latch on to commissions received by insurance agents that are the result of postpetition renewals of policies they sold before filing bankruptcy. The trustees' argument is based on the premise that all the work was done when the original policy was sold, so they want renewal commissions treated like accounts receivable owed on the petition date.

Insurance agents counter that policyholders won't renew unless the agent continues to service the account. Therefore, renewal commissions, in the view of insurance agents, result from work they perform after the petition date, and thus aren't property of the estate.

Some courts accept the trustee's argument, some lean toward the agent's, and others try to strike a Solomonic balance by attempting to figure out how much of a commission is attributable to prepetition work and how much to postpetition efforts.

Under this approach, only that portion of the commissions resulting from prepetition efforts is property of the estate. The rest goes to the debtor.

Similar to real estate commissions, the next question becomes whether renewal commissions are exempt as wages. Again, courts disagree. Some say that the exemption for wages is limited to the classic employer/employee relationship and that commissions are more like business profits. Other courts aren't as strict and say that commissions qualify as wages for exemption purposes.

Suits to recover money

If you had the right to sue someone when you filed bankruptcy, any recovery you receive from that suit is considered property of the estate, even if you didn't receive the money until after bankruptcy.

However, determining if part or all personal-injury awards qualify for an exemption depends on whether the award is for past earnings, medical bills, pain and suffering, or future earnings. If at all possible, you need to settle the claim before filing bankruptcy. Doing so enables your attorney to structure a settlement that maximizes the amount that you can claim as exempt.

Many exemption statutes say that personal-injury awards for loss of future earnings *are* exempt but yet those for pain and suffering *are not*. Your lawyer can devise a settlement agreement in which most of the award is allocated to items that normally are exempt. Be sure to tell your personal-injury lawyer that you're thinking about bankruptcy and insist that he have a bankruptcy specialist review any settlement documents before you sign them.

Depending on local law, your lawyer may advise you to file bankruptcy after reaching a settlement but before you receive the money. In any event, funds received from the settlement need to be placed in a separate bank account so they can be identified as the proceeds from your personal-injury claim.

If the claim can't be settled before bankruptcy, a Chapter 7 trustee can conversely take over the prosecution of the suit and thereby control the structure of the settlement so that it maximizes the part that is not exempt.

So, one strategy is to file Chapter 13 to control prosecution and settlement and then dismiss and file under Chapter 7. However, this strategy is pretty tricky and needs to be thoroughly reviewed by your lawyer.

Income tax refunds

An income tax refund attributable to the year in which bankruptcy is filed — and for any tax year ending before that — is property of the estate, even though you don't receive the refund until after the petition date. (Actually, a refund will be prorated for the year in which the bankruptcy is filed. If, for example, you filed November 18, which is the 323rd day of the year, roughly 88% of the refund would be property of the estate.)

You can sometimes avoid this problem by delaying bankruptcy until you've received your refunds and spent the money. Another possibility would be to elect, prior to bankruptcy, to apply your refund to the next year's taxes. A few courts have said that doing so prevents the refund from becoming an asset of the bankruptcy estate, but that sentiment isn't necessarily universal. Before relying on this strategy, be sure to check with your lawyer.

Unfortunately, things aren't quite as simple when you owe the government money.

The IRS has the right to deduct any taxes you owe from your refund. Furthermore, several federal statutes give other government agencies this same right. If you're in default on a guaranteed student loan, the government will try to take your refund. Additionally, if you owe back child support, local support enforcement agencies (such as the district attorney's office) may be able to snatch your refund. In fact, refunds to which you become entitled for tax years after the petition date may be in jeopardy, unless you're able to eliminate the debt in bankruptcy (see Chapter 14).

Earned income credits

The earned income credit (EIC) was designed as an incentive for poor people to work. It creates a refundable tax credit for low-income workers who have dependent children and maintain a household. Whenever you fall into this category, the government essentially pretends that you had more pay withheld than you actually did and then gives some of it back to you. The money is refunded as though it was part of a tax overpayment. So, even if you didn't have any taxes withheld, you still may be able to claim to a refund. Keep in mind that the same brainiacs who came up with that logic wrote the bankruptcy laws.

The courts haven't quite decided how to handle EICs. Although they resemble income tax refunds, EICs are actually a form of government assistance for needy individuals.

Typically, no exemption specifically covers earned income credits. But some courts have applied exemptions for welfare benefits or public assistance. Some have said that EICs are exempt as child support. One court held that an EIC was covered under the state's exemption for personal earnings. But recently, the consensus appears to be leaning toward not covering EICs by any exemption at all.

Retirement accounts

Retirement accounts are particularly complicated. After 11 years of debate in lower courts, the United States Supreme Court, in a 1992 case (*Patterson v. Shumate,* 504 US 753) ruled that pensions, which are *qualified* under the federal Employment Retirement Income Security Act (ERISA) don't become property of the estate. Therefore, bankruptcy trustees can't touch them.

Nevertheless, even though the Supreme Court has spoken on the matter, debtors, creditors, and trustees still split hairs about just what "ERISA qualified" means. More than 20 courts considering the question have reached different conclusions. Trustees and creditors have successfully argued in some cases that for a pension to be exempt and thereby excluded from the estate as ERISA qualified, it must satisfy not only the requirements of the federal ERISA statute but also the hypertechnical provisions of the Internal Revenue Code.

If your retirement plan isn't covered by ERISA, which is true of government pensions, pensions that primarily benefit only the owners of a business, and private plans such as IRAs, then the plan is property of the estate and is protected only to the extent that any federal or state exemption applies.

Lacking any exemption for IRAs in your state, these plans simply aren't protected, even though the Internal Revenue Service (IRS) can impose a tax penalty whenever you withdraw the money prior to retirement.

Fortunately, most states exempt at least a portion of IRAs; however, some actually limit the exemption to an amount that is reasonably necessary for a retiree's support.

Roth IRAs

Watch out for Roth IRAs, because they fall through the cracks of some state exemption schemes.

In some states, regular IRAs are exempt, but Roth IRAs may not be. This is because Roth IRAs are created under Section 408-A of the Internal Revenue Code. The problem is, many state statutes only exempt IRAs established under Section *408.* Applying the exemption statute literally would mean that Roth IRAs are not exempt.

Nevertheless, your chances are pretty good that your bankruptcy won't affect your retirement plan. (However, you probably won't be allowed to contribute to your retirement plan during a Chapter 13 case.)

The story can turn out much different if you made any unusual contributions to your retirement account, such as taking a large sum of nonexempt cash and depositing it into your account. Courts also won't allow you to get away with borrowing money and socking it into an exempt retirement plan.

Pension "rollovers"

Pension rollovers are especially dicey.

Suppose, for example, that you had a regular ERISA pension, left your job, and you were given the choice of leaving the money in the fund, rolling it over into a private retirement plan like an IRA, or receiving the money in cash. If you leave the money in the ERISA plan, most courts probably will say that it still is completely protected, even when you have the right to request an immediate distribution.

Similarly, if you decide to roll over the pension without actually receiving the money, most courts will allow the exemption, but the total may be limited to amounts necessary for support or, depending on the state law involved, only part of the rollover may qualify.

However, when you actually receive a distribution of the funds, you may not be protected at all, even if those fund eventually are reinvested into another retirement plan.

Creating Exemptions

To a limited degree, the law allows some prebankruptcy planning to maximize exemptions.

For example, if you had $1,000 in a bank account that wasn't covered by an exemption, you'd lose it to a Chapter 7 trustee. If, however, you make extra payments on your mortgage with that $1,000 before you file for bankruptcy, the increase in your homestead may be exempt.

Exemption planning is an extremely complicated and unsettled area of the law. If you go too far, you can face serious consequences, including denial of discharge (your debts don't get wiped out), denial of the exemption, or reversal of the transaction.

Courts frequently render a finding of fraud whenever someone liquidates all his assets and pays off a mortgage, especially in states with unlimited homestead exemptions. One court recently denied a debtor's discharge for using all his money to purchase a Florida house and then moving there from New York when he was being sued for $250,000.

A court reached the same kind of result in a case where a debtor, while living in Illinois, encumbered nonexempt assets to raise funds for a down payment on a homestead in Kansas, where the homestead exemption is unlimited. Ditto where debtor took $45,000 in nonexempt assets and purchased exempt property. In that case, the court ruled that a little exemption planning is all right, but a wholesale sheltering of assets that would otherwise go to creditors isn't permissible, saying: "When a pig becomes a hog, it is slaughtered." In this case — *In re Zouhar*, 10 B.R. 154, 157 (Bankr.D.N.M.1981) — the debtor became a hog.

And yet the results aren't consistent.

In one case, a debtor got away with selling $60,000 of nonexempt property and paying down the mortgage on his homestead in Arizona, which has a $100,000 exemption. Another debtor was successful in a case where he liquidated $80,000 in nonexempt assets over a two-year period and then used the funds to increase exempt equity in his homestead. And still another court ruled that a debtor didn't act improperly by using $3,500 to purchase an exempt asset shortly before filing for bankruptcy.

The bottom line is: Be sure to consult a bankruptcy attorney *before* engaging in any prebankruptcy planning.

The difference between converting your property into exempt assets that you continue to own and placing property in someone else's name is a huge one.

Transferring property to someone else is considered fraudulent if the court thinks that you did it just to keep assets out of the reach of creditors. Don't make any gifts or sell any property for less than it's worth before you file for bankruptcy. If you've already done so, be sure to tell your bankruptcy lawyer. We discuss this topic more in Chapter 18.

Chapter 10

Dealing with Secured Debts

. . . .

In This Chapter

▶ Looking at liens

▶ Wiping out liens through bankruptcy

▶ Handling liens on your household goods

▶ Dealing with liens on your car

. . . .

*T*he three people who may have an interest in one of your assets are

- ✔ You (obviously)
- ✔ The bankruptcy trustee as a representative of unsecured creditors (those who don't have dibs on your car, house, or other belongings)
- ✔ A *secured creditor* — one who holds a lien

In simplest terms, a *lien* is a legal claim in which someone else owns a portion of a particular asset that serves as collateral for the debt. You voluntarily create some liens like your mortgage or car loan. Others are *imposed* against you. For example, if you lost a lawsuit and a judgment was entered against you, that judgment probably created a lien against your home. Similarly, if you fail to pay property taxes, the local government may obtain a lien against your property.

Bankruptcy won't automatically make a lien disappear. So, if you file bankruptcy, you may end up wiping out the debt but still losing assets that have liens on them. Consider your car loan, for example. Filing bankruptcy wipes out your obligation to pay the loan, but the lender can still get the car when you don't pay.

This chapter spotlights liens, the headaches they can cause when they "lien on you," and how in some instances you can cast them aside. In Chapter 11, we explore how this works when the lien is against your home.

Getting the Lowdown on Liens

Generally, you face two types of creditors, unsecured and secured, in bankruptcy cases.

An *unsecured creditor,* such as a credit-card company or medical provider, has no specific claim or right to your property. A *secured creditor* has some leverage. Your debt to him is backed up, or secured, by a specific asset that serves as collateral for the debt. That security interest, in legalese, *encumbers* your property with a *lien.* Put another way, your ownership of the property is conditional — the condition being that if you don't repay the loan, the creditor can go after the *collateral,* or property that secures your debt.

When you finance a car, you and the lender share ownership of the vehicle. As long as you continue making the payments, you're entitled to possession. You don't have the right to sell it out from under the lender, and if you don't make the payments, the lender can take the car. After the debt is paid off, the lender no longer has a claim on the car; the lien is released, and the vehicle is yours free and clear.

Perfecting liens

When a lien is placed on your asset, the law usually requires the lienholder to take certain steps to warn others that it possesses some of the ownership rights associated with the collateral. When these steps are taken, the lien is considered *perfected.* Some sort of public recording or notation is usually required.

For example, your home mortgage isn't perfected until the mortgage document is recorded with the county. Likewise, in most states, a security interest in a motor vehicle isn't perfected until the creditor is listed as a lienholder on the certificate of title.

Perfection is an important concept to understand because bankruptcy trustees have the power to eliminate unperfected liens and take over that creditor's (the lienholder's) ownership rights (see Chapter 18).

Seeing liens as double-edged swords

A lienholder's firepower comes from two sources: you and the collateral. By promising to pay the debt, and most likely signing a *promissory note,* you accept personal liability. And by agreeing to a lien, you have given the lender an actual ownership interest in your property.

Putting it into practical terms, if you owe $10,000 on a car that's worth only $7,000, and you don't make the payments, the lender can:

- ✔ Forget about the car and sue you for the full $10,000.
- ✔ Take advantage of the lien and repossess the car.
- ✔ Do both, which, in general, is the most likely avenue of pursuit by the lender.

  And why not? Then, the lender can repossess the car and sell it for, say, $7,000, apply the money to the debt, and come after you for the balance on the promissory note. Talk about having their cake and eating it too!

Ordinarily, bankruptcy wipes out your personal liability on the debt, but it won't eliminate the creditor's lien. Although the creditor can no longer go after your personal obligation, it can go after its collateral. Using the example in the previous bulleted list, after you file bankruptcy, the creditor can still repossess the car but can't come after you for the debt itself. So, the cash in your wallet is safe; the car in your garage is not.

The Bankruptcy Code enables you to eliminate liens on household goods and tools of your trade in some situations and to reduce liens in other cases — depending on what kind of lien it is.

Identifying Different Kinds of Liens

Liens can take a variety of forms, including mortgage liens, mechanic's liens, artisan's liens, judicial liens, and tax liens. However, all liens fall in one or the other of two categories — consensual or nonconsensual. And to complicate matters a little more, there are two types of consensual liens — purchase-money liens and nonpurchase-money security liens. These types of liens are typically called purchase-money and nonpurchase-money security interests.

Consensual liens

Consensual liens are liens that you voluntarily grant to someone else. When they involve personal property, such as your car or television, they're called *security interests.* In the case of real property (like your house), they're usually called *mortgages* or *deeds of trust.*

Here's how consensual liens work.

First, start with the understanding that the bank doesn't give you a mortgage to buy a home, but rather you give the bank a mortgage. When you signed your mortgage papers, you gave the lender a lien, thereby giving away some of your ownership rights. You retained the right of possession and granted the lender the right to some of the proceeds if you decide to sell the property. Got that?

Now, by giving the bank a mortgage, you also made your ownership conditional. So, because the bank lent you money, you, in turn, agreed that it could take possession and sell the property if you didn't pay back the loan. As a result, you and the mortgage holder simultaneously have ownership interests, albeit different and sometimes competing ones. Similarly, whenever you grant a lender a security interest on your car, you give up some of your ownership rights.

Consensual liens come in two varieties:

- **Purchase-money security interests,** in which proceeds of a loan are used to purchase a specific item

- **Nonpurchase-money security interests,** which attach to property you already own

When you charge items at some department stores, you often give the store a purchase-money security interest in the merchandise that you buy. Similarly, if you borrow money from a finance company for the express purpose of buying a car that you'll use to secure the loan — that too is a purchase-money security interest.

If, for example, you charge a microwave oven on your department store account, you probably agree that the store can take back the appliance if you don't pay off what you owe. On the other hand, if you charged the oven on a general-purpose credit card (such as MasterCard or Visa), to which typically no security interest is attached, neither the store nor the credit-card company can repossess the oven, even if you don't pay for it. You still owe the money, however, and you can surely be sued for what you owe, but nobody can take your microwave or force you to sell it to cover the debt.

Lenders who specialize in relatively small loans to consumers typically require that the borrower give them a lien (security interest) in all their (the borrowers) household goods. This is a nonpurchase-money security interest because you didn't borrow the money to purchase the household goods; you already owned them. In theory, this stipulation gives the loan company the right to seize and sell all these items. As you see in the "Applying Lien Laws to Household Goods" section later in this chapter, it doesn't usually turn out that way in practice.

Nonconsensual liens

Sometimes the law gives creditors a lien on your property without your consent. The gall! These legal shackles are called *nonconsensual liens*.

Real property taxes, for instance, are liens against your property even though you never directly consent. The same is true of a judgment lien. When a judgment is entered against you in some courts, it becomes a lien against your real property, which secures payment of that judgment. See the "Banging the Gavel on Judgment Liens" section later in this chapter to find out how to eliminate this type of lien in bankruptcy.

Dealing with Liens in Bankruptcy

Although liens can seem indelible, the Bankruptcy Code provides you with special powers to remove them from exempt household goods, tools, and homesteads. See Chapter 9 for more on exempt assets.

Freeing your household goods and tools from liens

Recognizing the difference between *purchase-money* and *nonpurchase-money security interests* can help you hang on to your household goods and tools. See the section, "Consensual liens," earlier in this chapter.

Generally, you can't avoid a purchase-money security interest when you file bankruptcy, but, as you discuss in the following sections, you can redeem, reaffirm, or pay the value of the collateral over three to five years in a Chapter 13 repayment plan.

On the other hand, you can eliminate nonpurchase-money security interests in exempt household goods and tools. See Chapter 9 for more on which items are exempt. We go over this a little later in this chapter, too, in the "Applying Lien Laws to Household Goods" section.

Redeeming (getting back) your property

If you can't simply remove a lien, you can still *redeem* consumer goods by paying the creditor not the amount of the debt, but rather its value. Personal property depreciates so quickly that its value almost is always less than the amount of the debt. Say, for example, that you charged a $1,000 home entertainment system and gave the store a purchase-money security interest in the unit. Instead of paying the full $1,000 to keep the system, you can pay the store only its value, which, by the time you take it home, is probably half what it was in the store.

In Chapter 7 bankruptcy, this payment must be made in a lump sum shortly after your case is filed, unless the creditor agrees otherwise. If you and the creditor can't agree on how much the item is worth, a bankruptcy judge decides.

If you file Chapter 13 bankruptcy, you can stretch out payments over five years.

Reaffirming your debts

If you can't eliminate a lien, don't have the cash to redeem it, and don't want to tether yourself to a Chapter 13 repayment plan, you can reaffirm and promise to pay the debt even though it would otherwise be wiped out during bankruptcy. However, that means if you fall behind on the payments after bankruptcy, the creditor can repossess the collateral, sell it, and come after you for any shortfall.

If you were in default on the loan when you filed bankruptcy, the secured creditor can insist that you reaffirm or surrender the collateral.

If, however, you weren't in default on the petition date, many bankruptcy courts will rule that you *don't* have to reaffirm. All you have to do is to keep up with the payments. If it turns out that you can't keep up with the payments after bankruptcy, all you need to do is surrender the car to the lender with no further obligation. Be sure to discuss this situation with your lawyer before taking action.

Lenders hate it when borrowers keep collateral by making payments but don't reaffirm their debts. All they have to look forward to is the ever-depreciating collateral. They'll often try to trip you up by getting you to miss payments so they can repossess the collateral as soon as possible by not sending you payments reminders. Many won't give you so much as a single day's grace period if you're late.

The bottom line: Keeping collateral by remaining current on the debt — when you have that option — is usually a better deal than reaffirming. But you really must stay on your toes.

Dealing with rent-to-own contracts

Rent-to-own contracts are similar to purchase-money security interests, but they are set up as leases.

With these contracts, you lease a specific item, make periodic rent payments, and, at the end of the contract, end up owning whatever it is you rented. When a transaction is a true lease, the only way you can keep the item is to make all the payments. You can't redeem the property in a Chapter 7, and you can't just pay its value in a Chapter 13. However, in a Chapter 13, you can make up back payments and make all future payments on time if you want to keep the item.

Lenders know that they make out better if a transaction is a lease rather than one involving a security interest and frequently label transactions "leases" when they actually are security interests. Most courts say that a transaction is not a true lease unless you're allowed to cancel the deal at any time and return the merchandise without further obligation. Your lawyer needs to examine the fine print to see whether a transaction is a true lease or a cleverly disguised security interest.

Figuring Out What Will Happen to Your Car

Car loans are, of course, typically secured by the automobile itself. The fate of your vehicle in bankruptcy is determined by several Bankruptcy Code principles.

The following examples apply these rules so you can see what's going to happen to your car when you file bankruptcy. Assume that the value of your car is $12,000, and the allowable exemption is $3,500.

Example 1: All the equity is exempt, and loan payments are current

Say that you owe $11,000. Your equity is $1,000 ($12,000 – $11,000 = $1,000), which is within the $3,500 exemption, so you don't have to worry about the trustee.

Your options are:

- Kissing off the car and the debt by giving the vehicle back to the lender.
- Continuing to make payments.

  In many jurisdictions that's all you have to do. You don't have to reaffirm, and down the road you still can surrender the car without any further obligation. In other jurisdictions, however, you must sign a reaffirmation agreement. If you reaffirm, and later can't make payments, the lender can repossess the car, sell it at auction, and sue you for the difference. If you can't afford the payments, don't reaffirm. After all, the goal of bankruptcy is to free you from your debts, not merely to postpone the day of reckoning.

Chapter 13 bankruptcy doesn't offer any advantages over filing Chapter 7 in this example.

Example 2: All the equity is exempt, but you're behind in payments

If you have fallen behind on your $11,000 loan for your $12,000 car, you can file Chapter 13 to catch up on the $900 owed on back payments over the life of a repayment plan. In most jurisdictions, you can even retrieve your car if it has already been repossessed, provided that the lender has not yet auctioned it off.

If you file Chapter 7, however, you put the lender in the driver's seat (figuratively if not literally). Because the loan is in default, the lender can insist that you reaffirm the debt but doesn't even have to offer that option. The creditor may agree to allow you to make up back payments but, again, doesn't have to.

If the lender won't be reasonable, at least you can convert your case to Chapter 13 and force the lender to accept back payments over three to five years.

If you're behind on payments, don't tip off the finance company in advance about your bankruptcy plans, because it may try to beat you to the punch by snatching the car before you file.

Example 3: You owe more than the car is worth

If you owed $15,000 on the same $12,000 car, the same rules apply, except that in Chapter 7 you can also *redeem* it by making a lump-sum payment of $12,000 equal to the value of the vehicle.

In Chapter 13, you can *cram down,* or pay the $12,000 value of the car over the life of the plan instead of paying the entire debt.

Example 4: You have nonexempt equity in one car

Assume that you owe only $4,000 for the $12,000 car. You'd then have non-exempt equity of $4,500 ($12,000 – $4,000 – $3,500 = $4,500).

In a Chapter 7 bankruptcy, the trustee can sell the car, pay the creditor off, pay you $3,500 for your exemption, and distribute the rest to unsecured creditors.

In a Chapter 13, the trustee can't sell the car. However, the $4,500 in non-exempt equity can increase your monthly payment or the length of the plan under the *best-interests* test, which requires that creditors eventually receive as much from your Chapter 13 case as they would if you had filed under Chapter 7 (see Chapter 4.)

Another possible option is selling the car before bankruptcy, buying another one worth no more than $3,500 (the amount of the exemption), and using the rest of the money for some necessary item, such as home repairs. Or you may use the money to pay some of the debt that won't be wiped out in bankruptcy. But be sure to check it out with your lawyer first.

Be wary of using any of the money from the sale of your car to pay old debts. Whenever you pay any nondischargeable debts before bankruptcy, you may have to wait 90 days before filing bankruptcy; otherwise, the trustee can get the money back for the benefit of other creditors, leaving you with the bulk of the nondischargeable debt to pay after bankruptcy.

Furthermore, don't try selling the car to a friend or relative for less than it's worth. That can be considered a fraudulent transfer and thus cause you all kinds of grief (see Chapter 18).

Example 5: You have more than one car

Your options don't change that much. You just have to choose which car to claim as exempt.

Generally, states will allow you only one car exemption. Consequently, if you had $1,500 equity in one car and $2,000 in another car, you can lose one to a Chapter 7 trustee. In a Chapter 13 bankruptcy, the value of one of the cars increases your plan payments.

Other options include selling one car and spending the money, as in Example 4. Or you can sell both cars and use the $3,500 for a single car, which would be wholly exempt.

Example 6: Your car is leased

If you are leasing rather than buying your car, the rules are about the same in a Chapter 7, except that you can't *redeem* a leased vehicle.

In a Chapter 13, you can catch up on back lease payments and resume future payments, but you can't keep the car by paying its value (cramming it down) the same way you can with a vehicle that is financed.

Applying Lien Laws to Household Goods

You have a few more options where a lender's collateral is your household goods instead of your car because:

- ✔ The Bankruptcy Code allows you to eliminate nonpurchase-money security interests in exempt household items altogether.

- ✔ Creditors really don't want to repossess this stuff, so it's easier to negotiate with them.

With household goods, the secured creditor in a Chapter 7 bankruptcy will almost always allow you to make up back payments under a reaffirmation agreement. Unlike automobiles, there is little market for used household goods. So the creditor would much rather work with you to establish a repayment plan than seize the property and then have to deal with the problem of selling it.

Consider the following examples, which assume that the allowable exemption for household goods is $3,000.

Example 1: A creditor holds a purchase-money security interest in exempt household goods

Say that you have a stove purchased on a department store charge account where you gave the store a security interest in purchased items. The stove is presently worth only $200, but you still owe $900 for it.

In a Chapter 7, you have three options:

- ✔ Surrender the stove and wipe out the debt

- ✔ Reaffirm and pay the full amount of the debt under the terms of the original credit agreement

- ✔ Redeem the refrigerator by paying only its $200 value

In a Chapter 13, you can cram down the debt by paying $200 over the life of the plan.

Example 2: A finance company has a nonpurchase-money security interest

Let's say that the total value of your furniture and appliances is $2,500, well within the $3,000 exemption. However, prior to bankruptcy, you borrowed money from a finance company and gave it a security interest in the stuff that you already owned. No problem. Because this is a nonpurchase-money security interest, you simply wipe out the debt and eliminate the security interest in either Chapter 7 or Chapter 13.

Example 3: Your household goods exceed the exemption, but none are subject to security interests

Let's say your furniture is worth $5,400 and you own it all free and clear. Here, you must choose which items to exempt. In theory, a Chapter 7 trustee can insist that you surrender the items that you did not exempt, but he'd probably accept an offer from you to pay him the value of those items. In a Chapter 13, the value of nonexempt items would be paid over the life of the plan. Another alternative would be to sell some of these items before bankruptcy and use the money for living expenses.

Banging the Gavel on Judgment Liens

If you lose a lawsuit and the other side is awarded money, a *judicial lien* (a form of judgment lien) may be imposed. Sometimes, a lien is automatically placed on all your real estate the moment a judgment is entered against you. Under the Bankruptcy Code, you can eliminate a judgment lien to the extent that it impairs your homestead exemption.

Consider this example. Assume that your home is worth $75,000, is subject to a mortgage lien of $55,000, and that your state's homestead exemption (which protects at least some of the value of your home) is $30,000. Further assume that you owe $15,000 in medical bills.

If the equity in your home is $20,000, you can file bankruptcy, discharge the medical bills, and keep your home by continuing to pay the mortgage. Neat and clean!

But, say that the hospital sued you before you filed bankruptcy and obtained a judgment lien for $15,000. That lien would devour all but $5,000 of your homestead exemption, and you'd have to pay your mortgage and the judgment if you wanted to keep your home.

Congress thought that this was too harsh, especially because a judgment lien is nonconsensual. As a result, the Bankruptcy Code allows debtors to eliminate judgment liens that interfere with homestead exemptions. If the debtor in our example took advantage of these provisions, it would be as if no judgment lien had ever hit his property. In other words, to keep his house, all he must do is pay the mortgage. The hospital bill gets wiped our along with all the other debts.

A provision in the Bankruptcy Code enables debtors to avoid such a judgment to the extent that it impairs a homestead exemption.

Beware, however, that the rules about avoiding judgment liens *do not* apply to judgment liens entered by divorce courts for alimony or child support. Forget about avoiding those kind of judgment liens.

Chapter 11

Saving Your Home

- -

In This Chapter

▶ Owning and owing — the blessings and curses of home ownership

▶ Discovering the homestead exemption

▶ Addressing jointly owned property

▶ Comprehending foreclosures

▶ Hanging on to your home in Chapter 7 and Chapter 13 bankruptcies

▶ Using truth-in-lending laws to save your home

▶ Watching out for due-on-sale clauses

- -

Home ownership is an integral part of the American Dream. The Bankruptcy Code recognizes the importance of owning a home and strives to strike a delicate balance between the sometimes competing interests of mortgage companies that finance home purchases, other creditors, and, of course, the homeowners.

In this chapter, we look at what can happen to your home when you file bankruptcy and explain how bankruptcy can prevent *foreclosure* — that nasty situation when lenders take your home.

When you're struggling to make ends meet, refinancing your home or taking out a home-equity loan may seem like a great option — and maybe it is. However, we suggest that you explore your bankruptcy options first. See Chapter 6 for more about refinancing.

Your Home, Your Castle — and Sometimes Your Hassle

You probably see your home as a memory-filled place of refuge for you and your family, but others view it through different eyes — cold, calculating ones. Typically, they focus on the *equity* in your house — the difference between its value and the amount owed on mortgages and liens against it.

Three entities that may claim an interest in your home are

- ✔ You
- ✔ Secured creditors — including mortgageholders and other lienholders, such as judgment creditors
- ✔ The bankruptcy trustee, to the extent that its value exceeds the allowable homestead exemption

The three things that you need to know before assessing your options are

- ✔ The value of your property
- ✔ The amount of any mortgages or other liens against the property
- ✔ The homestead exemption that applies to your situation

Figuring out how much your home is worth

Bankruptcy offers various options with regard to your homestead. But before you can figure which works best for your situation, you need an objective appraisal of the dollars and cents value of your home. That can be a tough number to find. If you recently purchased your home, the selling price is some indication of its value. *Some*. Depending on where you live, a good starting point for determining the value of your real property *may* be the tax assessment. Unfortunately, in some parts of the country, values used by tax assessors bear almost no relationship to reality.

Be wary, however, of estimates from real estate brokers who may be more inclined to overstate the value of your home hoping to land a selling job. Similarly, don't blindly accept appraisals made in connection with home-equity loans. Home-equity appraisals routinely are inflated so the lender can justify giving you a larger loan that you probably can't afford.

If you did not recently purchase your home or if you live in a community where property tax assessments are out of whack, you'll have to hire a real estate appraiser. This way you'll get an expert opinion from someone with no ulterior motives.

Deducting mortgages and other liens that affect your share of the pie

Liens for mortgages, real property taxes, federal taxes, or judgments go against the value of your home and lienholders have first dibs on any proceeds if you sell the property. They must be paid in full before you or other creditors get anything from the sale of your home. The amounts of any liens need to be deducted from the value of the property so you can determine how much equity you have. You may want to review Chapter 10, where we take an up close and personal look at liens.

Understanding the homestead exemption

Homestead-exemption laws protect a person's home from those creditors who don't have liens against the property. For example, if your home is worth $120,000 and you owe $100,000 on the mortgage, your equity in the home is $20,000. So, if the applicable homestead exemption were $20,000 or more, your home would be protected from the bankruptcy trustee and creditors other than the mortgage holder.

Almost every jurisdiction has some type of homestead exemption; however, notable exceptions include Delaware, Maryland, New Jersey, and Pennsylvania. Some jurisdictions permit you to choose exemptions contained in the U.S. Bankruptcy Code or those provided by your state law. In other places, you are restricted to the exemptions recognized by your state and the federal exemptions aren't available. Appendix B summarizes the exemptions state-by-state and provides a list of federal exemptions.

Arkansas, the District of Columbia, Florida, Iowa, Kansas, South Dakota, and Texas have unlimited homestead exemptions. If you live in one of those states, your home is sheltered regardless of its value. In other words, you can sit in your million-dollar Florida mansion and thumb your nose at any creditor who doesn't have a lien against the property. In addition, your home would be off the table if you file bankruptcy.

But if you don't live in an unlimited-homestead state, the picture may not be so rosy. While some states have a homestead exemption as high as $300,000 (Massachusetts), homestead exemptions in some states don't amount to a hill of beans. In Michigan, for example, the homestead exemption is a measly $3,500.

Sometimes, the effective amount of your exemption may actually be more than the amount specified in exemption statutes. The reason? When the trustee sells your property, he is responsible for paying a commission to any real estate agent he hires. Commissions and other costs of sale can be as high as 10 percent of the selling price of your home and they must be paid from the trustee's share of the sale proceeds, not from the share covered by your homestead exemption.

Occasionally, a court must decide whether an unusual type of residence qualifies for homestead exemption. Not surprisingly, courts frequently disagree. Houseboats, for example, seem to confound the courts. Some judges say they're exempt as homesteads; others say they're not.

Another frequent question is whether you can exempt living quarters where you've rented out part of your abode or used another part of your residence for income-producing activities. Most courts agree that the mere fact that a person rents out a room or portion of his home doesn't impair the exemption. Other courts, however, differ.

Some states require you to actually reside in the dwelling, but others permit temporary absences or require only that a family member live there. Sometimes determining whether someone lives on the property is difficult. For example, does a debtor actually live on vacant land when he's staying in a camper on the property but intends to build a home? Some courts would rule that he doesn't live there; therefore, the land is not exempt.

Table 11-1 helps determine if a bankruptcy trustee has any claim to your home — whether or not you have nonexempt home equity that could be seized for your creditors.

Table 11-1	Nonexempt Home Equity
1. The value of your home	$
2. The costs of selling it (roughly 10 percent of its value)	$
3. Amount owed on mortgages	$
4. Amounts owed on other liens, for example judgments, real estate taxes, federal tax liens	$
5. Total deductions (add Lines 2, 3, and 4)	$
6. Your equity (Subtract Line 5 from Line 1)	$
7. Homestead exemption	$
8. Nonexempt home equity (Subtract Line 7 from Line 6)	$

Dealing With Jointly Owned Property

In noncommunity-property states (all except Arizona, California, Idaho, Louisiana, Nevada, New Mexico, Texas, Washington, and Wisconsin), when a married couple jointly owns a homestead, but only one spouse files bankruptcy, the other spouse's interest in the property doesn't come into play in the bankruptcy. Although courts disagree about how to calculate a dollar figure for the interest of one spouse, you can come up with a ballpark figure by deducting mortgages and liens from the value of your property, dividing the remainder by two, and applying your homestead exemption against this figure. The following sections show you what happens in some practical examples.

If you own property solely in your name, don't try to put it in the names of both you and your spouse (without first talking to a bankruptcy lawyer). Doing so can be considered a fraudulent transfer (see Chapter 18).

Example 1: When the homestead exemption is larger than your equity

Assume that your home is worth $100,000 and you owe $70,000 on the mortgage, which means that the equity in your home is $30,000 and your half would be $15,000. If your state's homestead exemption is $20,000, your property is entirely exempt, because the amount of your equity is less than the amount of the homestead exemption.

Example 2: When your equity is larger than your homestead exemption

Assume that your property is worth $160,000 and that you owe $70,000 on the mortgage, meaning that the equity in your property is $90,000, with your half being $45,000. If the homestead exemption still is $20,000, you have nonexempt home equity available to creditors.

In the example in the previous paragraph, if a Chapter 7 trustee can find a buyer for your one-half interest for, say $45,000, the buyer can pay you $20,000 and distribute $25,000 to creditors to become a joint owner with your spouse. The trustee must, however, give your spouse a chance to match this offer before actually selling the property.

When a buyer for your one-half interest can't be found, the trustee can ask the court for permission to sell the entire interest in the property, pay the mortgage, give your spouse his or her share, pay you your exemption, and distribute the balance to creditors. In this situation, instead of sharing ownership with a new buyer, your spouse receives cash for his or her share.

As a practical matter, the likelihood that a trustee can find a buyer for a one-half interest in your homestead is minimal, or even less. Furthermore, courts are reluctant to grant a trustee's request to sell a nondebtor spouse's interest in the marital home. So, a nondebtor may be able to buy the estate's interest in the property from the trustee for significantly less than the previous examples suggest, especially when you consider that the trustee has to pay a real estate agent's commission whenever the property is listed for sale.

From a debtor's perspective, things are even better in jurisdictions that recognize a *tenancy by the entireties* exemption. In Delaware, the District of Columbia, Florida, Hawaii, Illinois, Indiana, Maryland, Massachusetts, Michigan, Mississippi, Missouri, North Carolina, Pennsylvania, Vermont, Virginia, and Wyoming, when only one spouse files bankruptcy and no creditors have claims against both spouses, the property is fully exempt. Regardless of its value or whether it qualifies as a homestead, you can keep your home.

The bottom line: One spouse filing for bankruptcy with the other one avoiding it can prove advantageous. Be sure to discuss this angle with your lawyer.

The rules pertaining to jointly owned property are different — and somewhat less favorable — when you live in Arizona, California, Idaho, Louisiana, Nevada, New Mexico, Texas, Washington, or Wisconsin, the nine community property states, where even the nondebtor's interest in community property becomes property of the estate. If the community property isn't fully covered by an exemption, the trustee can sell it. Your home probably is considered community property when it's obtained during the marriage, unless one spouse inherits the property.

Understanding How Foreclosures Work

In weighing your bankruptcy options, you need to know a little about the nitty-gritty of foreclosure. Although procedures vary from state to state, foreclosure typically begins when the lender commences a lawsuit initiating what's known as a *judicial foreclosure* or files documents with the county clerk or another local official and mails copies to you, the borrower, in the case of a *nonjudicial foreclosure*.

But that's only the beginning. State laws require a public auction, referred to as a *foreclosure sale,* and public notice of that auction. In other words, the mortgage gremlin can't just auction off your house to his relatives at a no-contest auction. But even though a foreclosure sale is open to public bidding, the lender typically places the only bid. The time between commencement of a foreclosure proceeding and the actual sale rarely is less than three months and frequently is longer. During this period, you still own the property.

In some situations, depending on the method of foreclosure and requirements of state law, the borrower still may be able to *redeem* the property after a foreclosure sale by paying the full amount bid at the sale. After the foreclosure process is complete, however, the successful bidder can evict the borrower from the premises.

Heading Off the Homewreckers

Because holding on to your home may be a number-one priority, evaluating the differences between filing Chapter 7 and Chapter 13 makes sense. We designed the following sections to clarify the distinctions.

Keeping your home in Chapter 7

If you're current with your mortgage payments, and the value of your home is covered by your state's homestead exemption, Chapter 7 bankruptcy may be the way to go. By getting rid of most of your other debts, keeping up with the mortgage will be just that much easier.

Filing Chapter 7 usually is quick, easy, final, and helps you avoid the repayment responsibility that comes with Chapter 13 bankruptcy.

Keeping your home in Chapter 13

If you need time to catch up on back mortgage payments, Chapter 13 is probably the recipe you're looking for, because you then can make up late payments over the three- to five-year life of your bankruptcy plan. But remember that you must keep up with all future mortgage payments.

Additionally, whenever your equity is more than your state's allowable exemption, you don't want to file Chapter 7 because you'd probably lose your home to the trustee.

For example, say your house is worth $100,000, your mortgage balance is $60,000, and the homestead exemption is $25,000. If you file Chapter 7, the trustee can sell your house, pay off the mortgage, hand you $25,000 for your homestead exemption, and distribute the remaining $15,000 to creditors. In Chapter 13, you keep your home and pay creditors the same $15,000 they would have received in Chapter 7, but you have three to five years in which to do it.

Making up back payments: The "cure" for your ailment

A *cure* is the process of paying the amount that you're behind on your mortgage (*arrearage*) over the course of a Chapter 13 case. For example, if you're behind by five $1,000 mortgage payments as of the date of your bankruptcy, you can gradually pay off the $5,000 arrearage over the three to five years of a Chapter 13 bankruptcy plan.

After you file Chapter 13, in addition to chipping away at the arrearage, you must also resume your current payments. Continuing with the previous paragraph's example, say that your mortgage payments are due on the tenth of the month, that you file Chapter 13 on May 15 and that the arrearage consists of payments you missed for January, February, March, April, and May. Under those circumstances, you have to make your regular payments, starting with the one due on June 10, in addition to your payments on the arrearage.

If foreclosure proceedings already were started, you still can proffer a cure by filing Chapter 13 before the property is sold at a foreclosure sale. (See "Understanding How Foreclosures Work" section earlier in this chapter.) One problem is that courts disagree on precisely when this sale occurs. A foreclosure, by its baser nature, is a public auction. When the bidding stops, the auctioneer declares the property "sold to the highest bidder," (which is usually the mortgageholder bidding all or part of the amount it is owed). However, depending on local procedures, additional steps may be required to complete the process. In some places, a state court judge must confirm that the foreclosure was properly conducted. In addition, a deed must be delivered to the high bidder, who must properly record it in public records.

That said, some courts rule that if you don't file a Chapter 13 before the winning bid is accepted, it's too late for a cure. Others say that cure remains a possibility when a Chapter 13 is filed before all the additional steps are completed.

Filing a Chapter 13 well in advance of the foreclosure sale date usually is best because you're assured that it won't be too late. Filing early also saves you money. Mortgage documents typically require you to pay the lender's costs and attorney fees for the foreclosure proceedings. When you file late in the process, these amounts are added to the arrearage.

Even after a foreclosure sale, you may still have a shot at saving your house if your state provides for a *right of redemption,* an opportunity for you to redeem real property, even after it's sold at foreclosure. Depending on the state and method of foreclosure, you may have a period of time, usually six months to a year, to exercise a right of redemption. *Note:* A right of redemption is not to be confused with the right to redeem personal property under the Bankruptcy Code, which we explain in Chapter 10.

Remember, however, the difference between redemption and cure. When you cure, you only have to make up the missed payments; you don't have to pay the whole loan. And you can take up to five years to make up the back payments.

Redemption, on the other hand, essentially requires you pay the entire out-standing balance of the loan, and you can't stretch payments over the life of the plan. The entire debt has to be paid before the redemption period, which in some states may be only a few months, expires. Your only option in this situation would be to try to find a lender who would advance you the amount needed to redeem the property.

The answer to the question of whether you have redemption rights following a foreclosure depends on local law, so don't count on having the right to redeem without first checking with a local lawyer.

With all this to consider, contacting a lawyer as soon as possible after fore-closure procedures are threatened is essential. Then you and your attorney can discuss the pending deadlines and plan your strategy accordingly.

Modifying home mortgages: Special restrictions

Sometimes you can restructure mortgages in a Chapter 13, but special restrictions sometimes apply when modifying residential mortgages. If they do apply, the only modification allowed is making up back payments under the plan and continuing to make all future regular monthly payments after the petition date.

The following mortgages aren't entitled to special residential mortgage protection:

✔ **Loans secured by other property in addition to your home:** For example, a lender may take a security interest in your $100 junk car in addition to the mortgage. That decision — and it's not all that unusual — can cost the bank a bundle. If your home was worth $75,000 and you owed $100,000 on a mortgage that was not entitled to protection as a residen-tial mortgage, a Chapter 13 can enable you to reduce the principal amount of the loan balance to the value of your home ($75,000). If the mortgage were entitled to protection, you'd eventually end up paying the entire $100,000 to keep your home.

Sometimes lenders, sensing an approaching bankruptcy, will discover their blunders and magnanimously offer to release collateral like the junk car. Don't let them do this without first talking to a lawyer.

✔ **Loans that are due, or will come due, during the next five years:** This is common with home-equity loans requiring *balloon payments* where you make really small payments for a few years, basically covering only the interest, and then having to pay off the entire balloon portion of the loan in a lump sum.

✔ **Loans that in reality are completely unsecured because the property is fully encumbered by prior mortgages:** Lenders of first mortgages usually won't approve loans that are more than the property is worth.

Lenders of second mortgages, on the other hand, are more inclined to gamble, often stupidly. These home-equity lenders are so blinded by the prospect of making a highly profitable loan that they don't seriously consider whether the property already is fully encumbered.

When your home isn't worth more than the first mortgage, many courts conclude that a second mortgage isn't protected and may be eliminated. But if your property is worth as little as a buck more than the amount due on the first mortgage, the entire second mortgage is protected and must be paid if you want to keep your home. For example, if you owe $75,000 on a first mortgage and $25,000 on a second, you can eliminate the second mortgage if your home was worth $75,000 or less, but if it was worth $75,001, the second mortgage is protected. *Note:* Courts disagree on whether the property should be valued as of the time the loan was made, or as of the petition date.

Your options when the restrictions on modifying home mortgages don't apply

In situations where the restrictions on modifying home mortgages don't apply, you can actually restructure and possibly reduce your mortgage. You can:

- Propose to suspend payments until you can sell the property to pay off the secured claim
- Restructure the debt and reduce the interest rate
- Reduce the balance of the loan through *bifurcation* (also known as cramming down)

In Chapter 10, we explain the idea of *cramdown,* a situation in which a Chapter 13 debtor pays the value of collateral rather than the full amount of the debt.

When the collateral is real property, this technique is frequently called *bifurcation,* which means "division into two parts," a secured claim equal to the value of the property and an unsecured claim for the balance of the debt.

The practice of reducing the secured claim to the value of the collateral is sometimes referred to as *stripoff.* Paying the value of the collateral under a Chapter 13 plan is known as *cramdown.* For our purposes, stripoff, cramdown, and bifurcation mean the same thing.

Here's a practical example of bifurcation:

Assume that your property is worth $30,000 but a creditor has a mortgage for $50,000 with monthly payments of $483 for the next 20 years. The creditor has two claims: a secured claim equal to the value of the collateral, or $30,000, and an unsecured claim for the balance, which is

$20,000. The $50,000 claim can be bifurcated by dividing it into a secured claim of $30,000 and an unsecured claim of $20,000. If your plan, like many, proposes only nominal payments to unsecured creditors, bifurcation enables you to reduce the principal amount due on your mortgage from $50,000 to $30,000.

If you continue to make the regular monthly payments of $483, your mortgage will be paid off in 7 years — 13 years ahead of time.

Not bad! Too bad that this option is available only in situations where the special restrictions on modifying home mortgages don't apply.

Comparing Chapter 7 and Chapter 13

Table 11-2 provides a bird's eye view to help you decide whether a Chapter 7 or Chapter 13 is the best way to save your home.

Table 11-2	Saving Your Home — Chapter 7 versus Chapter 13	
Situation	*Chapter 7*	*Chapter 13*
Mortgage payment current, equity within the exemption	Home shouldn't be affected. Regular payments continue.	Home shouldn't be affected. Regular payments should continue, outside the plan if possible to avoid trustee's commission.
Mortgage payments behind, equity within the exemption	The trustee won't assert an interest, but you will have to make up all the back payments immediately unless the mortgage company agrees otherwise.	Must resume regular monthly payments and make up back payments over the life of the plan. (The Bankruptcy Code requires that back payments on residential mortgages be brought current within a "reasonable time" under the Chapter 13 plan. Some courts have said that back payments must be brought current in the early stages of the plan, but most say that they can be stretched over the full three to five years of the plan.)
Equity is greater than exemption	Trustee can sell your home, pay you the amount of the exemption, and pay the rest to your creditors.	Trustee can't sell your home. However, plan payments will be higher to cover the amount of your nonexempt equity over the life of the plan.

(continued)

Table 11-2 (continued)

Situation	Chapter 7	Chapter 13
No equity, mortgage is more than property is worth and is in default (you're behind in payments)	Temporarily stops foreclosure. Chapter 7 won't save home, but it will extinguish personal liability on the loan.	If mortgages don't qualify for special protection given residential mortgages, bifurcation is an option. (Despite the rule against modifying residential mortgages, many courts have allowed bifurcation in cases where the creditor has other collateral in addition to your home, where there is no equity in securing the loan, where the home is other than a single family residence, where the entire loan balance will come due within the next five years, or possibly where in the case of mobile and manufactured homes are concerned.)

ANECDOTE

"Due on sale" — A snake in the grass, and a pain in your . . .

Most mortgages contain a *due-on-sale clause* that says if the property is sold or liens attached to it, the entire loan becomes due now . . . right now. Generally, nobody pays any attention to these clauses — not even the lender — and they are routinely ignored. In fact, just about everyone who obtains a second mortgage violates this provision. Regardless, it's a hazard lurking in the tall grass, like a venomous snake.

Although most lenders won't bother attempting to enforce these clauses, a few mortgage creditors scour loan documents searching for due-on-sale clauses whenever a borrower files Chapter 13. If you bought your house subject to an existing mortgage and the seller didn't obtain the mortgage company's consent, or if you have allowed other liens to attach to the property, the mortgage company may claim that the loan is in default and can't be remedied, even in a Chapter 13. Many courts are siding — rather unhappily — with creditors on this issue.

When Archie and Edith bought their home from Fred and Ethel, they didn't get their own mortgage. Instead they just started making payments on the existing mortgage. Although the mortgage company accepted payments from Archie and Edith, it never gave its official consent to their purchase of the home. The bank neglected to complain until after Archie and Edith filed Chapter 13, and then it asked for court permission to foreclose on the grounds that the due-on-sale clause had been violated. While acknowledging that most courts would go the other way, the bankruptcy court in this case ruled against the bank, so Archie and Edith kept their home.

It was, however, a close call.

So far, only a few mortgage companies have made this argument, but you still should have your mortgage documents carefully examined by a lawyer for possible violations of a due-on-sale clause so that a strategy for dealing with the issue can be developed if it ever comes up.

Chapter 13 saves the day after injury

Grant and Nicole lived from paycheck to paycheck the way many couples do. When Grant fell off his bike and broke his shoulder, he couldn't work for three months. Nicole's salary wasn't enough to put food on the table and pay the mortgage, so they fell behind. Later, when Grant got back on his feet, they dutifully resumed their payments, but the bank still wanted to foreclose because of the three missed payments.

Like a growing number of people, Grant and Nicole were virtually pushed into bankruptcy by the foolish policy of their mortgageholder. As would be expected, they filed Chapter 13 bankruptcy and the court protected their home and allowed them to make up the missed mortgage payments over three years. The lender got its money, Grant and Nicole kept their house, and, thanks to sensible bankruptcy laws, everybody's happy.

Preserving your homestead isn't always a simple matter, and you can unwittingly lose your exemption if you're not excruciatingly careful. Consult a bankruptcy lawyer before refinancing your home, renting it out, moving, signing a contact to sell, making improvements, or allowing a judgment or tax lien to be filed. And keep in mind that while a Chapter 13 bankruptcy is open — that is, while you're making payments — moving, renting your home, or entering into a contract to sell your home are risky steps to be taking.

Using Truth-in-Lending Laws

So far, we've addressed powers provided under the Bankruptcy Code, but another federal law gives you the power to cancel liens on your home. It's called the Truth-in-Lending Act (TILA), which is doubly powerful when used in conjunction with a Chapter 13 filing.

When you borrow money against your home, the TILA gives you a three-day cooling off period in which to cancel the transaction. The lender must give you written notice that you have this right. The TILA also requires the lender to provide you with written disclosures of finance and other charges related to your loan.

If a lender doesn't disclose the required information in connection with a *non*purchase-money loan, you can cancel the transaction at any time within the following three years or whenever you sell your home, whichever comes first.

ANECDOTE

The Truth-in-Lending Act: An arrow in your quiver

When Claude received a $22,000 home-equity loan, he agreed to pay a $3,000 fee to the lender's agent for arranging the loan. The lender violated the Truth-in-Lending Act by not including this fee in the finance-charge category on the disclosure statement. Two years later, when the lender called the loan, Claude's lawyer gave notice he was *rescinding* the loan and filed a Chapter 13 bankruptcy for Claude. The bankruptcy court canceled the mortgage and wiped out the debt.

Likewise, if you want to cancel a lien against your home under TILA without bankruptcy, you must return the money to the lender. However, if you were to file bankruptcy, some courts allow you to cancel a lien without returning the money. That's a great deal — if your local court will play ball. Some do, some don't. So don't make any assumptions.

In addition to the TILA, your state's truth-in-lending law may cover you. If your state has such a law, your rights are likely to be greater under the state statute than they are with the federal provision. Some states enable you to cancel a lien even though it may be too late to do so under the TILA. Others aren't quite so forgiving. Your lawyer can advise you on the best course of action for your particular case.

Coping When Your Dream Home Becomes a Nightmare

Regrettably, more and more people are discovering that they can't handle their mortgage payments because they were suckered into taking second mortgages (home-equity loans) to pay off their credit cards. Paying the first mortgage and the home-equity mortgage is just too much. They may also realize that they've used up all the equity in their home and now owe more on mortgages than their houses are worth.

If you're in this predicament, you have our sympathy. You may have used your life savings to buy the home, put down roots, and enroll your children in the schools of your choice, but now you must think about giving it all up because you were conned into taking a second mortgage.

So, now it's time to bite the bullet and be brutally honest with yourself. If you try to keep your home when you really can't afford to make your mortgage payments, keeping your home may not put you on the road to financial recovery. Struggling to keep up with overwhelming mortgage payments will likely drag you down again.

Your best choice may be to file under Chapter 7 and allow the mortgage-holder to foreclose. What's the point in making further payments, provided that you have someplace to go and the funds to do so? Instead, use the money that you'd normally pay on the mortgage to find a new place to live or to pay for moving expenses.

Creditors sometimes are willing to pay you something for a *deed in lieu of foreclosure,* so they can avoid the expenses of foreclosure. In that situation, you relinquish your interest in the property in exchange for a modest payment, perhaps $1,000, and agree to move out within a specific period of time. Although this may be a good deal, don't take it without first exploring the income tax consequences (capital gains taxes) of making such a transaction (or sale).

Nevertheless, you may still want to keep your home even though you have no established equity, especially if you think its value will appreciate or if you're worried about finding a place to live after your bankruptcy. We explore ways of saving your home without filing bankruptcy in Chapter 6.

Part IV
Getting Rid of (Most of) Your Debt

The 5th Wave — By Rich Tennant

"I don't care what chapter of bankruptcy I file for, as long as it doesn't read like a Stephen King novel or end with a cliffhanger."

In this part . . .

Your aim is to get rid of your debts, and to a large extent, bankruptcy does that. For the most part, debts incurred before you file bankruptcy are eliminated, and debts that arise after you file are not. But when you're dealing with credit cards — and you almost certainly are — the game's a little different. Ditto with taxes, fines, child support, and student loans. This section goes into the nitty-gritty of what debts that hang on like a bad cold you can cure in bankruptcy and how to put yourself in the best position for receiving the most relief possible.

Chapter 12

Lingering Obligations

In This Chapter

▶ Distinguishing debts from other obligations

▶ Living with the 60-day bar date

▶ Borrowing to cover nondischargeable debts

▶ Knowing about reaffirmation agreements

▶ Watching out for the ultimate bankruptcy bummer — denial or revocation of discharge

*B*ankruptcy may not provide an escape route for each and every one of your financial obligations. Some debts are much like fly paper. They seem to stick to you no matter what. Your left foot gets stuck, and when you try to free that one, the right gets stuck. Try pushing away with your hands, and your tootsies come free, but now your paws are snared.

Escaping some debts would defy even the talents of Harry Houdini. But escape from others is possible if you just have the key. This chapter is that key. In it, we identify obligations that are just plain immune from bankruptcy and others that you may be able to shuck. You'll also discover rare situations in which *all* a person's debts survive because his bankruptcy discharge is denied or revoked.

Recognizing (Possibly) Indelible Debts

In Chapter 10, we look at *secured debts,* such as those backed up by your house or car, and explain that auto finance companies and mortgage lenders can still repossess or foreclose after you file bankruptcy. A handful of other obligations also survive bankruptcy and stick to you like hot tar, including:

- ✔ Those that are *not* technically "debts"
- ✔ Debts arising *after* bankruptcy

- Specific types of debts that the Bankruptcy Code preserves — *nondischargeable debts*

  We devote entire chapters to the most common of these: fraud and credit card abuse — Chapters 13, 15; taxes — Chapter 14; divorce obligations — Chapter 16; student loans — Chapter 17.

- Some debts that were not properly listed on bankruptcy documents

- Any debt you reaffirmed (or reagreed to after bankruptcy)

- All your debts if the court denies or revokes your bankruptcy discharge

However, you can escape some of these sticky debts in some cases:

- By successfully completing a Chapter 13 repayment plan

- By watching for creditors who are asleep at the switch in a Chapter 7 case and miss the deadline (the *60-day bar date*) for challenging your bankruptcy

- By filing a proof of claim (a document that must be filed with the court before a creditor can receive any payments from the trustee) so that at least part of the nondischargeable debt is paid by the trustee

But before going on, you must get a handle on the nature of the debt beast, so that you're better able to tell when you have a real tiger which bankruptcy can't tame or only a paper feline, which merely requires a little special handling.

Confronting obligations enforceable by court orders

Start with this premise: Courts usually don't force people to perform most contracts; they merely assess damages for nonperformance. For example, courts won't order you to pay a loan under penalty of contempt. They simply enter a judgment against you for some amount of money.

Monetary damages are inadequate where some contracts are concerned. For example, if you sold someone your business and signed a *noncompete covenant* (agreeing not to open a new competing business) and then turned around and set up shop across the street, the court may grant an *injunction,* which is just a court order where the judge says, with a bit more tact, "Yo, wise guy, get outta town or I'm gonna slap you with a fine or toss your butt in jail!"

Similarly, famous performers and prizefighters often agree to work exclusively for one promoter — a promise, enforced by an injunction, not to work for anyone else.

Most courts say promises that are enforceable by injunctions can't be avoided by bankruptcy, because no debt — as the law defines it — needs to be wiped out.

Debts arising after bankruptcy

For the most part, bankruptcy wipes out debts that arise prior to bankruptcy, but not those arising afterward. Therefore, it is a good idea to carefully decide not only *whether* you need to file bankruptcy, but also *when*.

Debts arise when the events causing the liability occur and not when you get the bill. When you buy something on credit, the debt *arises* at the moment of purchase, not when your credit-card statement comes in the mail. Similarly, if you cause a car wreck, your liability arises when the accident occurred, even though claims aren't made against you until much later.

Occasionally, people discover that they filed bankruptcy too soon. For example, if you file bankruptcy right before undergoing extensive medical treatment, the medical bills resulting from your treatment won't be included in the bankruptcy. Most of the medical bills, it is hoped, are covered by insurance and you'll be able to pay the balance. But you can never be sure. In a situation like that, postponing bankruptcy until the dust settles and you know exactly where you stand may be best.

Postpetition charges on prepetition contracts

Charges arising after bankruptcy (*postpetition charges*) under a contract that you made prior to bankruptcy (a *prepetition contract*) are usually wiped out. For example, if you surrender your car to the finance company before bankruptcy and the lender sells it at auction after bankruptcy but doesn't receive the total amount owed, tough beans. The lender can't come after you, because the debt was discharged as a prepetition debt because you borrowed the money when you signed the loan papers. See Chapter 5 for an explanation of how events occurring prior to a bankruptcy filing (prepetition) frequently have different ramifications than those occurring after the filing. In Chapter 9, we describe how and why most things you acquire after the day your bankruptcy is filed aren't affected by your bankruptcy.

However, courts disagree about when certain contractual debts arise.

Say, for example, that prior to bankruptcy, your dad let you use his credit card because you promised to make the payments and *indemnify* (reimburse him) if the credit-card company ever came after Pop. When you file bankruptcy and stop making the payments to the credit-card company, your dad has to step up and pay off the card. In this case, your promise to indemnify kicks in after bankruptcy. Does that mean your promise to reimburse Dad is nondischargeable? Most — but definitely not all — courts will let you off the hook because the actual promise was made prior to bankruptcy.

Divorce awards

Sometimes divorces are pending when bankruptcy is filed. Divorce decrees commonly require one spouse to pay certain bills and indemnify the other for any losses. The final divorce decree, however, is often not entered until after the bankruptcy petition date. This raises the question of whether the obligations created by the divorce decree are pre or post bankruptcy. See Chapter 16 for more on that chicken-and-egger.

Condo charges

If you intend to give up a condominium as part of your bankruptcy, watch out for condo fees that are assessed after bankruptcy. Fees already assessed at the time you file are dischargeable, just like most debts. But fees arising after bankruptcy, while you were still in possession of or received rents from the property, aren't wiped out in a Chapter 7.

Say that you stopped making $700 mortgage payments on your condo, but planned to live there until foreclosure was complete. That way, you'd save money that you'd otherwise use to pay the mortgage (see Chapter 11). You'd also stop making your $300 monthly condo fee. When you file bankruptcy, you wipe out both obligations, and mortgage payments that come due after bankruptcy. By contrast, you're still on the hook for condo fees that accrue after bankruptcy while you're still living in the condo.

After you find a new place to live, get out of the condo as quickly as you can so condo fees don't stack up against you. You also need to send a letter (certified mail, return receipt requested) to the condo association notifying them that you're vacating the premises and providing them with the name and address of the mortgageholder.

Unlisted debts

Sometimes, folks forget to list all their debts on their bankruptcy papers.

In a Chapter 13, debts not listed on your bankruptcy papers aren't discharged unless you amend your filing to include the creditor within 90 days of the 341 meeting. For more about the 341 meeting, see Chapter 5.

In a Chapter 7 *asset case* (where assets are sold and proceeds are paid to your creditors), an unlisted debt isn't discharged unless you can prove that the creditor had notice or actually knew about your bankruptcy in time to file a proof of claim — generally within 90 days of the 341 meeting.

Rock star can't use bankruptcy to dump record company

Rock star Demonic Dan signed with Moon Records, even though he was under an exclusive contract with Goon Recordings. When Goon asked a court to enter an injunction forbidding Dan from performing for Moon, Dan filed bankruptcy to discharge the recording contract with Goon.

The bankruptcy judge said, "No dice!"

The bankruptcy court ruled that Dan's obligation to Goon under the exclusive recording contract wasn't a debt subject to discharge in bankruptcy. So, despite his bankruptcy, Dan must still honor his commitment and can only perform for Goon Records.

Most courts say that debts not listed in *no-asset cases* (where no assets are actually liquidated: This category accounts for 96 percent of all bankruptcies) are discharged because the creditor wouldn't receive any money even when the debt was listed. Keep in mind, though, that this stipulation isn't an invitation for sloppiness.

When the time comes to clean up your credit reports after bankruptcy, you can easily show credit bureaus that a particular debt was included in bankruptcy by providing a copy of your bankruptcy schedules. In the case of unlisted debts, you have to prove that in your jurisdiction unlisted debts in no-asset cases are eliminated and that yours was a no-asset case. Sometimes you even have to hire a lawyer to make this point.

Another reason to be as careful as possible when listing all your debts is to obtain the benefit of the *60-day bar date*. See the "Sweating Out the 60-Day Bar Date" section later in this chapter.

Debts preserved under sections of the Bankruptcy Code

The Bankruptcy Code says certain types of debts are nondischargeable. Some debts that are nondischargeable in a Chapter 7 may still be discharged whenever you complete a Chapter 13 plan in which you receive a super discharge. See Chapter 4 for more on the benefits of choosing a Chapter 13 over Chapter 7. Table 12-1 lists nondischargeable debts and how they're respectively treated in Chapter 7 and Chapter 13 bankruptcies.

Table 12-1   Nondischargeable Debts: Chapter 7 versus Chapter 13

Type of Debt	Chapter 7	Chapter 13
Income taxes (see Table in Chapter 14)		
Employment taxes	Not dischargeable unless barred by the ten-year statute of limitations	Same as Chapter 7 and also must be paid in full under Chapter 13 plan
Loans to pay nondischargeable federal (but not state) taxes	Not dischargeable	Dischargeable
Debts from fraud (including credit-card charges made with no intention of paying and those made on the eve of bankruptcy)	Not dischargeable	Dischargeable
Welfare and unemployment benefits wrongfully received	Not dischargeable if benefits received fraudulently. Even if dischargeable, may be deducted from future benefit payments.	Dischargeable, but future benefits may be reduced to recoup payments wrongfully received.
Real and personal property taxes	Not dischargeable if assessed against the property owner rather than just the property and were incurred less than one year before bankruptcy.	Same as Chapter 7 and also must be paid in full under Chapter 13 plan
Claims for willful and malicious conduct	Not dischargeable	Dischargeable
Claims for theft or embezzlement	Not dischargeable	Dischargeable
Criminal fines and criminal restitution	Not dischargeable	Same as Chapter 7
Noncriminal restitution	Dischargeable unless restitution is considered a fine	Dischargeable

Type of Debt	Chapter 7	Chapter 13
Noncriminal fines nonand penalties (other than tax penalties)	Not dischargeable	Dischargeable, but payment may result in criminal prosecution
Personal-injury claims from drunk driving	Not dischargeable	Same as Chapter 7
Marital property divisions	Dischargeable if debtor lacks ability to pay or would suffer more than ex-spouse if forced to repay	Dischargeable
Marital and domestic support obligations	Not dischargeable	Not dischargeable, and must be paid in full under Chapter 13 plan
Student loans	Not discharged unless undue hardship can be proved	Same as Chapter 7
Motor-vehicle tickets and fines	Not dischargeable	Dischargeable if offense was a minor infraction such as a parking ticket or equipment violation. But local authorities may give you grief for wiping them out. Nondischargeable where the conduct was criminal. For example, driving with a suspended license.
Unlisted debts	*May* be dischargeable in a no-asset case	Not dischargeable

Sweating Out the 60-day Bar Date

Some debts listed in Table 12-1 actually are only *potentially* nondischargeable. A creditor with one of these types of debts must file an *adversary proceeding* — a minilawsuit filed in the bankruptcy court — within 60 days of your 341 meeting with creditors (don't confuse this with filing a *proof of claim,* which requests funds from the bankruptcy estate). An adversary proceeding to except a debt from discharge seeks to keep the debtor on the hook for the debt despite bankruptcy.

If a creditor wants to use any of the grounds in the following list to try to keep its debt from being discharged, that creditor must meet the 60-day deadline.

- ✔ Fraud
- ✔ Embezzlement or theft
- ✔ Willful and malicious conduct
- ✔ Marital property divisions

When the creditor misses this deadline, you're off the hook, provided that the creditor:

- ✔ Was properly listed on your bankruptcy papers, or
- ✔ Knew of your bankruptcy in time to file an adversary proceeding

The *60-day bar date* applies only in Chapter 7 liquidation cases. That's because these types of debts aren't excepted from a Chapter 13 discharge, unless you request a *hardship discharge* in your Chapter 13 case. See Chapter 19 for the scoop on undue hardship.

If you owe one of these potentially dischargeable debts, you may still want to file Chapter 7 and sweat it out. If the creditor doesn't file an adversary proceeding in time, you're home free. But when the creditor files an adversary, you still can convert your Chapter 7 case to Chapter 13 and get rid of the debt that way — although doing so commits you to a partial repayment program for at least the next three years. In other words, don't sign on to a Chapter 13 repayment plan unless you have to.

You need to discuss this strategy fully with your lawyer before you file. A few judges think this approach prevents the debtor from satisfying the "good faith" requirement for a Chapter 13 and would refuse to allow conversion.

Avoiding the Urge to Borrow to Pay Nondischargeable Debts

Most loans are dischargeable. So, some people are tempted to take out a bank loan or a cash advance on a credit card to pay a would-be nondischargeable debt, with the aim of discharging the new loan in bankruptcy and essentially trying to replace nondischargeable debt with dischargeable debt.

Bad idea.

If the lender can prove that was your plan all along, the new loan wouldn't be discharged in a Chapter 7 — because of fraud — and could be grounds for dismissing any Chapter 13 filing on bad faith grounds.

Remember that the trustee can also recover some kinds of payments made before bankruptcy and distribute the funds among all your creditors (see Chapter 18). So, not only do you risk the lender's wrath, but also the nondischargeable debt you intended to pay is revived — a double whammy!

Funds borrowed to pay nondischargeable federal income taxes aren't dischargeable in a Chapter 7, even though you weren't planning to file bankruptcy when you took out the loan. See Chapter 14 to find out which taxes are nondischargeable.

Understanding Reaffirmation Agreements

Any debt that is reaffirmed is not eliminated.

Reaffirmation is a process by which you agree to pay all or part of a debt that otherwise is wiped out in bankruptcy. It's as if you never filed bankruptcy on that particular debt; the creditor has all the remedies available before bankruptcy. He can sue you, repossess collateral . . . whatever.

In the old days, creditors used a number of ploys to trick people into reaffirming their debts. Sometimes, if a debtor merely acknowledged the existence of the discharged debt, it automatically was revived. The 1978 Bankruptcy Code sought to put an end to those shenanigans by requiring that reaffirmation agreements be in writing, filed with the court, and subject to cancellation by the debtors for 60 days. In addition, the bankruptcy court must conclude, based on information from the debtor or the debtor's attorney, that reaffirmation doesn't impose an undue hardship and is in the debtor's best interest.

Reasons to reaffirm

Why on earth would someone file Chapter 7 to wipe out her debts and then turn around and reaffirm? Isn't that the ultimate hair-of-the-dog? Good point. But people do reaffirm, and sometimes for good reasons. The reasons folks typically reaffirm are so they can:

- **Keep collateral that secures the debt.** In some jurisdictions, you must reaffirm any time you want to keep collateral subject to an unavoidable lien (see Chapter 10) — unless you *redeem* by paying the value of the collateral in a lump sum. In other places, however, you don't have to reaffirm if you're current on a secured debt when you file bankruptcy. You can continue to make future payments without reaffirming the debt. That's a good deal because you have only to continue making postpetition payments as long as you want to keep the collateral. Down the road, if you decide that you no longer want to keep the collateral, you can simply surrender it to the creditor and you won't be responsible for any deficiency. Creditors, however, hate it when consumers keep goods without agreeing to pay the full amount of the loan, and some courts insist that debtors actually sign a reaffirmation agreement on the loan or redeem the collateral if they want to keep it. Your lawyer will be aware of local practices.

✔ **Maintain credit privileges.** Creditors often offer to extend new credit when you agree to reaffirm a portion of an existing account. Accepting such credit rarely is a good idea. By recognizing that the amount you reaffirm is essentially a finance charge for the new loan, you can see how ridiculously expensive the new credit is. Besides, you probably won't have that much trouble getting new credit anyway.

✔ **Compromise a debt to a creditor claiming to have grounds for declaring the debt nondischargeable.** Often a creditor will go away if you reaffirm just a portion of the disputed debt rather than the whole thing. Reaffirming to settle a potentially nondischargeable debt makes sense only if a creditor has a good case. Your lawyer will know when the creditor is bluffing.

Changing your mind

Even when you sign a reaffirmation agreement, you still can change your mind if you write to the creditor before your discharge is entered or within 60 days after the agreement is filed with the bankruptcy court, whichever is later.

Some creditors don't bother filing reaffirmation agreements with the court, so be sure to find out whether a reaffirmation agreement was filed whenever a creditor tries to sue you on a reaffirmation agreement after bankruptcy. If the agreement was never filed with the bankruptcy court, you still can cancel it.

Having Your Discharge Denied or Revoked

The bankruptcy court has the power in a Chapter 7 case to deny your discharge altogether so that *none* of your debts are erased. That's obviously a stinker. You already surrendered any nonexempt property, your credit record is besmirched with a bankruptcy, and you still owe all your debts. And, to make matters worse, you can never file Chapter 7 on these debts. Now why would a judge do such a nasty thing? Read on.

Grounds for denial of a Chapter 7 discharge

A Chapter 7 discharge can be denied if you:

- ✔ Consciously fail to list an asset on your bankruptcy schedules
- ✔ Intentionally give false information in your schedules
- ✔ Lie to the trustee at the 341 meeting
- ✔ Refuse to cooperate with the trustee
- ✔ Disobey an order of the bankruptcy court
- ✔ Fraudulently transfer property within one year before bankruptcy
- ✔ Act too aggressively in converting nonexempt assets into exempt assets (see Chapter 9)

Protecting your discharge

The best way to ensure that you receive a discharge is to be completely truthful and make a full disclosure to your lawyer before you file.

If you put property in someone else's name, money into someone else's bank account, or otherwise try to protect any assets from creditors, be sure to tell your lawyer. These errors usually can be repaired when action is taken *before* you file bankruptcy. Afterward, it may be too late. So, remaining silent and hoping that no one finds out about these kinds of transfers is very dangerous. Don't risk it.

Your lawyer needs to give you copies of all the schedules filed with the bankruptcy court. Review them to make sure that all your assets are listed. Innocent mistakes can easily be fixed if you act promptly, especially when you correct your bankruptcy papers before the 341 meeting with creditors. If someone else points out the error, you may have trouble claiming that the mistake was an innocent one.

The good news is that courts rarely deny a discharge. When denials do occur, it's usually in cases of obvious misrepresentation or refusal to cooperate.

When you're completely truthful with your lawyer right from the beginning, she can give you a pretty good idea whether there's any real danger of your discharge being denied.

Revoking your discharge

Although extremely rare, a Chapter 7 or Chapter 13 discharge may be revoked whenever it is obtained by fraud, and the party asking for the revocation did not know about the fraud prior to discharge. *Note:* We're referring to fraud in the bankruptcy case, *not* fraud in incurring the debt in the first place.

A Chapter 7 discharge may also be revoked if you:

- ✔ Fail to report or surrender property of the estate
- ✔ Intentionally refused to obey an order of the court

Chapter 13

A House of Cards: Wiping Out Credit-Card Debts

In This Chapter

▶ Drowning in a plastic sea

▶ Looking at your motivation when you incurred debt

▶ Recognizing bogus charges of fraud

▶ Turning the tables on credit-card bullies

▶ Avoiding the pitfalls of credit-card balance transfers

▶ Risking dismissal for credit-card abuses

Almost every consumer who faces bankruptcy has some credit-card debts, and most are up to their gills in it. You'd think that credit-card companies, instead of perpetually whining about the relatively meager losses that are attributable to bankruptcy, would instead dispense credit more responsibly.

And you'd be wrong.

Although bankruptcies force some lenders to be a little more careful, most continue dispensing credit with reckless abandon. Because credit-card debt is such a pervasive element in bankruptcy, understanding the fact, fiction, nuances, and implications surrounding it is important. In this chapter, we reveal how creditors play the game, how they sometimes try to pin you for fraud, and how you can avoid getting stuck with the Old Maid card.

Playing the Credit-Card Game

Credit-card lending is the most profitable segment of banking — which is no surprise given the heads-we-win/tails-you-lose way lenders play the game.

Credit companies: Their home is your hassle

Did you ever wonder why most credit-card companies claim Delaware or South Dakota as their home state? No? Well maybe you should. It's pretty clever.

In 1978, the U.S. Supreme Court opened the floodgates for consumer lending with its decision in what's known as the *Marquette Case*. The Court ruled that national banks can export the interest rate of the state in which the bank is located to its out-of-state customers and credit-card holders without running afoul of the usury laws of the customers' home states. This decision, in effect, deregulated control of interest rates by individual states and emasculated state usury laws.

Delaware and South Dakota figured they could attract big lenders by eliminating interest rate restrictions in the wake of *Marquette*.

They were right.

All too often, people accept unsolicited, preapproved credit-card offers that, simply put, make getting into credit trouble all too easy. Borrowers max out their credit cards but find themselves making only the minimum monthly payments at interest rates of around 15 percent (and often higher). Fifteen percent is the average. With this kind of dutiful payment practice in place, credit-card companies happily skim off profits of double, triple, or even quadruple the prime-lending rate. Oh, happy days!

And these unsolicited, preapproved credit-card offers never seem to stop coming (even when your credit report tanks), tempting people to apply for *another* credit card that promises an *additional* credit limit and *increased* borrowing power with which they can cover the monthly minimum payments on their first credit card. Ah, yes, this vicious circle truly is how the credit-card game works. And, you know what? Consumers rarely win.

Whenever you find yourself on the losing side of the credit-card game, consult a bankruptcy lawyer to explore your options and develop a comprehensive plan for handling the problem before it gets worse.

Don't give in to the temptation of paying off your debts by using the equity in your home. Sure, the interest rate on a home-equity loan may be lower and the interest you pay may be tax deductible, but when you're struggling to make only minimum payments on credit cards, you'll probably have the same kind of trouble making payments on a home-equity loan and face losing your most important asset in the process. Before taking a home-equity loan, your homestead may well be off-limits to credit-card lenders, even if you don't file bankruptcy. When you take out a home-equity loan, you put your house on the line for debts that probably can be eliminated in bankruptcy, or maybe just ignored.

Watch out for debt-consolidation outfits that may try to convince you to make futile attempts at repaying your debts without clearly informing you that your creditors are paying them a percentage of the money they collect from you. Some borrowers succeed in paying their debts through consolidation, but many people make payments for years only to eventually end up in bankruptcy.

Seeing What Judges See

Bankruptcy judges are growing increasingly unsympathetic with credit-card predators who have the gall to come into their courts and claim that *they* were the ones defrauded. Although your odds of finding a sympathetic judge seem to be increasing, the rule of law reigns, and few judges will violate their legal and ethical obligations to apply that rule just because they don't like the way a credit-card company operates. That said, what you need is an understanding of the legal framework so that you can judge for yourself whether a credit-card company has a legitimate complaint against you.

Ordinarily, credit-card charges are dischargeable, meaning they disappear when you go through bankruptcy proceedings. But in Chapter 7 cases, credit-card issuers sometimes try to prevent the discharge of their claims by charging that a debtor used a card fraudulently.

Creditors argue that when someone uses a credit card, he implies that he has the ability and intent to pay. If it turns out that the customer couldn't afford to pay the charges, he's guilty of fraud . . . or so goes the theory of creditors.

Some courts buy this argument, but most find it simplistic, and absent additional circumstances, not terribly persuasive, for reasons that are all but self-evident: Although a customer's use of a credit card may imply that he *intends* to pay, it should not imply that he has the present *ability to pay*. After all, many folks use credit cards precisely because they're short of cash — which is precisely what credit-card companies encourage in their endless solicitations.

Remember that Chapter 13 bankruptcy offers a *super discharge* for debtors who successfully complete a Chapter 13 plan. In other words, debts from fraud are wiped out in Chapter 13.

Whenever you're in serious danger of being accused of credit-card abuse, you need to consider filing Chapter 13 rather than Chapter 7. You may find that committing to modest payments under a Chapter 13 plan is less stressful (and possibly even less expensive) than defending against fraud charges in Chapter 7 — even if you eventually win. In the majority of cases, filing

Chapter 13 avoids the problem altogether. But you nevertheless must file in good faith. If you maxed out your credit cards thinking that you'd just eliminate your obligations through bankruptcy, you may have a tough time convincing the judge that you're filing Chapter 13 in good faith.

Examining Your Mind-set When You Incurred the Debt

Figuring out whether you acted fraudulently, or just foolishly, takes something of a mind-reading act for the court to accomplish. The court isn't really looking for an excuse to slam you, but if you give the judge a reason, there's a good chance you'll get whacked with a fraud judgment. In addition to the obvious subjective element, a number of objective questions come into play. You may want to ask yourself:

- **Did I make a bunch of charges right before bankruptcy?** It's obvious that the closer to bankruptcy that the charges occur, the more likely that a judge may think that you never intended to pay.

  In fact, luxury purchases or cash advances totaling more than $1,150 (the amount changes every three years, with the next change scheduled April 1, 2004) to a single creditor within 60 days of bankruptcy are presumed by the courts to be fraudulent.

  A number of small charges within a very short time when an account is in default or over the limit may suggest that the customer purposely kept charges below levels where a merchant is likely to check the card (knowing that the lender would never authorize them). Particularly damning are multiple small charges on the same day. Changes in your charging habits may also indicate an intention not to pay. If, for example, you typically charged about $150 per month, and then a few months before bankruptcy you started charging like crazy, a court may be inclined to think that you bought things on credit while planning to file bankruptcy.

- **Did I make charges after talking to a bankruptcy lawyer?** Whenever you charge purchases after talking to a bankruptcy attorney, appearances point to your already having decided to file bankruptcy when you bought the stuff on credit. However, courts realize that many people visit a bankruptcy attorney just to find out their options and many never end up filing or, at best, wait as long as possible before doing so. So, the mere fact that you charge some purchases after talking to a bankruptcy attorney is not conclusive evidence of a fraudulent mental state.

✔ **What was my financial condition when I made the charges?** The fact that a person is in dire financial straits when incurring debt is relevant as to whether he intended to pay but, again, it isn't definitive. If you honestly believed that things would turn around, that a new job would come through, that you'd be able to refinance your home, that your business would take off, and yes, even that your luck would turn around at the gambling casino, you're probably not in trouble.

In the eyes of most judges, the key determination isn't whether you realistically expected to come up with the cash, but whether you honestly (even if foolishly) believed your ship would come in.

✔ **Did I buy luxury items?** The concept here is that someone buying necessities is more likely to repay the debt than someone who purchases luxury items. But a luxury for one person is a necessity for another.

Forcing the Credit-Card Company to Prove Its Case

Courts don't merely consider whether a debtor was at fault in making excessive credit-card charges, they also consider the degree to which creditors irresponsibly push credit cards on folks who can't afford to pay. In keeping you from wiping out the debt, the creditor must prove that it had no reason to know that you were drowning in debt at the time it authorized the charges.

Several courts have ruled that creditors who issue cards to people whose lack of creditworthiness would have been revealed by an ordinary credit report claim that they were defrauded. In other words, if it had exercised just a little prudence, the credit-card company would have known that the last thing you needed was yet another credit card.

The same is true for many creditors that rely on statistical credit scores like the ones prepared by the three national credit bureaus — Equifax, Trans Union, and Experian. Each company has a protocol for its scoring system, but all are based on a computer credit model called the Fair, Isaac credit bureau score, sometimes called "FICO." Like it or not, anyone who uses credit cards has a FICO score.

Courts have observed that FICO scores reveal little more than whether a prospective borrower has made timely minimum payments on his account and whether a creditor is justified in basing its decision to extend credit solely on those scores. These courts are less than understanding in cases where credit-card companies conduct no meaningful investigation into creditworthiness before issuing cards. Only when the debtor files bankruptcy does the creditor come up with so many reasons why it wouldn't have extended credit if had it only been aware of the debtor's financial condition — and argues, therefore, that the court should not allow the debtor to wipe out this particular debt.

Explaining Presumptively Fraudulent Charges

Luxury purchases or cash advances totaling more than $1,150 to a single within 60 days of bankruptcy are *presumed fraudulent*. What that means is that you must convince the court that you intended to pay for the charges, but the creditor doesn't have to prove your intentions were fraudulent. In other words, the burden of proof shifts to you, and it can be a heavy one.

However, every judge has a different idea of how to define "luxury," and you can rebut the presumption of fraud by proving that you intended to pay. A prudent bankruptcy attorney attempts to sidestep any problems with presumptively fraudulent charges by simply waiting at least 60 days from the client's last significant credit purchase before filing the bankruptcy. However, the client may have other reasons and considerations that make an immediate filing necessary. For example, if a foreclosure sale is imminent and you want to keep your house, you probably can't afford to wait, but you can anticipate that your recent credit purchases may be called into question.

Defending Against False Financial Statement Allegations

Occasionally, a creditor, seeking to prevent its account from being wiped out by bankruptcy, claims fraud on the grounds that the customer obtained credit privileges through the use of a false financial statement.

Most modern credit-card applications ask for little more than a name, address, Social Security number, and income. As credit companies request less and less information on their loan applications, claiming that you committed fraud by not revealing what wasn't asked becomes more and more difficult for them.

The creditor doesn't necessarily win just because your income was not as high as you indicated on the credit-card application. The creditor must also establish that you knew that your statement was false, that you intended to deceive the company, and that it would not have approved credit privileges if it otherwise had known about your actual income. This gambit is next to impossible to prove, especially when a creditor made its decision based on credit scores and not on the credit application.

Using Credit-Card Advances for Gambling

Many people who get into credit-card trouble are gamblers and, for many problem gamblers, the credit-card industry behaves like an all-too-eager-to-please bartender in a room full of binge drinkers. Some creditors even put ATM machines in gambling casinos, thereby encouraging customers to gamble with cash advances. Then, when a customer ends up in bankruptcy, these same companies try to keep the advances from being wiped out by alleging that the debtor was guilty of fraud for using cash advances for gambling — the very thing that the company encouraged them to do in the first place.

If your only hope of paying your debts was to hit the jackpot, you may be looking at an allegation of credit-card abuse. But, the criteria employed by most judges is not an objective analysis of whether your dream of hitting the big one made sense but rather is a subjective analysis of whether that scenario made sense to you. Your case would be even stronger if, in the past, you used winnings to pay debts.

Bottom line: Even if you used credit cards for gambling, most courts would still allow you to wipe out the charges provided that you honestly believed that you would win enough to repay the charges.

Bullying the Credit-Card Bullies

Creditors are well aware that many debtors are essentially broke and that the last thing they want to do, or are able to do, is pay extra for their bankruptcy attorney to defend them against an allegation of fraud. Sometimes creditors claim fraud in a bankruptcy case regardless of whether the claim has merit, hoping that the debtor settles by agreeing to repay part of the debt.

The Bankruptcy Code, however, provides you with a measure of protection against this sort of arm-twisting. If you put up a fight and win, the creditor can be ordered to pay your attorney fees and, in extreme cases, be fined.

Credit-card company pays the price for bullying

As her credit report duly noted, Claire was buried in debt when a credit-marketing company sent her a preapproved line of credit. Not surprisingly, Claire used the new line of credit in a desperate and misguided attempt to pay off her older bills. When she ended up filing bankruptcy, the credit-card company that extended the credit line tried to prevent the debt that was owed from being wiped out by alleging that Claire fraudulently accepted and used the loan knowing full well she could not pay. Because Claire certainly couldn't afford to pay any more money to her bankruptcy attorney to defend against the fraud, she figured that she'd just have to settle.

Not so fast!

Claire's attorney promptly directed the court's attention to the fact that the credit-card company initiated a frivolous fraud claim in an attempt to extort a settlement from his client. The court not only dismissed the fraud allegation, it also ordered the credit-card company to pay Claire's legal bills.

Transferring Credit-Card Balances

Just about everyone with a mailbox is constantly bombarded with pleas from credit-card lenders to use their low-interest cards to pay off balances on competitors' cards. Odd that these solicitations avoid using words like "borrow" or "loan," isn't it? Instead, they euphemistically label these transactions "balance transfers." Predictably, many people fail to fully realize that the "transfer" actually is a new loan — but that's exactly what it is.

If you're excruciatingly careful and diligent and able to essentially juggle your books without dropping any balls, (and if you were that good at financial gymnastics, you probably wouldn't be reading this book), it is possible to play the transfer game to your advantage. For instance, you can pay off one loan with another loan that carries a lower "teaser" interest rate and save money as long as you pay off the second loan before the interest rate jumps, which it will. In our experience, however, most people who play this game lose, and the people who promote these transfer gimmicks obviously know the odds are against you. In fact, they literally bank on it.

Recognize balance transfers for what they are, and fully explain to your attorney any transfers you've made so that he can decide whether delaying your bankruptcy for a few months would be better.

There are two reasons to delay bankruptcy:

✔ Because a balance transfer is a loan, if you file within 60 days of the transfer, the debt might be presumed to have been fraudulent. See "Explaining Presumptively Fraudulent Charges" earlier in this chapter.

✔ Because a balance transfer is also a payment on an existing debt, if you file bankruptcy within 90 days of the transfer, the trustee could recover the money and thereby complicate your bankruptcy. (See Chapter 18.)

Having a Bankruptcy Dismissed for Credit-Card Abuse

So far in this chapter, we've examined whether a creditor in a Chapter 7 can prevent its particular claim from being wiped out. Folks with massive credit-card debts have something else to worry about. Some courts are now dismissing Chapter 7 cases in which debtors are living extravagant lifestyles (in the eyes of the judge) at their creditors' expense. When it appears that the debtors can repay a significant portion of their debts by merely exercising some spending restraint, a few judges are rejecting Chapter 7 liquidations and pushing debtors into Chapter 13 repayment plans.

Still, these cases are relatively rare and involve pretty extreme situations. Here are a few examples:

✔ Debtors had more than 20 credit cards and owed $224,000. They ran up $14,700 in credit-card debt during the year preceding bankruptcy.

✔ During a six-month period, while unemployed, a debtor incurred $170,000 in credit-card debt, including $60,000 worth of luxury items and $50,000 that was loaned to his traveling companion. The balance was lost gambling.

✔ A debtor owed $79,236 on credit cards, but with a little belt-tightening could probably pay half of her debts within five years.

✔ Debtors owed $59,000, more than $39,000 of which was credit-card debt. Their household income was $65,000. The court thought that their lifestyle was extravagant and, if they tried, the debtors could pay 68 percent of their debts over five years.

The bottom line: If you've been living the lifestyle of the rich and famous at your creditors' expense, you may have more trouble shucking these obligations than someone who unwittingly played and lost the credit-card game.

More than you need to know

If you really want the full scoop on discharging credit-card debts, Jim Caher, who happens to be an attorney and coauthor of the book you're reading, has devoted an entire book to helping lawyers with just that subject. See *Discharging Credit Card Debts in Bankruptcy,* James. P. Caher, LRP Publications, 1998 (www.lrp.com/index.html). *Warning:* The book is very thorough and technical and should be read only by figureheads, eggheads, insomniacs, insufferable nerds — and all lawyers, lawmakers, law professors, and bankruptcy judges.

Chapter 14

Give unto Caesar: Using Bankruptcy to Deal with Tax Debts

• •

In This Chapter

▶ Wiping out federal and state income taxes in bankruptcy

▶ Dealing with other kinds of taxes

▶ Considering a loan to pay your taxes

• •

Sometimes you can get rid of your tax obligations through bankruptcy, but doing so isn't an easy task. Taxes generally can't be discharged in a Chapter 7 bankruptcy and must be paid in full over the life of a Chapter 13 repayment plan. Nevertheless, under a complicated set of rules and court decisions, you may be able to escape paying taxes, if enough time passes between the time you incurred the tax liability and the time that you file bankruptcy.

In this chapter, we explain the circumstances under which you can wipe out your federal and state income taxes and certain other kinds of taxes. We also look briefly at the tactic of borrowing to pay your taxes. See Chapter 8 for nonbankruptcy solutions to your tax problems.

Dealing with the Federal Tax Man

As a general proposition, if you filed a timely, nonfraudulent income tax return and haven't engaged in tax evasion other than simply failing to pay the tax, your debt to Uncle Sam is dischargeable in a Chapter 7 or a Chapter 13 — assuming, that is, the taxes are more than three years old. Simple, right? Of course not.

Nothing is simple when dealing with that veritable monument to Murphy's Law — the good ol' tax statutes.

For example, if a tax return for 1998 was due April 15, 1999, you may reasonably think that if you filed bankruptcy after April 15, 2002, the taxes would vanish, right? But reasonable thinking doesn't necessarily apply. After all, you're dealing with the Internal Revenue Service. If you received an extension of time to file your return, the three-year period starts on the date that the extension (or extensions) expires, or the day you file, whichever comes first. It doesn't start on the date the return originally was due.

Besides extensions, certain events can also interrupt the three-year period, giving the IRS even more time to collect your taxes. For example:

- ✔ If you filed a bankruptcy case prior to your current bankruptcy, the time that the earlier case was open isn't counted and, in the view of some courts, six months more is added to the three years.

- ✔ Any amount of time during which a taxpayer assistance order (where the IRS is ordered to lay off you by the taxpayer advocate) is in effect doesn't count toward the three years. See Chapter 8 for more information on the taxpayer advocate and taxpayer assistance orders.

When you neglect to file a return, file it late, submit a fraudulent return, or otherwise evade taxes, you've really made your life more complicated.

If you filed no return at all, your taxes never will be discharged in a Chapter 7 bankruptcy, regardless of how old they are. The IRS can, and often does, file a *dummy return* — a return filed by the feds in your name so the government can at least assess a tax, but that won't get you off the hook. Some courts even say that a return filed by a taxpayer for whom the IRS already has prepared a dummy return still doesn't start the clock ticking. In other words, unpaid taxes for the year for which a dummy return was filed are nondischargeable in Chapter 7, even though you eventually file your own return.

Even if the taxes are more than three years old, they still aren't dischargeable in Chapter 7 if you filed your return late and if you file bankruptcy less than two years from the date your late tax return was filed. Let's assume, for example, that you owe taxes for 1997, but didn't file your tax return until July 21, 2001. Even though the taxes were more than three years old, they would still not be dischargeable in Chapter 7 if you filed bankruptcy prior to July 22, 2003.

Even if the taxes are more than three years old and you've filed your return more than two years ago, your income taxes would still not be dischargeable in Chapter 7 if the return was fraudulent or if you intentionally tried to evade assessment or collection of the tax.

Taxes are treated in a different way in a Chapter 13 repayment plan. Taxes that are more than three years old can be discharged even when you filed a late or fraudulent return, willfully tried to evade the taxes, or never filed a return at all.

Although taxes (provided they are more than three years old) are dischargeable in Chapter 13 even though you've never filed a tax return, you will still be required to file delinquent returns shortly after filing Chapter 13. So, you should have the returns ready to file as soon as you file your bankruptcy petition because the IRS routinely checks Chapter 13 filers to ensure that they have filed all necessary tax returns. When you haven't submitted all your returns, the IRS can obtain a court order requiring you to file them within a short period, like only 15 days. If you don't file the returns, your bankruptcy case can be dismissed.

Table 14-1 offers an at-a-glance view of various tax scenarios and their consequences in a Chapter 7 and Chapter 13 bankruptcy.

Table 14-1	Discharging Federal Income Taxes	
Situation	*Chapter 7*	*Chapter 13*
Taxes less than three years old (measured from the date the return was due — usually April 15 of the following year, unless the taxpayer got an extension to file)	Not discharged. Must make payment arrangements with IRS after bankruptcy is closed	Not discharged, *unless* the IRS fails to file a proof of claim. But the taxes can be paid over the life of the plan without further penalties, and without postpetition interest (unless a Notice of Tax Lien has been filed; see below).
Taxes more than three years old but for which return was filed late, and within two years of the petition date	Not discharged	Discharged *unless* taxes are assessed within 240 days of the petition date
Taxes more than three years old, but return never filed	Not discharged.	Discharged *unless* the IRS filed the return for you and assessed the tax within 240 days of the petition date

(continued)

Table 14-1 *(continued)*

Situation	Chapter 7	Chapter 13
Taxes more than 3 years old fraudulent tax return filed or other intentional tax evasion	Not discharged	Discharged unless the IRS can convince the court to dismiss your case for "bad faith"
IRS Notice of Tax Lien filed.	Even if the taxes are discharged, any property owned on the petition date, including exempt property, remains subject to the tax lien. If the taxes are discharged, any property acquired after the petition date will not be subject to the lien	*Regardless* of whether the taxes are discharged, a Notice of Tax Lien gives the IRS a secured claim up to the value of all your property on the petition date. The secured claim must be paid, with interest, over the life of the plan
Prepetition interest.	Discharged *only* if the underlying taxes are discharged	Discharged *only* if the underlying taxes are discharged
Postpetition interest.	Continues to accrue on nondischargeable taxes	Does not accrue, even though the taxes are not dischargeable, *unless* a Notice of Tax Lien has been filed.
Prepetition penalties.	Discharged if the underlying tax is discharged, or the event giving rise to the penalty occurred more than three years before the petition date. But if a Notice of Tax Lien has been filed, the penalties are covered by that lien.	Discharged. It makes no difference whether the prepetition taxes to which the penalties relate are discharged. But if a Notice of Tax Lien has been filed, the penalties are included in the amount of the government's secured claim.
Postpetition penalties.	Not assessed *if* the tax is discharged. Not assessed while the case is open (usually about four months).	*Possibly*, but not definitely, assessed if the case is dismissed. Not assessed if the plan is completed.

Don't actually file the delinquent returns before reading the next section "Watching out for recently assessed taxes," and talking to your lawyer.

Watching out for recently assessed taxes

There's another requirement for discharging taxes in bankruptcy — the taxes must have been assessed more than 240 days before bankruptcy. This is usually not a concern with a Chapter 7. Taxes are typically assessed shortly after the return is filed. Because, in a Chapter 7, the return must have been filed more than two years prior to bankruptcy, the taxes most likely have been assessed for more than 240 days.

But the 240-day rule can be a booby trap if you're contemplating a Chapter 13. If you file your return prior to filing Chapter 13, the IRS will then assess the tax and you'll have to wait another 240 days to file bankruptcy if you want to discharge that tax. If you file the tax return after you file bankruptcy, the 240-day rule doesn't come into play and you can discharge the taxes (provided, of course, that they are more than three years old).

Coping with interest and penalties

The government charges interest and imposes heavy penalties when you don't pay your taxes on time. Sometimes, interest and penalties add up to more than the tax itself.

Interest is treated differently than penalties in bankruptcy. There are also different rules for interest and penalties accruing before you file for bankruptcy ("prepetition") and those arising after you file ("postpetition").

Prepetition interest charged on unpaid taxes is, for the most part, treated the same as taxes in both a Chapter 7 and a 13. When the tax is nondischargeable, so is the interest. Penalties, on the other hand, are discharged in a Chapter 7 if they are more than three years old. In a Chapter 13, however, prepetition penalties are dischargeable regardless of when they arose.

Postpetition interest on nondischargeable taxes continues accruing during and after a Chapter 7 case. Interest stops accruing in a Chapter 13 case when it is filed. And yet, whenever a Chapter 13 bankruptcy is dismissed or converted to a Chapter 7, interest is added as if no Chapter 13 had been filed.

Here's a wrinkle: If you filed a joint return for taxes included in your Chapter 13 case, but your spouse didn't join you in filing Chapter 13, the IRS still can come after her for interest that accrues while your Chapter 13 case is open.

Penalties on nondischargeable taxes aren't assessed while a Chapter 7 or a Chapter 13 case is open. Keep in mind that a Chapter 7 case is usually not open very long, typically just a few months, unlike a Chapter 13, which ordinarily lasts for at least three years.

Confronting federal tax liens

If you owe taxes, the IRS can record a Notice of Tax Lien in the pubic records. Doing so gives it a lien (See Chapter 10 for the lowdown on liens) on all your earthly belongings. Although the IRS periodically issues guidelines as to when a Notice of Tax Lien should be filed, the decision rests largely with the tax collector handling your case.

If a Notice of Tax Lien has been lodged before you file bankruptcy, the rules in the previous section don't apply and discharging taxes becomes even more difficult.

Taxes due, together with associated interest and penalties, are secured by all your prepetition assets (including your retirement plan, which is usually protected from most other creditors). Even when these obligations are dischargeable, they still encumber prepetition assets. If you suspect that a tax lien is about to be filed, contact a bankruptcy specialist IMMEDIATELY.

Making the trustee pay your taxes

If you think that you'll owe federal income taxes for the current year, and you have assets that will be liquidated in your bankruptcy, you may be able to get the trustee to pay the taxes.

The Tax Code enables Chapter 7 debtors to divide the year in which they file bankruptcy into two short years. For example: If you filed Chapter 7 bankruptcy September 2, 2000, you can elect to divide the tax year 2000 into two parts — the first running from January 1, 2000, to September 2, 2000, and the second running from September 3, 2000, to December 31, 2000. Consequently, liabilities that accrued up to September 2, 2000, are considered prepetition priority claims, which the trustee must pay ahead of other creditors.

Claiming too many dependents was tax evasion

Joe told his employer he had eight dependents, but he really had only one. As a result, Joe took home more money from each paycheck. When tax time rolled around, Joe discovered that he couldn't pay his whopping tax obligation because he'd already spent all his extra take-home pay. And yet, Joe still properly filed his income tax return; however, he didn't pay the taxes.

Four years later, when Joe filed Chapter 7 bankruptcy, the court refused to wipe out his taxes, saying that Joe was guilty of tax evasion for claiming too many dependents and spending the money on other things.

This "short-year election" must be made shortly after filing bankruptcy. So, discuss this with your lawyer before you ever file. In addition to making the election, you or your lawyer need to make sure that a timely *proof of claim* is filed by or on behalf of the IRS. See Chapter 5 to find out more about the claims process.

Paying taxes over time in Chapter 13

Even when the income taxes you owe aren't old enough to be discharged, you can still pay them over three to five years in a Chapter 13 — and, if no Notice of Tax Lien has been filed, without interest or penalties. While you're in a Chapter 13, the IRS can't bug you about prepetition taxes and it can't file a Notice of Tax Lien. See Chapter 8 for a discussion of payment arrangements outside bankruptcy.

Keeping on top of postpetition taxes

Of course, income taxes arising after bankruptcy aren't discharged, so you should plan on keeping up with future tax obligations. If you can't pay postpetition taxes immediately, you can submit a payment proposal to the IRS when you file your return. If you propose to pay the postpetition tax within three years, the IRS will probably go along. See Chapter 8 for more on submitting payment plans to the IRS.

In a Chapter 13, if you don't keep up with postpetition taxes, your bankruptcy plan may fall apart. See Chapter 19 to see why is it so important to stay on top of postpetition taxes in a Chapter 13.

Paying taxes before bankruptcy

If you owe nondischargeable taxes, consider selling nonexempt property and paying off the tax debt before filing bankruptcy. If part of your tax obligation is dischargeable, you can force the IRS to apply the payments to the nondischargeable part. However, you lose this option after you file bankruptcy. (See Chapter 8 for more about the benefits of allocating tax payments.) But, as we explain in Chapter 18, paying large debts shortly before bankruptcy sometimes can backfire, so don't pay any taxes without first consulting with your lawyer.

Using the statute of limitations to escape taxes

Time heals many wounds, including some tax debts. Generally if more than ten years go by after income taxes are assessed (which is usually shortly after you filed your return), the taxes vanish even if you don't file bankruptcy. But certain factors will suspend or extend the statute of limitations. (See Chapter 8.)

Facing the consequences if you've been a tax protestor

The courts are fed up with tax protestors. If you have a history of opposing income taxes on constitutional, religious, or philosophical grounds, don't expect much sympathy. The IRS considers you a CPA — Certified Pain in the . . . — and it's going to strenuously object to the discharging of old taxes in a Chapter 7, arguing that you're guilty of intentional tax evasion. If you file a Chapter 13, it may try to get your case dismissed on "bad faith" grounds. A tax protestor who wants to discharge her taxes in bankruptcy has to prove that she has seen the light and her protesting days are over.

Dealing with the State Tax Man

For the most part, the same rules that apply to federal taxes also cover state income taxes — with one peculiar glitch. Most, if not all, states require you to file an amended state tax return whenever your federal tax liability for a given year changes (perhaps as a result of an audit). Some courts hold that when you fail to file an amended state return in this situation, your initial state return is deemed "unfiled." The result is that your entire state tax — and not just the amount that would have been added had you amended the state return — can no longer be discharged in a Chapter 7 filing.

Addressing Taxes Other Than Income Taxes

As a general rule, nonincome taxes (with the exception of trust fund taxes, which we discuss in the following section) are dischargeable in a Chapter 7 or a Chapter 13, if whatever caused the tax liability occurred more than three years before the bankruptcy filing date.

Paying trust fund employment taxes

Employers are required to withhold certain taxes from employees' paychecks and turn them over to the government on a regular basis throughout the year. These are referred to as *trust fund taxes*.

If these taxes aren't paid, the government can go after the company, the owners of the company, and the company employees who were responsible for remitting the funds to the government and intentionally failed to do so. These taxes aren't dischargeable in any type of bankruptcy unless they're barred by the statute of limitations.

When a business is going down the tubes, paying trade creditors and letting employment taxes slide to continue to operate is tempting. This strategy almost always is a mistake. Employment taxes should be the *first* thing paid, not the last.

Deciding whether to pay real and personal property taxes

Certain advantages and disadvantages can be realized when deciding between paying or not paying real and personal property taxes, and you need to make a smart decision about what you're going to do.

Real property taxes

Real property taxes — taxes imposed on land and buildings, — are typically a problem only when you want to keep the property. That's because these taxes are assessed against the property, not against the owner personally. Nonetheless, the taxes are liens and must be paid if you intend to keep the property. In addition, failure to pay real property taxes probably constitutes a default under your mortgage, the same as when you fail to make your mortgage payments.

Personal property taxes

Personal property taxes — taxes paid on items that aren't real estate (such as cars) — aren't dischargeable if, under local law, they are assessed against the owner personally rather than against only the property, and are less than one year old.

Obtaining Loans to Pay Your Taxes

Lenders (not to mention tax collectors) may encourage you borrow money to pay taxes. Be careful.

Loans taken to pay nondischargeable federal taxes aren't dischargeable in a Chapter 7. They're treated similarly to any debt incurred while contemplating bankruptcy. See Chapters 13 and 15 concerning debts from fraud.

If you're contemplating a Chapter 13, you may be tempted to borrow money to pay nondischargeable taxes with the aim of wiping out this new loan in bankruptcy (because debts from fraud get discharged in a Chapter 13). In our view, this is a lousy stunt if indeed you are intending to defraud that lender. And it may even cause your Chapter 13 to get dismissed if the judge thinks you acted with suspicious motives. See Chapter 4 for an explanation of the "good faith" requirement for a Chapter 13.

In any event, don't pay any large debts prior to bankruptcy before reading Chapter 18 to see how a bankruptcy trustee can sometimes recover this money, leaving you worse off than if you had never paid the debt in the first place.

Chapter 15

The Devil Made Me Do It: Fines, Fraud, and Other Foibles

In This Chapter

▶ Addressing fraud debts

▶ Seeking redemption for other intentional misconduct

▶ Coping with fines, penalties, and restitution orders

▶ Accepting responsibility for injuries you cause by driving drunk

*B*ankruptcy is designed to give honest debtors a second chance, not to provide a safe haven for crooks and scalawags. So, for the most part, if you intentionally cheat someone or purposely hurt someone, the U.S. Bankruptcy Code isn't your safety net. Still, bankruptcy law coexists with other laws and balances competing interests — legally, politically, and morally. That's always a difficult balancing act.

For instance, society has a powerful interest in seeing you get back on your feet. Only then can you rejoin the productive and taxpaying citizens who serve as cogs in the economic and social engine. At the same time, society has an interest in ensuring that those whom you've harmed don't get short-changed simply because you're now broke. So how can the law put you back on your feet, without kicking the legs out from under innocent bystanders? Sometimes it takes the Wisdom of Solomon — plus a dose of sincere remorse on your part.

Many debts that arise from intentional misconduct can't be wiped out in a Chapter 7 bankruptcy, but you have a shot at getting out from under that cloud by filing a Chapter 13. If you demonstrate your contrition and genuinely pay as much as you can under a Chapter 13 repayment plan, even your debts for intentional wrongdoing may be eliminated.

In this chapter, we look at debts stemming from fraud and other misdeeds and explore your options.

Dealing with Debts Resulting from Fraud

So, what's fraud? It doesn't mean that you're merely unable to pay your debts. Just because you're broke doesn't mean that you committed fraud, or anything of the sort. If that were the case, no one ever would get bankruptcy relief. Still, creditors may accuse you of fraud if they think that doing so prevents the elimination of your debt to them. But they have to prove:

- That you knowingly made a false representation
- That you intended to deceive the creditor
- That the creditor actually and justifiably relied on your representation
- That as a result of your misrepresentation, the creditor suffered damage

That may be a bunch to prove, but it can be done — as we explain in the following sections.

Charges on the eve of bankruptcy

Congress and the courts aren't particularly fond of people accumulating new debts right before they file bankruptcy. It just smells like you racked up debts with no intention of paying your bills. Eve of bankruptcy spending binges is really bad karma. Debts racked up in this manner may not get wiped out (at least in a Chapter 7), and in extreme cases can cause your Chapter 7 or Chapter 13 case to be rejected. Don't risk it.

Luxury purchases and credit cash advances are presumed fraudulent when they're made within 60 days of filing bankruptcy and total more than $1,150. For that reason, putting bankruptcy attorney fees on your credit card (even as a cash advance) isn't a good idea. (See Chapter 13 for more about credit cards and fraud.)

False financial statements

Did you ever wonder why some lenders require such a complicated financial statement even though you own only a few items? The answer is simple: Debts obtained through falsely written financial statements aren't dischargeable in a Chapter 7. Creditors know this and some try to provide the rope with which to hang yourself in the event you end up in bankruptcy.

Some lenders actually encourage you to exaggerate your income or the value of your assets. Then, if you ever file bankruptcy, they dig out the financial statement, point to any inaccuracies and claim that their debt isn't discharge-able because you provided false information on your financial statement. Sneaky, huh?

The courts think so, and fortunately they require the creditor to prove that you intentionally lied and that the creditor reasonably relied on the misrepre-sentation in making the loan. In other words, they must show not only that the information was inaccurate, but also that you knew it was inaccurate and that they wouldn't have given you a loan had they known the truth.

Be on your guard whenever a lender asks for a financial statement. Be scrupulously honest, and don't ever let anyone coax you into exaggerating. The loan officer may be setting a trap. (See Chapter 13 for more information on whether the information you put on a credit-card application ever is deemed a false financial statement.)

Bad checks

Writing bad checks is considered fraudulent only when the creditor can prove that you knew, or should have known, that the check would bounce.

Most creditors won't bother unless the check is a big one. So, as a practical matter, debts from rubber checks frequently are discharged. Just the same, banks blacklist people who don't make good on checks, and you may have trouble obtaining a new checking account. Keeping your checkbook balanced is definitely a good idea.

In any case, never let a creditor talk you into signing a postdated check. If it turns out that you can't cover the check, the creditor may claim that you knew the check was bad and, for that reason, claim that the debt shouldn't be wiped out. Or, even worse, the creditor may file criminal bad-check charges against you and have you carted off to the hoosegow in the paddy wagon.

Receiving undeserved welfare and unemployment benefits

Someone receiving more Social Security, unemployment, welfare, or other government benefits than they should have is not all that uncommon. If the bankruptcy court is convinced that you fraudulently obtained these benefits, your obligation to repay them won't be dischargeable in a Chapter 7 but can be eliminated in a Chapter 13.

If getting more than your fair share was just a mistake — theirs or yours — any repayment obligation can be wiped out. The key wrinkle is whether you're still receiving benefits.

Chapter 7: No escape for coverup

When Zeke sold his house to Brenda, he assured her that his humble abode was solid as a rock, but that wasn't exactly true.

Actually, the foundation had shifted and the walls were cracking, and Zeke knew it. In fact, he covered the cracks with paint so Brenda and her real estate agent couldn't see the evidence.

Brenda bought the house, and soon discovered she was facing thousands of dollars of repair work. She sued, so Zeke filed a Chapter 7 bankruptcy to escape liability. The judge wasn't about to let Zeke play the system for a sucker and gave Brenda the green light to pursue her fraud claim.

Under a principle called *recoupment*, some courts enable the offended government agency to effect a reduction in your future benefits to recover its loss even though any obligation to repay was discharged in bankruptcy.

Willful and malicious behavior

Damages from *willful and malicious conduct* aren't dischargeable in a Chapter 7, but may be dischargeable in a Chapter 13, provided that you convince the court you're doing your best to pay as much of the damages as possible under your Chapter 13 plan.

As you may expect, determining whether conduct is so awful that it is willful and malicious usually isn't very easy.

The United States Supreme Court has ruled that simple negligence doesn't rise to the level of malice, even if you really screwed up. [(*Kawaauhau v. Geiger*, 523 U.S. 57, 118 S.Ct. 974 (1998).] For example, if you were stirring your coffee while driving and accidentally rear-ended a school bus, that's *negligence*. Although you didn't mean to cause an accident, you nevertheless did so because you weren't paying attention. On the other hand, if you intentionally rammed the bus in a fit of road rage, that's *malice*.

Creditors sometimes claim that a debtor was guilty of willful and malicious conduct when she sold or gave away the collateral she used to secure her loans — an allegation known in legal circles as *conversion of collateral*.

Some department stores take a security interest (which gives them the right to repossess if you don't pay; see Chapter 10 for more on security interests) in items purchased on the charge accounts their stores offer to customers. These stores sometimes claim that someone who sells or gives away an item before it's paid off acted willfully and maliciously. Say, for example, that you charged a lawn mower on an ABC Store account, and the store retained a security interest in that item. Sometime later, you sell the mower at a garage sale, even though you haven't paid off your ABC Store account, and spent your proceeds. ABC may later accuse you of acting with malice if you don't pay off the account.

In a situation like this one, most bankruptcy courts reject the store's conversion of collateral claim, unless ABC can prove that you were aware of the fine print in the charge account agreement and knew that you weren't supposed to sell the mower until it was paid for. Few consumers actually have any clue what's in the fine print of their charge-card documentation; however, in exceptional cases where the customer clearly is fully aware that she's doing a bad thing, courts rule in favor of the stores.

Even though some liabilities from alleged willful and malicious conduct are potentially dischargeable in Chapter 13, the judge will scrutinize your case, making sure that it's filed in a good faith attempt to repay as much as possible and not just to stiff the victim. Remember, when criminal charges are brought and a conviction results in a fine or restitution, these obligations aren't dischargeable (see "Covering Fines, Penalties, and Restitution Orders" later in this chapter).

Whenever someone sues you claiming that you're guilty of fraud or other misconduct, see a lawyer immediately. If you do nothing, the person suing you automatically wins, possibly preventing you from later claiming your innocence.

Payday loans

Payday loans are an epidemic of New Age loan sharking that are spreading at an alarming rate.

Here's how they work. Outfits accept a post-dated check in exchange for cash, with the understanding that you'll buy back the check for the amount of cash advanced, plus a hefty fee, whenever you receive your paycheck. The effective interest rate on these loans can run up to 500 percent, and even higher!

They do this knowing full well that when you wrote the check, you didn't have enough money in your account to cover it. In fact, they hope that you won't be able to redeem your check for a long time, because each time payday rolls around and you don't buy back the check, they charge additional fees. The underlying threat is that if you don't eventually pay, you'll be charged with fraud.

That's baloney! There's no fraud here — at least not on the customer's part. These loans should be dischargeable in bankruptcy the same as any other debt.

If you think that the only people engaging in this type of lending have thick necks and crooked noses, you're wrong. Some of our nation's largest banks are in the payday loan business. They're in the lobbying and political contribution business, too.

ANECDOTE

Rolex scheme falls through

Brad charged a $14,000 diamond-studded Rolex watch at Acme Jewelers. Because the purchase was so large, the store manager carefully explained to Brad that the watch was collateral for the account. He then had Brad sign papers to that effect.

Three weeks later, Brad sold the watch for $1,500 and used the money to catch up on car payments. Shortly thereafter, he filed Chapter 7. The court found Brad guilty of willful and malicious conduct and his debt to Acme wasn't discharged.

Theft

Congress wanted to make doubly sure that thieves can't escape liability by filing Chapter 7 bankruptcy. So, in addition to addressing obligations arising from willful and malicious conduct, Congress enacted a separate provision excepting from discharge in a Chapter 7 any debts arising from larceny and embezzlement. As is true of liabilities from willful and malicious conduct, these types of debts may be dischargeable in a Chapter 13, if the court is convinced of your good faith.

Covering Fines, Penalties, and Restitution Orders

The courts and Congress are like ships passing in the night when it comes to addressing court-ordered fines, penalties, and *restitution* (monetary compensation paid to the victim of a crime). Neither seems to understand exactly what the other is talking about. Making matters worse is the fact that these types of debts frequently arise from efforts by the states to enforce criminal or regulatory laws, and federal courts generally don't like stepping on a state's toes in these matters. The first problem in figuring out what impact bankruptcy has on these debts is identifying the nature of the obligation as accurately as possible.

Criminal fines

Fines that are assessed upon conviction of a crime can't be wiped out in a Chapter 7 or a Chapter 13.

Although you may propose paying off the fine in full during a Chapter 13 case, you still can be confronted with problems. First of all, most courts won't allow you to pay them off while other unsecured creditors are left holding the bag. Second, prosecutors may seek to incarcerate you for failure to pay a criminal fine, even though it's included in your Chapter 13 plan.

It may be better for you to pay the fine before filing bankruptcy, but don't forget that's potentially dangerous. The trustee may decide that you attempted to play favorites with whatever cash you have. (See Chapter 18.) Your lawyer's knowledge of the policies of local courts and prosecutors is critical in this situation.

Restitution

Courts commonly require anyone who injures another person or damages property to pay *restitution* to the victim. That simply means that if your neighbor has to shell out $300 for the vet because you kicked Fido in the head, you'll have to reimburse your neighbor. If you're ordered to pay restitution as part of a criminal conviction, the obligation is treated the same as a criminal fine.

Say, for example, you're convicted of vandalism in a criminal court and ordered to compensate the victim for damages as part of your sentence. This kind of obligation isn't dischargeable in a Chapter 7 or a Chapter 13. On the other hand, if criminal charges weren't brought against you, but the victim sued you and obtained a judgment, that kind of obligation would not be excepted from discharge (nondischargeable) as "restitution." However, it may be nondischargeable in a Chapter 7 on the basis of fraud, willful and malicious conduct, or embezzlement. Still, you may be able to discharge the claim in a Chapter 13.

Noncriminal fines and penalties

In most instances, penalties imposed on you for noncriminal wrongdoing — such as watering your lawn during a drought or (in some places) not cleaning up after your pooch — are dischargeable in a Chapter 13, but not in a Chapter 7.

But even when you can wipe out the debt, you still may be in for big trouble with the governmental entity imposing the fine or penalty. Many states have diversion programs where people avoid criminal prosecution by undergoing counseling. They're also expected to eventually pay for the services used in diversion programs. For example, the court may give you a break on a marijuana charge if you agree to undergo and pay for drug counseling. If you don't pay for the program, criminal charges may be revived.

Motor-vehicle fines

Unpaid traffic fines and parking tickets present a couple of questions. The first is whether the obligation is dischargeable, and that depends on whether your local courts consider the violation a crime or merely an infraction.

Parking tickets and equipment violations (broken headlight, noisy muffler, bald tires, and so on) typically are considered infractions, so fines for them are dischargeable in a Chapter 13, but not in a Chapter 7. Serious moving violations (reckless driving or driving with a suspended license) typically are considered crimes and fines for them aren't dischargeable in a Chapter 7 or a Chapter 13.

Many states will yank your driver's license for unpaid fines, even those involving infractions. If the fine is dischargeable, the Bankruptcy Code requires that the state restore your driving privileges. But that doesn't mean that the bankruptcy court will order the state to do so. You may find yourself in the middle of a huge power struggle between state and federal authorities.

For those reasons, it's better to file Chapter 13 before your license is actually suspended or revoked. Filing bankruptcy will halt suspension or revocation proceedings (see Chapter 5 for a discussion of the automatic stay), enabling you to keep your license while your lawyer tries to resolve any tug of war between the bankruptcy and state courts. However, if you're dealing with a criminal fine, the state doesn't have to restore your license, and bankruptcy won't interrupt suspension or revocation proceedings.

Accepting Responsibility for Drunken-driving Injuries

Patience for drunken or drugged drivers is at an all-time low. Getting blasted and mowing down a few mailboxes — let alone children — is no longer considered funny.

If you get drunk or high and injure someone in a car accident, you're going to pay for any personal damages. Liabilities for injuries caused by operation of a motor vehicle while under the influence of alcohol, drugs, or other substances *can't* be discharged in a Chapter 7 or a Chapter 13.

Chapter 16

Till Debt Due Us Part: Bankruptcy and Divorce

In This Chapter

▶ Preparing your game plan

▶ Working out a strategy that benefits you and your ex

▶ Figuring out the best time to file bankruptcy

▶ Dealing with support obligations in bankruptcy

▶ Dealing with property divisions in bankruptcy

Financial distress and divorce often go hand-in-hand. Sometimes, financial woes cause the divorce. Other times, divorce leads to financial disaster. In balancing your money concerns with your domestic issues, you need to carefully weigh your options, and their implications, in divorce court and bankruptcy court.

The two main reasons you may want to plow through this rather difficult and rather dour chapter are

✔ You owe money under a divorce decree that already has been entered and wonder whether bankruptcy can help you escape or at least manage these obligations.

✔ You're involved in a divorce right now, or thinking about it, and want to know how bankruptcy will affect things.

This chapter addresses these complicated issues.

Introducing Key Points

Because divorce can really complicate your bankruptcy (and vice versa), you need to know some basics. Although hard and fast rules are awfully hard to come by in this area, several constants to keep in mind are that:

- Bankruptcy deals only with debts in existence on the day you file. If a divorce decree creates financial obligations after the petition date, they won't be included in bankruptcy.

- Filing bankruptcy stops a divorce until the bankruptcy court grants permission to proceed. See the section entitled, "Using the automatic stay" in Chapter 5.

- Property divisions completed prior to bankruptcy aren't debts that can be avoided. For example, if a divorce court enters an order transferring an asset to you, it's yours even when your ex-spouse files bankruptcy. But if the divorce court orders your ex to transfer the property and he hasn't done so prior to bankruptcy, he may be able to escape this kind of debt through bankruptcy.

- Some liens imposed by divorce courts may be avoidable by your ex if he files bankruptcy, because they'll be deemed judicial liens impairing his homestead. Insisting that your ex sign a mortgage (which would not be avoidable as a judicial lien) to secure the debt would be a smart thing to do. See Chapter 11 for more on judicial liens.

- The fact that you or even the divorce court calls an obligation nondischargeable support isn't binding on a bankruptcy court, which looks at the underlying situation and makes its own determinations.

- If you're entitled to receive support when you file bankruptcy, most, if not all that money is exempt (off-limits to creditors) in your bankruptcy. On the other hand, if you expect to receive a property division, chances are that it won't be exempt. See Chapter 9 for more on exempt property.

- If you become entitled to a property division within 180 days of bankruptcy, you can lose it to the trustee.

Planning Your Strategy

If a divorce looms in your future, careful bankruptcy planning can:

- Reduce tensions between you and your soon-to-be ex-spouse
- Make divorce simpler
- Help produce a marital settlement that both parties can live with that will hold up in a future bankruptcy

On the other hand, blundering through a divorce without carefully considering the possible effects of bankruptcy may bring results that neither party wants, such as:

✔ An invalid divorce

✔ Unproductive and expensive fights about who's going to pay certain bills, especially when both are better off eliminating the debts in bankruptcy

✔ Hostilities resulting from one party believing he got the short end of the stick

✔ Unnecessary losses of assets to a bankruptcy trustee

Exploring your financial obligations

Basically two types of financial obligations arise from divorce: *support* to sustain the kids and your former spouse and the issue of property that's been divided between the two of you. Bankruptcy handles each commitment differently.

Generally, support obligations aren't wiped out in a Chapter 7 or a Chapter 13, while outstanding property division obligations *can* be wiped out in a Chapter 13 and *may* be eliminated in a Chapter 7 — if you won't have the ability to pay them after bankruptcy. Here are a couple of principles to keep in mind.

First, financial obligations arising from a *divorce decree* (or a marital settlement agreement adopted by the divorce court) may require payment of:

✔ Money for child support and schooling

✔ Life and health insurance premiums

✔ Alimony or maintenance for your ex-spouse

✔ Your ex-spouse's divorce attorney fees

✔ A sum of money to compensate your ex for his interest in joint property

For example, say that the divorce court awards you the marital residence worth $80,000 but requires you to pay your ex $40,000 for his interest in the property. As part of the deal, the court may actually impose a lien on the home to secure payment of the $40,000.

✔ Certain debts so that your ex doesn't have to pay them

If you're wondering which of these is support and which are property divisions, jump ahead to the section "Figuring out which obligations are in 'the nature of' support," later in this chapter.

Second, the decree may also actually transfer specific assets to your former partner. For example, the court may enter a Qualified Domestic Relations Order (QDRO) that gives your ex-spouse immediate ownership in part of your entire retirement plan. If the court enters a QDRO, your ex-spouse has an immediate ownership interest in your pension. In other words, he owns it. You don't.

Or the divorce court can award jointly owned property to one spouse. Say, for example, that you and your soon to be ex jointly own your home plus a rental house. A divorce court can rule that you own the home by yourself and your ex gets the rental property.

In other words, the divorce court can

- ✔ Order you to make payments in the future that represent either support or a property division. These payments may be secured or unsecured.
- ✔ Actually transfer ownership of certain assets to one party.

A little later in this chapter, we talk about how bankruptcy affects support obligations and property divisions.

Doing what's best for both spouses

If you and your mate were struggling financially when living together, things are just going to get worse when you have to maintain two households. Although a substantial emotional element is obvious, you'll both be much better off when you can work toward a financial solution that benefits each of you. Doing so isn't really that hard, assuming, of course, that you can respond rationally rather than emotionally. Work toward structuring a marital settlement agreement that:

- ✔ Both parties can live with
- ✔ Actually divides your existing property
- ✔ Ensures that sums to be paid by one spouse to the other will survive the bankruptcy of each and, it is hoped, will be exempt

Sure, you can play hardball and insist that your spouse pay all the bills, but you'll probably find out that you're doing nothing more than cutting off your nose to spite your face. Although the divorce court may order one party to pay the bill, that doesn't necessarily protect the other from creditors. Instead of playing one-upmanship, you and your mate need to reach an agreement where credit-card debts and other bills eventually are wiped out in bankruptcy. If you can do that, your mate will be in a far better position to handle any support obligations — and everyone will be happier.

Nevertheless, you still need to notify all creditors on joint accounts in writing that you won't be responsible for any future charges made by your spouse. Although doing so won't relieve you from charges that already were made, it should keep you off the hook for future charges.

ANECDOTE

A success story

Bob and Mabel own a home worth $100,000. It is subject to a mortgage of $80,000 ($20,000 equity). They also own an SUV worth $15,000 free and clear. However, they owe more than $50,000 in credit-card debts they racked up during their stormy marriage. The homestead exemption in their state is $25,000, and the vehicle exemption is $2,000. Their pensions are entirely exempt.

Bob and Mabel agree that because Mabel is getting custody of their two children, she also needs to have the house with its $20,000 equity.

Knowing that they'd lose the SUV in bankruptcy, they sell it, and Bob receives the $15,000 proceeds because he's giving up the house. To make things equal, Mabel gives Bob $5,000 from her pension.

Bob then takes the $20,000 and makes a down payment on a new home and buys a $2,000 car.

Bob agrees to make child support payments of $500 per month.

After the divorce is complete, Bob and Mabel each file separate Chapter 7 bankruptcies. (They can't file jointly even if they want to because they no longer are married.) The credit-card debts are eliminated, neither of them loses any property, and Bob's monthly support payments are manageable.

Completing property transfers

If a divorce court actually transfers an asset to your ex-spouse, you don't really have any debt to handle in bankruptcy, because you no longer own the property; your spouse does. Sorry. For example, if the court enters a QDRO, (see our earlier discussion of Qualified Domestic Relations Orders) your ex has an immediate ownership interest in your pension. There's simply no debt to wipe out or manage. Sorry.

Timing it right

When bankruptcy and divorce intersect, careful timing can make the difference between success and disaster. Although each situation is unique, as a general rule:

- ✔ When you have no assets to divide, no third-party debts (like joint credit-card accounts) to allocate, and no support issues, you need to file bankruptcy prior to filing for divorce. That way, you can file a joint bankruptcy, getting two for the price of one and making your divorce much simpler.

- ✔ In other cases, filing and completing your divorce before actually filing bankruptcy usually is best.

Sham divorces

You may be tempted to agree with your spouse that he gets the mine and you get the shaft so that creditors can't go after your assets. For example, if, as a couple, you have few joint debts and your spouse doesn't have many debts in his own name, it may be appealing to give him everything in the divorce and then file bankruptcy. Maybe you'll eventually settle up later but, in any event, you'd rather see him get your assets than your creditors.

Don't do it.

When you file bankruptcy after a divorce, the trustee makes sure that any property settlement was a fair transaction in which you received valuable property in exchange for property you gave up. If you didn't, the trustee can recover the property that your ex received. In addition, if you pulled this stunt within one year of filing bankruptcy, you may not be eligible for a Chapter 7 discharge (See Chapter 18).

Whenever you file bankruptcy while a divorce actually is pending, the automatic stay that puts an end to lawsuits and collection efforts ordinarily brings the divorce proceedings to a halt, too. So, if you proceed with the divorce without first getting the okay from the bankruptcy court, you may end up with a divorce that is void and not worth the paper it's printed on. That can come as an unpleasant surprise if you choose to remarry.

Although delaying bankruptcy until after the divorce is finished ordinarily is better, starting to make plans for your bankruptcy nevertheless makes sense.

Understanding How Support Obligations Are Treated in Bankruptcy

Although bankruptcy won't eliminate support obligations, it may ease your distress by erasing your other debts. Additionally, with a Chapter 13 repayment plan, you can gradually catch up with your outstanding support, paying during your three-to five-year plan.

Support obligations in Chapter 7

You can't do much with support obligations in a Chapter 7 liquidation bankruptcy. And the automatic stay doesn't protect you from collection efforts.

Chapter 7 still eliminates your other debts, and that makes meeting your support requirements easier. And if yours is an *asset case* — where property is liquidated and some money is paid to creditors — you can file a *proof of claim,* thus ensuring that the lion's share of the funds go toward your support obligation. The claims process is explained in Chapter 5.

Support obligations in Chapter 13

Although you can't wipe out support responsibilities in a Chapter 13, you can at least get your spouse off your back and pay accrued support during the three- to five-year duration of your Chapter 13 plan.

In a Chapter 13, support obligations are broken down into two categories:

- ✔ Back support that you owe when you file
- ✔ Support that accrues in the future

Back support can — and actually must — be paid in full over the duration of your plan from the payments you make to the trustee. As long as you keep up your end of the Chapter 13 bargain, you're shielded from attempts to collect support that was owed when you filed.

Support payments that are due after you file for bankruptcy are treated as a budgeted living expense that you pay directly, just like your rent or utility bill. But beware: The automatic stay doesn't provide much protection against support collection, and you may jeopardize your whole Chapter 13 case by letting postpetition support obligations slide. (For more about postpetition obligations, see Chapter 19.) If your postpetition support payments are unreasonably high, the place to look for relief is divorce court. Bankruptcy courts won't allow themselves to get dragged into the divorce business.

Figuring out which obligations are in "the nature of" support

Determining whether a particular obligation is support or a property division often is difficult.

Here's why: Assume that Grace agrees to accept less alimony because her husband, George, promises to pay all their joint debts (keeping in mind that even if the divorce court adopts this agreement and assigns these debts to George, the creditors can still come after Grace if George doesn't pay). Promises to pay third-party debts frequently are labeled as property divisions by the parties or by the divorce court. But, in this particular case, isn't it actually a form of support?

That depends.

Chapter 13 reduces marital obligations to manageable amounts

George and Donna divorce after seven years of marriage. George agrees to pay $1,000 per month alimony to Donna and $45,000 in exchange for her interest in the couple's vacation home. George then loses his job and doesn't pay either of these obligations.

After two years, George finally lands a good job, but by then he owes Donna $24,000 in back support, still owes her the $45,000, and he racks up $13,000 in credit-card debts to boot.

George files Chapter 13 and the court approves a plan where he pays Donna the $24,000 over five years and continues making current $1,000 payments to her. If George completes his plan, the $45,000 property division is wiped out along with his credit-card bills.

A bankruptcy judge can disregard labels, making up his own mind about the true nature of the obligation. In fact, a bankruptcy court doesn't even need to agree with the divorce judge's decision on the question. If the divorce court characterizes an obligation as being in the nature of support, specifically ruling that it can't be wiped out in bankruptcy, the bankruptcy court can reach the exact opposite conclusion, ruling that the obligation is actually a property division.

Bankruptcy is a federal law and, under our Constitution, national laws overrule inconsistent state laws.

Focusing on financial conditions at the time of your divorce

Although bankruptcy courts consider a number of factors, they like to zero in on the financial condition of the parties at the time of the divorce.

If the relative financial situation of the parties at that time indicates that support was necessary, bankruptcy courts usually find that an award is in the nature of support, regardless of how it is labeled.

If your spouse is barely able to meet basic expenses and has few job skills, while you have substantial earning ability, a bankruptcy court probably will rule that the disputed obligation is support, regardless of whether it consists of a lump-sum payment, periodic payments, or a promise to pay a third-party debt. For example, suppose that Jane supports Dan for ten years while he completes his medical training, and the divorce court orders Dan to make payments to her equal to a percentage of the value of his medical practice. Few courts ever conclude that the obligation is anything other than support, at least to the extent that such payments are necessary for Jane to support herself.

Certain third-party debts are more likely than others to fall under the support umbrella. For example, when a wife is awarded the marital home and her husband is ordered to make the mortgage payments, the obligation is probably support, especially if the wife has custody of children.

Many bankruptcy courts also deem as support a husband's obligation to pay a car loan on an essential vehicle awarded to his wife if, at the time of the divorce, she can't afford the payments herself. Similarly, courts almost always rule that when one spouse is ordered to pay the other's divorce attorney, this obligation is support, not a property division.

Looking at factors that some courts consider

Because the determination about whether an obligation is in the nature of support isn't always obvious, courts examine the circumstances to make those kinds of decisions. Bankruptcy judges consider a number of factors, including whether:

- ✔ There are children involved. Payments to an ex-spouse with custody of the parties' minor children are more likely to be deemed support.

- ✔ Marked differences existed between the relative incomes of you and your former spouse at the time of your divorce. A key question is whether the recipient actually needed (at the time of divorce) financial assistance from his ex-spouse in order to make ends meet.

- ✔ The obligation terminates on death or remarriage of the recipient spouse. Traditionally, support obligations end upon the recipient's death or remarriage, but property divisions don't.

- ✔ The obligation is subject to modification based on changes in circumstances. Support obligations tend to be modifiable, while property divisions don't.

- ✔ The parties treat the obligation as support on their income tax returns — with the person making payments deducting them and the person receiving them treating them as income. If the paying spouse claims that payments were tax-deductible support payments rather than nondeductible property division payments, the bankruptcy judge will be skeptical if he changes his tune and tries to claim that they are not support obligations.

All you need to know, and more

If you really want the full scoop on discharging marital obligations, Jim Caher, a coauthor with his brother, John Caher, of the book you're reading devotes an entire book for lawyers to just that subject. See, *Discharging Marital Obligations in Bankruptcy,* James. P. Caher, LRP

Publications, 1998 (`http://www.lrp.com/index.html`). Beware: This is a technical, lawyerly legal book; oceanfront reading it isn't. It nevertheless tells you everything you ever wanted to know, and more, about the topic.

Understanding How Property Divisions Are Treated in Bankruptcy

If a marital obligation is a property settlement, you can wipe it out in a Chapter 13, and *may* be able to eliminate it in a Chapter 7. In a nutshell, property divisions are dischargeable in a Chapter 7 if you can prove that:

- You lack the ability to pay.
- The benefit to you of discharging the obligation outweighs the harmful consequences that will befall your ex-spouse and/or children.

But you still may have to deal with any lien imposed by the divorce court. For example, if the divorce court orders you to pay $10,000 as a property division and imposes a lien on your home to secure payment, you must deal with that lien even when your personal liability on the debt is canceled.

As we discuss in Chapter 11, judgment liens that impair your exemption can be avoided (unless they secure a support obligation). When it comes to judgment liens securing property divisions, the Supreme Court [see *Farrey v. Sanderfoot.* 500 U.S. 291, 111 S.Ct. 1825 (1991)], in a rather convoluted fashion, has ruled that you can't avoid the judgment lien if it is imposed to secure payment for your half of jointly owned property awarded to you in the divorce.

Suppose, for a moment, that the divorce court awards you sole ownership of a $80,000 home — *owned jointly with your spouse* — and then imposes a lien on the property to secure payment to your spouse of $40,000 for his share of the home. That kind of lien isn't avoidable in bankruptcy.

On the other hand, suppose the divorce court imposes a lien against property that you own in your own name. That kind of lien can be avoidable in bankruptcy to the extent that it impairs your homestead exemption. See Chapter 11 for more on eliminating judgment liens on homesteads.

In 1994, Congress amended the Bankruptcy Code to make eliminating property division debts more difficult for debtors in a Chapter 7. Unfortunately, the amendment was so confusing that courts still struggle to figure out exactly what it means.

The amendment says that a property division is dischargeable when either of the following is true:

- ✔ "The debtor does not have the ability to pay such debt from income or property of the debtor not reasonably necessary to be expended for the maintenance or support of the debtor or a dependent of the debtor and, if the debtor is engaged in a business, for the payment of expenditures necessary for the continuation, preservation, and operation of such business."

- ✔ "Discharging such debt would result in a benefit to the debtor that outweighs the detrimental consequences to a spouse, former spouse, or child of the debtor."

If you're wondering just what *ability to pay* means and what types of *detrimental consequences* outweigh the benefit to the debtor of discharging the debt contemplates, join the club. Judges have tried to figure those nuances out since 1994 — Judge Francis G. Conrad, in fact, referred to these provisions as incomprehensible "sausage" in *Kessler v. Butler,* 186 B.R. 371, 372 (Bankr. D.Vt. 1995). In the following section and the "Tipping the relative suffering scales" section, later in this chapter, we give you our take on these two concepts.

When all is said and done, however, the individual views and prejudices of local bankruptcy judges largely determine which property divisions are dischargeable in a Chapter 7 and which aren't.

Determining your "ability to pay"

Just what does *ability to pay* mean?

Does it mean ability to pay right now? Or during the next 30 years? Or during some period of time in between? Are you supposed to live at a poverty level until the obligation is satisfied? Can the court consider your earning potential, or is its inquiry limited to current earnings? Whenever you remarry, is the income or property of your new spouse considered? To what extent should the bankruptcy court impose its values on you in deciding necessary expenses? Is the debtor expected to liquidate exempt property, such as his pension or homestead?

To a large extent, these questions go unanswered. In attempting to apply the law to those facts, judges have considered several factors, including:

- The debtor's disposable income, as measured at the time of trial

- The debtor's opportunities for more lucrative employment

- The extent to which the debtor's burden of debt will be lessened in the near-term

- The extent to which the debtor has made previous good faith efforts to fully employ himself and to satisfy the debt in question

Ability to pay — over what period of time?

When you have disposable income of $50 per month, do you have the ability to pay an $18,000 obligation, even though doing so would take 30 years? If the entire $18,000 is declared nondischargeable, may your ex-spouse immediately start garnishing your wages, drag you into court for debtor's exams, and otherwise torment you over an obligation that you can't immediately pay?

Or does ability to pay mean ability to pay within some reasonable time period? And if so, what's reasonable?

A number of courts come down on the side of ability to pay over a reasonable period of time. But they disagree on just what reasonable is. Some say it means ability to pay over three years. Others say that ability to pay over ten years is reasonable.

Some courts are willing to figure out how much a debtor can pay within some reasonable period of time, and wipe out the balance. Others impose repayment schedules by which the debtor pays part of or the entire obligation.

Tipping the relative suffering scales

Even when you can afford to pay a property division obligation, the court may still wipe it out if "discharging such debt would result in a benefit to the debtor that outweighs the detrimental consequences to a spouse, former spouse, or child of the debtor."

Not surprisingly, courts disagree on just what that quotation of the law means. But many look at certain factors, such as:

- Amount of disputed debt, including all payment terms

- Income and assets of the debtor and his new spouse, compared with the income and assets of his ex-spouse and her present mate

✔ Health, job skills, training, ages, and educational levels of the debtor, ex-spouse, and their respective spouses

✔ Number of dependents of the debtor, ex-spouse, and their respective spouses, their ages, and any special needs that they may have

✔ Any changes in the financial conditions of the debtor and the ex-spouse that occurred since the entry of the divorce decree

✔ Total amount of debt that is discharged in the debtor's bankruptcy

✔ The good faith of each party

With third-party debts that the ex-spouse escapes by filing bankruptcy, some courts say the complaining spouse should simply file bankruptcy himself and stop bugging the debtor. Other bankruptcy courts strenuously disagree, saying the ex-spouse shouldn't be pushed unwillingly into bankruptcy.

Remembering the 60-day bar date

The debtor's ex-spouse has to be on his toes to prevent discharge of property divisions in a Chapter 7. The rule states: If he wants to claim that the debt shouldn't be wiped out, he must file certain papers with the Bankruptcy Court within 60 days of the *341 meeting* (where you meet with creditors and they ask you questions); otherwise, the obligation will be discharged. You can find out more about the 60-day bar date in Chapter 12.

The 60-day bar date applies only to property divisions, *not* support obligations. If an obligation is support, it's automatically protected from being wiped out by bankruptcy.

Other grounds for bankruptcy-proof marital debts

Because more than one reason can exist for making a debt nondischargeable, you may encounter some other situations where a property division isn't dischargeable even in a Chapter 7.

A debtor may be guilty of fraud in negotiating a marital settlement agreement, or of some other type of intentional misconduct. When one spouse agrees to a marital settlement with no intention of performing, that may constitute fraud. Or if he withdraws and spends money from his pension after it was awarded to his ex-wife, he may be guilty of theft.

Chapter 17

Student Loans and Other Mind Games

In This Chapter

▶ Appreciating how student loans work

▶ Eliminating student loans in bankruptcy

▶ Eliminating student loans without bankruptcy

A college education is one of the best investments you can make in your future — sometimes. It can also be one of the very worst.

Today's college graduates earn 40 percent more than people with only high school diplomas. But the cost of a college education is well beyond what most people, or their parents, can afford without student loans. So, the lending of money for higher education has evolved into an industry unto itself. Today, one of every 12 Americans owes money on student loans.

When student-loan programs function as intended, everybody wins. With their enhanced earnings, graduates can pay off their loans without serious difficulty and, by earning more, they pay more in federal and state income taxes. It's a win-win-win situation for the borrower, the lender, and society — when it works out that way. Unfortunately, that doesn't always happen. When you buy a house, the bank assesses the property, ensuring not only that you're paying a reasonable price, but also that the home is worth enough to cover the loan if you happen to default. But with educational loans, no one seems to care whether a particular course of study has any economic value.

Students often incur a fortune in debt to earn a personally fulfilling but economically worthless degree. After that, they're saddled with enormous debt from their school loans, and an earning potential that's no better than it was before they went to school. Frequently, they're up to their necks in debt, and have no realistic prospect of paying it off in the foreseeable future.

Bankruptcy, however, isn't always — or even usually — the best way to deal with student loans. For a number of reasons, some better than others, lawmakers have made discharging student-loan obligations in bankruptcy very difficult.

This chapter explains the complicated workings of the student-loan industry, your bankruptcy options, and your nonbankruptcy options.

Members of Congress want to ensure that everyone seeking a college education has that option, and they have a vested interest in appeasing the lending industry, which is ever so generous with campaign donations and lobbying dollars. So, Congress creates and sustains an environment where lenders are willing to make loans because chances are good that they'll make money from them.

If you're to have even a fighting chance of eliminating your student loans, you need a firm understanding of how the process works, generally and with regard to your unique situation. The first step is figuring out who holds your loan, which isn't nearly as simple as you may think. Next you need to know just what the loanholder can do if you don't pay.

Tracing Your Loans

Student loans frequently are moving targets, because they constantly are assigned to various players in a huge and hugely complex industry. Although the guaranteed student-loan program is federal, these loans may originate from any of three sources:

- Private lenders (Federal Family Education Loans, or FFEL)
- Schools (Perkins Loans)
- The United States Department of Education (Federal Direct Loans)

After your loan goes into default, figuring out who to deal with can be tough — a guarantee agency, a private collector hired by a guarantee agency, the Department of Education, a collection agency hired by the department, or the school. So, you need to keep these points in mind:

- If a private lender makes the loan, it frequently turns right around and sells it to a lender specializing in student loans, such as the Student Loan Marketing Association (*Sallie Mae*).
- Either the original lender or the purchaser of a loan may hire a loan servicer to receive payments and keep track of how much is owed.
- When a loan is delinquent for at least 270 days and therefore deemed in default, the loanholder (except where the original lender was the Department of Education) is paid off by state guarantee agencies. The state guarantee agency then goes after you or hires a private bill collector to do the dirty work.
- If the guarantee agency can't collect, the federal government bails it out and inherits the problem.

> ✔ The Department of Education also hires private agencies to collect the loans it holds, regardless of whether the loans originated with the department or were acquired through the guarantee process.

When the loan isn't yet in default, you may find at least a temporary fix for your student loan burden by checking out repayment plans available from the original lender (or the purchaser of the loan, such as Sallie Mae), the school (in the case of Perkins loans), or the Department of Education where the loan originated from the government.

If you've recently received a collection letter, that's a pretty good starting point in hunting down the holder of your loan. You can call the Federal Student Aid Information Center at 800-433-3243, which likely will yield the name and address of the holder of your loan. If your loan came directly from the Department of Education, you can call the Direct Loan Servicing Center at 800-848-0979. If you're still having trouble, you can contact the ombudsman office in the Department of Education at www.sfahelp.ed.gov or call 877-557-2575.

What They Can Do If You Don't Pay

If you're behind on your student loan payments, you won't receive any more student loans without reestablishing your eligibility or rehabilitating the loan. (See the section entitled, "Requesting a reasonable and affordable payment plan" later in this chapter.) Collection can be enforced by:

> ✔ Lawsuits
>
> ✔ Garnishment (where money is taken from your wages even without filing a lawsuit) of up 10 percent of your net income
>
> ✔ Interception of your income tax refunds

Likewise, after your loan goes into default, collection costs of up to 43 percent may be added.

Managing Student Loans with Bankruptcy

The statute of limitations on student loans is pretty much gone. So, no matter how old the loan is, you may still have to pay it back. And, if that isn't bad enough, you can't wipe it out ("discharge" it) in any kind of bankruptcy without first showing that repayment poses an "undue hardship" — a term the Bankruptcy Code left for the courts to define.

The whole ball of wax

Although written primarily for lawyers and judges, an entire book is devoted to the subject of discharging student loans. Information about acquiring the book, *Discharging Student* *Loans in Bankruptcy*, by David J. Light (LRP Publications 1998), can be obtained at the publisher's Web site: www.lrp.com/index.html.

Absent proof of "undue hardship," the following educational obligations are considered nondischargeable student loans:

- ✔ A loan made, insured, or guaranteed by a governmental unit, or made under any program, funded in whole or in part by a governmental unit or nonprofit institution

- ✔ An obligation to repay funds received as an educational benefit, scholarship, or stipend

- ✔ Overpayments made on grants and other educational benefits

Nevertheless, not every education-related expense is protected from discharge. Some courts have ruled that debts for things like books, supplies, and student housing are dischargeable in bankruptcy. Another court may say that Congress didn't intend "to elevate any garden variety indebtedness that a student may incur to an educational institution, be it cafeteria charges, bookstore charges, parking lot charges, or room and board charges, to the category of excepted educational debt." So, getting to know the views of your local bankruptcy judge is critical.

What if someone else lends you money to pay off your student loan? Is that new debt dischargeable? It may very well be. A couple of courts have said that a loan from an employer to pay off student loans is dischargeable. But this stipulation isn't an invitation to borrow money to pay student loans while intending to bankrupt the new loan. As we discuss at length in Chapters 13 and 15, borrowing money without intending to repay it is fraud, and claims of fraud aren't dischargeable.

Proving your insufferable need for a break

If you want to discharge a student loan in bankruptcy because repayment would impose an undue hardship on you or your family, you have to convince the judge of each of the following:

- ✔ You can't maintain a minimal standard of living for you and your family if you're forced to repay the student loan.

> ✔ Your situation is likely to continue.
>
> ✔ You've made a good-faith effort to repay the loan.

Here's a closer look at these requirements.

Defining financial hardship

Although you needn't be poverty stricken to satisfy this requirement, you do have to be pretty severely strapped. One court ruled that a household income of about $45,000 can provide a family of five with more than a minimum living standard and, as a result, the debtor was able to pay at least $175 per month on student loans.

When determining undue hardship, most courts consider all household income and household expenses. But beware. Many courts won't consider the household expenses for a live-in lover or his children if you have no legal obligation to support them.

Determining whether repayment imposes an undue hardship raises the question of how long a person is expected to pay. Some courts look to the original term of the loan, frequently ten years, to assess whether a debtor can repay a loan over that period of time. But others adopt a much stricter view, saying that debtors need to be required to pay on student loans for up to 25 years and, if that's possible, then the loan isn't discharged.

Courts don't just look at how much money you're earning right now, they also look at how much you *could* earn in the foreseeable future if you put your mind to it.

Forecasting that your circumstances are unlikely to improve

In addition to proving your inability to pay the loan, you must also show that your financial plight is likely to continue into the foreseeable future. Temporary hardship isn't enough.

ANECDOTE

Noble intentions aren't enough

Mary chose to use her costly law degree to represent indigent clients who were unable to pay her legal fees. Consequently, she couldn't afford to pay off her student loans. Is bankruptcy the answer?

As noble as Mary's efforts were, the court wasn't willing to cut her any slack on her student loans. The judge flatly rejected Mary's argument that she couldn't afford to repay her loans because she was supporting a 20-year-old daughter attending college.

ANECDOTE

Judges' ideas of good/bad faith

Case law provides some guidance into what judges are likely to accept, or not accept, as a good-faith argument:

When Joanne tried getting out of her student loans by filing bankruptcy right after graduation, the court not only refused to wipe out the loans, but also scolded her for abusing the bankruptcy process.

Ruby, a single mom living with her mother in public housing, barely earned enough to get by. Although she paid only $180 of $9,000 in student loans, the court found that she acted in good faith by paying as much as she could and waiting for several years to file bankruptcy rather than heading directly to bankruptcy court as soon as her loans came due.

Mackenzie was able to discharge $100,000 in student loans, part of which was for law school. On the petition date, she was working as a law clerk, earning $30,000, and her husband stayed home to care for their children. Their monthly income exceeded expenses by only $71. The court agreed that Mackenzie's husband probably couldn't earn enough to offset child-care expenses and concluded that the situation was likely to continue for six years, when the youngest child would be in school full time. Finally, the court held that the good-faith test was met even though no payments had been made on the loans, because Mackenzie was doing her best to minimize expenses and had found the best job available.

This requirement can be met when the debtor suffers from a permanent physical or mental disability or disease. Several courts ruled that a bipolar condition (manic-depression) qualifies, and at least one believed that chronic fatigue syndrome is a permanent disability. But not all judges are receptive to claims of mental illness.

Although the fact that the education was worthless doesn't by itself justify discharging the loan, it may be taken into consideration when determining whether a debtor's financial plight is likely to improve.

Demonstrating good faith

The third prong of the hardship test requires proof that you acted in good faith regarding your student loans. Essentially, that means you:

- ✔ Made all reasonable efforts to maximize income and reduce expenses
- ✔ Didn't file bankruptcy solely to evade student loans
- ✔ Tried nonbankruptcy alternatives
- ✔ Made some effort, if at all possible, to repay the loans

Good faith is one of those eye-of-the-beholder concepts and, in bankruptcy, the judge has the beholding eye.

Wiping out part of your student loans

Even when you're unsuccessful in discharging the entire loan, some courts will wipe out part of the loan, forcing the creditor to accept a repayment plan. For example, courts have:

- ✔ Examined the debtors' budget, determined that the debtor can afford to pay $10 per month, and discharged the balance of the loan

- ✔ Reduced a Chapter 7 debtors' student loans by more than 50 percent and instructed the parties to propose a schedule for repaying the balance within six years

- ✔ Deferred collection for a period of one year

- ✔ Ruled that repayment of the principal balance would not impose undue hardship, but discharged attorney fees and interest, and ordered the creditor to accept a repayment plan of $50 per month

- ✔ Held that repayment of the total balance of several student loans imposed undue hardship and discharged all but about one-fifth of the total balance, reducing each loan proportionately

Other judges, however, don't think the Bankruptcy Code empowers them to partially discharge or restructure student loans. In their view, discharge is an all-or-nothing proposition, and that sort of ruling cuts both ways for student lenders. A court that can't reduce or restructure a loan is left with only two choices: preserve the entire obligation or wipe the whole thing out. Faced with this dilemma, it may opt to erase the whole thing even though it would have preferred to wipe out only a part of it.

A few courts say that although student loans may not be restructured, each loan can be considered separately so that one or two of a person's student loans can be wiped out and the others preserved. If your local court takes this approach, consolidating all your loans before bankruptcy may be a mistake, because doing so can eliminate the possibility of discharging one of your more costly loans. After all, consolidation combines all existing loans into a single loan.

Paying student loans under a Chapter 13 plan

Although student loans can't be wiped out in a Chapter 7 or a Chapter 13, absent proof of "undue hardship," you still can force the student loan creditor to accept payments in amounts you can afford to make through a Chapter 13 repayment plan. However, you need to remember that if the loan isn't paid in full during the Chapter 13, you still must pay the balance when your case is over, and interest on the loan balance continues to accrue during the bankruptcy. So, even if you pay the balance of a student loan in full under a Chapter 13 plan, you're still going to owe some interest after your case is complete.

If your student loan is but one of many debts, proposing a Chapter 13 plan in which more of your payment is earmarked for nondischargeable student loans than for dischargeable debts would be nice, but most courts won't permit that kind of discrimination. Some courts would go along if you voluntarily agreed to extend your plan so that other creditors receive as much as they'd receive under a regular 36-month payment schedule without the student loan receiving preferential treatment. For example, if you can propose a confirmable 36-month plan that pays all creditors, including the student loan, 30 percent of their claims, a court would approve a plan that pays a student loan in full if your plan was extended (to a maximum of 60 months) long enough so that other creditors still receive 30 percent of their claims.

If the remaining term of the student loan is longer than three years, you can propose making up all the missed payments on the student loan over the life of a Chapter 13 plan and resume regular monthly payments as they come due after the petition date. Of course, the balance remaining when your Chapter 13 is completed still has to be paid.

A number of courts have endorsed the approach described in the previous paragraph. One court points out that merely resuming regular payments on a student loan is okay, but paying off the entire debt under the plan improperly discriminates in favor of the student loan.

A downside to curing a student loan and maintaining payments as a long-term debt stems from the fact that long-term debt is excepted from discharge in a Chapter 13 without regard to whether repayment imposes undue hardship. By choosing to treat the loan in this fashion, you may lose the right to claim that it should be discharged on undue-hardship grounds.

Using a "Chapter 20" strategy

One way around the rule forbidding Chapter 13 plans from discriminating in favor of student loans is colloquially known as *Chapter 20 bankruptcy* (filing Chapter 7 and Chapter 13 in succession).

For this strategy to work, you first file a Chapter 7 to discharge all debts other than the student loan, and then you file a Chapter 13 case where you propose paying the entire student loan. No discrimination problem exists, because you now only have one debt left; the others were discharged in the Chapter 7.

Discharging student loans by stealth and ambush

We (and a number of courts) view one way of getting out of student loans in a Chapter 13 as a dirty trick. Although this ploy has worked in some cases, we most certainly don't endorse it. Still, it is something to discuss with your lawyer who knows the views of your local bankruptcy judge. Here's how it works:

A crafty lawyer sticks a provision in a Chapter 13 plan essentially providing that court approval of your plan constitutes a finding that repayment of student loans imposes an undue hardship and that, as such, the debt will be discharged. A copy of the proposed plan is forwarded to the student-loan creditor. If the student-loan creditor lodges no objection, and the court approves the plan, Voilà! the debt is wiped out.

Keep in mind, however, that your victory here may be Pyrrhic, because you and your lawyer may well end up getting fined. Many aren't at all amused by what they view as an attempt to slip one past the court, and they often react with a vengeance.

Other courts, however, are more tolerant because they view the Chapter 13 as essentially a bargaining process where the plan is simply an offer to creditors. Under this view, fining a debtor or his counsel for simply making an offer to a student-loan creditor wouldn't seem proper.

Some courts take a dim view of this strategy, but they're more likely to go along if you don't file Chapter 13 until you first try working out a nonbankruptcy repayment arrangement. Actually, you may get a better deal outside bankruptcy. We cover these options in the "Managing Student Loans without Bankruptcy" section, later in this chapter.

Addressing medical school loans

Loans under the Health Education Assistance Loan (HEAL) program and repayment obligations under scholarships granted by the National Health Services Corporation (NHSC) program are even more difficult to discharge in bankruptcy than other student loans. A waiting period must be satisfied, and a court must decide that requiring repayment would be *unconscionable*.

The waiting periods are seven years for HEAL loans and five years for NHSC obligations. Both are measured from the date the obligation first became due to the date of the bankruptcy discharge.

Here's kind of a weird crinkle: The strict standards for discharging medical school loans apply only to a person's first bankruptcy. If he ends up having to file a second time, then dischargeability is determined according to the undue hardship standards applicable to ordinary student loans. See the earlier discussion in the section, "Proving your insufferable need for a break."

Choosing underemployment doesn't cut it

Edwin had a master's degree from Oxford but gave up teaching because of stress and started a pottery business, earning him less than $7,000 per year. The court said that a person can't qualify for discharge of student loan by voluntarily choosing to be underemployed and adopting a minimalist lifestyle.

Similarly, one court refused to discharge a $19,121 student loan, because the debtor, who was a teacher, could earn more if she chose to work during the summertime.

Getting stuck even when you're only a cosigner

Student loans aren't dischargeable even if you're only a cosigner. If you cosigned for your child's student loan, not only are you liable when he doesn't pay, you probably can't escape it by filing bankruptcy.

Clicking your clock into The Hardship Zone

Everyone's financial situation fluctuates, so timing can be critical. When considering undue hardship, the court tries to predict your future income and expenses, based on your current situation.

Obviously, asking the court to discharge the student loan is a question best posed when your financial situation is at its bleakest. In fact, you can even ask the court to discharge your student loans after your bankruptcy case has been closed. In fact, when your loan is held by a state agency, you may *have* to wait until your bankruptcy case is closed, and then file suit in state court (instead of bankruptcy) seeking discharge of your loan on undue hardship grounds. The Eleventh Amendment to the United States Constitution protects the rights of states, shielding them from unwillingly being dragged into a bankruptcy proceeding — or so a number of courts have found.

Bankruptcy can only affect debts existing at the time you file. Debts arising after bankruptcy aren't covered by the bankruptcy discharge. So, replacing a prebankruptcy student loan with a new consolidation loan (see "Consolidating your loans" a little later in this chapter) may undercut your bankruptcy options because the new loan would arise after you filed.

Bottom line: Check with a bankruptcy lawyer before getting a consolidation loan.

Managing Student Loans without Bankruptcy

If, after reading the earlier section entitled "Managing Student Loans with Bankruptcy," you're thinking that bankruptcy doesn't appear to be the answer to your prayers, other options include loan consolidation, deferment, forbearance, renewal of eligibility, and administrative discharge.

Consolidating your loans

Consolidation actually is a misnomer because you don't need to have more than one loan to qualify. Two programs that may prove helpful to you are

- Direct Consolidated Loans, which come directly from the federal government
- Federal Family Education Loans, which, although guaranteed by the federal government, are made by private lenders

Through these programs, your loans are paid off and a new, consolidated loan is created. Monthly payments are based on family income.

Don't confuse these special educational consolidation loans with ordinary pitches from private lenders to consolidate loans by balance transfers or cash advances on credit cards, which almost never are good ways to address a student loan.

The upside is that the consolidated loan may well carry a lower interest rate than the original loan(s), the monthly payment *probably* will be less, and the time to repay *probably* will be extended. It sounds like a great deal if you qualify: Old loans are eliminated, you're immediately eligible for new educational loans and grants, and you're no longer subject to garnishments or other collection efforts.

However, here are a few downsides to consider:

- If you think you'll ever want to challenge one of your student loans in court, consult with an attorney before you agree to any form of consolidation. A closed bankruptcy can be reopened to discharge a student loan if your financial condition worsens. You may give up that option whenever you obtain a consolidation loan after bankruptcy.
- Be aware that the consolidated loan carries an 18.5 percent collection fee, which is added to the loan principal after consolidation. Ouch, that hurts!

✔ If you've defaulted on any of your student loans, your credit report continues to reflect the fact that you were, at some point, in default, even when you consolidate the loan.

✔ As always, realize that extending your payments increases the total amount you have to pay, just as it does with a car loan or a home mortgage.

In almost every instance, the Federal Direct Consolidation loan is a better deal than a FFEL consolidation loan because Federal Direct loans:

✔ Don't have the FFEL requirement that you must make three payments to qualify

✔ Offer lower interest rates and payments (In fact, payments can be zero for families living at or below the poverty line. After 25 years, the remaining balance is wiped out.)

✔ May be easier to postpone if someday you need a deferment

After obtaining either type of loan, the borrower is eligible for new loans, and no longer is subject to tax intercepts, garnishments, or other collections efforts.

Only you, and perhaps your attorney, can decide whether consolidation is the appropriate route. If you think it may be, you can obtain a loan application and fact sheet by calling 800-557-7392. You can also download forms from the Department of Education Web site, www.ed.gov/DirectLoan/consolid2.html.

Spouses need to avoid combining their individual loans into a single consolidation loan; otherwise, each spouse becomes legally responsible for the other's student loans.

Requesting a reasonable and affordable payment plan

As an alternative to consolidation loans, you can request "a reasonable and affordable" payment plan and renew your eligibility (so you qualify for more student loans) or rehabilitate your loans (so your name is removed from the creditor's deadbeat list).

Guarantee agencies or collectors for the federal government are required to offer this type of payment plan, but only when you specifically request it by using the magic words: "renew eligibility" and/or "rehabilitate the loans."

Additional resources

Relieving your student-loan obligations without bankruptcy is extremely complicated, and few lawyers are knowledgeable in this area. The best resource is a book entitled *Student Loan Law.* Written for lawyers by the National Consumer Law Center, you can find out more about this book by calling 617-523-8089, or visiting www.consumerlaw.org. The Northwest Justice Project also sponsors a Web site that provides similar information at www.nwjustice.org/docs/1170.html.

You can also obtain information from two very helpful publications. One by Robin Leonard and Shae Irving is *Take Control of Your Student Loans* (Nolo Press). The other, by Jonathan Sheldon and Gary Klein is *Surviving Debt* (The National Consumer Law Center). The Federal Student Aid Information Center at 800-433-3243 may also be able to help, and the Department of Education maintains a Web site at www.ed.gov, which is very informative.

When you make six consecutive payments under such a plan, you renew your eligibility for student loans. When you make 12 consecutive payments, you can request that the loan be rehabilitated. In that case, the loan is essentially rewritten. The disadvantage of rehabilitation is that the amount of your payments will almost surely increase.

Guarantee agencies have authority to settle for less than the full amount of the loan by waiving collection fees and agreeing to a discount of up to 30 percent in exchange for a lump sum payment. Before agreeing to a compromise, however, you need to confirm that the Department of Education recognizes the deal and won't later try to collect the balance.

Getting a deferment

Depending on what type of loan you have and when the loan was made, many different grounds exist for justifying deferment of your loan. The most common grounds are that you're still in school, have lost your job, or are suffering economic hardship. Contact the holder of your loan to determine whether you may be eligible.

The nice thing about deferments is that you remain eligible for additional student aid and you won't be subjected to collection activity. The problem is that you're not eligible for a deferment if your loan is in default. Just the same, you can reestablish the right to deferment by renewing eligibility or getting a consolidation loan.

Accepting a forbearance

If you don't qualify for a deferment, the holder of your loan may still agree to a *forbearance*, which temporarily suspends your payment obligation. Forbearances are easier to obtain than deferments, but they aren't as good. If the loan is in default, you can still obtain a forbearance and stop collection activity. However, interest continues to accrue. You can also obtain a forbearance to prevent a loan from going into default, thereby preserving the right to a deferment at some point in the future. As is true for a deferment, contact the holder of your loan to find out whether you qualify.

Going for an administrative discharge

In some situations, student loans can be wiped out without bankruptcy through administrative procedures within the U.S. Department of Education. But the grounds for discharge are quite technical and vary among different types of loans. More information is available through the Department of Education Web site at www.ed.gov/finaid.html and www.ed.gov/offices/OSFAP/DCS/loan.cancellation.discharge.html. Those sites offer information about extinguishing student loans if:

- ✔ You become permanently and totally disabled.
- ✔ You were unable to complete an educational program because the school closed.
- ✔ The school admitted you without a requisite high school degree or otherwise improperly allowed you to enroll.
- ✔ The school improperly certified your ability to benefit from the training offered.

Or if you are:

- ✔ Engaged in full-time teaching
- ✔ In the military service
- ✔ Involved in the Head Start Program
- ✔ In the Peace Corps

Part V
Strategies for a Successful Bankruptcy

The 5th Wave   By Rich Tennant

"You'll notice in section 4 of your bankruptcy, the money owed your girlfriend has been discharged. However, she still holds a lien on your weekends."

In this part . . .

Now that you've filed for bankruptcy, or decided to file, you need to know how to function in this brave new world. This part tells you how. In the same way that a wedding ceremony doesn't ensure future blissful years or even weeks, filing for bankruptcy doesn't instantly eliminate all your troubles and responsibilities. You must put a little effort into making bankruptcy work for you and taking full advantage of your fresh start. In this part, we explain how to avoid ticking off the trustee assigned to your case and how to live comfortably and happily within the confines of a Chapter 13 repayment plan.

Chapter 18

Avoiding Troubles with Your Trustee

In This Chapter

▶ Protecting your fresh start by telling the truth and not playing games

▶ Appreciating how fraudulent transfers can cause you grief

▶ Anticipating situations where your bankruptcy can affect friends and relatives

Creditors can usually get only the benefit of those assets deemed *property of the estate* — which includes not only stuff you own on the petition date, but also property you've transferred just prior to filing bankruptcy (see Chapter 9 for more about transferring assets). Under certain circumstances, the bankruptcy trustee can grab property that you transferred and sell it for the benefit of your creditors.

In this chapter, we tell you some things that you shouldn't do before filing bankruptcy, if at all possible. If you've already done something that we talk about here, your lawyer probably can fix the problem — but only if she knows that the problem exists. You can find yourself in an awful mess when you file bankruptcy if you don't appreciate the trustee's ability to retrieve assets that you've transferred prior to bankruptcy, or if you haven't been completely honest and forthright with your lawyer.

Playing by the Rules and Telling the Truth

Quite simply, playing it straight is the best way to avoid headaches when filing bankruptcy. When you don't, the law arms the trustee with some pretty potent weapons, and you really don't want to stare down the barrel of that gun. Trust us on this one.

Debtor too smart for her own good

Joan thought she was being clever. She transferred her vacation house to her daughter but didn't bother telling her lawyer about the transaction and conveniently neglected to mention it in her bankruptcy papers. Who would know? Anyone who wants to, that's who.

A creditor discovered Joan's little maneuver in public records and brought it to the court's attention. Joan's daughter had to transfer the house to the bankruptcy trustee, none of Joan's debts were wiped out, and she barely escaped going to jail.

If Joan had been upfront with her lawyer from the get-go, a far better strategy could have been developed. For example, she may have been advised to sell the vacation house for a fair price and use the proceeds to fix the roof on her primary home and catch up with back mortgage payments.

Making sure that you play by the rules and that any assets that can and should go to creditors actually do go to creditors is the trustee's job. If you gave your kayak to your buddy right before bankruptcy just to ensure that the credit-card company wouldn't get it, the trustee can go after your pal for the return of the boat or payment of its value. Furthermore, and much more painfully for you, if the trustee in a Chapter 7 liquidation case thinks you're jerking your creditors around, she can ask the court to deny your discharge outright. When that happens, filing bankruptcy was for naught, because

- All your nonexempt property has been surrendered
- A bankruptcy is on your record
- None of your debts are eliminated
- You have no chance to eliminate those obligations through a Chapter 7 bankruptcy

In short, it's a lose-lose-lose-lose situation.

By now you're probably asking how you can avoid that headache.

The answer is real simple: Tell the truth, the whole truth, and nothing but the truth. Your parents were right; honesty is the best policy. And not only does truthfulness make you feel good, it may also keep you on the better side of prison bars.

Most documents filed in bankruptcy must be signed under penalty of perjury. If you intentionally lie on bankruptcy documents, or at the *341 meeting* with creditors, you've committed *perjury* — a crime that can land you in prison. Careless disregard for the truthfulness of your statements is the same as lying, so ignorance is not bliss.

Accurately Listing Your Assets

If avoiding criminal prosecution and protecting your discharge isn't enough to keep you on the straight and narrow, there's another reason to list all your assets. If you accurately describe an asset and the trustee doesn't sell it while the case is open, that asset is *abandoned* — meaning it's yours again when the case is closed. Conversely, whenever you omit an asset or don't accurately describe it, your case can be reopened, even years later, with a trustee demanding that you turn over the asset or pay for its value.

In addition, whenever you accurately describe an asset and claim it as exempt in your bankruptcy schedules, the trustee and creditors have only 30 days after the *341 meeting* to object. If no timely objection is filed, the property is deemed exempt even though a court would have ruled otherwise had a timely objection been filed.

Sometimes debtors forget to list a pending or potential lawsuit they have against someone (from which they hope to gain some money). Forgetting can prove to be a problem, especially when the debtor remembers the lawsuit after the bankruptcy is closed and tries to pursue the claim. If the party defending the claim is on the ball and discovers that you didn't list the claim, she may be able to have your suit dismissed.

Appreciating the Trustee's Ability to Recover Assets

The bankruptcy trustee has powers designed to help her recover assets and distribute proceeds fairly to unsecured creditors. Although powers wielded by Chapter 7 and Chapter 13 trustees are similar, they are most commonly invoked in Chapter 7 cases.

These powers include recovering concealed assets and *avoiding* or undoing:

- Fraudulent transfers
- Preferential transfers
- Unperfected liens

Fraudulent transfers

A transfer can be deemed a fraudulent transfer even when no actual fraud is involved. The law distinguishes between transfers that reek so bad that they are "actually fraudulent," and those that are only technically fraudulent.

A transfer that wasn't necessarily intentionally fraudulent, but was so far out of line that it may as well have been intentional is called a *constructively fraudulent* transfer.

Actually fraudulent transfers

When you're buried in debt, your first impulse may be to give away your valuable property to friends or relatives so that creditors can't get it. That's an *actually fraudulent* transfer, and it's cheating. If you transfer the property within the year before filing bankruptcy, your Chapter 7 discharge may be denied — leaving you in worse financial trouble than when you started.

Your discharge may be denied even when the actual transfer was more than one year before bankruptcy, if you concealed the transfer during the year before you filed for bankruptcy. Say, for example, that three years before filing bankruptcy you transferred all your belongings to a trust but continued using these assets within one year of bankruptcy just as if you still owned them. In that situation, many courts apply a doctrine known as *continuing concealment* to deny your discharge because you concealed the transfer within one year of the petition date.

Whenever you try to conceal transfers or property from your bankruptcy trustee, you may end up in jail.

In addition to having your discharge denied, the trustee can also go after the recipient of a fraudulent transfer to recover the transferred asset or its value. And we're not talking about transfers made just before bankruptcy. When taking this route, the trustee can challenge transfers you made up to six years before bankruptcy!

Constructively fraudulent transfers

In contrast to actually fraudulent transfers (see the previous section), *constructively fraudulent* transfers aren't intentional schemes to shield property from creditors. Instead, they involve gifts or legitimate transfers of assets for values less than they're actually worth. The problem, from the standpoint of creditors, is that these kinds of transfers leave you with fewer assets. For example, if you sell a $10,000 car for $10,000, you still have the same amount of assets to use for paying creditors. You simply transformed the car into another asset — cash. On the other hand, if you just gave the car away, you would have less for creditors. Here are a couple more examples that may help illustrate this rather counterintuitive concept.

> ✔ **Bob giving his sister $10,000 to help her through a nasty divorce.** This is a constructively fraudulent transfer because Bob transferred valuable assets ($10,000) that could theoretically have been used to pay his debts, but didn't receive anything in return. So, the bankruptcy trustee sued Bob's poor sister for $10,000. But at least Bob got his debts wiped out because he didn't intentionally try to stiff his creditors.

  ✔ **Mary paying $5,600 on her sister's credit card right before filing.** The court deemed the transfer constructively fraudulent because Mary wasn't getting anything for her $5,600 and ruled that the trustee could get the money back from Mary's sister or the credit-card company.

  ✔ **Joe paying $100,000 to attend a fund-raising dinner with the President of the United States shortly before filing bankruptcy.** When Joe filed bankruptcy, the court ordered the Republican National Committee to turn the money over to the trustee because the court decided that Joe received "less than reasonably equivalent value" for his investment.

Gambling losses present yet another conundrum. Trustees sometimes go after gambling casinos to recover a debtor's gambling losses for the benefit of creditors. But courts usually accept the casino's argument that a gambler *receives significant value* when gambling — the prospect of winning.

Until recently, whenever a debtor donated to his church, the trustee could retrieve that money for payment to creditors. The theory then was that no matter how laudable a person's motives, his creditors shouldn't subsidize his charitable impulses. That's changed.

In 1998, powerful religious organizations, pushed through the "Religious Liberty and Charitable Donation Protection Act," which protects good-faith charitable contributions of up to 15 percent of a debtor's gross income during the year before filing bankruptcy, or more when greater amounts are consistent with past practices of the debtor. However, if the bankruptcy court is convinced that a debtor's contributions are made for the purpose of shortchanging creditors, the money can be recovered and the debtor can be denied his discharge.

Preferential transfers

Congress considers it unfair for unsecured creditors to get paid on the eve of bankruptcy when others are left holding the bag. As a result, Congress gave bankruptcy trustees the power to recover these payments, which are called *preferential transfers*, for the benefit of all creditors.

For example, if you paid your dentist $1,000 on an overdue bill a month before bankruptcy, the trustee can get the money back from the dentist and distribute it among all your creditors. For you, it's a lose-lose situation. The dentist won't be happy about having to give up the money, and you'll be out $1,000 that you could have used for living expenses, car payments, or house payments. Even worse, if you paid that money toward a nondischargeable debt only to have the trustee retrieve it, you wasted the dough — and the nondischargeable debt that you intended to pay is revived and continues to haunt you after bankruptcy.

You need to understand the difference between preferential and fraudulent transfers. *Fraudulent transfers* are cheating; *preferential transfers* aren't.

Debtor loses homestead by trying to save it

Sneaky Pete owned his $75,000 Boston home free and clear, but he was buried in debt and afraid that his many creditors would go after the house. So, Pete gave the house to his mother and then filed a do-it-yourself bankruptcy, figuring his creditors couldn't take what wasn't his.

Pete was wrong. Very wrong.

When the trustee learned of Pete's stunt, she went on the warpath. The trustee sued Pete's mom, recovered the home, and sold it. Adding insult to injury, the trustee convinced the bankruptcy court to deny Pete's discharge. So, in the end, Pete lost the house he was finagling to save and still was up to his eyeballs in debt.

Pete's first (and very costly) mistake was attempting to handle his own bankruptcy. That's often about as sensible as a do-it-yourself appendectomy. Any lawyer worthy of her license would have told Pete that under Massachusetts law, Pete's home already was exempt in bankruptcy, provided that he owned it when he filed. So, Pete had no reason to transfer the house to his mother. Furthermore, if he already had given Mom the deed, the lawyer would've told him to get it back before filing bankruptcy. That way, Pete would keep his home, have his debts discharged, and avoid the embarrassment and indignity of getting his mother sued.

Whenever you pay a legitimate debt, the payment may be preferential but not fraudulent. The distinction is important because your discharge can be denied for making a fraudulent transfer but not for a preferential transfer. The former is malicious or sneaky and the latter is essentially an accident or error in judgment. Either can affect your bankruptcy, though in different ways.

Be aware that preferential transfers can be recovered only when they're made within a relatively short time before bankruptcy, usually 90 days.

However, when a transfer is made to an insider, the trustee may be able to recover all the payments made during the entire year prior to bankruptcy. Whether an individual qualifies as an insider is determined on a case-by-case basis. *Insiders* generally include relatives and others with relationships close enough to you to strongly influence your actions. If you're still friends with your ex-spouse, he or she may be considered an insider. If you're bitter enemies, probably not. A live-in lover is deemed an insider by some courts.

Most courts say that in the case of a regular check, *payment* occurs when the check actually clears; however, with a cashier's check or money order, payment occurs when it is mailed to the creditor.

Payments on cosigned loans and joint debts

If the potential exists for a friend or relative to be left holding the bag for one of your debts if you don't pay it (for example, a joint debt or your friend cosigned for you), you may be tempted to protect her by paying that debt before bankruptcy. That's usually a bad idea (see "Poor planning brings an ugly surprise" anecdote), despite your good intentions.

For example, if your dad cosigns for your loan, he promises the lender that if you don't pay, he will. Say that, before bankruptcy you caught up on the back payments on that loan. Because every payment you make to the lender also reduces the amount of your father's potential liability, the law also treats any payment to the lender as a payment to your dad — even though he doesn't actually receive any money. So a trustee can go after your dad for the money you paid to the *lender* during the entire year prior to bankruptcy, because your dad is an insider. If the cosigner wasn't an insider, the trustee can recover only the payments made during the 90 days before the bankruptcy.

Rather than making payments on joint or cosigned loans before bankruptcy, explaining things to the other person and having *her* make the payments until after you file bankruptcy is a better way to go. You can always reimburse her later. Obviously this situation may cause some hard feelings, but your lawyer may be able to help you explain how this strategy is best for both of you.

Payments that aren't preferences

The following payments aren't considered preferences and the trustee can't recover them:

- ✔ **Small payments:** Payments totaling less than $600 to any single creditor during the relevant time period (usually 90 days before bankruptcy, but one year for payments to insiders).

- ✔ **Payments on secured debts:** Payments for things such as your house or car aren't recoverable as preferences. You can and need to continue making these payments if you intend to keep your house or vehicle.

- ✔ **Payments for current expenses:** Regular payments on bills that aren't overdue aren't avoidable. For example, your rent payment for the current month isn't a preference. But if you paid back rent totaling more than $600, it would be a preference.

- ✔ **Payments of back alimony or child support.** The trustee can't recover payments to an ex-spouse for back alimony or child support.

Unperfected liens

The law requires lienholders to *perfect* their liens, or warn people that someone other than you claims an interest in your property. That's why mortgages must be filed as part of the public record, and security interests in motor vehicles are noted on the certificate of title.

If a lien isn't perfected by the time a bankruptcy petition is filed, it's too late for the creditor. The trustee can take over the creditor's interest in the asset.

Poor planning brings an ugly surprise

Patti's parents loaned her $20,000 to help get creditors off her back. Although the loan provided temporary relief, Patti still was buried deep in debt. A few months later, her parents needed their money back. So, Patti used money in her IRA to repay them. She filed bankruptcy two months later.

The trustee forced Patti's parents to cough up the $20,000 for distribution to all her creditors. If Patti had filed bankruptcy *before* withdrawing the IRA, the trustee couldn't have touched the money. Then, she'd have been free, after bankruptcy, to repay her parents if she chose.

Moral of story: Parents and relatives can wait.

For example, assume that you owe the bank $4,000 on a car worth $5,000, and the amount of the car that you can claim as exempt (property which is usually off-limits to creditors) is $1,500. Usually, your exemption covers any equity in the car, so the bank would have its security interest (meaning it could take the car if you don't pay) and there'd be nothing left over for the trustee. If you wanted to keep the car, you'd continue making the payments to the bank.

However, if it turns out that when the bank loaned you the money, it forgot to have its lien on your car noted on the certificate of title, the trustee can take over the bank's security interest and sell your car. The trustee then can take all the money that would have gone to the lender, and you'd be paid for the amount of your exemption only if any money was left over.

Here's another hurdle: The act of perfecting a lien also is considered a transfer of property. So, if a lien isn't perfected at the same time that the loan is made, trying to perfect it later on creates an avoidable preference if the borrower files bankruptcy within the preference period.

For example: The bank that made your car loan discovers that it failed to have its security interest noted on the certificate of title when it made the loan. If the bank tries to fix the error later by having its security interest added to the certificate of title, that attempt would be an avoidable transfer — if, that is, you file bankruptcy within 90 days of when the bank tried to fix its error.

Special problems with manufactured homes

In many states, manufactured homes begin life as personal property, subject to certificate of title laws. In other words, a security interest must be noted on the certificate of title. Whether the unit remains personal property covered by a certificate of title or becomes real property covered by a mortgage when it is installed and affixed to land, isn't clear.

As you can see, manufactured housing can be very tricky, and even major lending institutions sometimes mess up their paperwork in such a way that their security interest isn't properly perfected. Trustees know to watch for these kinds of circumstances and closely examine financing documents. When they're not done right, the trustee can swoop in, and you can lose your home.

Bottom line: Whenever you have a manufactured home, show all the financing documents to your lawyer so that she can determine whether the paperwork is in order. If it isn't, she then can try to have the lender fix it before you file bankruptcy. But remember the wrinkle we point out, 90 days must pass from the time that the paperwork is corrected until bankruptcy is filed. Otherwise, the trustee can nullify the act of fixing the paperwork.

When the trustee eliminates a lien because it's unperfected, new preference issues crop up.

Remember that payments on secured loans aren't avoidable preferences (see "Payments that are not preferences" earlier in this chapter), but payments on unsecured loans may be? Well, whenever the trustee avoids a lien, the loan is considered unsecured at the time, so all prebankruptcy payments to the creditor within the relevant time period (a year or 90 days) become avoidable preferences.

Finding out the hard way

Celeste talked her way into a 60-day jail term and four-month home detention after lying to the bankruptcy court and fraudulently concealing asscts — namely, artwork, furniture, and money she was making on the sly through her off-the-books escort service. Celeste now has a criminal record, and she owes $25,000 restitution to her creditors.

George and Rose got into trouble with the bankruptcy court for neglecting to list $200,000 worth of marijuana in their bankruptcy schedules. The court said that even though the illegal drugs had no value to creditors, they should've been disclosed.

Betty had authority to draw on her mother's bank account. Because all the money belonged to her mother, Betty didn't list this account on her bankruptcy papers. Later, an angry creditor yelled "fraud" and asked the court to deny her bankruptcy discharge. Ultimately, Betty prevailed because the funds, in fact, belonged to her mother, but her bankruptcy became much more expensive and complicated than it would have been had she revealed her situation to the court and her attorney.

Moral of the story: Tell your lawyer about every asset you own or control, and let your attorney decide how to use that information.

Assume, for example, your uncle cosigned your secured car loan and during the past year you paid $1,500 on the loan. Ordinarily, these payments wouldn't be avoidable preferences because they were made to a secured creditor.

But say that the bank forgets to note its security interest on the certificate of title, which enables the trustee to avoid it. In that situation, all the loan payments become preferences, and the trustee can recover the money from your uncle. What's more, your uncle still is on the hook for the car loan, because the trustee is selling the car for the benefit of other creditors.

Protecting Your Discharge

Your Chapter 7 discharge is in jeopardy if you:

- ✔ Consciously fail to list an asset on your bankruptcy schedules
- ✔ Intentionally give false information in your schedules
- ✔ Lie to the trustee at the 341 meeting
- ✔ Refuse to cooperate with the trustee
- ✔ Disobey an order of the bankruptcy court
- ✔ Fraudulently transfer property within one year before filing bankruptcy
- ✔ Go too far in converting nonexempt assets into exempt assets (see Chapter 9)

Honest errors usually can be repaired if action is taken *before* you file bankruptcy. Afterward, however, it may be too late. So remaining silent and hoping that no one finds out about your transfers is very dangerous. Don't risk it. If you put property in someone else's name, money into someone else's bank account, or otherwise tried to protect any assets from creditors, be sure that you tell your lawyer.

Your lawyer should give you copies of all the schedules filed with the bankruptcy court. Review them carefully to make sure that all your assets are listed. Innocent mistakes can easily be fixed if you act promptly (especially if you correct your bankruptcy papers before the 341 meeting with creditors). If someone else points out the error, you may have trouble claiming that it was only an innocent mistake.

That said, courts rarely deny a discharge. But when they do, it usually happens in cases of obvious misrepresentation or refusal to cooperate. If you're completely truthful with your lawyer right from the beginning, you have a good chance of avoiding problems.

Chapter 19

Living on the Edge in Chapter 13 Bankruptcy

In This Chapter

▶ Constructing a realistic plan

▶ Having a lawyer by your side

▶ Figuring out what to do if you blow it

▶ Dealing with car and mortgage payments outside the plan

▶ Addressing postpetition debts

▶ Getting lucky

*W*hen preparing your Chapter 13 financial reorganization plan, you have to gaze three to five years into the future, realistically calculate your income and expenses, and promise to make regular payments based on those guesstimates. Unless you have a pretty reliable crystal ball, or a resident soothsayer, that's an awfully tall order. Often adjustments must be made because of your mistakes or because something (like an unexpected medical expense) happens to muck up your plan.

This chapter provides you with pointers for getting started on the right foot with a plan that's realistic and sensible. It addresses the importance of having a lawyer who's willing to stand by you from A to Z, describes your options when your repayment plan implodes, and offers insights into the potential successes and pitfalls that arise when things suddenly turn around and a windfall comes your way. Finally, a chart at the end lists the various choices you can make whenever your plan isn't working, along with the implications of making those choices.

Creating a Realistic Plan

Stuff happens — good things and bad. It's no wonder that nationally less that one-third of all Chapter 13 bankruptcies succeed. But *your* Chapter 13 needn't fail. With a reasonable plan, the odds of your success aren't all that bad. In fact, they're pretty decent.

The key is remaining *reasonable*.

Face it. If your plan is so tight that macaroni and cheese becomes an extravagant delicacy, it won't work — at least not for long. On the other hand, if your plan imposes reasonable restraint but enables you to maintain a satisfactory, albeit disciplined, lifestyle, you have a good shot.

Although statistically most plans will fail, the raw stats don't tell the entire story, because they fail to take into account which plans were unreasonable, and therefore are virtually jinxed from the get-go, and which were reasonable, and therefore had a fighting chance.

The key: Don't be discouraged by the theoretical odds. When your plan makes sense, you're probably going to come out of this situation just fine, even with those little surprises that life tends to toss in your path.

Why Chapter 13 plans fail

A Chapter 13 reorganization usually fails for one (or more) of the following reasons:

- It's poorly designed, unrealistic, and doomed from day one.
- The debtor screws up and just won't live within a budget.
- Unexpected expenses pop up.
- One of the first three listed items happens, and the debtor neglects to advise his or her lawyer, who probably could have dealt with the problem before it got out of hand and before it was too late to deal with.

Avoid these pitfalls, and you're home free.

Paying the bare minimum

With a Chapter 13 plan, you can clear your slate of most debts by paying just pennies on the dollars that you owe. Still, you usually must pay a threshold minimum so that you obtain your fresh start. Typically, that minimum amount is the total of:

- ✔ Back payments on your mortgage (if you want to keep your home)
- ✔ Nondischargeable taxes
- ✔ Prepetition support obligations
- ✔ The value of any nonexempt assets

The total amount must be paid within 60 months, so any plan that's designed to last the full 60 months is precarious and suspect because it puts you right up against the wall from the start and offers you no wiggle room if things don't work out just the way you hoped. If the math doesn't add up under a 60-month plan, you may be tempted to propose a schedule where monthly payments start out relatively low but then increase in the latter stages of your plan. At first blush, such plans sound doable, and maybe they are. But . . .

In our experience, we find it more often is a prescription for disaster. When the time comes for plan payments to increase, the money inevitably just isn't there. Then, the Chapter 13 case is dismissed or converted to a Chapter 7 liquidation, and any payments that you made are frequently for naught.

Keeping Your Lawyer in the Loop

Because the Bankruptcy Code doesn't provide clear guidance for dealing with the unexpected — job losses, unforeseen medical expenses, and so on — judges and trustees have had to improvise. They're usually pretty reasonable, but absent any formal direction, they more or less fashion their own rules and practices.

Having payments deducted from your wages

If you want to, you can have your Chapter 13 payments automatically deducted from your pay and forwarded to the trustee. Doing so is a convenient way to go that obviously makes squandering the money much harder to do because you never see it. You can do this by signing what's called a *wage deduction order.*

We have mixed thoughts about wage deductions.

Although some studies suggest that the success rate is higher, experiencing financial discipline is part and parcel of the Chapter 13 process. Working with your plan is when it's time to take control of your finances, instead of allowing others to do it for you. You certainly won't get any mileage out of burdening your boss with special payroll procedures. It's your call, of course, but we recommend making the payments yourself.

What's kosher in some areas is taboo in others, so having a guide who really knows the local practices, preferences, and eccentricities truly helps.

A Chapter 13 plan has a much better chance of succeeding when your lawyer sticks with you through the entire case — not just until your plan is confirmed.

Your lawyer needs to be willing to bargain with the Chapter 13 trustee whenever circumstances change. A lawyer who stands by you for three to five years obviously expects to be paid, but that shouldn't be a big problem. Legal fees usually are covered in regular plan payments.

Blowing It . . . Again? Not!

Sometimes, even the best Chapter 13 plan falls through because you lose your job, get sick, or you're unable to make payments as a result of other unforeseen events. All isn't necessarily lost. Depending on the type of debts and payments you're facing, your options include:

- Suspending your payments
- Modifying your plan
- Requesting a hardship discharge
- Converting your case to a Chapter 7 liquidation
- Dismissing your case outright
- Dismissing your case and then filing a Chapter 7
- Dismissing your case and then filing a second Chapter 13 reorganization

Considering each of these options is enough to make your head spin. The table at the end of this chapter entitled "Comparing Your Options" provides a thumbnail (granted a very large thumbnail) sketch of what you have to think about. You may want to jump ahead and glance at this table right now just to get a general overview, and then refer back to it as you read through this chapter.

Whenever you miss payments to the trustee — and don't take advantage of any of the options in the previous bulleted list — the court will dismiss your case, enabling creditors to resume collection efforts against you and your property. Furthermore, you may be barred from filing another bankruptcy for 180 days — regardless of how bad things get. Yes, the law is pretty harsh. But if you watch your step, you'll be okay.

Pondering one fickle legal pickle

Nigel faithfully made all his Chapter 13 payments until the auto repair shop where he had worked for 15 years cut its workforce. To make ends meet, he got a job working nights in a convenience store and even moved into an apartment above the store so he could rent out his house. When Nigel filed a Chapter 13, no one objected to his assertion that the home was exempt.

Nigel's convenience store boss, Garfield, filed a Chapter 13 at about the same time.

When he filed a Chapter 13, Garfield owned his personal residence, which was exempted, and a rental property, which wasn't exempt. After his income dropped, Garfield cut expenses by moving into the smaller rental property and allowing foreclosure to progress on his former residence.

Neither Nigel nor Garfield can keep up with their Chapter 13 payments, so the question becomes one of whether Nigel's and Garfield's homes are exempt if their Chapter 13 cases are converted to Chapter 7 cases.

Most courts would say that Nigel's house would be exempt after the case converts to a Chapter 7, because it was exempt on the date he initially filed under the Chapter 13. However, Garfield's house wouldn't be exempt, because it wasn't his residence on the Chapter 13 petition date, even though it was when the case was converted.

But then, again, other courts may rule just the opposite, saying that Nigel's home wasn't exempt because he didn't live there on the date of conversion, but Garfield's home was exempt because that's where he lived when his case was converted.

Suspending your payments

If you miss payments because of a temporary crisis — say you get laid off or sick — the wise thing to do is to ask the trustee to allow you to suspend payments until the crisis subsides. In that situation, the suspended payments aren't forgiven; they are just paid later, and the time limit of the plan is extended.

As long as you have a good reason for suspending payments and can convince the trustee that your problem is only temporary, you'll probably be allowed some latitude.

But there's a hitch.

Because a Chapter 13 can't run any longer than 60 months, if your plan already is five years old, suspending payments and extending the life of your plan won't work. In that case, the plan must be modified, which can raise an entirely new set of problems (see the next section). This reason is just one of several why a 60-month repayment plan is inherently dicey. Quite simply, not much room is left for error.

Modifying your plan

When a suspension of payments won't work — because the change in your circumstances isn't temporary or because your plan already is 60 months long — it may be possible to modify your Chapter 13 plan. Doing so usually results in lower payments now and higher ones in the future.

Consider the case of Fred and Frederica.

The Chapter 13 repayment plan was working just great. Fred and Frederica were diligently making up the missed mortgage payments and, finally, could see some light at the end of the tunnel. Then, their teenage son fractured his skull in a car crash, and they had to use the mortgage money to pay doctor bills. The bank asked for bankruptcy court permission to foreclose on their house.

Fred and Frederica quickly called their lawyer, who immediately filed a modified Chapter 13 plan. The plan, accepted by the court, extended the previous schedule and established payments that Fred and Frederica could make. They kept their house. And their son is doing just fine, thank you.

Modification can solve your problem the same way it did for Fred and Frederica. Of course, any proposed modification must be feasible, so the court examines your situation to see whether it's likely you'll be able to make higher payments at a later date. In other words, a judge isn't going to cut you a break now unless he's pretty sure you'll be able to make good on it later. If you can't afford higher future payments under a modified plan, consider asking the court for a hardship discharge (see the next section).

Modifying a plan after confirmation may open a Pandora's box.

Remember that any Chapter 13 plan must propose to pay the value of your nonexempt property based on the value of the property when the plan is confirmed.

If the value of your nonexempt property increases and you ask to have a modified plan confirmed, the court may insist on payments based on the increase in value. That kind of a result certainly isn't a good one, especially when you're already having problems keeping up with payments. All courts don't see things that way, but changing property values is something you need to discuss with your lawyer before requesting a plan modification.

For example, when your plan was initially confirmed, the equity in your home was within the allowable exemption. But after a couple of years, when you request a plan modification, the increase in your equity may exceed the exemption, because of an appreciation in value or simply a reduction of the mortgage balance. In this situation, some courts will bump up your payments to cover the increased equity.

Requesting a "hardship discharge"

A *hardship discharge* stops the Chapter 13 dead and excuses all remaining payments. To understand how it works, look at what happened to Isaac.

Isaac filed a Chapter 7 five years ago, and lo and behold, is in trouble again, with $10,000 in new credit-card bills. Because Isaac's bankruptcy was less than six years ago, a Chapter 7 won't wipe out his debts, so he tried making payments under a Chapter 13, but no dice. He just couldn't keep up. So, Isaac's attorney convinced the court to award a hardship discharge. Once again, his slate is squeaky clean.

Good deal, huh?

To qualify for such a discharge, you must:

- ✔ Convince the court that your inability to make payments is for reasons beyond your control

- ✔ Show that modification of the plan isn't feasible

- ✔ Already have made payments equal to the value of any nonexempt property you had on the petition date

The major disadvantage of a hardship discharge is that you don't obtain the usual super discharge provided in Chapter 13 cases. We explain in the chapters of Part IV how some debts may be wiped out in a Chapter 13 but not in a Chapter 7. That's why a Chapter 13 discharge is called a *super discharge*. But you obtain a super discharge only if you complete all your plan payments. In a hardship discharge, the only debts that are wiped out are the ones that are eliminated in a Chapter 7.

Nonetheless, a hardship discharge has the following advantages over converting the case to a Chapter 7:

- ✔ You can wipe out your debts even though you've previously received a bankruptcy discharge within the last six years. Conversely, this earlier discharge would prevent your current debts from being discharged in a Chapter 7.

- ✔ The property you owned when your Chapter 13 was filed won't be re-examined the way it would if you convert the case to a Chapter 7. This issue can be an especially important issue if, for example, you move out of your home (which had qualified for a homestead exemption) or the law governing exemptions was altered. On the other hand, if you convert to a Chapter 7, the court can apply the new rules and your property may no longer be exempt. If you go the hardship discharge route, property that was exempt when you initially filed bankruptcy remains exempt despite changes of this kind.

Converting to a Chapter 7

Although a hardship discharge is frequently a better deal than converting your case to a Chapter 7, it may not be an option. Some courts interpret the "hardship" in hardship discharge strictly and literally, reserving it for debtors who have suffered some catastrophic disaster. Your lawyer should know if your judge takes this view.

Conversion does have one advantage over a hardship discharge, however. If you convert, you gain relief from debts arising after your Chapter 13 petition was filed that wouldn't be included in a hardship discharge. For example, if you incurred some new bills after filing a Chapter 13, they ordinarily won't be wiped out in your existing bankruptcy; however, if you convert to a Chapter 7, you can add these debts to the ones you can eliminate.

Dismissing your Chapter 13 and filing a new Chapter 7

Instead of converting your Chapter 13 to Chapter 7, you can dismiss your Chapter 13 bankruptcy and file a brand new one under Chapter 7. Choosing between these two alternatives can be devilishly complicated.

The advantages of filing a new Chapter 7 over converting an existing case to a Chapter 7 are:

- ✔ Beneficial changes in the law will apply in a new case.

- ✔ You can delay filing a new case so that any debts incurred on the eve of the first case aren't presumed to be fraudulent. See Chapters 13 and 14 for an explanation of why debts incurred on the eve of bankruptcy may not be covered by a Chapter 7 discharge.

- ✔ You may be able to sell assets that you'll lose in a Chapter 7 and use the money for living expenses. Chapter 9 contains more info on turning nonexempt assets into exempt assets. Chapters 6 and 18 provide more food for thought on the subject of selling assets prior to bankruptcy.

- ✔ You can reestablish your homestead exemption if you've changed your residence during the Chapter 13 case. We explore this option a little later in this chapter.

- ✔ If you dismiss your Chapter 13 and then file a new Chapter 7, you retain an option to convert the Chapter 7 into a Chapter 13 filing. When you convert to a Chapter 7, you can't convert back to a Chapter 13.

The disadvantages of filing a new Chapter 7 over converting an existing case to a Chapter 7 are:

- ✔ Attorney fees and costs will probably be higher.

- ✔ Unfavorable changes in the law will apply in a new case, but wouldn't if you converted an existing case.

- ✔ The 180-day rule (see the section "Understanding when the 180-day rule applies") may force you to wait about six months before filing your new Chapter 7 case.

When a case is converted, courts disagree about whether exemptions are determined as of the date of your Chapter 13 petition or the date that the case was converted.

In other words, your property may have qualified as a homestead when your Chapter 13 was filed, but if you moved out of the property and then converted to a Chapter 7, the property may no longer qualify as a homestead and, as such, would go to the trustee.

Sounds complicated, doesn't it? Well, it is . . . and it's further complicated by the fact that to some extent the rules that apply aren't uniform or consistent and are dependent on the way your local bankruptcy court does business.

Also, your property may have increased in value since you filed Chapter 13. For example, when you filed under a Chapter 13 reorganization, say that your homestead was worth $75,000 and subject to a $50,000 mortgage. Because your state allows a homestead exemption of $25,000, at the time you filed, your property was entirely exempt — no ifs, ands, or buts about it.

But when you converted to a Chapter 7 liquidation, the value of your property had increased to $90,000 and the mortgage balance had dropped to $47,000. As a result, your equity in the house is $43,000, a considerable amount more than your state allows for an exemption. If your home is still completely off-limits, then you get the benefit of this increase in value. But some courts would allow the Chapter 7 trustee to sell your home, pay you $25,000 for your exemption, and distribute the balance to creditors.

The answer's a crapshoot, because it depends on where you live and how your bankruptcy court views converting to a Chapter 7 versus dismissing a Chapter 13 and filing a new Chapter 7 case.

Kind of a bummer, isn't it?

Dismissing your Chapter 13 and filing a new Chapter 13

Sometimes you're better off dismissing your Chapter 13 and starting a new Chapter 13 instead of trying to modify your existing Chapter 13 plan.

The advantages:

- ✔ You get a brand-new 60-month period to repay your debts. When you're in the fourth year of a five-year plan and problems develop, you have only one year remaining to cure any problems. This way, a new Chapter 13 gives you another five years.

- ✔ Debts incurred since your original Chapter 13 filing can be included.

The disadvantages:

- ✔ When your Chapter 13 is dismissed, you lose the benefit of *cramdown* (restructuring the loan without needing the consent of the lender). Say, for example, that your car is worth $5,000 and you owe $11,000. You can keep your car in Chapter 13 by cramming down or paying its value — $5,000 during the life of the plan (See Chapter 10). Dismissing and filing a new Chapter 13 means having to pay for your $5,000 car all over again, because you receive no credit for payments made in your earlier case.

- ✔ Whenever you file more than one Chapter 13, the court eyes all the circumstances very carefully to determine whether the second case is filed in bad faith.

Understanding when the 180-day rule applies

Whenever you're contemplating a second bankruptcy filing after an earlier case is dismissed, watch out for a restriction known as the *180-day rule*, which forbids you from filing a second bankruptcy within — you guessed it — 180 days of dismissal of an earlier case. This rule kicks in when:

- ✔ You request a dismissal after a creditor asks the court for permission to foreclose (known as a motion for *relief from stay*).

- ✔ You, the debtor, intentionally fail to comply with a court order.

When a previous Chapter 13 case is dismissed because you can't make plan payments, some courts rule that the 180-day rule doesn't apply, because your inability to make payments doesn't represent intentional disregard for a court order. On the other hand, some courts forbid you from refiling right away and 180 days are enough time for an aggressive mortgageholder to foreclose on your house.

Tackling Car and Mortgage Payments Outside the Plan

Chapter 13 plans commonly provide that, in addition to payments to the trustee, the debtor must continue making regular house and car payments directly to the lenders for payments that come due after the date you file bankruptcy (the *petition date*). These payments are deemed *outside the plan*.

Whenever you fall behind on outside-the-plan payments, the lender will ask the court for a *relief from stay* so that it can foreclose on your home or repossess and sell your car.

At this point, your options are:

✔ Doing nothing

✔ Proposing a modified plan that includes missed payments

✔ Working out a drop-dead agreement (See the upcoming section entitled, "Working out drop-dead agreements.")

✔ Asking for time to sell your property

Doing nothing

If your attorney doesn't respond to a motion for relief from stay, the court will probably grant the motion by default.

You choose this option only when you're resigned to letting the property go. *Note:* You'll have to surrender your car immediately, but you can remain in your home for a while.

How long you can stay in your home depends on whether foreclosure proceedings were underway when you filed bankruptcy. If they were, you may not have much time because the mortgage company can simply resume foreclosure proceedings where they left off. On the other hand, if the foreclosure isn't already pending, you have at least three months before you have to get out.

Thoughtless revenuer creates problems for everyone

Joe thought he had it made in the shade.

He faithfully made all his Chapter 13 payments for four and one-half years and looked forward to his discharge in only a few months. Then disaster struck. A tax collector filed a proof of claim for postpetition income taxes that added up to far more than Joe could pay over the remaining life of the plan. The court dismissed Joe's case, which meant that all his previous efforts were for naught, sending him back to square one.

If only the tax collector had not filed that claim, Joe would have completed his Chapter 13 plan and received his well-deserved discharge. Likewise, he then would have had the ability to pay the postpetition taxes with ease.

The Bankruptcy Code arms the IRS and state income tax authorities with several options in dealing with postpetition taxes and, to put it bluntly, you're largely subject to the whims of the tax collectors. They can ignore your bankruptcy and collect the taxes from you immediately, wait until your plan is completed and then collect, or simply file a proof of claim in your case. Any way you add it up, it's a headache for you — but there is hope.

Your lawyer needs to try to persuade the tax collector to choose an option that benefits you and the government. For instance, whenever a tax problem arises early on in your case and the plan provides for relatively large payments to unsecured creditors, the best course is for the taxing authority to file a proof of claim immediately. That way, money for taxes comes out of the share designated for unsecured creditors.

If, as in Joe's case, the tax problem doesn't surface until late in the case, hopefully your lawyer can persuade the tax collector not to file a claim, and to wait until your Chapter 13 is complete and your other debts wiped out before trying to collect postpetition taxes.

You also need to consider whether you have any reason to remain in your Chapter 13 — especially when the only reason for filing bankruptcy was to save your home. If that's the case, you may be better off simply dismissing your case, or if you have other debts, converting to a Chapter 7. Choosing to remain in Chapter 13 after a creditor gets relief from the stay probably means that you'll have to modify your plan. Be sure to ask your lawyer about doing that.

Proposing a new plan that includes missed payments

If you still want to keep your house or car, the court may give you time to make up additional missed payments by adding them to the amount you're already paying to the trustee.

When your plan calls for monthly $500 outside-the-plan payments on your mortgage and you fall four payments behind ($2,000) with 24 months left on your plan, you can propose an increase in your plan payment to the trustee of about $90 per month to catch up on the missed postpetition payments.

This scenario is a feasible option only when the reason for missing postpetition payments was temporary and you're able to afford increased payments to the trustee and resume regular payments to the lender.

You must also have enough time left under the plan to make up the missed payments. Remember that Chapter 13 plans can't be more than 60 months long.

If you don't have enough time left in your plan, you may consider dismissing your Chapter 13 and filing a new one. Some of the pitfalls to this tactic are:

- That when a creditor moves for relief from the stay; you can't file a second case for 180 days. This rule gives the mortgage lender enough time to complete foreclosure if it acts quickly.

- That you risk being branded as a *serial filer*, someone who abuses bankruptcy by filing multiple cases to thwart foreclosure proceedings.

- That the bankruptcy court may enter an, *in rem order,* which means that any bankruptcy filed in the foreseeable future won't interfere with foreclosure.

Working out drop-dead agreements

Sometimes, a mortgage lender agrees to withdraw its challenge to the automatic stay, provided that you agree that any further missed payments result in virtually automatic foreclosure. This sword of Damocles is known as a *drop-dead agreement,* because if you blow it again, you're "dead." As chancy as it sounds — and is — it may be your only option for keeping your home.

Ordinarily, your lawyer negotiates the terms of such an agreement, but you need to pay close attention to make sure that everybody concurs on the date by which payments must be made, the amount of the payments, and whether payments are to be made directly to the creditor or to the trustee. Likewise, you need to try to get the creditor to agree to give you notice and a short time — ten days is reasonable — to make up any payment you accidentally miss.

Asking for time to sell your property

Finally, your lawyer may respond to a motion for relief from stay by asking the court to allow you a short time to sell the property and pay off the mortgage company. Doing so makes sense when you have substantial equity built up in the property. Although you don't get to keep the property, at least you won't lose your exemption.

For example, assume that your home is worth $100,000 and you owe $75,000 on the mortgage. Odds are that at a foreclosure sale, your mortgageholder will end up owning the property and you'll get nothing. However, if you sell the property yourself, you'd sell it for $100,000 — enough to pay off the mortgageholder and leave you with $25,000.

In some jurisdictions, Chapter 13 trustees claim that the $25,000 needs to be turned over to them for distribution to unsecured creditors and, regrettably, some judges agree. Your lawyer can fill you in on these local customs.

Addressing Debts Incurred After You File

When your budget is realistic and no unforeseen catastrophes occur after confirmation of your Chapter 13 plan, you shouldn't need any postpetition credit. In fact, you're not supposed to incur any postpetition debts without permission from the trustee. As a practical matter, incurring a new debt is occasionally necessary and sometimes even wise, but it's so potentially perilous that you never should do it without first consulting your attorney and the trustee.

The implications of postpetition debt vary, depending on whether the debt is for:

- Nonemergencies
- Emergencies
- An automobile
- Support obligations
- Income taxes

Nonemergencies

Whenever you find yourself in need of credit after filing your petition, you'll probably hear big-time warning bells going off. Before you rack up any new debts, you need to figure out why your plan isn't working. If your budget was unrealistic, admit it, and ask your lawyer about modifying your plan. Otherwise, things are just going to get worse. Trust us.

Postpetition debts may be dischargeable when you convert to a Chapter 7 or dismiss your Chapter 13 and file a new case, but if you incurred debts during a Chapter 13 case and you didn't tell the creditor that you were in bankruptcy, that creditor has a pretty good argument that the amount it loaned you should be excepted from discharge because of fraud.

Emergencies

True emergencies are different. If your wife got cancer and insurance covers only a fraction of the cost of her treatment, if your company downsized and you lose all your overtime hours, or if you live in Buffalo and your furnace blows in mid-January, accommodations are in order.

When something that causes your bankruptcy plan to fail truly is beyond your control, you can probably find a way to reasonably deal with it. But you need to contact your lawyer as soon as you can, preferably before incurring any expense. The Bankruptcy Code includes a procedure for obtaining trustee approval and modifications to your plan that include emergency expenses. It's in place to deal with just these sorts of things. If you need it, use it.

Automobiles

One of life's certainties is that cars die, often when you need them most. So what do you do when your car croaks while you are in the middle of a Chapter 13 bankruptcy?

If you own the late, great car outright, and don't owe anything, you can probably go out and buy a new one, assuming you have the cash, but be sure to check with your lawyer first about local rules and customs. Financing the new car isn't so easy. You need to contact your lawyer, who will have to convince the trustee and the judge that you can afford the payments and still live within your budget.

If, on the other hand, the car that died was financed, you have another problem. The creditor who financed the now deceased car was promised certain payments under your plan. Ideally, you can try modifying your plan, giving back the car, and avoiding payment of the balance of the loan. Some courts allow this kind of approach, but others will hold you to your original commitment. Again, you need to talk to your lawyer about this situation.

Support obligations

Nothing but trouble lies ahead when you start falling behind on support obligations that come due after the petition date.

The support creditor — be it an ex-spouse, child, or governmental support collection agency — may come after you without regard to your bankruptcy.

When your support payments are unreasonably high, the place to look for relief is the state court but beware. Figuring out how to pay a domestic relations lawyer is tricky because of restrictions on incurring postpetition debt. Your bankruptcy lawyer will have to forge some sort of arrangement that is acceptable to the trustee and the divorce lawyer. The specifics depend on the practices adopted in your locality.

Income taxes

Bankruptcy laws do *not* suspend your obligation to pay income taxes that accrue after filing your Chapter 13 petition. You need to pay them the same as if you hadn't filed bankruptcy.

Ideally, your employer withholds enough from your paycheck so that you won't owe additional taxes. However, consumers often are hit with unexpected tax bills on April 15, and the temptation to ignore that obligation is great because you're already on a tight budget. That's the worst thing to do. Call your lawyer instead.

The lesson: Make sure that you carefully consider the possibility of postpetition income taxes *before* filing for bankruptcy. And if an unexpected tax liability pops up after you file, call your lawyer immediately.

Sinking Your Ship before It Arrives

Sometimes a person's financial condition improves instead of falling apart. Funny thing, an arriving ship still may result in bad news when it isn't handled properly. Look what happened to Mary, for example.

Mary filed a Chapter 13 to save her home and relieve herself of $50,000 in credit-card debt. Her plan was confirmed and she cured her back mortgage payments during the first year of the plan, but she still owed most of the credit-card debt.

Then Mary's long lost Uncle Joe died, leaving her $20,000. When the Chapter 13 trustee learned of her inheritance, he tried to grab it for the benefit of credit-card lenders. Relying on a 1994 amendment to the Bankruptcy Code, Mary's lawyer responded by converting her case to a Chapter 7, figuring that doing so would enable her to keep the inheritance and wipe out the credit-card debt. The court, however, balked. Deeming Mary's conversion to a Chapter 7 bad faith, the court made her turn over the entire $20,000 to the Chapter 7 trustee.

Mary's story illustrates the fact that the Bankruptcy Code neither clearly explains what happens when a Chapter 13 debtor comes upon a valuable asset after filing bankruptcy nor adequately addresses the question of whether a Chapter 13 plan can be paid off early.

Paying off a plan ahead of time

In some areas, a Chapter 13 debtor is allowed to borrow against his homestead and pay off a Chapter 13 plan. But not all courts agree with this maneuver, and if you miscalculate, it can cost you an arm and a leg.

Consider the case of Miles.

Miles was in the middle of his Chapter 13 plan when a home-equity lender told him that he could take out a second mortgage on his home equity for $20,000, use $5,000 to pay off his Chapter 13 plan, and keep the rest for himself.

That sounded pretty good to Miles, who went ahead with the second mortgage and hoped to go happily on his way with his newfound wealth.

Well, the trustee in Miles' case was less than enamored with this maneuver and was no longer willing to accept only $5,000 to cover the Chapter 13 plan. Instead, she wanted all the money, claiming that every cent amounted to disposable income. The bankruptcy court agreed and Mile's miscalculation cost him 20 grand. Ouch!

In Mary's case, assume that her plan required monthly payments of $300 per month for 36 months and that she received her inheritance in the 16th month of the plan. Can Mary simply complete her plan and discharge her credit-card debts by paying the trustee $6,000 ($300 monthly payment × 20 months remaining on plan), thereby pocketing the remainder of the inheritance for herself?

The answer isn't real clear. Most, but not all, courts would say "No," ruling that Mary must pay the Chapter 13 trustee all her disposable income and that the inheritance constitutes disposable income.

In these jurisdictions, it may be best for Mary's lawyer to try to negotiate a deal with the Chapter 13 trustee where the debtor can keep a large portion of the windfall to offset increased expenses (especially deferred expenses such as home maintenance, medical or dental treatment, and car repair or replacement). Fashioning a fair settlement may be better than the all-or-nothing gamble of converting to a Chapter 7 — a gamble that Mary lost.

Tying Things Together

The rules, regulations, and nuances of bankruptcy can make your head spin, and sometimes having a scorecard to keep track of what ifs and what fors helps. This chart makes figuring out where you stand easier when your Chapter 13 plan isn't working out.

First, find your circumstance in the left-hand column, and then look at the four options in Table 19-1 (suspending payments, converting to a liquidation, dismissing your Chapter 13 and filing a new Chapter 7, and asking for a hardship discharge) to understand the implications.

Table 19-1	Comparing Your Options			
SITUATION	*OPTIONS*			
	Suspending Payments or Modifying Plan	*Converting to Chapter 7*	*Dismissing Chapter 13/ Filing New Chapter 7*	*Requesting a Hardship Discharge*
Debts incurred after filing Chapter 13	Not discharged	Discharged	Same as converting to Chapter 7	Not discharged
Discharge received in a bankruptcy filed within six years of current Chapter 13.	Discharge available despite the earlier bankruptcy	Discharge unavailable *unless* the first case was a Chapter 13 and creditors in that case received at least 70 percent of their claims	Same as converting to Chapter 7	Discharge available despite the earlier bankruptcy
Secured claim is being crammed down (value of collateral is being paid over the life of the plan). For example, if a car is worth only $2,000, and the debt is $5,000, the *cramdown* amount is $2,000.	Collateral *should* be released as soon as the cram-down amount is paid in full.	Collateral can be redeemed by paying a lump sum equal to the unpaid cram-down amount. If you paid $1,200 during Chapter 13, you can redeem the car by paying the creditor only $800.	Collateral is revalued as of the new Chapter 7 filing date. To redeem, you would have to pay the value of the collateral in a lump sum, with no credit given forcram-down payments made during Chapter 13 case.	Same as conversion to Chapter 7

SITUATION	OPTIONS			
	Suspending Payments or Modifying Plan	**Converting to Chapter 7**	**Dismissing Chapter 13/ Filing New Chapter 7**	**Requesting a Hardship Discharge**
Property acquired after Chapter 13 petition	Not affected *unless* trustee or a creditor gets the court to modify the plan prior to completion of payments.	Does *not* go to Chapter 7 trustee unless conversion is deemed in bad faith.	Goes to Chapter 7 trustee if not exempt at the time the new Chapter 7 is filed.	Same as sticking with current plan
Status of property changes during Chapter 13. Example: Debtor moves out of property that qualified as a homestead when Chapter 13 was filed, and property thereafter is unqualified as a homestead because debtor rents it out *after* the Chapter 13 is filed.	*Probably* no effect, but check with lawyer first	Courts disagree about whether property must be exempt on the date of conversion.	Exempt status determined as of the date new Chapter 7 filed	*Probably* no effect, but check with lawyer first

(continued)

Table 19-1 *(continued)*

SITUATION	OPTIONS			
	Suspending Payments or Modifying Plan	*Converting to Chapter 7*	*Dismissing Chapter 13/ Filing New Chapter 7*	*Requesting a Hardship Discharge*
Increases in value of exempt property more than the exempt amount. Example: When filing, Chapter 13 debtor's equity was $15,000 in homestead with an allowable exemption of $17,000. After Chapter 13 is filed, debtor's equity increases to $20,000, because of an overall increase in the property value or a reduction of the mortgage balance.	Not affected *unless* trustee or a creditor gets the court to modify the plan prior to completion of payments.	Courts disagree about whether value of property must be within exemption amount at the time of conversion.	Chapter 7 trustee claims nonexempt equity.	Same as sticking with current plan

Part VI
Enjoying Your Fresh Start

The 5th Wave   By Rich Tennant

"I'm sorry, Mr. and Mrs. Chuckles, but the only thing you seem qualified for is a balloon loan."

In this part . . .

You're almost there. You've survived the surgery of bankruptcy. Now you can build your strength back and get on with your life. In this part, we go over some strategies for restoring your credit and avoiding the pitfalls that can undermine all your good and hard work.

Chapter 20

Repairing Your Credit

. . . .

In This Chapter

▶ Realizing that you're already on the path to credit repair

▶ Ordering credit reports after bankruptcy

▶ Finding mistakes on your credit report

▶ Disputing items on your credit report

▶ Reestablishing credit

▶ Building credit in your own name if you're married

. . . .

*L*ike life insurance or aspirin, credit is something that's better to have than use. Knowing it's there if you really, really, really need it is nice. However, you don't want to use credit just because it's there any more than you want to die so you can finally make the insurance company fork over all those premiums you paid though the years or conk yourself on the head so you can use up that aspirin before the expiration date.

Granted, you'll probably have to borrow money if you intend to buy a home, but that isn't a big deal when you have a halfway decent job and don't set your sights on the snazziest house in town. Under current guidelines, if you have steady employment, you can qualify for a conventional mortgage (with the same interest rate and fees as everyone else) within four years of filing bankruptcy. If you're willing to pay a little more in interest and fees, you can get a mortgage sooner.

You *may* even need to borrow to buy a car, but it's usually better for you to save and pay cash for a reliable used car than to borrow heavily to finance a flashy new vehicle that drains your bank account for years to come. And you'll probably want a credit card so you can rent a video or reserve a hotel room.

Despite misgivings about credit in general, in this chapter, we explain how to get your credit back, point out how you've already taken the first step by filing bankruptcy, describe how to access and (if necessary) clean up your credit reports, and show you how to continue building a reputation for creditworthiness.

Recovering from bankruptcy

Today, so many people are on the rebound from bankruptcy that "prosperity advisor" Paula Langguth Ryan has devoted her life to helping recovering bankrupts "heal" their relationship with money. Ryan, who endured bankruptcy herself, authored *Bounce Back From Bankruptcy: A Step-By-Step Guide to Getting Back on Your Financial Feet* (Pellingham Casper Communications, 1998). Her book covers post-bankruptcy from soup to nuts and provides lots of comforting advice on putting your financial life back together. You can order the book by calling 1-800-507-9244. Also, you can e-mail her at: PaulaRyan@ArtofAbundance.com.

Realizing that You've Already Taken the First Step by Filing Bankruptcy

Counterintuitive as it may sound, bankruptcy is frequently the first step on the road to credit repair.

A decade ago, lenders avoided customers with bankruptcies on their records like the plague, but, now, they're making so much from their unconscionably high interest rates that they've become less discriminating. In fact, several companies specifically target folks who've recently obtained bankruptcy discharges. To these lenders, you're a financial virgin — squeaky clean, unable to file bankruptcy again in the near future, and ripe for picking.

Nevertheless, that doesn't mean you won't ever encounter some short-sighted, mean-spirited, vindictive type, dead set against giving you the benefit of the doubt and resentful of your fresh start. So, getting all your ducks in order makes sense. And one way of doing that is making sure that your credit reports are accurate. After you know your credit reports show that your debts were eliminated through bankruptcy and that your slate is clean, you can start writing a new chapter.

Using the Fair Credit Reporting Act to Your Advantage

The federal Fair Credit Reporting Act (FCRA) offers you some measure of protection against inaccurate credit reports by guaranteeing your rights to:

Knowing the score

Many lenders find it more efficient and cheaper to forego individual credit reports in lieu of statistical credit scores prepared by the three national credit bureaus. Each company produces its own score, but they're all based on the same computer-credit model developed by a California company, Fair, Isaac & Company, Inc.

Your Fair, Isaac Credit Bureau Score — sometimes called *FICO Score* — is the result of an intricate analysis of your credit history.

You can get your FICO Score by visiting `www.equifax.com`, and `www.myfico.com`. For general information about credit scoring, check out `www.creditscoring.com`.

✔ Know what is in your credit file

✔ Find out the name and address of any credit bureau that produces a report that results in a denial of credit or employment and obtain a copy of that report

✔ Force the credit bureau to verify any information that you claim is wrong and to delete incorrect information when it can't be verified within 30 days

✔ Insist that corrected reports be sent to anyone who received an incorrect version within the past six months (within the past two years when the incorrect report was ordered for employment-related reasons)

✔ Expunge adverse information after seven years (ten years after a bankruptcy)

✔ Include a written statement in your credit file explaining any issues that you dispute

Hopefully, you can use this information to make sure that your credit reports are reasonably accurate.

Getting Your Credit Reports after Bankruptcy

Your ability to secure credit is determined largely by credit reports issued by Equifax, TransUnion, and Experian. The reports of these three companies show who has extended credit to you, the amounts, your payment records, and other information that can be obtained from creditors or gleaned from public records (such as public filings of judgments and liens). Most major lenders and many smaller local ones subscribe to one or more of the credit bureaus. In return for receiving credit reports from the big three, subscribers agree to furnish current information about your account.

Credit reports do *not* contain subjective judgments or comments. The reports are supposed to include only the facts — your Social Security number, birth date, addresses, employers, the status of your accounts, and information from public records like bankruptcy, judgments, or tax liens.

A few weeks after your bankruptcy discharge is granted, you need to order credit reports from:

- Equifax, P O Box 74024, Atlanta, GA 30374-0241; phone 800-685-1111; Web site www.equifax.com.
- Experian, P O Box 2002, Allen, TX 75013; phone 888-567-8688, Web site www.experian.com.
- TransUnion, P O Box 1000, Chester, PA 19022, phone 800-888-4213, Web site www.transunion.com.

Getting credit reports for free

You're entitled to a free copy of your credit report whenever you:

- Have been denied credit during the past 60 days because of that report
- Are unemployed and intend to apply for work within the next 60 days
- Receive welfare assistance
- Believe that the report contains inaccurate information as a result of fraud

Although some companies offer reports that combine the information from all three credit bureaus (see Chapter 2), you may find that correcting mistakes is easier when you deal directly with each individual credit bureau.

You need to look for two things on the reports:

- Mistakes unrelated to your bankruptcy
- How your bankruptcy is reported

Correcting mistakes on your credit reports

Unfortunately, about half of all credit reports contain errors — such as adverse information about someone with a similar name, duplicate accounts, and obsolete data.

When you receive your report, check to make sure that it doesn't:

- Misstate your name, Social Security number, birth date, or marital status

- Include information about someone with a name similar to yours

- Contain obsolete information. Most items must be removed after seven years. Bankruptcies may remain for ten years. Judgments remain until the statute of limitations (which can be as long as 20 years) lapses

- Report the same account more than once

- Inaccurately indicate that you were party to a lawsuit

- Include credit inquiries older than two years

Mistakes usually are easy to address, but *you* must take the initiative. Completing the investigation request form that usually comes with a copy of your credit report is the first thing to do. You also may want to write a letter identifying each mistake and requesting an investigation. The credit bureau is supposed to respond within 30 days.

Deleted items have a nasty habit of reappearing on credit reports, usually because of some computer glitch. You need to order new reports a few months after adverse information has been deleted. If the same stuff pops up again, write another letter to the credit bureau and, with a little luck, this time they'll fix it for good.

Whenever a mistake isn't so obvious, or involves something that isn't verifiable as a matter of public record, the credit bureau checks with the creditor, and it tends to take the creditor's word. Subscribing creditors are the backbone of a credit bureau's business, so any time an issue comes down to your word versus the creditor's, guess who the bureau is going to believe?

When a creditor insists that the information is correct, the credit bureau won't remove it. In a situation like that, you must contact the creditor directly and in writing so that there's a paper trail. Under the FCRA, creditors who use credit bureaus are prohibited from intentionally reporting false information.

Among the other duties of creditors are

- Notifying the credit bureau whenever they discover that information they already provided is wrong

- Providing credit bureaus with corrected information

- Including notices of the dispute — if you're disputing that you owe the money — when reporting the debt to credit bureaus

If the creditor sends you a letter agreeing that information is incorrect, you need to send a copy of that letter to the credit bureau, requesting a correction.

When the creditor insists that the information is correct, call the credit bureau, asking whether it can provide any suggestions. You can at least prepare a written statement that explains your side of the story. In all likelihood, however, such a statement probably won't do any immediate good because most creditors are linked to credit bureaus by computer, and your statement isn't transmitted with the credit report. Nevertheless, submitting a written statement establishes a record. *Note:* The credit bureau may limit your statement to 100 words, but only if they help you write it.

Submit your statement using certified mail, with a return receipt requested, in all communications with credit bureaus or creditors concerning disputed issues. Doing so tends to focus their attention much more than regular mail and establishes a written record that proves useful if you eventually end up in court.

Although the FCRA gives you the right to sue in court or complain to the Federal Trade Commission (FTC), as a practical matter, polite persistence is probably your best tactic. And although credit bureaus naturally are biased toward their subscribing creditors, they really don't want any legal trouble or fights, particularly when it looks like you're going to win.

Creditors who report to credit bureaus, however, may not care quite as much about complying with their obligations under the FCRA. A well-drafted letter from your attorney may do the trick.

Making sure your credit reports properly reflect your bankruptcy

After receiving a bankruptcy discharge, all your prepetition accounts are supposed to show zero balances. If they don't, or if other mistakes are evident, follow the instructions for disputing issues that accompany your credit report. Send in the dispute form (always using certified mail, with a return receipt requested), copies of your bankruptcy schedules D, E, and F (which show all the debts you listed), the court's notice of your 341 meeting with creditors (which shows the date that you filed bankruptcy), and the court's order of discharge (which proves that your debts were wiped out). See Chapter 5 for an explanation of your bankruptcy schedules, the 341 meeting, and the order of discharge.

Be sure to specifically request a copy of the corrected report for you and insist on distribution of corrected copies to all creditors who potentially received the inaccurate version within the past six months (or within the past two years for reports requested for employment-related purposes).

Oops! Many credit reports are inaccurate

A study of credit bureaus by the U.S. Public Interest Research Group, entitled "Mistakes Do Happen," concludes:

- Nearly one-third of all consumer credit reports contain errors that are serious enough to cause a denial of credit, or even a job

- Seventy percent contained errors of some kind

- Twenty percent were missing information that could demonstrate that a consumer was in fact creditworthy

- Twenty-six percent of the accounts listed as active in reports actually had already been closed by the consumer

A copy of "Mistakes Do Happen" can be ordered from: U.S. PIRG Reports, 218 D. Street 8E, Washington, DC 20008.

Obtaining New Credit

You know how some recent college graduates complain that they can't get a job because they don't have experience, and they can't get experience because they can't get a job? Sometimes, obtaining new credit works the same way. You can't build a record of creditworthiness until you have credit, and some lenders won't give you credit until you've established a good record.

When your postbankruptcy credit reports show a clean slate, you're halfway home — but *only* halfway. Now, you must establish a good payment record and ensure that your efforts are reflected on the credit reports. Creditors want to know that you're now good for your debts, and if you continue making payments on a prepetition debt, such as a house or car loan, you're off to a good start. Check out the following sections for other things you can do to start building a solid credit record.

Applying for an unsecured credit card

At the moment, obtaining an unsecured credit card (one not secured by the items you purchase or anything else) with a modest limit is pretty easy. Many lenders target people who have recently obtained bankruptcy discharges.

If you obtain an unsecured credit card, keep the purpose for your card firmly in mind, remembering that the objective is to show that you can responsibly handle debt. Use the card only for small items and make sure that you keep up with all the payments (actually you'd be wiser using the card only when cash won't do, like when renting a car or making hotel reservations.) And if you find yourself only making minimum payments, watch out! You may be drifting into financial trouble all over again. See Chapter 21.

Beware of *catalog cards* that enable you to charge items from particular merchants. For one thing, the company probably doesn't sell anything that you should ever consider buying at this point. For another, you can't be sure that the company actually reports your payment history to credit bureaus. So, whenever you use one of these cards, you may end up buying stuff you don't need without doing diddly squat to improve your credit rating.

Settling for secured credit

If you can't get an unsecured credit card, you may be able to obtain some form of secured credit.

Local banks or credit unions may give you a small loan if you agree to maintain a specific balance in an account, which they of course promptly seize if you don't pay. If you go this route, however, make sure that the lender reports your good payment history to the credit bureaus.

You may also be able to get a secured credit card. Some credit-card issuers guarantee you a credit card as long as you keep enough money on deposit to pay off the account. If, for example, you have a $300 line of credit, you need to keep $300 on deposit.

Again, be certain that the issuing bank reports your diligence to the credit bureaus. Otherwise, what's the point?

Likewise, don't confuse secured credit cards with debit cards that allow only immediate deductions from your bank account. Because you don't borrow money with a debit card, nothing about your creditworthiness can be reported to credit bureaus.

Shopping around for a lender who won't flag the card as secured when reporting to the credit bureaus is another good idea. Similarly, you may want to look for a lender that's willing to convert the secured card to an unsecured card after a record of timely payments is established.

Several online outfits provide comparisons between secured cards and instructions for obtaining one. Keep in mind that because these companies are heavily dependent on cooperation from the credit-card industry, they provide a wealth of useful information about credit. Check out:

✔ **CreditComm Services LLC** — www.creditcom.com. CreditComm, in our opinion, is the best. In addition to their Web site, CreditComm can be reached by calling 800-777-9700. Or, you can write to: CreditComm Services LLC, 10400, Eaton Place, Suite 400, Fairfax, VA 22030.

- ✔ **Ram Research Group** — www.ramresearch.com
- ✔ **BankRate Monitor** — www.bankrate.com

You may also want to consider buying a used car from one of those we-don't-turn-anyone-down-for-financing outfits. But be real careful. Don't let them sell you a car that you can't afford, because you certainly won't accomplish your purpose that way. And, be prepared to pay sky-high interest rates on the loan.

Informing credit bureaus of your good work when the creditor doesn't

If you're making payments to a creditor that doesn't report to the credit bureaus, you still can write the agencies yourself, asking them to include that information on your report. They're not obliged to comply and chances are good they won't but, nevertheless, asking is worthwhile. When you do, be sure to include the creditor's phone number and your account number so that the credit bureaus can verify the information. After you've established a good payment history, you also have the option of using the creditor as a credit reference. Just make sure beforehand that the creditor is willing to back you up.

Taking it easy when building new credit

Although building a credit history is important, you need to begin slowly. If you go wild, applying for credit all over the place, your report probably is going to show that you tried to get credit and failed. That kind of report makes lenders nervous, and they begin thinking that you're headed toward trouble again or that they're missing some egregious problem.

After you reestablish credit and (despite our warnings about the evils of plastic) want to start regularly using credit cards, shop around for the best deal. Many lenders entice you with ads for low interest rates but, after they've got your attention, come up with some cockamamie reason why you don't qualify and try to sell you on a higher one. Others offer low teaser rates, but then hike the interest after a short period of time or when you miss a payment. Some impose outrageous fees for late payments, sticking you with a $25 fine when you're a day late on a $5 payment. Late fees represent as much as one-third of the income of some credit-card issuers.

The smartest move — other than avoiding credit cards altogether (Have we convinced you yet? We didn't think so . . .) — is paying off the entire balance every month. That way, you never have to pay interest. Of course, credit-card companies aren't particularly fond of folks who pay their bills in full because they lose out on collecting a ton of interest; and some even have the nerve to cancel your account.

Watching Out for Credit-repair Scams

Credit-repair companies can't do anything legitimate that you can't do for yourself. Some are shady, some are not, and you have to be on the lookout for scams. Run for cover whenever the company:

- ✔ Tries to loan you money
- ✔ Plans to sell your name to other lenders
- ✔ Boasts that it can remove truthful information from your credit reports

One common ploy that credit-repair hustlers use is repeatedly disputing negative but truthful information on your credit report, hoping that the credit bureau drops the ball, doesn't investigate the dispute and, as a result, has to delete the item. Credit bureaus are onto this game, and they don't like it. Even when your credit repairer succeeds in getting a legitimate item off your report, the chances are good that the credit bureau will look a little harder in the future and put it right back in.

Creating a new credit identity by applying for and then using a new Social Security number to obtain a new credit file is another *dumb trick*. That obtaining a Social Security number for fraudulent purposes is illegal is a no-brainer. And yet, some credit-repair advisors advise you to go that route. If you do, you'll pay the consequences. The judge just isn't going to care that you took the advice of some bonehead credit-repair advisor.

Sometimes, advisors suggest that you apply for credit using a Social Security number similar to but slightly different than your real number, hoping that the credit bureau won't match this fake number with an existing file but that it will create a new one. Taking this step is illegal and stupid.

Establishing Good Credit When You're Married

Each partner in a marriage needs to take responsibility for building his or her own credit history. Married people are considered an economic unit only in Arizona, California, Idaho, Louisiana, Nevada, New Mexico, Texas, Washington, and Wisconsin, the nine community-property states. In the other states, married folks are entitled to establish separate credit identities and can structure their finances so they're not legally responsible for the financial blunders of the other.

Still, if your husband or wife can't get credit in his or her own name, a joint card may be a good idea. If you're both legally responsible on an account and regular payments are made, that helps *both* of you establish a good credit record. Of course, the opposite is just as true — delinquencies also reflect badly on the credit of *both* spouses.

Bear in mind that this joint credit applies only when both spouses are legally responsible on the account and doesn't apply to cases when one spouse is merely an authorized user on the account. The *authorized user* isn't legally responsible on the account and payments help only the credit history of the spouse who is liable on the account.

The federal Equal Credit Opportunity Act (ECOA), and laws in many states, indicate that a creditor can't refuse to extend credit because of gender, marital status, race, religion, or because you're older than 62. In noncommunity property states, if you apply for credit in your own name, the lender isn't supposed to request information about your spouse — unless, of course, you're relying on your mate's income to qualify for a loan.

If you're about to get married, don't merge your credit-card accounts. Keep your spouse's separate from yours and, for good measure, each partner needs to maintain one checking account in his or her own name. Similarly, whenever you take your spouse's name, inform your creditors and the credit bureaus of the name change in writing. Creditors aren't supposed to cancel your credit simply because you got married.

The great number of people who end up in bankruptcy because of the misdeeds of someone who turned out to be Mr. or Ms. Wrong is a shame. Time and time again, we see folks with a lifetime of perfect credit financially ruined because of a spouse's spending or problems with drugs, alcohol, or gambling. After you discover these kinds of problems, you need to write to your creditors and cancel any joint accounts and, if you've given your spouse authority to charge on your accounts, terminate it right away. Doing so won't eliminate your responsibility for charges that already were made, but it should protect you from future charges.

The same applies when you consider splitting up with your spouse. Be sure to send the letter by certified mail, with a return receipt requested, and then save copies of the letter and receipt. That way you'll have proof for when a creditor claims that it was never notified.

If you and your spouse are bent on maintaining a joint account and are building a good payment record, at least make sure that each person's credit reports reflect this good record. If not, write a letter to your creditors requesting that they report this favorable information to the credit bureaus — under your name *and* your spouse's name.

Chapter 21

Staying Out of Financial Trouble

In This Chapter

▶ Dealing with compulsive spending

▶ Getting your family with the program

▶ Creating a workable budget

▶ Rejecting additional credit

▶ Changing your lifestyle

▶ Being aware of the danger signs

*Y*ou know how doctors and pharmacists always tell you to take *all* your antibiotics even after you're feeling better, lest the infection recurs and knocks the stuffing out of you? Well, the same is true with the debt bug. When you stop taking the medicine, even though you think you're cured, your problems almost certainly return with a vengeance. A painful financial relapse is probably as close as a single missed paycheck or one ill-advised spending binge.

But now that you're ahead of the pack, you need to maintain your lead. This chapter shows you how. It explains the importance of building a support network and creating a realistic budget. It offers suggestions for changing your lifestyle and reveals some telltale signs that the barbarians are again at the gate.

Addressing Compulsive Spending

Compulsive spending is very much like an addiction and often is as difficult to overcome. It has serious and often devastating consequences — emotional, financial, professional, social, and so on. Mental health professionals estimate that perhaps 25 percent of the American public has a buying problem, and as many as one in six are compulsive spenders. It kind of gives the "Shop 'til you drop!" slogan a literal meaning, doesn't it?

Experts on compulsive disorders say you can't really make progress without understanding the nature of the beast and directly confronting the host of personality traits and emotional needs that feed your compulsion. And that may require some uncomfortable soul-searching. Ask yourself:

✔ Why do I buy things I don't need and don't even particularly want?

✔ Why do I buy little, or big, gifts for people when it isn't their birthdays or Christmas?

✔ Am I afflicted with *affluenza*, the curse of consumption and materialism?

Admitting that you have a problem

If you've become guarded and secretive about your buying, if you routinely spend more than you intended to, if you buy to take your mind off other things (the same way an obese person may stuff him or herself after a marital spat), you may have a problem. If you're unable to pass up a "good deal," tend to live from paycheck to paycheck, and suspect you'd live that way no matter how much money you made, or you continually obsess over how you can juggle this debt or that bill to keep the collectors at bay, you already know that you have a problem. Know, however, that you have loads of company.

Enrolling in Debtors Anonymous

Admitting your problem is an important first step. So, getting help is a close second. Many compulsive spenders find aid through Debtors Anonymous (see Chapter 2). With its 12-step process and support groups, Debtors Anonymous helps you understand that your problem is common and that many people have found ways to cope quite nicely with it. Contact them by writing to Debtors Anonymous, General Service Office, P.O. Box 920888, Needham, MA 02492-0009; phone 781-453-2743; Web site www.DebtorsAnonymous.org.

If joining support groups just isn't your thing, you may look for a private counselor who works with compulsive disorders. In any case, this chapter identifies some ways to get your spending urges in check, regardless of whether you get outside professional help.

Building a Consensus with Loved Ones

You needed the support of your friends and relatives when you first thought about filing bankruptcy, and you need it just as much now. The people closest to you need to understand that the same way a person recovering from open-heart surgery isn't the best candidate to play center in a bruising pickup hockey game, you're not the one to grab the tab or the one to hit up for a donation every time little Buster sells candy bars for Little League. In short, the expectations that loved ones have for you need to conform with the new reality.

And you know what? They will. When you stay on the financial wagon, your pals and kin adjust accordingly. And so will you.

Establishing common ground with your mate on money matters

Regardless of whether your significant other filed bankruptcy with you, you are, to a large extent, in this together, for better or worse. Obviously, the household budget will implode if one of you is acting responsibly and the other isn't. It's kind of like riding a bicycle built for two — the stoker has to go where the pilot goes, or everyone's gonna get some boo-boos. So, remember that the project is a joint one and you need to tackle it in tandem.

Creating realistic expectations from your offspring

When you're deep in financial do-do, chances are your kids need to get real as much as you. Maybe that costly excursion to the amusement park needs to be a once-a-year treat rather than an every-weekend entitlement. Yeah, the kids may get cranky, but they'll get over it. And dollars to donuts you'll all find something to do that's much less expensive but just as satisfying — like going to the public park or the library or. . . .

Using a Budget

In Chapter 2, we recommend keeping a record of every penny you spend. That's good advice there, and it's good advice here. But you're more likely to succeed in budgeting when you view your spending plan not as something that restrains you, but rather as something that empowers you. In other words, look at a budget as your way of taking control, not as something that controls you.

Developing a system for tracking what you spend

Many computer programs can help you track expenses and create a budget. Although computer programs can make budgeting a game, they can also be a pain in the rear when the novelty wears off. In our experience, you're better off with a little notebook, and one big rule: Everything — and we mean *everything* — gets recorded. After you know exactly where your money goes, you'll almost certainly stop, or at least slow the bleeding.

The worksheets in Chapter 2 will help you create a budget. We're not going to suggest what you should spend on specific items. By now, you know enough to be sure you aren't spending more than you have coming in every month, and are saving for that inevitable rainy day.

Sticking to the plan

Sticking with any personal development schedule — whether it's an exercise plan, a diet, whatever — is difficult, and staying on a budget is particularly stressful. One good way to save money is to enroll in a payroll deduction program, like the kind offered through credit unions. That way, a certain amount of your paycheck goes directly into savings. It's right there if you really need it, and safely stashed until that need arises. Again, however, think *need*, not *want*.

Avoiding Temptation

Although offering credit to folks with obvious spending problems is the moral equivalent of providing booze to a recovering alcoholic, credit-card companies do it all the time. Everywhere you turn, you face temptation. Although resisting the lure of credit isn't easy, you *can* do it, but it nevertheless helps when you can eliminate at least some sources of enticement.

Reducing credit-card solicitations

Those credit-card offers that clutter your mailbox certainly are a pain, but you can try sending a note to the solicitor asking to be removed from its mailing list. That may work, but in all honesty you'll probably be ignored. One of our favorite jokes is stuffing all the crap they send you into their prepaid envelope and mailing it back. Turning the tables on credit-card companies, making them not only open junk mail, but also receive nothing in return, *and* pay the postage to boot is incredibly satisfying. Ah, revenge is sweet — particularly when it's justice personified! And solicitors listen much more carefully when something actually costs them money.

Removing your name from direct-marketing lists

As unlikely as it seems, those mosquitolike companies using the direct marketing tactic really don't want to get under your skin. The Direct Marketing Association even provides a service called the Mail Preference Service (MPS). When you sign up, your name is placed in a do-not-mail file. (Although signing up online at www.the-dma.org costs $5, you can register for free via snail mail by printing the online form set out at http://www.dmazconsumers.org/cgi/offmailinglistdave and mailing it to: Mail Preference Service, Attn: Dept: 7377757, Direct Marketing Association, P.O. Box 282, Carmel, NY 10512.)

Members of the Direct Marketing Association are required to check the list before sending solicitations. Doing so is a smart move on their part because they don't want to waste their time and money on people like you who aren't going to take the bait, and they realize no mileage can be gained from ticking you off.

Also, the Federal Trade Commission has set up a toll free number that allows people to stop ALL credit card solicitations: 888-567-8688 (888-5-OPTOUT).

Reigning in telemarketers

Some states now offer do-not-call registries. Telemarketers are required to check the registry before contacting you and, if your name is on it, they can't call. These programs usually include many caveats — for instance, political pollsters and charities often are exempt — but you can significantly cut down on junk phone calls by signing up. Check with your state's consumer protection bureau (it may be part of the attorney general's office) to see whether your state offers this service.

Making a Few Lifestyle Changes

When you keep track of what you're spending, you'll probably discover that many of your expenditures are simply a matter of habit — the $2 latte you get on the way to work, the $1 you plop in the soda pop machine, the $2.50 you spend for an afternoon snack. It all adds up, big time. But you can save a bundle by bringing your own coffee, soda, and snack — bought at supermarket prices. By simply tracking your expenses, you're sure to cut out many of these impulse buys.

Figuring out your priorities

Studies show that Americans spend 6 hours per week shopping, but only 40 minutes actively playing with their kids. Something is seriously askew about that ratio.

But more and more people are getting their priorities in order and opting out of the consumption rat race by *downshifting* — working less, spending less, making more meaningful use of their time, and devoting more energy to raising their children. The seminal downshifting organization is probably the Seattle-based New Road Map Foundation (`www.scn.org/earth/lightly/vsacpbak.htm`). You may also want to check out the Center for a New American Dream at `www.newdream.org`. Both of these Web sites provide links to tons of information on living a simpler and more rational life.

Thinking about ways to save money

Simple awareness of what you have and where it goes helps you save money. Can you save a couple bucks by parking a block farther away? Do you really want dessert with your meal? Can you get a better rate on a plane ticket through Priceline.com? When you train yourself to be more conscious of what things cost, you naturally cut your expenditures.

Discovering how to live without credit

Life without credit is as basic as forcing yourself to use cash. Give yourself a monthly cash allowance, and make your credit cards off-limits, or better yet, cut them up and throw them away. If you don't have the dough in your pocket to make a purchase, you know right away that you can't afford whatever you're thinking about buying. Granted, some expenditures require more than you have in your wallet, but you're still almost always better off using your savings than going into hock.

For example, car dealers try to convince you to finance a vehicle, new or used (or is *preowned* the preferred euphemism of the moment?). Now, why would they want you to do that? The answer's simple: They make a fortune on finance charges. On a five-year, $10,000 car loan at 10 percent, you'll end up paying nearly three grand (that's $3,000) in interest alone. Paying that much extra when you don't have to is a waste of money. When dickering with a car salesman, don't even go down the monthly payment path. The issue isn't how much it will cost you every month but rather how much you'll end up paying in the end.

If you absolutely must borrow money to buy a car, focus on the *total* amount you're borrowing, not the monthly payment.

Discovering cheap ways to have fun

After growing up poor during the Great Depression, our parents were experts at finding inexpensive ways of having fun and discovering myriad imaginative uses for cardboard boxes. We can all garner some lessons from our beloved parents, Big Jim and Fitz: Take a hike, literally. Rent a video rather than going to see a movie. Borrow a book from the library instead of buying it (except for this one, of course). Watch an amateur baseball game at the park rather than a pro game at the stadium. The possibilities are limited only by your imagination.

Recognizing Danger Signs

In the same way a scratchy throat signals an oncoming cold, plenty of telltale signs warn you that the debt demons are back on your track. You must keep your eyes open, but these gremlins are fairly easy to detect and stare down when you know what you're looking for.

Watching for telltale signals

At this point, you know when you're headed for trouble. If you're using one credit card to pay off another, buying junk you don't need, or ignoring your budget, cut it out! Remember, you're in control and the responsibility is yours. As soon as you adopt a victim's mind-set, you've ceded power to the creditors. Never forget that control of your finances is in your own hands — and the moment you feel like you're losing control, you probably already have.

If you get to this point, immediately stop buying on credit and borrowing money. Then, turn to Chapter 2 for pointers on stopping the financial hemorrhaging.

Living without savings

If you have nothing squirreled away for a rainy day, you're living on the edge. The best thing you can do with your extra cash is put it in a savings account used only for emergencies. Financial planners usually advise that you have at least six months' worth of income set aside. In other words, if you lost all sources of income today, you need to be able to rely on savings to exist for the next six months.

When developing a budget, (see our earlier discussion in this chapter and also Chapter 2) be sure to include an item for savings. We're not going to tell you how much to spend on any specific item. Instead, we have you decide for yourself which expenditures are reasonably necessary, then save all the rest. Simple.

Using debt-to-income and equity ratios

Financial advisors frequently suggest that you watch your debt-to-equity ratios to see if you're drifting too far into debt. In our view, that's great when you're a CPA or figurehead. But for most folks, using such formulas is pretty useless because most folks don't have realistic ideas about how much their assets are really worth. In any case, here are a couple formulas if you're the numbers-crunching type:

- **Debt-to-income ratio formula No. 1:** Many so-called experts say that you're okay as long as your debts are between 10 percent and 20 percent of your income. However, these same experts disagree about whether to include mortgages as a part of your total debts and whether using gross income or net income is appropriate. If you're taking this approach, we recommend including all mortgage debts, except the first mortgage on your home. We also suggest using net income rather than gross income.

- **Debt-to-equity ratio formula No. 2:** Taking the value of your assets into account is important in this method of determining how much debt you should carry. Divide the total amount of your debts, including all mortgages, by the value of all your assets. As a general rule, 30 percent is deemed acceptable.

Part VII
The Part of Tens

The 5th Wave   By Rich Tennant

"No, Mrs. Moskowitz. There's just no way we can list the unpaid debt of gratitude your son owes you on his credit history."

In this part . . .

This part includes some nifty lists of ten things you can do right now — regardless of whether you end up filing for bankruptcy — to ease your financial burdens, ten mistakes you want to avoid, and ten of the most common questions we hear from folks pondering whether bankruptcy is the route for them.

Chapter 22

Ten Common Bankruptcy Mistakes

In This Chapter

▶ Borrowing to beat bankruptcy rarely works
▶ Dealing with assets and debts

*O*ne mantra that we definitely preach: Play it straight and simple. Some debtors get into trouble because they try to manipulate the system or they outright lie and cheat. For them, we have no sympathy whatsoever. May a thousand red ants invade their armpits!

Many more people turn their lawyers' hair gray with well-intentioned but ill-conceived efforts at making the most of a bad situation. That's unfortunate, and unnecessary. Most pitfalls are easily avoided when you know where they are. This chapter lists the most common errors, so you can sidestep them now and avoid the hassles of dealing with them later.

Borrowing Money from Relatives

Asking your parents, children, or rich uncle for a loan is awfully tempting, but if you do, you'll probably live to regret it. For one thing, asking for a loan inevitably stresses relationships, and you're going to need the support and encouragement of your family as you undertake the bankruptcy process. For another, you simply can't borrow your way out of debt. Unless your benefactor has more money than she knows what to do with, filing bankruptcy and wiping out debts that you can't afford to pay just makes more sense to us than hitting up your loved ones.

Repaying Money Owed to Relatives

If you ignore our advice and end up accepting a loan from a relative, about the worst thing you can do is pay it back if you're planning to file bankruptcy within the next year. Strange as it may seem, a bankruptcy trustee can sue any relative who received $600 or more from you during the year prior to bankruptcy — even if the payment was on a perfectly legitimate debt. The rationale is that your relatives shouldn't be paid when other creditors are left holding the bag.

Chipping Away at Debts with a Home-equity Loan

We can't say it often enough: You can't borrow your way out of debt. It's pretty obvious that banks and other lenders are really pushing home-equity loans, and it's pretty obvious why. If they can get you to sign over the most valuable and most important asset in your life, they have you right where they want you — scared out of your wits and willing to eat regurgitated dog food if necessary to keep up with your payments. Don't yield that kind of power to lenders. Odds are that if you file bankruptcy instead of obtaining a home-equity loan, you'll not only wipe out those pesky debts, you'll also be able to keep your home.

Draining Retirement Accounts to Pay Debts

Read that heading again! That's a bad, bad idea — albeit one that some credit counselors advocate. If there's even a remote chance that you'll end up in bankruptcy court, there's no point in squandering your retirement account. Oftentimes, pensions are protected in bankruptcy — meaning that you get to keep your retirement benefit and creditors can't touch it. However, if you voluntarily sign over your pension or drain it to pay the credit-card company, that money's lost; it's gone forever.

Neglecting to Accurately List All Creditors

A bankruptcy petition is no place to wing it. Don't guess. Instead, get it right. Make sure that *all* your creditors are listed. If you screw up, you can amend your petition later . . . maybe. But that's a bunch of trouble, and if the judge thinks you tried to hide something or to mislead the court, she may well become very grumpy. Although some exceptions are in place, you nevertheless need to assume that if you fail to list a creditor with an accurate mailing address, that debt may not get wiped out.

Concealing Your Assets

People who monitor bankruptcies aren't stupid, and they generally don't have much of a sense of humor. When you go out of your way looking for trouble, you'll surely find it. Don't play games. Don't assume things will go unnoticed. Don't "forget" to mention the vintage Mercedes sitting in your garage. Just play it straight.

Transferring Assets to Keep Them Away from Creditors

Many people transfer their assets with the best of intentions, often shifting property to their children or other loved ones to keep it away from the groping paws of creditors. You can't do that. And, if you try, you'll almost certainly cause trouble for yourself and quite possibly for the relative or friend to whom you transferred property.

Making Payments that You Can't Afford to Make

Making payments to a bill collector that you can't afford to make is money down the drain, simple as that. Coming up with a few bucks here and a few there to temporarily pacify bill collectors puts a great deal of pressure on you. But the finger-in-the-dike approach quickly becomes overwhelming. You simply don't have enough digits, or dollars, to plug all those holes, and you'll probably stretch yourself to the breaking point if you try.

Thinking that Bankruptcy Is Your Last Resort

Much can be said for preventive medicine — in matters of health as well as in matters of finance. So, we urge you to look at bankruptcy as a financial-planning decision rather than as your fiscal funeral. You don't have to wait until your home equity is blown, your relationships are shot, and your pension is kaput before exerting your right to a fresh start. As a rule: If you can't fully pay off all your debts (except mortgages) within three years, while living a reasonably restrained lifestyle, you definitely need to consider bankruptcy.

Filing Bankruptcy Too Soon

Although filing for bankruptcy sooner rather than later usually is better for most folks, in some circumstances, delaying a bit is to your advantage. For instance, if you're contemplating divorce, expecting a sizeable income tax refund, in the process of repaying debts to family members (or have been in the recent past), or owing taxes that may be dischargeable in the near future, it can be better to wait. However, it's never too early to discuss your situation and your options with a good bankruptcy lawyer.

Chapter 23

Ten Things You Can Do Right Now to Ease Your Financial Woes

In This Chapter

▶ Getting your financial affairs in order

▶ Establishing what your assets are worth

*F*olks swimming against the high tide of debt frequently feel powerless. Some are even inclined to just let go and allow the current to take them wherever it may — even if it's smack into the jagged rocks. Don't do that.

No matter how bleak things may seem, you're still in control, and the list of what you can do to relieve the burdens on your bank account (if you still have one) and your psyche (we'll assume you have one) is a long one. Maybe you can't quite manage to swim upstream, but plenty of branches are jutting out from the banks for you to grasp so you at least won't go over the falls. You only need to grab hold, hang on tight, and keep your head up, even if — especially if — you're up to your neck in debt do-do.

Think of this chapter as your temporary lifeline. It shows you how to survive until you get your bearings and how to take those first tentative steps toward dry land.

Stop Feeling Guilty

Okay, so maybe you screwed up. Get over it. Although in our experience the far more likely scenario you'll encounter is that something unexpected pushed you over the edge. No matter how you ended up in your present predicament, you won't gain any mileage by beating yourself up. Keep in mind that making you feel as miserable, beholden, and dirty as possible is in your creditors' best interests. They've probably already half convinced you that you're some sort of worthless deadbeat. They're not dumb. They know full well that the more guilty you feel, the more you're under their thumb.

Chuck it.

If you develop coronary disease and suddenly become aware that your diet hasn't always been exemplary, are you going waste time fretting over your prior indulgences or do what you can to improve your life now and in the future? It's not like you can un-eat the double bacon cheeseburger and quart of eggnog that you had for breakfast, but you *can* go the veggie route at lunchtime. What has happened, has happened. The past is past, but tomorrow is money in the bank — literally and figuratively.

Cut Up Your Credit Cards

Start with this premise: You can't borrow your way out of debt (are we getting redundant on that? Good!). Using Card B to pay off Card A isn't going to solve the problem. It'll only make matters worse.

In all but a few situations, you don't really *need* a credit card. Sure a credit card makes shopping easier, especially from mail-order catalogs and online merchants, but the last thing you need right now is more temptation.

Pick *one* credit card to save — preferably one with a zero balance — and put it in a drawer, not your purse or wallet. Reserve that card for those few situations where only plastic will do, such as auto rentals and possibly hotel reservations. Now take a deep breath and cut up all the rest of your cards and put the pieces in an envelope so you can remind yourself of the commitment that you've made. Join the ranks of smart and happy campers who pay cash or do without. You'll be surprised how liberating escaping the yoke of credit cards can be. It just feels good, kind of like the way it feels to take a shower when you're all sweaty.

Again, take control.

Order Your Credit Reports

The first step toward taking control is knowing the score and understanding just where you stand. Of course, you can pluck the petals off a daisy, playing "she's loves me/she loves me not," but you'll probably get a more realistic answer from your credit reports. Obtaining them shouldn't cost any more than ten bucks. You can order your reports from the big-three reporting agencies:

- Equifax, P.O. Box 740241, Atlanta, GA 30374-0241; phone 800-685-1111; Web site www.equifax.com
- Experian, P.O. Box 2002, Allen, TX 75013; phone 800-682-7654; Web site www.experian.com
- Trans Union, P.O. Box 1000, Chester, PA 19022; phone 800-851-2674; Web site www.transunion.com

See Chapter 5 for more tips on tracking down your creditors.

Keep Track of Everything You Buy

Keep a list of everything that you buy. Write it down, write it all down — everything from donuts to dentists. Yeah, doing so is a definite pain in the rear, but that's actually the point. If you have to do some work every time that you buy a gumball, you may figure that impulse to buy is more trouble than it's worth. Besides, identifying the holes in your pockets so you can realistically consider what's needed, what's not, and what's in between is the smart thing to do.

Get Your Name off Any Joint Accounts

Joint accounts are often convenient, especially for married couples. But they can create plenty of headaches in times of financial distress. Keeping your credit accounts separate is better, because when you have a joint account, you're legally responsible for the debts of your mate (and vice versa).

Stop Making Partial Payments on Credit-card Bills

Whenever you're making only partial payments on your credit cards, bankruptcy may be on the horizon and, quite frankly, is more likely probable, although most people put off the inevitable as long as possible. In short, making partial payments on your credit-card debt is money down the flusher. Besides, you have no upshot for making payments now, for a couple of reasons. One main reason is if you file bankruptcy, you stand a good chance of not having to pay those debts (or at least not all of them). The second reason: At this point, you'd do better using that money for bare necessities, so you're better equipped to resist temptation to pull out your credit card for groceries.

Call a Lawyer Now If You're Being Sued or Foreclosure Is Underway

If you don't respond to a lawsuit, the other side automatically wins and obtains a judgment, which may limit your options if you end up filing bankruptcy. Have a lawyer look at the lawsuit papers while you still have time to respond.

If a foreclosure already has started and you want to keep the property, find out the date of the foreclosure sale and call a bankruptcy lawyer right away. If bankruptcy isn't filed before the foreclosure sale date, it may be too late to save the property.

Find Out How Much Your Home and Car Are Worth

Odds are your house and vehicles are among the most valuable assets you have. But you need to know just how valuable they are. For your home, you can check with the local assessor to obtain a ballpark figure of what it's worth. However, those figures are notoriously inaccurate, and you'd do better finding out what similar homes in your neighborhood are selling for. For your car, check out the *Kelley Blue Book*. The Blue Book, which is readily available in most libraries, is a bible of used-car values.

Empty Accounts in Banks Where You Owe Money

If you owe a bank money, and the bank is sitting on your cash, you can pretty well figure out what happens next. Before it dawns on the banker to seize whatever stash you have, pull it out of his reach. You need to decide where your assets will do the most good at this point (hint: not the mall), and you don't need the bank making that decision for you. Oh, it may, of course, go back to the bank at some point but, for now, you need to marshal your forces until you figure out how they'd be most effectively deployed.

Sharpen Your Pencil and Start Filling Out the Worksheets in Chapter 2

You have some homework to do, and we'll bet you'll feel much better when it's done. Filling out the worksheets in Chapter 2 gives you a firmer grasp of your situation. An enemy is much easier to overcome when you know the nature of the beast. Regardless of whether you eventually file bankruptcy, taking an inventory is crucial. We've tried to make that chore as painless as possible with our worksheets in Chapter 2.

Chapter 24

Ten Common Questions about Bankruptcy

In This Chapter

▶ Putting bankruptcy hobgoblins to rest

▶ Glimpsing the pros and cons of bankruptcy

*B*ankruptcy — the B-word — conjures up images of horror, torment, and eternal financial damnation. In this chapter, we lay many of these bugaboos to rest, and place others in proper perspective.

Will Bankruptcy Damage My Credit Rating?

Yes.

Credit bureaus are allowed to report your bankruptcy for up to ten years from the date bankruptcy is filed, and generally do just that in Chapter 7 cases. With Chapter 13 cases, major reporting agencies usually delete mention of your bankruptcy after seven years, assuming, that is, you successfully complete the court-approved repayment plan. In either case, for seven to ten years, any time you seek credit — for a house, a car, for anything — your bankruptcy will factor in.

Under the Federal Fair Credit Reporting Act, only certain people and entities are allowed access to your credit information, including credit-card companies, insurance firms, and prospective employers who sometimes review credit reports to determine whether a job applicant is financially stable. No one else is entitled to look at your credit report.

On the other hand, bankruptcy filings are public court records, available forever to anyone who wants to scour the files. The record is there in the courthouse or in federal archives whenever anyone cares to see it, and as more and more records are stored on computers, searching that kind of data will become easier and easier.

Nevertheless, even with a bankruptcy, the odds of your obtaining credit are very good. With a little work and perseverance, you can reestablish credit almost immediately. (Some credit-card companies actually *target* folks right after bankruptcy, because they know their slates are clean.) So, don't lose any sleep worrying about your credit. Instead, see Chapter 20 and get to work restoring your good credentials.

Will Bankruptcy Affect My Job?

It shouldn't.

Employers are barred by federal law from firing or in any way discriminating against you because of a bankruptcy petition. And unless you volunteer information about your bankruptcy, your employer probably won't even know. That said, remember that *prospective* employers are among the entities legally entitled to check out your credit reports. A poor credit rating or a bankruptcy may lead a potential employer to reject you.

Will I Lose My Home?

Probably not.

Few people ever lose their homes solely because of bankruptcy, but it can happen. It all boils down to how much your house is worth, your mortgage balance, how far you're behind in your payments, and which state you live in. See Chapter 11 for more information.

Will I Lose My Personal Belongings?

Probably not.

Debtors are allowed to keep all their stuff in about 94 percent of personal bankruptcies. The reason debtors keep their stuff is that most personal belongings are off-limits to creditors or simply aren't worth enough to bother with.

Will I Ever Be Able to Buy a House?

Probably.

As a general rule, you stand a pretty good chance of getting a conventional mortgage about four years after your debts have been wiped out in bankruptcy, assuming, of course, your income is high enough for you to qualify. You may qualify even sooner when you're willing to go through a finance company and pay more fees and higher interest rates.

Does My Spouse Have to File Bankruptcy Too?

Not necessarily.

You're usually not responsible for your spouse's debts, unless, of course, you cosigned and promised the creditor that you'd cover for your wife or husband. A divorce decree sometimes will also make you liable for your ex's spending.

However, when you live in one of the nine community property states (Arizona, California, Idaho, Louisiana, Nevada, New Mexico, Texas, Washington, and Wisconsin), the story is different. In those states, so-called community property belonging to both spouses is subject to debts incurred by either spouse. *Community property* includes the earnings of you and your spouse, and any property acquired by either of you (except for gifts and inheritances) during the marriage.

Can I Keep Some Debts Off My Bankruptcy and Deal with Them Separately?

No.

Your bankruptcy petition must list every one of your creditors.

If you mistakenly forget to list a creditor, you can amend your bankruptcy papers. But doing so is a hassle, and life's much simpler when you get it right from the get-go. Additionally, if the court somehow thinks you intentionally excluded a creditor, you can find yourself in a heap of trouble.

You can voluntarily repay any creditor *after* you file. And you can always continue regular house or car payments so that those creditors aren't affected by your bankruptcy.

Can I Cancel My Bankruptcy If I Change My Mind?

That depends.

You can't dismiss a Chapter 7 — or a Chapter 13 that was converted from a Chapter 7 — unless you convince the court that dismissal is in the best interest of creditors. But, absent fraud or other misconduct, you can dismiss a Chapter 13 that was never in Chapter 7 without court permission. However, remember that even if your case is dismissed, the bankruptcy still may show up on your credit reports.

Is Filing Bankruptcy a Long, Protracted Process?

Not at all.

Your petition can be filed within a matter of days and, after that happens, the automatic stay kicks in, collection activities cease, and you're on your way.

About 40 days later, you and your lawyer meet with creditors (the 341 meeting). (See Chapter 5.) At that hearing, you take an oath and answer some questions about your financial affairs.

Most Chapter 7 cases are closed within four months of the petition date. Chapter 13 repayment cases remain open for the length of your plan (basically three to five years). But, as a practical matter, after the judge approves your repayment plan, the procedural stuff is dispensed with as long as you continue making your payments.

Does It Cost a Bundle to File?

No: Court fees for a Chapter 7 are $200, and $185 for Chapter 13.

Legal fees vary, depending on where you live. A Chapter 7 filing usually costs $500 to $1,000. Fees for a Chapter 13 typically are about twice as much. See Chapter 3 for some ideas about how to free up some cash to pay the court and your attorney.

Appendix A

Glossary

• •

*T*he terms that appear in *italic type* within the definition are defined in this glossary.

341 meeting: Named for a section of the Bankruptcy Code, this session is a meeting attended by you, your lawyer, a trustee, and any creditors who choose to appear.

adversary proceeding: A legal proceeding filed in a pending bankruptcy case that carries all the formalities of a full-blown lawsuit, including a trial before a bankruptcy judge. For example, when a creditor in a Chapter 7 case believes that her debt should not be *discharged,* she can bring an adversary proceeding and have the bankruptcy judge decide. Most consumer bankruptcies are completed without any adversary proceedings being filed.

arrearage: The total of missed payments, late charges, and attorney fees you owe on a long-term debt. An arrearage usually isn't the entire amount of a debt, just the amount you're behind. For example, say you owe $50,000 on your mortgage and are behind three monthly payments of $500. The arrearage is $1,500, plus late charges, and anything else the creditor can add on.

automatic stay: A court order that automatically kicks in the moment you file bankruptcy and stops most lawsuits, foreclosures, garnishments, repossessions, and may even prohibit creditors from contacting you. Theoretically, any action a creditor takes in violation of the automatic stay is void; nevertheless, making sure that aggressive creditors know of your bankruptcy the moment you file is better than waiting until the court sends out bankruptcy notices. That way, if the creditor doesn't stop in his tracks, you can recover damages against him, plus your attorney fees.

avoidance powers: Special powers given to debtors and trustees under the Bankruptcy Code to cancel certain liens and property transfers. A trustee uses these powers to increase *property of the estate* and distributions to creditors. Debtors use them to enhance *exemptions.*

balance transfer: A euphemism for the practice of borrowing money on one credit card and using the money to pay other credit cards. Credit-card companies figure that you're more likely to borrow money from them if they call it something other than a loan.

balloon payment: A payment (sometimes amounting to the entire loan balance!) that is made some time after a series of initially smaller payments on a loan like a home-equity mortgage. In taking out such a loan, you know that somewhere down the line you have to come up with a huge lump sum. Loans carrying balloon payments are dangerous, because when the balloon comes due, you're at the complete mercy of a lender who can dictate the terms of any refinancing unless you can find an alternative source of funds to pay off the balance.

bankruptcy: The word *bankruptcy* evolved from an Italian phrase, *banca ratta*, which means a broken bench or table. In medieval times, when a merchant failed to pay his debts, creditors would ceremoniously break the bench or table from which he conducted his business. But the forgiveness of debts has biblical roots. Over the years, bankruptcy has evolved from a debt- collection tool for creditors to a system of providing honest, but unfortunate, debtors with a financial fresh start in life.

bankruptcy court: A federal court established by Congress to hear bankruptcy cases and related proceedings. If you don't agree with the judge, you can appeal to a bankruptcy appellate panel or a federal district court. If you lose there, you can appeal your case to the U.S. Court of Appeals. And if you're still unhappy, you can ask the U.S. Supreme Court to hear your case (which is really unlikely).

bankruptcy law: Includes the Bankruptcy Code and thousands of opinions written by federal judges interpreting the Code. These opinions are published in more than 300 bound volumes of the 1,000-page Bankruptcy Reporter, which comes out every month. You can look up a case if you have the citation. For example, you'd find *In re Morgan*, 274 B.R. 776, in volume 274 of the Bankruptcy Reporter at page 776. Our judicial system is based on a hierarchy. Decisions of the U.S. Supreme Court bind all judges. Those of the Circuit Court of Appeals bind all federal judges in their respective circuits (12 of them in all across the country, each responsible for a certain geographical region). Decisions of other federal courts may influence bankruptcy judges but aren't necessarily binding on them. In other words, until or unless a higher court says otherwise, the bankruptcy judge in your case has the final word.

bar date: Deadlines for creditors to challenge some of the bankruptcy benefits debtors receive. The bar date for challenging your claim of *exempt property* is 30 days from the *341 meeting*. The bar date for a creditor to allege that its claim arises from fraud, intentional wrongs, or a *marital property division* (and therefore shouldn't be wiped out) is 60 days from the *341 meeting*.

best-efforts test: One of two tests (see *best-interest test*) that must be met for a Chapter 13 bankruptcy plan to be approved by the court. Like most people, if you can't pay all your unsecured debts in full, you must pay all your *disposable income* to the trustee during the length of the plan. Disposable income is all the money coming into your household. It can include your spouse's income, even if you don't file a *joint bankruptcy*, pension and Social Security benefits you presently receive, and just about anything else that represents a stream of income. From your disposable income, you deduct all reasonable living expenses. As you'd expect, judges have different ideas about what expenses are reasonable.

best-interest test: One of two tests (see *best-efforts test*) that must be met for a Chapter 13 bankruptcy plan to be approved by the court. It requires that you pay unsecured creditors as much under the Chapter 13 plan as they'd receive if the case were filed under Chapter 7. For example, if you have no nonexempt assets, creditors in a Chapter 7 get nothing. Under that scenario, unsecured creditors receiving nothing in your Chapter 13 filing is okay; however, if you had a nonexempt asset — say a travel trailer worth $10,000 — and you filed Chapter 7, creditors would receive a distribution after the trustee sold the trailer. All creditors would probably share in about $7,000 after deducting the costs of selling the trailer and the Chapter 7 trustee's commission. Thus, if you file Chapter 13 instead, the best-interest test would require that your plan provide for payment of at least $7,000 to unsecured creditors.

bifurcation: The practice of splitting debts that are backed by *collateral* into two parts in situations where the amount of the debt exceeds the value of the collateral. For example, if your $10,000 car loan, secured by an $8,000 car, was bifurcated, the debt would be split into an $8,000 secured claim and a $2,000 unsecured claim. In some situations, you can keep the car by paying only its value — $8,000 — while wiping out the balance. See *cramdown* below. Bifurcation may enable you to reduce the balance of your mortgage to the value of the property. For example, if your investment property is worth $50,000 and you owe $80,000 on the mortgage, a Chapter 13 plan can reduce the mortgage balance to $50,000. You may even be able to eliminate a mortgage altogether. For example, if your home was worth $100,000 and the first mortgage was $105,000, you can eliminate any second mortgage.

Chapter 7: Sometimes referred to as *straight bankruptcy* and frequently what people think of when they hear the term *bankruptcy*. Under Chapter 7, your nonexempt property can be sold, with the proceeds distributed among creditors and most debts eliminated without a repayment plan of any sort. Ninety-six percent of all Chapter 7 cases are no-asset cases.

Chapter 7 panel trustee: The person who represents the interests of the bankruptcy estate and creditors. The trustee is responsible for liquidating the estate and distributing the proceeds to creditors. She also has the power to take action against you or others to recover *property of the estate.*

Chapter 11: The chapter of the U.S. Bankruptcy Code that provides for extremely complex reorganizations, usually used only by large businesses seeking to restructure under the direction of the court.

Chapter 12: The chapter of the U.S. Bankruptcy Code reserved for reorganizations of family farms.

Chapter 13: The chapter of the U.S. Bankruptcy Code that enables most consumers to reorganize their financial affairs. With Chapter 13, you pay off your debts, in whole or part, over a three-to-five-year period.

Chapter 13 standing trustee: A Chapter 13 trustee who has duties and powers similar to a *Chapter 7 trustee*, with the added responsibility of receiving your payments, making distributions to creditors, overseeing the repayment plan, and keeping tabs on your financial situation during the life of the case.

Chapter "20": Although no Chapter 20 exists in the Bankruptcy Code, the phrase nevertheless is slang for the strategy of filing a Chapter 13 shortly after a Chapter 7 case (7 +13 = 20) to accomplish things that aren't possible under either individual chapter alone. For example, you can file Chapter 7 to wipe out all *dischargeable* debts, and then file a Chapter 13 to pay off a nondischargeable debt over time. A few courts frown on this practice, even though it seems perfectly legitimate under the Bankruptcy Code.

collateral: An asset that backs up a specific debt because the item is subject to a *lien*. For example, your home is collateral for your mortgage debt and your car is collateral for your auto loan. A debt backed by collateral is called a *secured debt*.

collateral estoppel: A legal doctrine that prevents retrying an issue that was already litigated in another court. For example, if a creditor wins a lawsuit against you claiming that you're guilty of fraud or other misconduct before you file bankruptcy, collateral estoppel may prevent you from disputing those allegations when you do file. It can arise even when the only reason you lost is because you didn't contest the suit and a *default judgment* was entered against you before bankruptcy. The lesson here: Don't ignore lawsuits even if you're planning to file bankruptcy. See a lawyer as soon as possible whenever you're sued so that he can determine whether bankruptcy should be filed immediately.

Collection Information Statement (CIS): An extensive financial disclosure statement that must be submitted to the Internal Revenue Service (IRS) in support of an *offer in compromise* or request for an installment payment plan. The CIS shows the IRS your financial condition and tells it where all your assets are located. Don't provide the IRS with a CIS without first talking to a tax professional.

community-property states: In nine states (Arizona, California, Idaho, Louisiana, Nevada, New Mexico, Texas, Washington, and Wisconsin), the earnings of either spouse are deemed the property of both, and any property obtained during the marriage — with the usual exception of gifts and inheritances — is considered property of both the husband and wife. If you live in a community-property state, your stuff is automatically your spouse's, and vice versa.

confirmation: A court order making a Chapter 13 plan binding on the debtor and all creditors. If the trustee or a creditor objects to a proposed plan, a court hearing is required. But in most cases, plans are approved as a matter of course.

consensual lien: *Liens* that you voluntarily grant to someone else. When they involve personal property, they are called *security interests*. In the case of real property, they are usually *mortgages* or *deeds of trust*.

contempt of court: An act of disrespect toward the court, such as deliberate disobedience of a court order or conduct that tends to obstruct the court from carrying out its responsibilities. Although debtors' prisons are a thing of the past, you can still end up in jail for contempt of court.

conversion of a bankruptcy case: Switching a pending bankruptcy from one chapter to another. Sometimes, this occurs when a debtor realizes she can't maintain payments set up in a Chapter 13 and seeks to convert the case to a Chapter 7. Other times, it is the creditor who seeks conversion, usually when the debtor fails to live up to his Chapter 13 promises. Chapter 13 cases frequently are converted to Chapter 7 when debtors can't maintain payments required under the Chapter 13 plan. Less frequently, Chapter 7 cases are converted to Chapter 13 when an unexpected development pops up and the debtor wants to regain control of his property.

conversion of collateral: The wrongful act of disposing of property that is *collateral* for a debt without the lender's consent, which may give rise to a debt that is *nondischargeable* in Chapter 7. For example, if you financed the purchase of a piece of jewelry then turned around and sold it for the cash and knew your maneuver wasn't kosher, that would be conversion of collateral. In most cases, however, consumers avoid trouble simply by explaining that they didn't know they weren't supposed to sell the item or items.

cramdown: Reducing a *secured debt* to the value of its *collateral* and paying the reduced amount over the life of a Chapter 13 plan. If, for example, you still owe $10,000 on a car that's worth only $6,000, you can reduce the car loan to $6,000 and pay that sum over three to five years.

credit reports: Your ability to obtain credit is determined largely by credit reports issued by three companies: Equifax, TransUnion, and Experian. These reports show who has extended you credit, the amount, your payment record, and other information that can be obtained from creditors or gleaned from public records (such as public filings of judgments and liens). Most lenders subscribe to one or more of these credit bureaus. In exchange for receiving your credit reports, they agree to provide information about your account.

credit scoring: Many lenders find it more efficient and cheaper to forego individual credit reports in lieu of statistical credit scores prepared by the three national credit bureaus. Each company produces its own score, but they are all based on the same computer credit model developed by a California company, Fair, Isaac & Company, Inc.

cross-collateralization: When an asset is *collateral* for more than one loan with the same lender under loan documents that contain a *dragnet clause.*

cure: Making up missed payments (*arrearages*) on a loan gradually over the life of a Chapter 13 plan. Say your mortgage payment is $800, you've missed three months, and you owe $100 in late fees. The arrearage as of the *petition date* is $2,500 ($800 × 3 + 100 = $2,500). In Chapter 13, you'd reduce the arrearage gradually during a three-to-five-year period.

debtor: A person who owes money to another person. In the context of a bankruptcy case, the debtor is the person who files bankruptcy.

debtor's exam: A state court proceeding where a creditor who's won a *judgment* against you hauls you into court and asks questions about your assets. Although you usually can't be put in jail for not paying a debt, you can be jailed for *contempt of court* if you don't show up for a debtor's exam.

deed in lieu of foreclosure: A deed that you give to a mortgageholder to save the time and expense of foreclosing. Sometimes a creditor is willing to pay a modest amount of cash, and may be willing to let you stay on the property until you find new place to live.

deed of trust (or trust deed): A method, commonly used in some states, to secure a loan with real property. It is quite similar to a *mortgage* and, for your purposes, needs to be considered one and the same.

default judgment: A judgment that can be entered against you whenever you don't respond to a lawsuit within a specified period of time, frequently 30 days after you receive the initial lawsuit papers. Don't ignore lawsuits. See *collateral estoppel.*

denial of discharge: When a bankruptcy court refuses to erase your debts. That can happen if you conceal assets, disobey an order of the court, or commit fraud in connection with the bankruptcy. If discharge is denied, you have a bankruptcy on your record and still are on the hook for your debts. In short, it's a lose-lose situation — so avoid it.

discharge: The term used to describe what happens to debts when they're wiped out by bankruptcy.

discharge injunction: A court order kicks in the moment you receive your *discharge,* forbidding creditors from coming after you to collect any *dischargeable debts.* Creditors who violate a discharge injunction can be ordered to pay damages and your attorney fees and can even be fined. However, a discharge injunction doesn't prevent a creditor from repossessing or foreclosing on its *collateral* when its *lien* wasn't wiped out in bankruptcy. Neither does it forbid creditors from coming after you to collect any debt that you *reaffirmed.*

dischargeable debt: A debt that can be wiped out by bankruptcy.

dismissal: Ending a bankruptcy before it's complete. After a bankruptcy is dismissed, creditors are free to resume collection efforts. A Chapter 13 debtor can usually choose to dismiss her case, and the trustee or creditors may request dismissal if the debtor isn't living up to her obligations. By comparison, a Chapter 7 debtor must obtain the court's permission for dismissal.

disposable income: The amount of income that you have left over after paying all routine expenses other then *unsecured debts* (deduct mortgage and car payments because they're *secured*). In most cases, the Chapter 13 *best-efforts test* requires you to contribute your disposable income to the plan for at least 36 months.

dragnet clause: A contractual provision that says a particular asset stands as collateral for more than one account with the same lender. For example, if you have your car loan and a credit-card account with the same credit union, the fine print in the auto finance contract may contain a provision that says something like: "This car is security not only for this loan, but for all other loans you have with us." This dragnet clause is a result of loans that are *cross-collateralized*.

due-on-sale clause: A provision lurking in the fine print of many mortgages that says, essentially, that if the property is sold or becomes subject to a *lien*, the entire mortgage becomes due immediately. These clauses are routinely violated and mortgage companies usually don't care as long as you're making payments. Occasionally, when a borrower files Chapter 13, mortgage companies argue that if the due-on-sale clause has been violated, they can *foreclose* even if an *arrearage* is being *cured* under the plan.

dummy return: A tax return that the IRS files on behalf of someone who doesn't file his own return. It is filed so that taxes can be assessed. It doesn't excuse your failure to file.

earned income credit: A form of public assistance for low-income workers who have dependent children and maintain a household. Typically, no *exemption* specifically covers earned income credits. You may want to delay filing bankruptcy until you've received your earned income credit for the current year and spent the money on some essential items.

equity: Your interest in property after subtracting what you owe on mortgages and other *liens* on the property. For instance, if you have a house worth $100,000 and you owe $80,000 on the mortgage, your equity is $20,000.

exceptions to discharge: Specific types of (nondischargeable) debts that aren't wiped out in bankruptcy. Compare *objections to discharge* where *no* debts are eliminated.

exempt property: Property that is protected by state or federal law from the claims of creditors. Different states have different exemptions, but most exempt homesteads, pensions, wages, a car, and household goods.

family farmer: In the case of an individual, a farmer whose debts aren't in excess of $1.5 million, 80 percent of which arises from farming, and who in the past year received more than 50 percent of her income from farming. Family farmers receive special treatment under the Bankruptcy Code.

foreclosure: The way a lien creditor collects on its *lien*, usually by a forced sale of the *collateral*. When the collateral is *real property*, an actual lawsuit is sometimes required. Many states provide a method of nonjudicial foreclosure where real property is sold at public auction. When the collateral is *personal property*, a nonjudicial sale can take place with as little as ten days' notice. Foreclosure needs to be distinguished from *repossession,* which, by itself, doesn't terminate your interest in the collateral — at least in most states.

fraudulent transfer: A transfer of property made by a debtor with the intention of shielding it from creditors, or even without fraudulent intention whenever property is transferred for less than it's worth. If you've made what may be considered a fraudulent transfer, be sure to tell your bankruptcy lawyer about it so corrective measures can be taken before you file. Otherwise, you may encounter serious problems in your bankruptcy. The *trustee* can recover the transferred property or its value for the benefit of creditors. In some instances, your *discharge* can be denied for having made a fraudulent transfer.

fresh start: The central theme of American-style bankruptcy is that an honest but unfortunate debtor is entitled to a fresh financial start in life. Despite the effort of influential creditor groups doling out huge campaign contributions, the fresh start principle remains firmly embedded in our law.

garnishment: A legal procedure where a creditor obtains a court order to have money taken directly out of your paycheck or bank account. Creditors (other than taxing authorities and holders of student loans) may not garnish your money without first suing you and obtaining a *judgment.*

hardship discharge: A Chapter 13 discharge that may be available if you're unable to complete plan payments. The court must conclude that you did your best and that creditors received at least as much as they would have if the case originally were filed under Chapter 7. However, a hardship discharge isn't as broad as the discharge you'd receive whenever you completed your Chapter 13 plan — you don't obtain the *super discharge,* but instead only the discharge you'd receive from a Chapter 7 case.

home-equity loan: Any loan secured by your home other than the one used to purchase the property. For example, say you bought your house for $100,000, put $20,000 down and borrowed $80,000. Then, several years down the road you got another loan for $20,000 and put your home up as *collateral*. This second loan is a home-equity loan. Regardless of whether it's called a "home-equity loan," "second mortgage," or "line of credit mortgage," the result is the same: Your home is in jeopardy whenever you can't cover the payments.

homestead exemption: Laws that protect your home, or a portion of its value, from creditors. The extent of your homestead exemption is determined by where you live. In some states, the homestead is unlimited. You can sit in your multimillion-dollar estate, declare bankruptcy, and thumb your nose at creditors. On the other hand, some states limit homesteads to only a few thousand dollars. Some don't offer any protection at all.

in rem order: An order sometimes issued when a court dismisses a bankruptcy and has reason to suspect that you may attempt to refile to stop a foreclosure. These orders provide that any bankruptcy filed within a specified time period won't impede a foreclosure. *In rem* orders are designed to stop an abusive practice where debtors thwart legitimate foreclosure proceedings by repeatedly filing and then dismissing Chapter 13 cases.

insider: Relatives and others who have a strong influence on you. If you have repaid a total of $600 or more to an insider within a year before your *petition date*, the bankruptcy trustee can make that person pay the money back. For that reason, repaying debts to friends or relatives prior to filing bankruptcy is a mistake. You can always pay them after bankruptcy if that's what you want to do.

installment agreement: An agreement with the IRS where you pay back taxes over a specified period of time. If you owe less than $25,000, getting the IRS to agree to an installment agreement is pretty easy. If you owe more, you'll probably need help from a tax professional. An installment agreement requires that all payments be made on time, that future tax returns must be filed, and the tax shown on those returns paid in full. Even if you make an installment agreement, penalties and interest continue to accrue, and the IRS wants all your future tax refunds until the balance is paid off. Sometimes you may want to make payments under an installment agreement until enough time passes to enable you to eliminate the taxes altogether by filing bankruptcy.

joint bankruptcy: A bankruptcy petition filed by a husband and wife. Just because one spouse files doesn't necessarily mean that the other must file. And even if both must file, filing separately may be better than filing jointly.

judgment: If someone wins a lawsuit against you, they obtain a judgment. In most states, a judgment results in a *lien* on *real property* you own in the state where suit was brought. A few additional steps are required to extend that *lien* to property in other states. A judgment entitles the creditor to *garnish* your bank account and part of your wages.

lien: An interest in another's property (*collateral*) that secures payment of a debt and remains in effect until that debt is paid. For *consensual liens,* such as mortgages, the collateral is *real property.* For security interests, the collateral is *personal property. Nonconsensual liens* are imposed without your consent and include judgment liens and tax liens.

marital property divisions: Financial obligations arising from a divorce that are *not* in the nature of spousal or child support. For example, if a divorce court rules that you get to keep your marital home, but you first have to pay your spouse $30,000 for his interest in the property. This ruling probably is considered a property division unless this $30,000 was awarded to enable your spouse to put food on the table and otherwise support himself. Some so-called property divisions are actually designed to function as support, so it is sometimes tough to determine which is which. Property divisions may be *discharged* in bankruptcy, but spousal and child support can't.

mortgage: A *consensual lien* on *real property* that is essentially the same as a *deed of trust*.

motion for relief from stay: Although an *automatic stay* puts the brakes on collection efforts, in a few situations the bankruptcy court enables a particular creditor to take some action against you or your property. But that creditor must obtain permission ahead of time by filing a motion for relief from stay and satisfying certain conditions. Relief from stay usually is granted only to *secured creditors* whose *collateral* is in jeopardy. For example, when your car is worth less than you owe and you're not keeping up with payments (remember that in Chapter 13 you can make up back payments but must also resume future payments), the car lender may file a motion for relief from stay requesting permission to *foreclose* on the car. But even if the court grants relief, that doesn't mean the car lender can come after you personally. Your personal liability on the debt still is *discharged* by the bankruptcy. A motion for relief from stay is entirely different than an *adversary proceeding* to have a debt declared *nondischargeable*.

no-asset case: A Chapter 7 case where the debtor doesn't lose any property to the trustee because the debtor's assets are subject to *liens, exempt*, or simply aren't worth enough to bother with (which is the situation in 96 percent of all Chapter 7 cases). Usually, at the conclusion of your *341 meeting* the trustee declares the case to be a no-asset case. Your *discharge* will be entered and the case closed as a matter of course within about 60 days. If the trustee determines that your case is an *asset* case, she has plenty of paperwork to complete, even when the value of those assets is small. The trustee may allow you to keep even *nonexempt* property, if the property is more trouble than it's worth. If, for example, you have a second car worth several hundred dollars the trustee will probably let you keep it if you have no other *nonexempt* assets.

nonconsensual lien: A *lien* on your property without your consent. Real property taxes, for instance, are liens against your property even though you never directly consent. The same holds true with a judgment lien. When a judgment is entered against you in some courts, it becomes a lien against your real property, which secures payment of that judgment.

nondischargeable debt: A debt that bankruptcy doesn't eliminate. For the most part, recent taxes, support obligations, criminal fines, and personal-injury claims arising from drunk driving are nondischargeable in any kind of bankruptcy. Claims for fraud, credit-card abuse, embezzlement, theft, some marital-property divisions, and other intentional misconduct aren't dischargeable in Chapter 7, but can be discharged if you complete a Chapter 13 plan.

nonexempt assets: Assets that aren't specifically made off-limits to creditors by state or federal law. If, for example, you owned a rental house in addition to the home you live in, the rental unit can be taken and sold by a Chapter 7 trustee, who then distributes the proceeds to your creditors. In a Chapter 13 case, you pay the value of your *equity* over the life of your Chapter 13 plan. Even an *exempt* asset may have nonexempt equity. For example, if your home was worth $100,000, you had a $50,000 mortgage, and the *homestead exemption* in your state was $20,000, then you'd have $30,000 of nonexempt equity in your home ($100,000 − $50,000 − $20,000 = $30,000). A Chapter 7 trustee can sell your home, pay off the mortgage, pay you your $20,000 exemption, and distribute the balance to creditors. In Chapter 13, the total of your plan payments would be roughly $30,000.

nonpurchase-money security interest: A *security interest* you grant to a lender in property you already own. Consumer-finance companies typically insist on taking a security interest in all your household goods when they lend you money. Theoretically, if you don't pay, the company can take your stuff. But they seldom bother. These types of security interests usually can be eliminated when you file bankruptcy.

notice of tax lien: A filing in the public records giving the IRS an enforceable lien on essentially all your earthly belongings. If the notice is filed before your bankruptcy petition, taxes can be much more difficult to discharge.

objection to discharge: An *adversary proceeding* filed by a creditor or the trustee in a Chapter 7 case requesting the bankruptcy court to declare that none of your debts are wiped out. Compare an *exception to discharge* where a creditor commences an *adversary proceeding* to prevent only its debt from being wiped out. If the creditor prevails on an exception to discharge, your other debts still are eliminated.

offer in compromise: A formal offer to the IRS that satisfies a tax obligation for less than the full amount owed, if accepted and performed properly.

perfection of lien: For a *lien* to take effect against third parties and bankruptcy trustees, it generally must be filed in the public record. For example, *mortgages* must be recorded in local land records and *security interests* in motor vehicles must be noted on the certificates of title. If a lien isn't perfected, a bankruptcy trustee can eliminate it.

personal property: Everything that is neither land nor permanently attached to land. Whether something is real or personal property usually is pretty self-evident but not always. For example, some states treat mobile homes as personal property; others treat them as real property.

petition date: The date when a bankruptcy petition is filed. The precise date is important in determining exactly when bankruptcy takes effect, which debts are eliminated, and what property is affected.

postpetition debts: Debts that arise after the *petition date*. If you borrow money on the day after your bankruptcy papers are filed, that is a postpetition debt. For the most part, postpetition debts aren't wiped out by your bankruptcy. Whether a debt is a prepetition or postpetition debt sometimes isn't clear, but it's determined by when the debt was incurred. For example, if you were in an auto accident before bankruptcy, financial obligations arising from the mishap are prepetition debts even though no actual claim is made against you until afterward.

preferential transfer: When some creditors get paid shortly before bankruptcy while others are left holding the bag, those kinds of payments are considered unfair or preferential transfers. Within 90 days of the *petition date*, a creditor who receives $600 or more on a past-due debt can be made to repay that money to a bankruptcy trustee, who then parcels it out to all your creditors. When a debt is repaid to an *insider,* the time period is not merely 90 days but rather an entire year. For example, if you repaid a $3,000 debt to your mom nine months before filing bankruptcy, a bankruptcy trustee can sue your mom to recover the money. However, if you wait only three months longer to file bankruptcy (so more than a year had passed from the date of the $3,000 payment), your mom is safe.

prepetition debts: The opposite of *postpetition debts*.

presumption of fraud: Debts from fraud are *nondischargeable* in a Chapter 7. If you make luxury purchases, take cash advances, or make credit-card charges totaling more than $1,150 to a single creditor within 60 days of bankruptcy, this debt is presumptively fraudulent. If such a creditor files an *exception to discharge* proceeding, you have a tough row to hoe, convincing a bankruptcy judge that you intended to pay these charges. If you delay bankruptcy until 61 days after making the charges, the complaining creditor must prove that you didn't intend to pay the charges when you made them, which is so hard to do that many creditors simply write off the debt when the presumption doesn't apply.

priority debts: Certain nondischargeable debts that receive special treatment under the Bankruptcy Code. The most common are support obligations, some taxes, and claims for personal injuries caused by drunk driving or boating. These obligations can and must be paid in full during the course of any Chapter 13 plan.

proof of claim: A document that must be filed with the court before a creditor can receive any payments from the trustee. Creditors usually have 90 days after the 341 meeting to file a proof of claim. In some situations you may want to file a proof of claim on behalf of a creditor to make sure debts that can haunt you after bankruptcy are paid by the trustee. If, for instance, you owe $7,000 in spousal support, you want to make sure that a proof of claim is filed by or on behalf of your spouse.

property of the estate: Property that is subject to the bankruptcy process, including all property rights owned as of the petition date, plus inheritances, life insurance benefits, and divorce settlements received within 180 days thereafter. In a Chapter 13, it also includes postpetition income received during the case.

pro se: When a person represents himself instead of being represented by a lawyer, he acts pro se (for himself).

purchase-money security interest: Where you use an item that you're purchasing as *collateral* for a loan for the purchase price. A common example is financing the purchase of a washing machine and giving the lender a *security interest* in that appliance. You can't simply eliminate purchase-money security interests in bankruptcy the way you can *nonpurchase-money security interests.* Sometimes what starts out as a purchase-money security interest transforms into a *nonpurchase-money security interest* because of a refinancing or subsequent purchases that are added as security for the loan.

reaffirm: A procedure where you agree to pay a debt that otherwise is wiped out in bankruptcy. People usually reaffirm so they can keep property on which a creditor has a lien. Sometimes debtors reaffirm so they can preserve credit privileges with a particular creditor or settle an *exception to discharge* proceeding.

real property: Land and things permanently attached to land, such as buildings, fences, built-in swimming pools — essentially the opposite of *personal property.*

redemption: It literally means "to buy back." In a Chapter 7 bankruptcy, redemption refers to the practice of freeing property from a *security interest* by paying that creditor only the value of the collateral, instead of the entire debt. Outside of bankruptcy, redemption describes the right of a property owner to retrieve his property from foreclosure sale by paying the entire amount of the debt.

relief from stay: When a creditor receives bankruptcy court permission to pursue collection activities after the petition date. In Chapter 7, the court may allow a secured creditor to foreclose on your home or repossess and sell your car when you don't keep up with your payments, or when you're not making payments required under your Chapter 13 plan. See *motion for relief from stay.*

repossession: When a creditor obtains possession of collateral after a default. (Compare *foreclosure,* which actually terminates your interest in the collateral.) Repossession more often involves personal property and a creditor's rights are quite limited. Unless the creditor obtains a court order (which rarely happens), it can't "breach the peace" to repossess collateral. Courts differ on what constitutes a breach of the peace, but a creditor certainly can't enter your home to seize possessions and can't break into a locked garage to repossess a car. A creditor can, however, repossess a car from a public street and probably from a private driveway. And nothing says that a creditor has to give you advance notice of its plan to repossess.

restitution: A court order requiring you to pay compensation to a victim for injuries or property damage that you have caused. Sometimes, restitution is ordered as part of a criminal conviction and, if so, is *nondischargeable* in Chapter 7 and Chapter 13.

reverse mortgage: A way for folks, usually senior citizens, to draw *equity* from their homes. You use your home as *collateral* in exchange for regular monthly payments from a lender up to the full amount of the loan that typically do not have to be repaid until you move or die. Fees connected with these loans can be quite high. Selling your home, pocketing the cash, and moving to cheaper quarters can be a better alternative.

schedules and statement of affairs: Official documents that are filed with the bankruptcy court setting forth your financial situation.

secured credit card: A credit card backed up by a cash deposit with the card issuer. For example, you provide a credit-card company $500 of your money in exchange for a credit card with a $500 credit limit. If you don't make payments on the card, the company simply takes your deposit. However, when you make all your payments on time, you're establishing a good credit record for the future. If you're having trouble getting a regular credit card after bankruptcy, you almost certainly can obtain a secured card.

secured debt: A debt that is backed by *collateral.* Your home is collateral for a mortgage, and your car is collateral for your car loan.

security interest: A *lien* on personal property that you voluntarily give a creditor.

short-year election: When you file a Chapter 7 case in which assets will be distributed to creditors, you can divide the year in which you file bankruptcy into two short years. For example: When you file Chapter 7 on September 2, 2003, you can elect to divide tax year 2003 into two parts — the first runs from January 1, 2003, through September 2, 2003, and the second runs from September 3, 2003, through December 31, 2003. Liabilities that accrued up to September 2, 2003, are considered *prepetition priority* claims that the trustee must pay ahead of other creditors. If you think you'll owe federal income taxes for the current year, and you have nonexempt assets, you may be able to get the trustee to pay those taxes. Be sure to talk to your lawyer about it, because election must be made shortly after filing bankruptcy. Likewise, make sure that a *proof of claim* is filed by or on behalf of the IRS.

spendthrift trust: A type of trust established for the benefit of another person that provides that the trust property can't be seized by the beneficiary's creditors.

statute of limitations: Laws that limit the amount of time that a creditor has to collect a debt. For example, the IRS has ten years to collect taxes. States differ on how much time creditors have to collect on credit cards, medical bills, and loans. Usually the limits are between four and six years. If a creditor obtains a *judgment* against you, the time limit typically extends for as many as 20 years. Theoretically, when the statute of limitations expires, you're off the hook. But relying on the statute of limitations can be tricky because making payments or otherwise acknowledging a debt can start the clock running all over again.

substantial abuse: In the unusual situation in which you have enough money to eventually pay off your part of your debts, courts will dismiss your Chapter 7 for substantial abuse of the bankruptcy process. However, you still have the option of switching to Chapter 13 and repaying a portion of your obligations over time.

super discharge: An advantage that completing a Chapter 13 repayment plan has over filing Chapter 7. Certain debts (commonly claims for fraud, credit-card abuse, embezzlement, theft, marital property divisions, and other intentional misconduct) can be discharged in Chapter 13 but are not dischargeable in Chapter 7.

support obligations: Obligations from a divorce that are designed to provide financial support for children or an ex-spouse — in effect, the opposite of *marital property divisions*. Support obligations are *nondischargeable* in bankruptcy, but in Chapter 13 you can catch up on back support payments during the three-to-five-year plan. Support obligations are also *priority debts*.

taxpayer advocate: A federal government employee who's supposed to be on your side when the IRS is coming down too hard on you. The taxpayer advocate can issue a taxpayer assistance order suspending arbitrary collection or other activities of the IRS whenever they're causing a "significant hardship." On the downside, a taxpayer assistance order suspends the *statute of limitations* and may increase the waiting period before which taxes become *dischargeable* in bankruptcy.

tenancy by the entirety: An ancient concept, still embraced by some states, where property owned jointly by a husband and wife can'tt be seized by creditors with a claim against only one spouse.

trust fund taxes: Taxes that an employer is supposed to withhold for the government from an employee's pay, including the employee's share of federal unemployment and Social Security (FICA). An employer who files bankruptcy can't discharge these taxes unless they're more than ten years old. If the employer is a corporation, these taxes can be collected from the corporate officer or employee who is responsible for withholding them.

undue hardship: What you must prove to be able to *discharge* student loans. You must show that you can't maintain a minimal standard of living if forced to repay the loan, that your financial condition isn't likely to improve, and that you've made a good-faith effort to repay your student loans.

United States Trustee: An official of the U.S. Department of Justice responsible for overseeing the administration of bankruptcy cases.

unsecured debt: The opposite of a *secured debt*, an unsecured debt isn't backed up by *collateral*. Although a creditor with an unsecured debt can sue you, that creditor can't repossess or foreclose on your asset without a *judgment*. Most debts, including those for credit-card charges and medical services are unsecured unless that creditor has sued you and gotten a *judgment lien*.

Appendix B

Exemption Laws

Choosing between Federal and State Exemptions

Although bankruptcy law is generally the province of the federal government, a number of states have their own provisions with regard to exemptions, giving people the chance to choose between exemptions offered under the Bankruptcy Code (federal exemptions) and those provided by their own state legislature.

Debtors can choose local or Bankruptcy Code exemptions, based on the jurisdiction where they lived for the longest period during the 180-day span immediately preceding the petition date, in the following places: Arkansas, Connecticut, District of Columbia, Hawaii, Massachusetts, Michigan, Minnesota, New Hampshire, New Jersey, New Mexico, Pennsylvania, Puerto Rico, Rhode Island, Texas, Vermont, Virgin Islands, Washington, and Wisconsin.

Generally, you have to stick with one set of exemptions; the law usually doesn't allow debtors to shop for the best deal. Also, joint debtors must both agree to choose local or federal exemptions. In other words, one spouse can't pluck the state exemptions if the other elects to go the federal route.

You can claim some federal exemptions in statutes other than those in the Bankruptcy Code in addition to state or federal bankruptcy exemptions. They include:

- Social Security benefits
- Civil service employee's retirement benefits
- Veterans' benefits
- Veterans' life insurance benefits
- Railroad Retirement Act benefits
- Railroad unemployment benefits
- Longshoreman's and Harbor Worker's Compensation Act benefits

- ✔ Foreign service retirement and disability payments
- ✔ Retired servicemen's annuities
- ✔ Federal employee's workers compensation benefits
- ✔ Compensation payments from war risk hazards
- ✔ Seaman's wages
- ✔ Judicial survivors annuity for survivors of federal judges
- ✔ Pensions awarded to Medal of Honor winners
- ✔ Military survivor annuities

The federal Employment Retirement Security Act of 1974 (ERISA) covers most private pensions. ERISA shields these pensions even if a debtor doesn't claim an exemption because the pensions don't become property of the estate.

You have to rely on an exemption only if your retirement plan isn't covered by ERISA, a problem that crops up with IRAs, public employee pensions, and pensions that benefit primarily only a business owner. Then, plans are protected only to the extent that there is an applicable federal or state exemption.

To find out more about exemptions for your particular state, log on `http://www.bankruptcyaction.com`.

Identifying Bankruptcy Code Exemptions

The exemptions listed in the Bankruptcy Code are available only if a debtor lives in a certain state. (Check for your particular state later in this appendix.) Remember that you can't find all federal exemptions in the Bankruptcy Code, but that they're sprinkled throughout the whole United States Code. And these non-Bankruptcy Code exemptions are available in all states.

The amount allowed under the most important Bankruptcy Code exemptions is set forth in this appendix. Keep in mind that at each three-year interval ending on April 1, the exemption allowed under the Bankruptcy Code is adjusted to reflect changes in the Consumer Price Index. The Judicial Conference of the United States publishes the dollar amount in the Federal Register 30 days before the change takes effect. (See 11 U.S.C. '104.) The amounts will next change on April 1, 2004.

Married debtors may each claim the full amount for separate property and double these amounts for jointly owned property. The exemption amounts at present are:

- **Homestead:** $17,425. Isn't limited to real property (land and buildings), so mobile homes, and possibly even travel trailers qualify. But the property must be the actual home of debtor or a debtor's dependent.

- **Motor vehicle:** $2,775.

- **Household goods:** $9,300, with no single item worth more than $450. Covers household furnishings, household goods, clothes, appliances, books, animals, crops, or musical instruments that the debtor or a debtor's dependent utilizes primarily for personal, family, or household use.

- **Jewelry:** $1,150. If held primarily for personal, family, or household use of debtor or a debtor's dependent. Note that although jewelry may also qualify as wearing apparel, jewelry isn't subject to the $450 limit for individual items.

- **Any property, wild card exemption:** $925, plus any unused amount of the homestead exemption up to $8,725. The latter is intended to give renters the same treatment as homeowners. This exemption is also sometimes called the spillover exemption because it can be applied to any other exemptions exceeding the specific limits. For example, if the debtor's car was worth $4,000, this exemption could be applied to protect the $1,225 that would otherwise exceed the $2,775 limit for motor vehicles.

- **Tools of trade:** $1,750. Applies to any implements, professional books, or debtor's tools of the trade or the trade of a debtor's dependent.

- **Term-life insurance:** Term-life insurance applies only to policies, other than credit life policies, which have no case value. The amount is unlimited but term policies usually have only nominal value. This exemption is designed to allow a debtor to continue life insurance coverage under policies that have no real value to creditors, but may be important to debtor.

- **Life insurance with cash value:** $9,300. Exemption applies only if debtor is owner of the policy and the insured person is the debtor or a dependent of the debtor.

- **Health Aids:** Unlimited. Covers professionally prescribed health aids for debtor or a debtor's dependent.

- **Disability, retirement, and similar benefits:** Covers the right to receive Social Security benefits; veterans' benefits, unemployment compensation (with no limitation as to amount); alimony and support to the extent reasonably necessary for the support of debtor and any debtor's dependent; retirement plans to the extent reasonably necessary for the support of debtor and any dependent for non-ERISA plans (unlimited as to ERISA plans).

✔ **Compensation for injuries:** Covers any award under a crime victim's reparation law, with no monetary limitation; life insurance benefits or wrongful-death award resulting from the death of a person upon whom debtor was dependent at the time of death (to the extent reasonably necessary for the support of debtor and any dependent of the debtor); personal injury awards up to $17,425 plus any additional amount of a personal injury award representing loss of future earnings to the extent reasonably necessary for the support of debtor and any dependent of the debtor.

Surveying State Exemptions

Alabama

Bankruptcy Code exemptions aren't available.

Homestead: Up to $5,000, and land can't exceed 160 acres. Husband and wife may double.

Vehicle: None.

Household belongings: Wearing apparel — all necessary clothing for debtor and his family. Unlimited books and pictures.

Miscellaneous other exemptions: General personal property — $3,000. Most pensions.

Alaska

Bankruptcy Code exemptions aren't available.

Homestead: $64,800. Although joint debtors may each claim exemption, combined amount may not exceed $64,800.

Vehicle: $3,600.

Household belongings: Household goods, furniture/clothing — $3,600. Jewelry — $1,200. Tools of trade — $3,360. Pets — $1,200.

Miscellaneous other exemptions: Most pensions except for contributions to retirement plan within 120 days of bankruptcy.

Arizona

Bankruptcy Code exemptions aren't available.

Homestead: $100,000 real property or mobile home. Joint debtors may not double.

Vehicle: $5,000.

Household belongings: Household furniture up to $4,000.

Miscellaneous other exemptions: Tools of trade and books up to $2,500. Most pensions except for contributions made within 120 days of bankruptcy, spousal and child support.

Arkansas

Debtor may choose between state and federal bankruptcy exemptions.

Homestead: Unlimited in amount for married persons and heads of households, but can't exceed ¼ urban acre or 80 nonurban acres. Otherwise, value is limited to $2,500. If debtor isn't head of a family, exemption is limited to $800 for single debtors or $1,250 for married debtors.

Vehicle: $1,200.

Household belongings: $200. If married or head of household, $500.

Miscellaneous other exemptions: Tools of trade professional books up to $750. Most pensions.

California

Debtor may not choose between the exemptions in the Bankruptcy Code and those under state law, but the debtor does have two alternative sets of exemptions. One is quite similar to the exemptions under the U.S. Code. The following list of exemptions includes some of those available if the debtor doesn't select the set of exemptions that are similar to the Bankruptcy Code exemptions.

Homestead: $50,000 if single and not disabled; $75,000 family residences; $125,000 if debtor is: 65 or older; disabled; or if 55 or older and, if single, earns $15,000 or less or, if married, joint income of less than $20,000.

Vehicle: $1,900.

Household belongings: Household items, wearing apparel, food and personal effects, to the extent reasonably necessary.

Miscellaneous other exemptions: Tools of trade — $5,000.

Colorado

Bankruptcy Code exemptions aren't available.

Homestead: Real property, certain manufactured home or mobile homes — $45,000. Husband and wife may not double. House trailer used as residence — $3,500. Mobile home used as residence — $6,000.

Vehicle: $3,000.

Household belongings: $3,000.

Miscellaneous other exemptions: Child support. Tools of trade — $10,000, $25,000 if debtor is a farmer. Most pensions.

Connecticut

Debtor may choose between state and federal bankruptcy exemptions.

Homestead: $75,000. Husband and wife may double.

Vehicle: $1,500.

Household belongings: All necessary household goods.

Miscellaneous other exemptions: All necessary tools of trade. Most retirement plans. Child support, 75 percent of spousal support, $1,000 for any property.

Delaware

Bankruptcy Code exemptions aren't available.

Homestead: None, but debtor may exempt up to $5,000 of any property. Husband and wife may double.

Vehicle: None, but debtor may exempt up to $5,000 of any property.

Household belongings: Any personal property up to $500 for a head of a family.

Miscellaneous other exemptions: Tools of trade — $75 if debtor lives in some counties, $50 in others, most retirement plans.

District of Columbia

Debtor may choose between these and federal bankruptcy exemptions.

Homestead: Unlimited.

Vehicle: $500 if used in trade. Professional office equipment — $300.

Household belongings: $300.

Miscellaneous other exemptions: Teachers' and judges' pensions.

Florida

Bankruptcy Code exemptions aren't available.

Homestead: Unlimited value, up to 2 acres in municipality or 160 contiguous acres elsewhere.

Vehicle: $1,000.

Household belongings: Any personal property up to $1,000.

Miscellaneous other exemptions: Most retirement plans. Annuity contracts. Alimony and child support to extent necessary for support.

Georgia

Bankruptcy Code exemptions aren't available.

Homestead: $10,000. Husband and wife may double.

Vehicle: $3,500.

Household belongings: $5,000 but no single item can be worth more than $300.

Miscellaneous other exemptions: Tools of trade — $1,500. Most pensions to the extent necessary for support. Wildcard exemptions. $600, plus unused portion of homestead exemption up to $5,000.

Hawaii

Debtor may choose between state and federal bankruptcy exemptions.

Homestead: $30,000 for head of family or individual 65 or older, all others $20,000.

Vehicle: $2,575.

Household belongings: Household furnishings, books, and wearing apparel to extent necessary.

Miscellaneous other exemptions: Tools of trade to extent necessary. Most pensions except for contributions made within three years of bankruptcy.

Idaho

Bankruptcy Code exemptions aren't available.

Homestead: $50,000.

Vehicle: $3,000.

Household belongings: $5,000, no item worth more than $500.

Miscellaneous other exemptions: Tools of trade — $1,500. Most pensions.

Illinois

Bankruptcy Code exemptions aren't available.

Homestead: $7,500. Husband and wife may double.

Vehicle: $1,200.

Household belongings: Any personal property — $2,000.

Miscellaneous other exemptions: Tools of trade — $750. Alimony and child support to extent necessary for support of the debtor or a dependent.

Indiana

Bankruptcy Code exemptions aren't available.

Homestead: $7,500. Husband and wife may double.

Vehicle: None, but can use general exemption of $4,000.

Household belongings: Any personal or real property up to $4,000, however total of homestead plus personal property exemption may not exceed $10,000.

Miscellaneous other exemptions: Most pensions.

Iowa

Bankruptcy Code exemptions aren't available.

Homestead: Unlimited value, up to 40 rural acres or one-half acre in city.

Vehicle: $5,000.

Household belongings: $2,000.

Miscellaneous other exemptions: Tools of trade — $10,000. Most pensions to the extent necessary for support. Alimony and child support to the extent necessary.

Kansas

Bankruptcy Code exemptions aren't available.

Homestead: Unlimited in amount, up to 160 rural acres or one acre in town or city.

Vehicle: $20,000.

Household belongings: Household goods to extent necessary.

Miscellaneous other exemptions: Tools of trade — $7,500. Most pensions, alimony, and child support.

Kentucky

Bankruptcy Code exemptions aren't available.

Homestead: $5,000. Husband and wife may double.

Vehicle: $2,500.

Household belongings: $5,000.

Miscellaneous other exemptions: Wildcard applicable to any property — $1,000. Tools of trade — $300. Library, office equipment, and instruments of minister, doctor, lawyer, chiropractor, or dentist — $1,000. Most pensions. Alimony and child support to extent necessary.

Louisiana

Bankruptcy Code exemptions aren't available.

Homestead: $25,000 may not exceed 5 acres in city or town, 200 acres elsewhere. Husband and wife may not double.

Vehicle: Unlimited value but exemption applies only if vehicle is used in trade.

Household belongings: Household goods and personal items — to the extent actually used by debtor or family.

Miscellaneous other exemptions: Tools of trade — unlimited amount. Most pensions, except for contributions made within one year of bankruptcy.

Maine

Bankruptcy Code exemptions aren't available.

Homestead: $25,000; if minor dependents live with debtor, $50,000; if debtor is 60 or older or disabled, $60,000. Husband and wife may double.

Vehicle: $5,000.

Household belongings: Unused portion of homestead exemption up to $6,000, $12,500, if dependents live with debtor; $25,000, if debtor is 60 or older or disabled, $60,000.

Miscellaneous other exemptions: Tools of trade — $5,000. Any property — $400. Most pensions to the extent necessary for support. Alimony and support to extent necessary.

Maryland

Bankruptcy Code exemptions aren't available.

Homestead: No specific exemption, but some general exemptions totaling $6,000 may be applied to homestead.

Vehicle: None, but may use $5,500 exemption for any property (see Miscellaneous other exemptions later in this entry).

Household belongings: Household goods, wearing apparel and other personal property — $500

Miscellaneous other exemptions: Tools of trade — $2,500. Any property — $5,500.

Massachusetts

Debtor may chose between state and federal bankruptcy exemptions.

Homestead: $300,000. Husband and wife may not double.

Vehicle: $700.

Household belongings: Furniture — $3,000.

Miscellaneous other exemptions: Tools of trade — $500. Most pensions.

Michigan

Debtor may chose between state and federal bankruptcy exemptions.

Homestead: $3,500 with a maximum of 40 rural acres or one lot in town. Husband and wife may double.

Vehicle: None.

Household belongings: $1,000.

Miscellaneous other exemptions: Tools of trade — $1,000.

Minnesota

Debtor may choose between state and federal bankruptcy exemptions.

Homestead: $200,000 up to 160 rural acres or one-half acre in city. Husband and wife may not double.

Vehicle: $2,000.

Household belongings: Household appliances and wearing apparel — $5,000.

Miscellaneous other exemptions: Tools of trade — $5,000. Pensions — unlimited for public employees, $51,000 plus additional amounts necessary for support of debtor or dependent for employees of private employers.

Mississippi

Bankruptcy Code exemptions aren't available.

Homestead: $75,000 up to 160 acres.

Vehicle: None but may use general exemption (see Miscellaneous other exemptions later in this entry).

Household belongings: None but may use general exemption (see "Miscellaneous other exemptions" later in this entry).

Miscellaneous other exemptions: Any personal property — $10,000. Most pensions.

Missouri

Bankruptcy Code exemptions aren't available.

Homestead: $8,000. Husband and wife may not double.

Vehicle: $1,000.

Household belongings: Household goods and wearing apparel — $1,000.

Miscellaneous other exemptions: Tools of trade — $2,000. Any other property — $400, plus $1,250 for head of household and $250 for each dependent under 18. Most pensions to extent necessary for support. Alimony and support — up to $500 per month.

Montana

Bankruptcy Code exemptions aren't available.

Homestead: $60,000. Husband and wife may not double.

Vehicle: $2,500

Household belongings: Household goods, wearing apparel, jewelry and other personal property of an individual value of $600 or less — $4,500.

Miscellaneous other exemptions: Tools of trade — $3,000. Most pensions.

Nebraska

Bankruptcy Code exemptions aren't available.

Homestead: $12,500 if debtor is married or head of a household. Husband and wife may not double.

Vehicle: None but debtors may use general exemption (see Miscellaneous other exemptions later in this entry).

Household belongings: Household furnishings — $1,500.

Miscellaneous other exemptions: Any personal property — $2,500. Tools of trade — $2,400. Most pensions to extent necessary for support.

Nevada

Bankruptcy Code exemptions aren't available.

Homestead: $125,000. Husband and wife may not double.

Vehicle: $4,500.

Household belongings: Household goods — $3,000.

Miscellaneous other exemptions: Professional libraries and tools of trade — $4,500. Most pensions up to $500,000.

New Hampshire

Debtor may choose between state and Bankruptcy Code exemptions.

Homestead: $50,000.

Vehicle: $4,000.

Household belongings: Household furniture — $3,500. Stove refrigerator, and utensils — unlimited.

Miscellaneous other exemptions: Tools of trade — $5,000. Any property — $1,000 plus up to $7,000 of any unused exemptions. Most pensions.

New Jersey

Debtor may choose between state and Bankruptcy Code exemptions.

Homestead: None.

Vehicle: None.

Household belongings: Household goods — $1,000.

Miscellaneous other exemptions: Any personal property — $1,000. Most pensions.

New Mexico

Debtor may choose between state and Bankruptcy Code exemptions.

Homestead: $30,000. Husband and wife may double.

Vehicle: $4,000.

Household belongings: Clothing, furniture, books, medical-health equipment — unlimited.

Miscellaneous other exemptions: Any personal property — $500, plus $2,000 if debtor doesn't own a homestead. Most pensions.

New York

Bankruptcy Code exemptions aren't available.

Homestead: $10,000. Husband and wife may double.

Vehicle: $2,400.

Household belongings: Household furniture, refrigerator, radio, television, and necessary utensils.

Miscellaneous other exemptions: Total exemption for personal property may not exceed $5,000. If debtor doesn't have a homestead and doesn't exceed the $5,000 limit, debtor may exempt cash in the amount of the lesser of $2,500 or the unused limit for personal property. Tools of trade — $600. Most pensions to the extent necessary for support. Alimony and support to the extent necessary.

North Carolina

Bankruptcy Code exemptions aren't available.

Homestead: $10,000. Husband and wife may double.

Vehicle: $1,500.

Household belongings: Household goods, wearing apparel, books, animals, crops, musical instruments — $3,500 plus an additional $750 for each dependent, up to $3,000.

Miscellaneous other exemptions: Any property — $3,500 less any amount claimed as homestead. Most pensions.

North Dakota

Bankruptcy Code exceptions aren't available.

Homestead: $80,000. Husband and wife may not double.

Vehicle: $1,200.

Household belongings: Household furniture — $1,000.

Miscellaneous other exemptions: Head of family — any property up to $5,000 total, or books and musical instruments up to $1,500. Farm implements up to $4,500. Tools of trade and professional libraries up to $1,000. Single person, any property up to $2,500. Any property in lieu of homestead — $7,500. Most pensions.

Ohio

Bankruptcy Code exemptions aren't available.

Homestead: $5,000. Husband and wife may double.

Vehicle: $1,000

Household belongings: Household goods — $1,500 if homestead exemption claimed, otherwise $2,000. Stove and refrigerator — up to a value of $300 each.

Miscellaneous other exemptions: Tools of trade — $750. Most pensions. Alimony and child support to extent necessary.

Oklahoma

Bankruptcy Code exemptions aren't available.

Homestead: Unlimited for property outside city limits up to 160 acres, up to one acre within city limits.

Vehicle: $3,000.

Household belongings: Unlimited for furniture and appliances. Clothing — $4,000.

Miscellaneous other exemptions: Tools of trade — $5,000. Most pensions. Alimony and child support to the extent necessary.

Oregon

Bankruptcy Code exemptions aren't available.

Homestead: Real property — $25,000, $33,000 if owned by joint debtors. Mobile home with land — $23,000, $30,000 if owned by joint debtors. Mobile home without land — $20,000, $27,000 if owned by joint debtors.

Vehicle: $1,700.

Household belongings: $3,000.

Miscellaneous other exemptions: Tools of trade — $3,000. Most pensions. Alimony and child support to the extent necessary.

Pennsylvania

Debtor may choose between state and Bankruptcy Code exemptions.

Homestead: None.

Vehicle: None, but may use general $300 exemption.

Household belongings: None, but may use general $300 exemption.

Miscellaneous other exemptions: Any personal property — $300. Most pensions.

Puerto Rico

Debtor may choose between local and Bankruptcy Code exemptions.

Homestead: $1,500, available to persons who are head of a family.

Vehicle: $6,000, but only if used for work.

Household belongings: Chairs, tables, desks, and books up to $100. Necessary household furnishings up to $200.

Miscellaneous other exemptions: Farming implements — $200 for tools, two horses, one wagon, and $200 in seeds. Tools of trade — $300. Professional libraries, and implements of doctors, lawyers, judges, and ministers. Certain pensions of public employees.

Rhode Island

Debtors may choose between state and Bankruptcy Code exemptions.

Homestead: $150,000. Husband and wife may not double.

Vehicle: $10,000.

Household belongings: $8,600.

Miscellaneous other exemptions: Tools of trade — $500. Most pensions.

South Carolina

Bankruptcy Code exemptions aren't available.

Homestead: $5,000. Husband and wife may double.

Vehicle: $1,200.

Household belongings: $2,500.

Miscellaneous other exemptions: Tools of trade — $750. Most pensions.

South Dakota

Bankruptcy Code exemptions aren't available.

Homestead: Unlimited value. Area limited to one acre in municipality or 160 acres elsewhere.

Vehicle: None, but debtor may use general personal property exemption (see Miscellaneous other exemptions later in this entry).

Household belongings: None, but debtor may use general personal property exemption (see Miscellaneous other exemptions later in this entry).

Miscellaneous other exemptions: Any personal property valued up to $6,000. Most pensions.

Tennessee

Bankruptcy Code exemptions aren't available.

Homestead: $5,000, joint owners are entitled to $7,500.

Vehicle: None, but debtor may use general personal property exemption.

Household belongings: None, but debtor may use general personal property exemption.

Miscellaneous other exemptions: Tools of trade — $1,900. Any personal property — $4,000. Most pensions. Alimony and support.

Texas

Debtor may choose between state and Bankruptcy Code exemptions.

Homestead: Unlimited value, limited in area to one acre of urban property or 100 acres (200 for families) of rural land.

Vehicle: None, but debtor may use general personal property exemption.

Household belongings: None, but debtor may use general personal property exemption.

Miscellaneous other exemptions: Personal property of debtor's choice including tools of the trade and motor vehicles, up to a value of $30,000 for an individual or $60,000 for head of family.

Utah

Bankruptcy Code exemptions aren't available.

Homestead: $20,000. Husband and wife may double.

Vehicle: Motor vehicle — $2,500, must be used for work.

Household belongings: Household furniture — $500.

Miscellaneous other exemptions: Tools of trade — $5,000. Most pensions. Alimony — to extent necessary. Child support — all.

Vermont

Debtor may choose between state and Bankruptcy Code exemptions.

Homestead: $75,000. Husband and wife may not double.

Vehicle: $2,500.

Household belongings: One stove, heating appliances, one refrigerator, one freezer, one water heater and one sewing machine — unlimited value. Other household goods — $2,500.

Miscellaneous other exemptions: Any property — up to $7,000, which isn't used for other personal property exemptions, plus any property up to $400. Tools of trade — $5,000. Most pensions. Alimony and child support to the extent necessary.

Virgin Islands

Debtor may choose between local and Bankruptcy Code Exemptions.

Homestead: $30,000.

Vehicle: None.

Household belongings: $3,000.

Miscellaneous other exemptions: Tools of trade — unlimited. Pensions for public employees.

Virginia

Bankruptcy Code exemptions aren't available.

Homestead: $5,000, plus $500 for each dependent. Husband and wife may double.

Vehicle: $2,000.

Household belongings: $5,000.

Miscellaneous other exemptions: Tools of trade — $10,000. Most pensions.

Washington

Debtor may choose between state and Bankruptcy Code exemptions.

Homestead: $40,000. Husband and wife may not double.

Vehicle: Two motor vehicles — $2,500 total for both.

Household belongings: $2,700.

Miscellaneous other exemptions: Tools of trade and professional libraries — $5,000. Most pensions. Any personal property — $2,000.

West Virginia

Bankruptcy Code exemptions aren't available.

Homestead: $25,000. Husband and wife may double.

Vehicle: $2,400.

Household belongings: $8,000.

Miscellaneous other exemptions: Tools of trade — $1,500. Any property — $800, plus any unused portion of homestead exemption. Most pensions. Alimony and support to the extent necessary.

Wisconsin

Debtor may choose between state and Bankruptcy Code exemptions.

Homestead: $40,000. Husband and wife may not double.

Vehicle: $1,200.

Household belongings: $5,000.

Miscellaneous other exemptions: Tools of trade — $7,500. Most pensions.

Wyoming

Bankruptcy Code exemptions aren't available.

Homestead: $10,000. Husband and wife may double.

Vehicle: $2,400.

Household belongings: $2,000.

Miscellaneous other exemptions: Tools of trade and professional library — $2,000. Most pensions.

Index

• *Numerics* •

60-day bar date, 179, 227
180-day rule, 264–265
240-day rule, 201
341 meeting
  Chapter 7, 79–80
  Chapter 13, 84
  court notice, 282
  deadlines, 81
  definition, 54, 326
  divorce, 227
  preparing for, 78

• *A* •

ABI. *See* American Bankruptcy Institute
ABI World, 49
ability to pay, divorce, 225–226
accounts receivable, asset worksheet, 38
ACS. *See* Automated Collection System
actually fraudulent transfer, 248
administrative discharge, student loan, 242
adult educational expenses, disposable
    income equation, 61
adversary proceeding, 181–182, 311
Alabama, exemptions, 330
Alaska, exemptions, 330
alcohol, expense worksheet, 32
alimony
  asset worksheet, 37
  collecting, 15
  failing to pay, 22
  nondischargeable debt, 16
  property of the estate, 135
allowance, expense worksheet, 33
American Bankruptcy Institute (ABI), 49
American bankruptcy law, compared to
    other countries, 8
American Consumer Credit Counseling, 104
antibankruptcy propaganda, 46
antidiscrimination law, 76
appliances, 30, 37

appraisal, 132
Arizona, exemptions, 331
Arkansas, exemptions, 331
arrearage, 60, 163–164, 311
assessed value, 132
asset. *See also* property of the estate
  abandoned, 247
  accurately listing, 247
  concealing, 301
  determining whether to pay value of, 128
  documenting, 36–37
  exempt, 17
  lawyer checklist, 71
  losing, 18
  selling, 19, 93–94
  transferring, 301
  worksheet, 37–39
attorney
  contacting, 305–306
  finding money to pay, 49–50
  hourly rate, 48
  legal fees, 48
  locating, 47
  preparing documentation for first
      meeting, 70–72
audio equipment, asset worksheet, 37
Automated Collection System (ACS),
    117–118
automatic stay
  benefits, 15, 75–76
  codebtor stay, 77
  definition, 53, 311
  exceptions, 76–77
automobile
  debt, 40
  determining value of, 132, 306
  exempt equity with late payments, 152
  exempt equity with up-to-date payments,
      151–152
  exemption, 134, 329
  fines, 214
  insurance, 32
  lawyer checklist, 71

automobile *(continued)*
  leased, 154
  loan, 31
  maintenance, 31
  monthly expenditure, 35
  more than one, 153
  nonexempt equity, 153
  owing more than it's worth, 152
  payments, 99–100
  repossession, 22
avoidance powers, 311

• *B* •

back alimony, 33, 251
back child support, 33, 251
back taxes, expense worksheet, 32
bad check, 209
balance transfer, 311
balloon payment, 97, 312
bank account, 137–138, 306
BankRate Monitor, 285
Bankruptcy Act of 1841, 11
Bankruptcy Act of 1867, 11
Bankruptcy Act of 1898, 8, 11
Bankruptcy Code of 1978, 8, 20, 328–330
bankruptcy court, 312
bankruptcy, definition, 312
bankruptcy judge, 50–51
bankruptcy law, 46, 312
bankruptcy myths
  filing to avoid bill paying, 12
  negative impact on honest citizens, 13–14
  negative impact on society, 12–13
  rate of bankruptcy, 10
  stereotypes, 10–11
Bankruptcy Reporter, 48
bar date, 179, 312
beauty products, expense worksheet, 33
best-efforts test, 21, 312–313
best-interest test, 21, 313
biblical roots, debt forgiveness, 9
bifurcation, 166–167, 313
bill collector
  cease-and-desist letter, 111
  contacting others about your debt, 112

Fair Debt Collection Practices Act,
    108–111
  filing lawsuit against, 113
  intimidation, 107
  limitations placed upon, 108, 111–112
  obtaining advice of, 46
  paying, 109
  protecting yourself against, 115–116
  unfair practices, 113
bills. *See* creditor; debt
bonds, asset worksheet, 38
bonus, employment, 38, 72
books, expense worksheet, 32–33
Bounce Back From Bankruptcy: A Step-By-Step Guide to Getting Back on Your Financial Feet (Paula Langguth Ryan), 278
budgeting, 92, 291–292
bug-off letter. *See* cease-and-desist letter
business expenses, 33
business inventory, asset worksheet, 39
business partners, paying back, 26
business reorganization. *See* Chapter 11 bankruptcy

• *C* •

cable TV, expense worksheet, 30
Caher, James, P.
  Discharging Credit Card Debts in Bankruptcy, 196
  Discharging Marital Obligations in Bankruptcy, 224
California, exemptions, 331–332
caller ID, bill collector use of, 115
car. *See* automobile
case trustee, 51–52
cash advance, 121–122, 208
CCCS. *See* Consumer Credit Counseling Services
cease-and-desist letter, sending to third-party bill collector, 111
cell phone, expense worksheet, 32
Center for a New American Dream, 294
Chapter 7 bankruptcy
  ability to pay, 57
  asset case, 82

assets, 57
backing out, 67
Chapter 13, compared to, 85–86, 167–168
credit card fraud, 189
creditor, adding to list after filing date, 81
deadlines, 81
definition, 313
denial of discharge, 185
discharge hearing, 82
discharge, protecting, 254
divorce, 220–221, 224–225, 227
eligibility requirements, 65
good faith, 58–59
homestead exemption, 163
legal fees, 48
liquidation, 20–21
no-asset case, 82
panel trustee, 51, 313
paperwork, amending, 81
Schedule I, 58
Schedule J, 58
secured creditor, making arrangement with, 80–81
substantial abuse, 57–58
341 meeting, 79–80
when to select, 62
Chapter 11 bankruptcy
business reorganization, 20
definition, 313
when to use, 66
Chapter 12 bankruptcy
definition, 314
eligibility requirements, 66–67
family farmer, 20
Chapter 13 bankruptcy
advantages, 63–64
automobile, purchasing, 269
best-efforts test, 21, 60
best-interest test, 21, 60
bifurcation, 166–167
Chapter 7, compared to, 85–86, 167–168
compared to nonbankruptcy repayment plan, 64–65
confirmation hearing, 84–85
converting to Chapter 7, 262

cramdown, 272
definition, 314
disadvantages, 64
discharge received, 272
dismissing, 67, 262–263
disposable income, 60–61
divorce, 221, 224
drop-dead agreement, 267
eligibility requirements, 65
emergency postpetition debt, 269
exempt property, increase in value, 274
failure, reasons for, 256
filing new Chapter 13 instead of modifying, 264
foreclosure, 164
full repayment, 17
hardship discharge, 261
homestead exemption, 163
income taxes, 270
inheritance, disposition of, 270–271
lawyer, importance of consulting, 257–258
legal fees, 48
minimum payments, 256–257
missed payments, 258, 266–267
modified payment plan, 260
mortgage arrearage, 163–164
mortgages, restructuring, 165–166
nonemergency postpetition debt, 268
nonexempt assets, 60
Notice of Tax Lien, 203
180-day rule, 264–265
outside-the-plan-payments, 265
partial repayment, 16
payment plan, 83–84
payments outside the plan, 59
postpetition debt, 272
postpetition property acquisition, 273
priority claims, 60
priority debt, 85
proof of claim, 85
property status change, 273
relief from stay, 265–266
reorganization, 20–21
repayment over time, 16
right of redemption, 164–165

Chapter 13 *(continued)*
  secured debts, 60
  selling property, 267–268
  standing trustee, 51–52, 314
  student loan, 235–236
  super discharge, 59, 189
  support obligations, 269–270
  suspending payments, 259
  341 meeting, 84
  time limit, 257
  trustee, 59
  240-day rule, 201
  unsecured debts, 60
  valuation hearing, 84–85
  wages, deducting payments from, 257
  when to select, 63
Chapter 20 bankruptcy, 67, 236–237, 314
charitable contributions, 34, 61, 249
child support
  asset worksheet, 38
  collecting, 15
  failing to pay, 22
  nondischargeable debt, 16
  property of the estate, 135
children, discussing bankruptcy with, 44
CIS. *See* Collection Information Statement
citizenship, 17
civil service retirement benefits, 327
clothing expenses, 31
Coast to Coast Information Services,
    obtaining credit report from, 73
codebtor stay, 77
collateral, 53, 314
collection due process, Internal Revenue
    Service, 120
Collection Information Statement (CIS),
    121, 314
collection ploys, recognizing, 115–116
Colorado, exemptions, 332
commissions, asset worksheet, 38
common law, 114
community property, 56, 130, 314
compensation payments from war risk
    hazards, 328
compulsive spending, 35–36, 289–290
computer, asset worksheet, 37

concerts, expense worksheet, 32
condo charge, 178
confirmation, 53, 315
confirmation hearing, 84–85
Connecticut, exemptions, 332
consensual lien, 147–148, 315
Consolidated Credit Counseling
    Services, 104
consolidator, 100
Constitutional Convention of 1787, 11
constructively fraudulent transfer, United
    States Trustee, 248–249
Consumer Credit Counseling Services
    (CCCS), 103
consumer goods, redeeming, 150
Consumer Price Index (CPI), 133
consumer reorganization. *See* Chapter 13
    bankruptcy
consumption, prevailing attitudes
    about, 43
contempt of court, 15, 315
contingency funds, disposable income
    equation, 61
contributions to pension, 28
conversion of a bankruptcy case, 315
conversion of collateral, 210–211, 315
copyrights, asset worksheet, 39
cosigned debt, 77, 250–251
CPI. *See* Consumer Price Index
cramdown, 166–167, 272, 315
credit
  living without, 294
  obtaining after bankruptcy, 283
  secured, 284–285
  unsecured, 283–284
credit card
  abuse, 195
  balance transfer, 71, 94, 194–195
  cutting up, 304
  debt consolidation, 189
  dischargeable debt, 16
  expense worksheet, 31
  fraudulent use of, 189–191
  gambling with cash advances, 193
  interstate rate restrictions, 188
  monthly expense, 34
  partial payment, 305

paying off with home-equity loan, 188
paying taxes with, 121–122
payments, 99
solicitations, reducing, 292
credit counselor
   Consumer Credit Counseling Services, 103
   home equity loan, 100
   obtaining advice of, 45
   online debt counseling, 104
credit industry, attempts to change
   bankruptcy law, 8
credit rating
   married couple, 286–287
   negative effect upon, 18, 307–308
   rebuilding, 285
   repairing, 83
credit report
   correcting mistakes on, 280–282
   definition, 315
   free copy, 280
   obtaining copy of, 72–73, 279–280, 304–305
credit scoring, 315
CreditComm Services LLC, 284
creditor
   adding after 341 meeting, 81
   contacting, 26
   failing to list, 301, 309
   ignoring, consequences of, 104–105
   informing about bankruptcy filing, 27, 76
   negotiating with to reduce debt, 19, 101
   role of, 53
   work-out agreement, 102
credit-repair scam, 286
criminal fine, 180, 212–213
criminal prosecution, 15
cross-collateralization, 316
cure, 316
current child support, expense
   worksheet, 33
current gross wages, salary and
   commissions, 28

• *D* •

daily spending habits, 35
danger signs, recognizing, 295–296
day care, expense worksheet, 33

deadlines
   after 341 meeting, 81
   bankruptcy process, 310
   when creditors miss, 176
debt
   calculating, 39–40
   mortgage, 40
   repayment, 71
   typical causes of, 7
   vehicle, 40
   worksheet, 40–41
debt collector
   cease-and-desist letter, 111
   contacting others about your debt, 112
   Fair Debt Collection Practices Act, 108–111
   filing lawsuit against, 113
   intimidation, 107
   limitations placed upon, 108, 111–112
   obtaining advice of, 46
   paying, 109
   protecting yourself against, 115–116
   unfair practices, 113
debt consolidators, obtaining advice of, 46
debt forgiveness, biblical roots, 9
debt from fraud, nondischargeable debt, 16
debt payment expenses, 31
debtor, 316
Debtor's Anonymous, 35–36, 49, 290
debtor's exam, 316
debtors' prison, abolishment of, 11
debt-to-income ratio formula, 296
deed in lieu of foreclosure, 171, 316
deed of trust, 147, 316
default judgment, 316
Delaware, exemptions, 332
denial of discharge, 316
dentist, expense worksheet, 31
depreciation, personal property, 150
determining whether to file, 90–91
detrimental consequences, divorce, 225–227
Direct Consolidated Loans, 239–240
Direct Loan Servicing Center, United States
   Department of Education, 231
Direct Marketing Association, 293
disability benefits, exemptions, 329
discharge
   definition, 53, 316
   denial of, 184–185

discharge *(continued)*
  hearing, 82
  injunction, 316
  order of, 282
  protecting, 185–186
  received, 272
  revocation of, 186
dischargeable debt, 16, 316
Discharging Credit Card Debts in Bankruptcy
    (James P. Caher), 196
discharging federal income taxes. *See also*
    income tax; Internal Revenue Service
  Chapter 7, 198
  Chapter 13, 199
  extensions, 198
  fraudulent tax return filed, 200
  Notice of Tax Lien, 200, 202
  paying before filing bankruptcy, 204
  postpetition interest, 200–201
  postpetition penalties, 200
  prepetition interest, 200–201
  prepetition penalties, 200–201
  short-year election, 202
  taxes less than three years old, 199
  taxes more than three years old, 199
  240-day rule, 201
*Discharging Marital Obligations in
    Bankruptcy* (James P. Caher), 224
Discharging Student Loans in Bankruptcy
    (David J. Light), 232
discrimination, as result of bankruptcy, 19
dismissal, 67, 262–263, 310, 317
disposable income, 60–61, 317
disputing debt, 115
distributions from estate, asset
    worksheet, 39
District of Columbia, exemptions, 333
divorce
  ability to pay, 225–226
  automatic stay, 220
  award, 178
  Chapter 7, 220–221, 224–225, 227
  Chapter 13, 221, 224
  constraints, 216
  detrimental consequences, 225–227
  financial condition, at time of, 222–223
  fraud, 220, 227
  impact on filing, 27

lawyer checklist, 71
  mutually beneficial settlement, 218–219
  obligation, determining nature of, 221–223
  planning, importance of, 216–217
  property division, 217–218, 224–225
  property transfer, 219
  Qualified Domestic Relations Order, 217
  settlement, property of the estate, 135
  support obligations, 217
  when to file, 219-220
doctor, expense worksheet, 31
doctrine of necessaries, 56
documentation. *See* paperwork
do-it-yourself bankruptcy service, 46
do-not-call registry, 293
downshifting, 294
dragnet clause, 317
driver's license
  expense worksheet, 31
  lawyer worksheet, 70
  preventing loss of, 15, 78
driving under the influence, 16, 214
drop-dead agreement, 267
drugs, expense worksheet, 31
due-on-sale clause, 168, 317
dummy return, 198, 317

earned income credit (EIC), 141, 317
eating out, expense worksheet, 30
ECOA. *See* Equal Credit Opportunity Act
electric, expense worksheet, 30
eligibility requirements, bankruptcy, 65
embezzlement, 180
employer, informing about bankruptcy, 76
Employment Retirement Income Security
    Act (ERISA), 141, 328
employment tax, Chapter 7 compared to
    Chapter 13, 180
Equal Credit Opportunity Act (ECOA), 287
Equifax, 72–73, 191, 280, 304
equipment violation, vehicle, 214
equity, 95, 317
estate, administration of, 82
estimated overtime pay, 28
estimated tax payment, expense
    worksheet, 31

eve of bankruptcy spending binge, 208
eviction, 14, 70
exceptions to discharge, 317
exemptions
  definition, 53, 127, 317
  disability benefits, 329
  federal compared to local, 327–328
  health aids, 329
  homestead, 329
  household goods, 329
  injury compensation, 330
  jewelry, 329
  life insurance with cash value, 329
  listed by state, 330–346
  maximizing, 143–144
  property of the estate, 131
  retirement benefits, 329
  term-life insurance, 329
  tools of the trade, 329
  vehicle, 329
  wild card, 329
expenditures
  extravagant, 35
  importance of writing down, 29, 305
  worksheet, 30–34
Experian, 72–73, 191, 280, 304
eyeglasses, expense worksheet, 31

• F •

failure, Chapter 13, 256
Fair Credit Reporting Act (FCRA),
  278–279, 282
Fair Debt Collection Practices Act (FDCPA)
  bill collector, limitations placed upon, 110
  consumer protection, 108–109
  lawsuit, filing against bill collector, 111
Fair, Isaac & Company, Inc. (FICO score),
  191–192, 279, 315
false financial statement, 192–193, 208–209
false information, lawyer checklist, 72
family
  accepting help from instead of filing, 92
  borrowing money from, 19, 299
  changing spending habits, 290–291
  repaying, 26, 70, 99, 300
family farmer, 318. *See also* Chapter 12
  bankruptcy
Farmers Home Administration (FmHA), 95

FCRA. *See* Fair Credit Reporting Act
FDCPA. *See* Fair Debt Collection
  Practices Act
federal employee's workers compensation
  benefits, 328
Federal Family Education Loan (FFEL), 230,
  239–240
Federal Housing Administration (FHA), 95
Federal Student Aid Information Center, 231
Federal Trade Commission (FTC), 282, 293
fees, for filing, 310
FFEL. *See* Federal Family Education Loan
FHA. *See* Federal Housing Administration
FICO score. *See* Fair, Isaac & Company, Inc.
filing bankruptcy papers, 74–75
finance companies, paying, 99
financial obligation related to criminal
  conviction, nondischargeable debt, 16
fines
  criminal, 180, 212–213
  failing to pay, 23
  lawyer checklist, 71
  motor vehicle, 181, 214
  noncriminal, 181, 213
  paying, 99
firearms, asset worksheet, 38
Florida, exemptions, 333
FmHa. *See* Farmers Home Administration
food expenses, 30
forbearance, student loan, 242
foreclosure
  averting, 14, 22
  compared to selling, 95
  contacting lawyer, 305–306
  definition, 54, 318
  lawyer checklist, 70
  sale, 27, 76, 162
  service, 15
  types, 162–163
foreign service retirement and disability
  payments, 328
Form 433-A, 121
Form 433-B, 121
Form 433-F, 121
Form 656, 123
Form 656-A, 123
Form 911, 124
Form 9465 Installment Agreement
  Request, 120

fraud-related debt
Chapter 7 compared to Chapter 13, 180
credit card use, 190–191
frivolous claim, 193–194
fraudulent transfer, 318
fresh start, 318
friends
obtaining loans from, 19
repaying, 26, 71, 99
FTC. *See* Federal Trade Commission
furniture, asset worksheet, 37
furniture purchases, expense worksheet, 30

• G •

gambling, 32, 193
garnishment, 14, 71, 318
gasoline, 30–31
Georgia, exemptions, 333
gifts
expense worksheet, 32
lawyer checklist, 71
overspending, 27, 35
good faith, 234
government regulatory proceeding, 15
groceries, expense worksheet, 30
gross income, 29
guarantee agency, 241
guilt, 303–304

• H •

haircuts, expense worksheet, 33
hardship discharge, 182, 318
Hawaii, exemptions, 333–334
Head Start Program, extinguishing
student loan, 242
health aids, exemptions, 329
Health Allies, 104
health club membership, expense
worksheet, 33
Health Education Assistance Loan, 237
health insurance, 27, 32
hidden cost, refinancing, 97
history, debt forgiveness, 9
hobby equipment, asset worksheet, 38

home
asset worksheet, 37
determining value of, 158, 306
liens, 158–159
losing, 308
real estate appraiser, 158
selling, 27
tax assessment, 158
home maintenance and repairs, expense
worksheet, 30
home-equity loan
avoiding, 19, 96–97
definition, 318
reducing debt with, 300
homeowners insurance, expense
worksheet, 32
homestead exemption
definition, 319
determining, 133
joint ownership, 160–162
nonexempt home equity, 160
state law, variability of, 159–160, 329
honest debtor, 14
household goods
determining value of, 132
exemptions, 134, 329
nonpurchase-money security interest, 155
purchase-money security interest, 154–155
housing expenses, 30
HUD. *See* United States Department of
Housing and Urban Development

• I •

Idaho, exemptions, 334
ignoring creditor, consequence of, 104–105
Illinois, exemptions, 334
impulse purchase, 35, 293
in rem order, 267, 319
income
calculating, 28
prorating, 28
worksheet, 28–29
income tax. *See also* discharging federal
income taxes; Internal Revenue Service
arrearages, 60
borrowing money to pay, 206

Chapter 7 compared to Chapter 13, 180
expense worksheet, 31
lawyer worksheet, 71
nondischargeable debt, 16
not deducted from pay, 31–32
paying past due, 27
payments, 99, 101
refund, 80, 140–141
state tax, 124
indemnify, 177
Indiana, exemptions, 334
individual retirement account (IRA), 142
inexpensive entertainment, 295
inheritance, 71, 135, 270–271
injunction, 176
injury compensation, exemptions, 330
innocent spouse, 120
insider, 319
installment agreement, 120–121, 319
insurance. *See* automobile, insurance;
        health insurance; homeowners
        insurance; life insurance
insurance commission, property of the
        estate, 139
intention to file bankruptcy, revealing to
        creditor, 27
Internal Revenue Service (IRS). *See also*
        discharging federal income tax;
        income tax
    Automated Collection System, 117–118
    collection due process, 120
    Form 982, 102
    installment agreement, 120–123
    local offices, 118
    Notice of Tax Lien, 200, 202
    offer in compromise, 123–124
    seizure, 15
    Service Centers, 117
    statute of limitations, 119
    tax lien, 122–123
    taxpayer advocate, 124
    time restrictions, 122
    undue hardship, 122
    Web site, 102, 119
Internet, expense worksheet, 32
interstate rate restrictions, credit card, 188

intervivos trust, 136
investments, asset worksheet, 38
Iowa, exemptions, 335
IRA. *See* individual retirement account
IRS. *See* Internal Revenue Service

jewelry, 37, 329
job, impact of bankruptcy upon, 27, 308
joint account, removing name from, 305
joint bankruptcy, 54–56, 319
joint debt, 27
joint ownership, 129–130, 160–162, 224–225
judgment, 319
judgment lien, 149, 155–156
judicial foreclosure, 162
judicial lien, 155
judicial survivors annuity for survivors of
        federal judges, 328

• K •

Kansas, exemptions, 335
Kelley Blue Book, 306
Kentucky, exemptions, 335
Klein, Gary *(Surviving Debt),* 100

• L •

laundry, expense worksheet, 31
lawsuit
    default judgment, 23
    halting, 14
    ignoring, 27
    lawyer checklist, 70
lawyer
    contacting, 305–306
    finding money to pay, 49–50
    hourly rate, 48
    legal fees, 48
    locating, 47
    preparing documentation for first
        meeting, 70–72
legal aide counselor, 95
legal comments, regarding bankruptcy, 13

lien
consensual, 147–148
definition, 54, 319
perfected, 146
promissory note, 146
repossession, 147
secured creditor, 145
unperfected, 251–252
life insurance
asset worksheet, 39
benefit, 135
cash value, 38
determining value of, 132
exemptions, 329
expense worksheet, 32
lawyer checklist, 71
premium, 61
Light, David J. (*Discharging Student Loans in Bankruptcy*), 232
liquidation. *See* Chapter 7 bankruptcy
living trust, 136
loan cosigner, proceedings against, 15
loans, dischargeable debt, 16
loans to pay nondischargeable federal taxes, Chapter 7 compared to Chapter 13, 180
local offices, Internal Revenue Service, 118
Longshoremen's and Harbor Worker's Compensation Act, 327
Louisiana, exemptions, 335–336
luxury purchase, preceding bankruptcy, 208

• M •

machinery, asset worksheet, 39
Mail Preference Service (MPS), 293
Maine, exemptions, 335–336
makeup, expense worksheet, 33
malicious conduct, damages resulting from, 210–211
manufactured home, 252–253
marital property divisions, 181, 320
marriage, 27
married couple, joint bankruptcy, 55–56
Maryland, exemptions, 335–336
Massachusetts, exemptions, 336–337
medical expenses, 16, 31, 56, 71, 99

Michigan, exemptions, 337
military service, extinguishing student loan, 242
military survivor annuities, 328
minimum payments, Chapter 13, 256–257
Minnesota, exemptions, 337
missed payments, Chapter 13, 258, 266–267
Mississippi, exemptions, 337
Missouri, exemptions, 338
Mistakes Do Happen (U.S. Public Interest Research Group), 283
modified payment plan, Chapter 13, 260
money
borrowing more, 26
recovered in lawsuit, property of the estate, 140
saving, 294–295
Montana, exemptions, 338
mortgage
arrearage, 163–164
consultant, 15
definition, 320
expense worksheet, 30
home-equity loan, 96–97
lawyer worksheet, 71
payment, 35, 99–100
rate, shopping for, 96
refinancing, 96
restructuring, 19, 94–95, 165–166
reverse, 97–98
motion for relief from stay, 320
motor-vehicle fine, 181, 214
movies, expense worksheet, 32
MPS. *See* Mail Preference Service
Myvesta, 104

• N •

National Association of Consumer Bankruptcy Attorneys (NACBA), 73
National Consumer Law Center (NCLC), 49, 100, 241
National Foundation for Consumer Credit, 103
National Health Services Corporation (NHSC), 237
Nebraska, exemptions, 338
negative consequences of filing, 90

negative feelings about bankruptcy, overcoming, 7
negligence, 210
Nevada, exemptions, 338–339
new clothes, expense worksheet, 30
New Hampshire, exemptions, 339
New Jersey, exemptions, 339
New Mexico, exemptions, 339
New Road Map Foundation, 294
New York, exemptions, 340
no-asset case, 21, 54, 82, 320
noncompete covenant, 176
nonconsensual lien, 149, 320
noncriminal fines, 181, 213
noncriminal restitution, 180
nondischargeable debt
   borrowing to pay off, 182–183
   Chapter 7 compared to Chapter 13, 180
   definition, 16, 321
nonemergency postpetition debt, 268
nonexempt assets, 55, 57, 60, 80, 321
nonjudicial foreclosure, 162
nonpurchase-money security interest, 148, 321
North Carolina, exemptions, 340
North Dakota, exemptions, 340
Notice of Intent to Levy, Internal Revenue Service, 118
Notice of Tax Lien, Internal Revenue Service, 200, 202, 321

• O •

objection to discharge, 321
objective advice, importance of obtaining, 45–46
offer in compromise, 123–124, 321
official documents, reviewing, 74
offspring expenses, 33
Ohio, exemptions, 341
oil, expense worksheet, 30
Oklahoma, exemptions, 341
On Time (Payment Protection Systems, Inc.), 101
180-day rule, 264–265
Oregon, exemptions, 341
outside-the-plan-payments, Chapter 13, 265
The Overspent American (Juliet B. Schor), 43

• P •

panel trustee, 5
paperwork
   amending, 81
   forms, viewing on the Web, 75
   preparing for first meeting with lawyer, 70–72
parents, discussing bankruptcy with, 42
parking, expense worksheet, 31
parking ticket, 214
patents, asset worksheet, 39
payday loan, 211
payment plan. *See* Chapter 13 bankruptcy
Payment Protection Systems, Inc. *(On Time)*, 101
payments, prioritizing, 99
payroll deductions, 28–29
payroll taxes, 28
Peace Corps, extinguishing student loan, 242
Pennsylvania, exemptions, 342
pension
   asset worksheet, 39
   borrowing against, 19, 98
   determining value of, 132
   disposable income equation, 61
   Medal of Honor winners, 328
   rollover, property of the estate, 142–143
   withdrawal, 27
perfection of lien, 146, 321
perjury, 246
personal education expenses, 33
personal injury damages, nondischargeable debt, 16
personal item expenses, 33
personal property, 54, 308, 322
personal property tax, 180, 206
personal relationships, stress upon, 19
personal-injury claims from drunk driving, Chapter 7 compared to Chapter 13, 181
petition date, 54, 74, 322
pets, expense worksheet, 32
phone charges, dischargeable debt, 16
postdated check, 27, 115, 209
postpetition charge, 177–178
postpetition debt, 272

postpetition property acquisition, 273
postpetition taxes, 203
prebankruptcy planning, 143–144
preferential transfer, 249–250, 322
prepetition contract, 177–178
prepetition debts, 322
presents. *See* gifts
presumption of fraud, 192, 322
priority debt, 85, 322
private school costs, disposable income
    equation, 61
pro se, 323
professional license, revoking, 22
proof of claim
  definition, 323
  filing, 85, 176
  short-year election, 203
property division, divorce, 217–218, 224–225
property of the estate
  alimony, 135
  bank account, 137–138
  child support, 135
  community property, 130
  definition, 54, 127, 323
  determining, 128–129
  divorce settlement, 135
  earned income credit, 141
  exemptions, 131
  income tax refund, 140–141
  individual retirement account, 142
  inheritance, 135
  insurance commission, 139
  joint ownership, 129–130
  life insurance benefit, 135
  money owed to you, 130
  money recovered in lawsuit, 140
  pension rollover, 142–143
  real estate commission, 139
  rent receipts, 136–137
  retirement account, 141–142
  sales commission, 138
  security deposit, 137
  severance pay, 138
  vacation pay, 138
  wages, 137
property status change, 273
public record, 18

public transportation, expense
    worksheet, 31
public-interest law office, 95
Puerto Rico, exemptions, 342
purchase-money security interest, 148, 323

• *Q* •

Qualified Domestic Relations Order
    (QDRO), 217

• *R* •

Railroad Retirement Act, 327
Railroad unemployment benefits, 327
Ram Research Group, 285
reaffirm
  changing your mind, 184
  definition, 54, 323
  discharge hearing, 82
  importance of, 150–151
  reasons to, 183–184
real estate appraiser, 158
real estate commission, property of
    the estate, 139
real property
  asset worksheet, 37
  definition, 323
  determining value of, 132
  tax, 30, 149, 180, 206
reasonable-relief maxim, 14
recoupment, 210
recreation expenses, 32
redemption, 54, 323
refinancing, 71, 96
relatives. *See* family
relief from stay, 265–266, 323
Religious Liberty and Charitable Donation
    Protection Act, 249
rent, 30, 99
rent receipts, property of the estate,
    136–137
rental property, expense worksheet, 33
rent-to-own contract, 151
reorganization. *See* Chapter 11 bankruptcy;
    Chapter 13 bankruptcy
repayment of pension loan, 28, 61

repossession
  averting, 14
  definition, 54, 324
  lawyer checklist, 70
  vehicle, 22
resident-alien status, 17
restitution, 212–213, 324
retired serviceman's annuities, 328
retirement account. *See also* pension
  borrowing against, 98
  individual retirement account, 142
  paying debt with, 300
  property of the estate, 141–142
  Roth IRA, 142
retirement benefits, exemptions, 329
retirement income, 29
reverse mortgage, 97–98, 324
Rhode Island, exemptions, 342
right of redemption, Chapter 13, 164–165
Roth IRA, 142
Ryan, Paula L. *(Bounce Back From Bankruptcy: A Step-By-Step Guide to Getting Back on Your Financial Feet),* 278

• S •

sales commission, property of the estate, 138
Sallie May. *See* Student Loan Marketing Association
saving money, 294–295
Schedule A, 75
Schedule B, 75
Schedule C, 75
Schedule D, 75, 282
Schedule E, 75, 282
Schedule F, 75, 282
Schedule G, 75
Schedule H, 75
Schedule I, 58, 75
Schedule J, 58, 75
schedules and statement of affairs, 324
school supplies, expense worksheet, 33
Schor, Juliet B. *(The Overspent American),* 43
seaman's wages, 328
second job, 19
second mortgage, 19, 170–171

secured credit card, 284, 324
secured creditor, 80, 146
secured debt, 324
security deposit, property of the estate, 137
security interest
  consensual lien, 147
  definition, 324
  rent-to-own, compared to, 151
selling property, 267–268
serial filer, 267
Service Centers, Internal Revenue Service, 117–118
severance pay, property of the estate, 138
Sheldon, Jonathan *(Surviving Debt),* 100
short-year election, 324–325
sick time, lawyer checklist, 72
Silverman, David *(Taxes For Dummies),* 120
60-day bar date, 179, 227
Social Security
  disposable income equation, 61
  exemptions, 138, 327
  payments, 28
  receiving fraudulent benefits, 209
South Carolina, exemptions, 342–343
South Dakota, exemptions, 343
spendaholic. *See* compulsive spending
spendthrift provision, 135
spendthrift trust, 325
sporting events, expense worksheet, 32
spouse
  discussing bankruptcy with, 42–44
  filing bankruptcy, 309
standing trustee, 51–52
state income taxes, discharging, 204–205
state law, bill collector practices, 114
state tax debt, 124
Statement of Financial Affairs, 75
Statement of Intention, 75
statute of limitations, 23, 119, 231, 325
stigma, attached to bankruptcy, 19
stocks, asset worksheet, 38
straight bankruptcy. *See* Chapter 7 bankruptcy
stripoff, Chapter 13, 166–167
student loan
  administrative discharge, 242
  Chapter 7, 181

student loan *(continued)*
Chapter 13, 235–236
consequences of not paying, 231
consolidation loan, 238–240
cosigner, 238
deferment, 241
discharging, 232–233
expense worksheet, 31
failing to pay, 22
Federal Direct Loan, 230
Federal Family Education Loan, 230
Federal Student Aid Information
Center, 231
forbearance, 242
good faith, 234
Health Education Assistance Loan, 237
National Health Services Corporation, 237
nondischargeable debt, 16
payment plan, 99, 240–241
Perkins Loan, 230
statute of limitations, 231
Student Loan Marketing Association, 230
undue hardship, 231–233
United States Department of Education,
230–231
wiping out part of, 235
Student Loan Law (National Consumer
Law Center), 241
Student Loan Marketing Association
(Sallie May), 230
substantial abuse, 325
super discharge, 59, 189, 325
support obligations, 28, 33, 217, 325. *See
also* alimony; child support
Surviving Debt (Jonathan Sheldon and
Gary Klein), 100
suspending payments, Chapter 13, 259

● *T* ●

take-home pay, 29
tax. *See* discharging federal income tax;
income tax; Internal Revenue Service
tax assessment, home, 158
tax protester, 204
tax refunds, asset worksheet, 38
Taxes For Dummies (Eric Tyson and
David Silverman), 120

taxpayer advocate, 124, 325
teacher, extinguishing student loan, 242
telemarketer, 293
telephone conversation, tape-
recording, 116
telephone, expense worksheet, 30
telephone number, blocking while
dialing, 115
tenancy by the entirety, 133, 325
Tennessee, exemptions, 343
term-life insurance, exemptions, 329
testamentary trust, 136
Texas, exemptions, 343–344
theft, 180, 212
third-party bill collector, sending cease-
and-desist letter to, 111
threatening to file bankruptcy, 102–103
341 meeting
Chapter 7, 79–80
Chapter 13, 84
court notice, 282
deadlines, 81
definition, 54, 326
divorce, 227
preparing for, 78
TILA. *See* Truth in Lending Act
timing, of filing, 91
tobacco, expense worksheet, 32
tools of the trade, 39, 134, 329
toys, expenses, 33, 61
Trans Union, 72–73, 191, 280, 304
transportation expenses, 31
travel, expense worksheet, 32
True Credit, obtaining credit report
from, 73
trust, 71, 135–136
trust deed. *See* deed of trust
trust fund taxes, 205, 326
truth, importance of telling, 245–246
Truth in Lending Act (TILA), 95, 169–170
tuition, expense worksheet, 33
240-day rule, Chapter 13, 201
Tyson, Eric *(Taxes For Dummies),* 120

● *U* ●

unconditional discharge, 11
undue hardship, 122, 326

unemployment, 180, 209
unfair practices, bill collector, 113
union dues, 28
United States Attorney General, 52
United States Bankruptcy Code, 8, 20, 328–330
United States Code, 95
United States Constitution, references to bankruptcy, 8, 11
United States Department of Education, 230–231, 242
United States Department of Housing and Urban Development (HUD), 95
United States Department of Justice, 52
United States Trustee
    actually fraudulent transfer, 248
    back alimony, 251
    child support, 251
    constructively fraudulent transfer, 248–249
    cosigned debt, 250–251
    current expenses, 251
    definition, 52, 326
    manufactured home, 252–253
    preferential transfer, 249–250
    secured debt, 251
    small payments, 251
    unperfected lien, 251–252
United States Trustee Program (USTP), 52
unlisted debt, 178–179, 181
unsecured creditor, 146
unsecured debt, 326
unused vacation, lawyer checklist, 72
U.S. Public Interest Research Group (Mistakes Do Happen), 283
Utah, exemptions, 344
utility expenses, 30, 99

• V •

VA. *See* Veteran's Administration
vacation, expense worksheet, 32
vacation pay, property of the estate, 138
valuation hearing, 84–85
vehicle. *See* automobile
Vermont, exemptions, 344
Veteran's Administration (VA), 95
veterans' benefits, 327

vice expenses, 32
video equipment, asset worksheet, 37
Virgin Islands, exemptions, 344–345
Virginia, exemptions, 345
voluntary petition, 75

• W •

wages
    deducting payments from, 257
    garnishment, 14, 71, 318
    property of the estate, 137
Washington, exemptions, 345
water, expense worksheet, 30
Web sites, recommended, 49
welfare
    Chapter 7 compared to Chapter 13, 180
    disposable income equation, 61
    receiving fraudulent benefits, 209
West Virginia, exemptions, 345
when to file, 91, 177, 302
wild card, exemptions, 329
willful and malicious conduct, 180, 210–211
Wisconsin, exemptions, 345–346
work-out agreement, 102
Wyoming, exemptions, 346

FOR DUMMIES®

The easy way to get more done and have more fun

PERSONAL FINANCE

0-7645-5231-7

0-7645-2431-3

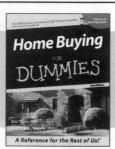

0-7645-5331-3

Also available:

Estate Planning For Dummies
(0-7645-5501-4)
401(k)s For Dummies
(0-7645-5468-9)
Frugal Living For Dummies
(0-7645-5403-4)
Microsoft Money "X" For
Dummies
(0-7645-1689-2)
Mutual Funds For Dummies
(0-7645-5329-1)

Personal Bankruptcy For
Dummies
(0-7645-5498-0)
Quicken "X" For Dummies
(0-7645-1666-3)
Stock Investing For Dummie‌
(0-7645-5411-5)
Taxes For Dummies 2003
(0-7645-5475-1)

BUSINESS & CAREERS

0-7645-5314-3

0-7645-5307-0

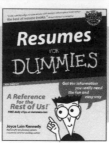

0-7645-5471-9

Also available:

Business Plans Kit For
Dummies
(0-7645-5365-8)
Consulting For Dummies
(0-7645-5034-9)
Cool Careers For Dummies
(0-7645-5345-3)
Human Resources Kit For
Dummies
(0-7645-5131-0)
Managing For Dummies
(1-5688-4858-7)

QuickBooks All-in-One Desk
Reference For Dummies
(0-7645-1963-8)
Selling For Dummies
(0-7645-5363-1)
Small Business Kit For
Dummies
(0-7645-5093-4)
Starting an eBay Business F‌
Dummies
(0-7645-1547-0)

HEALTH, SPORTS & FITNESS

0-7645-5167-1

0-7645-5146-9

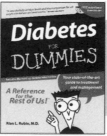

0-7645-5154-X

Also available:

Controlling Cholesterol For
Dummies
(0-7645-5440-9)
Dieting For Dummies
(0-7645-5126-4)
High Blood Pressure For
Dummies
(0-7645-5424-7)
Martial Arts For Dummies
(0-7645-5358-5)
Menopause For Dummies
(0-7645-5458-1)

Nutrition For Dummies
(0-7645-5180-9)
Power Yoga For Dummies
(0-7645-5342-9)
Thyroid For Dummies
(0-7645-5385-2)
Weight Training For Dummie‌
(0-7645-5168-X)
Yoga For Dummies
(0-7645-5117-5)

Available wherever books are sold.
Go to www.dummies.com or call 1-877-762-2974 to order direct.